John Mitchel

The Crusade of the Period

And, Last Conquest of Ireland

John Mitchel

The Crusade of the Period
And, Last Conquest of Ireland

ISBN/EAN: 9783337107284

Printed in Europe, USA, Canada, Australia, Japan

Cover: Foto ©ninafisch / pixelio.de

More available books at **www.hansebooks.com**

THE CRUSADE OF THE PERIOD:

AND

LAST CONQUEST OF IRELAND

(PERHAPS.)

BY
JOHN MITCHEL.

NEW-YORK:
LYNCH, COLE & MEEHAN, 57 MURRAY STREET.
1873.

INTRODUCTION.

THE controversy provoked by the lectures of Mr. James Anthony Froude, in this country, and by the publication of his book, "The English in Ireland, in the Eighteenth Century," elicited no abler reply or more convincing refutation than the papers devoted to those subjects by Mr. John Mitchel, which are compiled in the present volume in chapter form. Those incisive articles have been reprinted wherever the Irish race extends, or the English language is spoken; and it is intimated, in addition, that one or two European Continental houses (French and German,) intend bringing them out in a translated form, as affording a valuable store of information relative to a most important epoch of Irish history. So that, no matter how extensively Mr. Froude's calumnies against the Irish nation may have been circulated, the antidote to them will be present in the shape of the exact historical truth, to counteract their malignant influence.

The chapters on "The Last Conquest of Ireland (Perhaps)," which are added, will be found not less important or interesting, as dealing with a more recent era, in which Ireland (whether from her struggles for national independence, or the unparalleled sufferings of her people) occupied much of the world's attention. This is, unquestionably, the most complete history of the "Repeal" struggle that has yet been given; and as the work of one who was prominently identified with that struggle, and in immediate and most intimate association with the leading spirits by whom it was directed and impelled, it possesses a double value for the Irish people.

Originally given in the shape of a series of letters to an eminent American statesman, (Hon. Alexander H. Stephens, of Georgia,) the papers have been, since their first appearance, carefully collated and revised by the author, so as to make them, as far as possible, a complete and accurate history of the events of which they treat. The scope and intent of the work cannot be better expressed than in the following extract, which is taken from Mr. Mitchel's announcement of the design of the Letters:—

"These Letters were first published with the purpose professed in the Letters themselves;—namely, to give information to Americans, on Irish authority and from an Irish point of view, concerning a series of events in Ireland, which have been studiously presented to all mankind by the British Press from precisely the *opposite* point of view. . . . . There has not been, to my knowledge, any other attempt to give a connected narrative of the Decline and Fall of 'Repeal,'—of the English Famine policy, and its complete success, —and of the steady progress of demoralization and denationalization, which have brought Ireland into her present abject state. These Letters may fill up that *desideratum*, at least provisionally,—till the task shall be better accomplished by somebody else.

"The title of the Letters,—LAST CONQUEST, (PERHAPS,)—is sufficiently descriptive; as was also the title of that song of Béranger,—'*Ma dernière chanson, peut-être.*' The song was his last song, until the next came. Whether our latest conquest is to remain, or not, the 'Last Conquest,' will depend upon ourselves altogether."

THE CRUSADE OF THE PERIOD.

CHAPTER I.

FROUDE *versus* IRELAND—THE MOCK TRIAL—PLAN OF THE "CRUSADE"—ITS MEANING—THE "CRUSADER" HIMSELF—"TAKING CHARGE" OF THE IRISH—THE "INVERTED COMMAS."

The "First of Living Historians," as several newspapers designate this gentleman, is only now really opening his batteries. He has by no means done with his victim, but presses on, "blow on blow." Even since the termination of the lectures and counter lectures, by the Historian and by Father Burke, there has been published, in this country and in England, the first volume of a new and elaborate work:—*The English in Ireland, in the Eighteenth Century: By James Anthony Froude, M.A.*, a work which sheds additional darkness on a subject which the author has already done much to overwhelm in obscurity. This darkness I shall endeavor presently to dispel in some degree. Meantime the pens not only of national writers in Ireland, but of many fair-minded journalists both in England and in the United States, are busily employed in making indignant exposures of the spirit and tone of the Historian, as well as of his alleged facts and authorities. The controversy, then, is only beginning.

This grand plea, lately brought forward so gravely by the Historian, and as gravely tried before the imaginary tribunal of our American public, *this* indeed is finished, and got out of the way. Now that all those pleadings are before us, as well as the fresh and formidable indictment set forth in the new book, it may be expedient to review the whole matter. The lectures are carefully reported on either side, and the reports are doubtless generally correct; but still (at least so far as Mr. Froude's share in them is concerned,) they do not seem to have been revised by the author and published as his very words, so that you cannot absolutely hold him to words, figures, dates, and citations of authorities. Here, in this book, we have him, with his *litera scripta*, "inverted commas" and all. It may indeed be regretted that the eloquent Father Burke gave any countenance to the Sham Trial; that he innocently accepted the tribunal and pleaded to the declaration, in the name of his country; thus materially helping the general plan of the crusade: also that, after bandying compliments with the learned gentleman on the other side, gratuitously affirming and proclaiming that person's honesty, and saying that he *loved* him, Father Burke ended by giving up the whole case, concurring in his adversary's practical conclusion, turning to his countrymen and telling them plainly that they can do nothing, *nothing*, at home or abroad, to relieve their native island of British domination; and in short that they had better "wait for the *New Zealander!*" "*Attendez sous l'orme*" is the ironical French proverb to this same effect. "Wait for the New Zealander" will become proverbial in Ireland, in the same derisive sense. When that predestined savage shall be seen squatting upon the broken arch and sketching the ruins of London, *then* Ireland will arise, great, glorious, and free, first flower, etc.! Also, when the sky falls, shan't we have larks?

And so, at the end of the sham "trial," the Historian comes forward with a kind of playful insolence, and seizes on his small triumph with a sneer; congratulates everybody that "for practical objects" he and his opponent are agreed, offers him his hand, and kindly says, "any how, I hope we part in good humor." Oh! certainly; all the good humor in life, so far as he and Father Burke are concerned: and the sham court rises, with a laugh—*solvuntur risu*.

But there are others concerned in this crusading mission of the Historian. And there is, and was, no tribunal at all: it was only the agreeable Englishman's device to flatter this great American people, by presenting a sort of mimicry of a Geneva Arbitration to settle international differences by the high and mighty award of American public opinion. I decline to plead at all before the American public: because Irishmen are themselves the best and sole judges of the rights and the wrongs of their own land. Neither can I be a client of the excellent and eloquent Father Burke in this cause; indeed he excludes me; for, in his second lecture, he accepts with thanks and effusion Froude's statement, that, after the "Reformation," "the cause of the Catholic Religion and Irish independence became inseparably and irrevocably one." As a non-Catholic, then, I am ruled out of court, as well as Grattan and Tone and O'Brien and Davis. We are not quite Irish, under this rule. Counsel on the other side, indeed, is willing to take us under *his* protection: he treats the Irish Protestants as his peculiar and favored clients; but I repudiate his advocacy even more earnestly than the Dominican's. He has obliging things to say concerning Irish Protestants when they are useful slaves of British policy: and not being a slave to that policy, I cannot hope to profit by the author's advocacy. From my own point of view, then, I shall adventure to survey the whole field on which our Irish cause lately *appeared* to be debated so earnestly, but from which the two adversaries have walked off together almost hand-in-hand, with all the complacency in the world.

The truth is, and it may as well be said, that many of Father Burke's countrymen have felt disappointed at the soft and tender usage which he gave, throughout, to that loud and furious enemy of our native island. Surely, the Dominican could have struck heavier blows, but that something held his hand. Yet it is not easy to understand what moved Father Burke to such tenderness of courtesy: for, assuredly, the First Living Historian prepared the campaign of this foray of his in a manner irritating enough to provoke a saint.

The Historian had written his book, and had sent it to the press, a book full charged with venomous loathing and contempt of the Irish name and nation; and seems to have judged it expedient, for some reason or another, to condense the substance of it into lectures, and to come over and discharge them in American cities, where he supposed he would be sure of a favorable hearing for any abuse of Irish and Catholics amongst the preponderating masses of American

Protestants. I suppose he had been told so by some "Christian young men." At any rate, the thing would make a stir, and advertise his book. At the very moment when it was convenient for him he was invited by the "Literary Bureau." Whether this was a happy coincidence, or whether he invited the Bureau to invite him, cannot now be guessed; nor is it worth while. His subject was to be "The Relations between England and Ireland;" and his coming was heralded by a pamphlet containing first a fac-simile of his letter of acceptance, and then many pages presenting selected passages from his works, entitled "Gems from Froude." This pamphlet was largely circulated gratuitously. In the letter he considerately says—"I should like it to be understood by the Irish in New York generally, that I am neither going to flatter them nor flatter England." Were "the Irish in New York generally" fondly soothing themselves with the idea that Froude was coming to flatter them? Who saw any sign of such pleasing anticipations? In truth, we are not much used to flattery,—save from a politician, now and then, about election times. And those who know very much of the "First Historian's" previous writings could scarcely have looked for anything very fulsome in the way of sycophancy at his hands. Indeed in these very "Gems," strung together on the thread of this pamphlet, there is but one passage referring to Ireland, which begins thus—

"Sadder history, in the compass of the world's great chronicle, there is none than the history of the Irish: so courageous, yet so like cowards: so interesting, yet so resolute to forfeit all honorable claims to interest. In thinking of them, we can but shake our heads," etc.

I do not well know how courageous men contrive to be "like cowards:" yet after all, it seems our people are "interesting:" he never denies this: "interesting" yet "resolute to forfeit honorable claims to interest!" Not only a dishonorable people, but resolutely and irrevocably determined that no honorable person can concern himself about any of them. Differ, we Irish may, on politics, on religion, on many matters of human conduct and life, but at least on one point we are agreed—we are unanimously and irremediably resolved to be *dishonorable!* This is bad indeed. Let me add to this "Gem" another jewel of my own selection from the new volume just published—

"The sun never shone on a lovelier country, as nature made it. *They have pared its forests to the stump*, till it shivers in damp and desolation. The perceptions of taste which belong to the higher orders of understanding are as completely absent as truthfulness of spirit is absent, or cleanliness of person and habit."

No: assuredly the First Living Historian had no mission to flatter the Irish race. But let readers bear in mind the phrase, "They have pared its forests to the stump," until we have advanced a little further with this modest review.

England, the country of the Historian, is in these days disquieted once more by a revival of national spirit and national pretensions in Ireland. "Home-Rule" has become a political test. "Irish ideas," even, which England has so often before felt it her duty to stifle in blood—these very Irish ideas are now again put forward as the only just basis on which the island should be governed: and, worse than all, many of the best of the Protestants are cordially uniting with their Catholic fellow-countrymen in demanding some approach to self-government. British policy had often been interfered with by such demonstrations before; and had usually, at least since the "Reformation," found its best safety in promoting religious animosities. The same course must be taken now again: hatred and spite of Protestant against Catholic must be kindled again and fed with fresh fuel, or all is lost. Prudent British Statesmen look anxiously around and survey the situation; they see a considerable Protestant recrudescence in several parts of the world, provoked ostensibly by the late Council of the Vatican, with its definition of the ancient doctrine of Papal Infallibility. They see prosperous and triumphant Germany girding up its loins to do battle with the dreadful Pope; and Prince Bismarck is prosecuting bishops and thundering against Jesuits. And so in the very latest Irish papers I read, without surprise—

"On Monday, criminal informations were filed in the Crown Office, Dublin, in the names of Mr. Christopher Palles and Mr. W. Lane Joynt, against his Lordship the

Bishop of Clonfert, twenty-three Catholic clergymen of the county Galway, Captain Nolan, and Mr. Sebastian Nolan. All these gentlemen are charged with the use of undue influence, and the Court of Queen's Bench is asked to 'award due process of law' against them. The venue is laid in the county Galway, and it appears that, as the informations are equivalent to bills found by a Grand Jury on an indictment, the next step will be to put the Bishop of Clonfert and his fellow-defendants in the dock of the County Court-house, in Galway, and call on them to plead."

The "undue influence" was in representing to their flocks that it would be committing a sin to vote for Gladstone's candidate : and a crying sin it certainly would have been; and who could more properly warn them against sin than their clergy? However, the prosecution itself will excite spite and rage, unmanly exultation amongst the Orangemen, bitter and vindictive wrath amongst the Catholics; and thus a great point is gained, to begin with. Next, it is at any time easy to create exasperation amongst the more ignorant Protestants, by pointing out the so-called presumption of the Catholic Church; and facilities are given to carry on the unholy work of lashing the two parties to fury by the agitation now existing on the question of public education. Shall the education of children be made carefully irreligious? or shall all the people be required to pay for an irreligious education, though they cannot use the article? Or shall parents be at liberty, if they choose, to give to their children a separate denominational education, without being compelled also to pay for the State-education of other people's children? Easy enough to alarm the ignorant persons aforesaid, by a suggestion that this latter plan is nothing but a device of the Jesuits to bring back the Inquisition. Then, in turning their eyes anxiously around the horizon, those prudent English Statesmen take careful note of the signs of the times in the United States. Here, also, the State and denominational school systems are eagerly debated. Here, also, the ignorant masses have been taught to believe that the Infallibility of the Pope, and especially the "Syllabus," are only an insidious machinery for troubling the peace of States and Governments, and making us all vassals to "the Woman who sitteth upon Seven Hills." The English know, also, (for they have both spies and agents busy here,) that, ever since the close of the war, there has been gradually reviving a strong, anti-Catholic and anti-Irish feeling, which awaits only a good stirring example, set *in England*, to follow suit as usual. An excitement can always be stirred up in America on this principle. It was the "Ecclesiastical Titles Act" to restrain Papal Aggression, that gave birth to our shabby Know-Nothing crusade; and a few bloody riots were duly enacted, a church or two wrecked, a good priest "ridden on a rail," and tarred and feathered by the principal inhabitants of a New England town. A renewal of all this would be invaluable for exasperating the so-desirable religious rage in Ireland.

And there is more in it. Certain millions of the Irish people, extirpated out of their own land, and escaped from the British famines, are now dwelling, they and their children, upon this continent; and everybody knows that they watch with keen interest every National movement of their kindred at home, with the stern determination to bear a hand in the final settlement of that question. Nothing could possibly be more serviceable to Gladstone's policy than the successful arousing of strong dislike and contempt on the part of the Protestant-American people against their Catholic and Irish fellow-citizens. Now no man in all England could be found so fitted for this dreadful office as the First Living Historian.

Froude's qualifications for his mission (besides a most fluent and sensational rhetoric) are twofold. First, he hates the Catholic Church, and has at his fingers' ends all the foulest imputations and all the diabolical language of abuse usually employed these last three hundred years to cover that Church with a robe of blackest horror:—second, he claims for his own country an absolute right to possess and govern Ireland at her own will and for her own profit. As I read these pages of the "First Historian," I confess that I warm towards him a little: he does not cant much, for an Englishman, but pours forth his insults upon the people and upon their religion with a rather honest kind of cynical brutality. He tells us in plain words that "superior strength is the equivalent of superior merit:" in other words it *is* "superior merit:" and referring to Ireland and her *rights*, forsooth, he says:—

"There neither is nor can be an inherent privilege in any

person or set of persons to live unworthily at their own wills, when they can be led or driven into more honorable courses ; and the rights of man—if such rights there be—are not to liberty, but to wise direction and control : "—that is, control by us English. There is another passage (page 609,) which I like even better—

"The consent of man was not asked when he was born into the world : his consent will not be asked when his time comes to die. As little has his consent to do with the laws which, while he lives, he is bound to obey. Let a nation be justly governed," etc.,

—that is, by us English. *hurra —*

As for the Catholic Church in Ireland, the only defect he finds in the course of English policy is, that there was not persecution violent enough and constant enough exercised upon that Church. Here are his words (p. 213)—

"No government need keep terms with such a creed when there is power to abolish it. To call the repression of opinions which had issued so many times in blood and revolt by the name of *religious persecution,* is mere abuse of words ; while at the same time the best minds in England really believed that, besides its treasonable aspects, the Roman Catholic religion was intellectually degrading and spiritually poisonous."

These, you observe, were not the worst minds in England, but the best ; and the Historian most heartily agrees with them. But the author is not altogether averse from " reconciling the loyal priests and the Government, by subsidizing a power which had proved too strong to be violently overthrown " (p. 565). On the same page he cites with approbation the words of a pamphlet which seems one of his favorite authorities—

" Possibly it might be a good plan to abolish the payment of dues, offerings and fees from the poor Papists to the priests, and settle salaries for them. Their interests would then be closely tied to those of the State, and they might be managed like cannons, *whose mouths are still pointed as they please who fill their bellies.*"

The reader has now a clear enough idea of the high qualifications of this Historian to do the Queen's business in Ireland.

The adventurers under Henry II., came to "take charge" of the Irish, says this Historian, in his preliminary chapter. "The Normans," he assures us, were a people "whose peculiar mission was to govern men:" and it seems they could not help it. Who can resist his fate?—

"They were born rulers of men, and were forced, by the same necessity which has brought the decrepit kingdoms of Asia under the authority of England and Russia, to take the management, eight centuries ago, of the anarchic nations of Western Europe."

It was hard on the Norman people! For these poor devoted rulers of men were forced "by the same necessity," to do much forgery, perjury and murder to carry out their missioned task. Neither will our rulers of men altogether give us up when we escape from under their clutch: their care and sympathy follow us round the world. Here, for example, the Irish-Americans who have been living on good enough terms with native American and other citizens, and who have been doing much honest work here, making themselves independent, marrying and giving in marriage, procreating a good breed, which is to have its full share in the labor and the thought and the honorable effort of every kind upon this Continent in the future,—these Irish-Americans find themselves followed, even here, from time to time, by agents and emissaries of those blessed governors of men, whose task is to lower us in the eyes of our fellow-citizens, and to make them understand that we are not fit to be trusted as citizens of this or any other country. These English have taken direction of our people, once for all, and cannot without a pang give up the management of us. Though we take the wings of the morning and flee to the uttermost ends of the earth, even there will their hand lead us and their right hand hold us! Even here we find, at every turn, a vigilant English "ruler of men" cooling our friends, heating our enemies, carefully warning our neighbors that we are false, treacherous, cowardly, and cruel, that we never knew what to do with our own country, when we had one, and will surely do what in us lies to ruin America as we ruined Ireland.

I cannot but admire the Historian when, in one of his lectures, he comes to deal with the apparently simple suggestion that, inasmuch as England has shown nothing but imbecility and stupidity in her dealings with Ireland for seven hundred years, and has brought the island to be a world's wonder for its long agony of misery, famine, and discontent, she had better perhaps relieve herself of the charge and let Ireland alone. At this idea he breaks out into a foam of rage. What! let Ireland govern herself! No, never! Anything but that. England will never consent either to Home Rule, or to any altered arrangement which might put Ireland into the way of being able to extort Home Rule:—never, until England is beaten to her knees: *never! never!*

Bravo! First Historian! Beaten to her knees, quotha? Beaten to her mouth and nose must she be. It is precisely the sentiment which I have myself often written and uttered. The British Empire must utterly perish, that is, be dismembered as an Empire,—or "Ireland must die a daily death, and suffer an endless martyrdom."

Mr. Froude seems to admit all this: confesses with a charming ingenuousness that Ireland has been always not only unjustly and cruelly, but stupidly, governed by England: that she is now so governed, and is likely to be: nay that Ireland has ample provocation and perfect right to take up arms and establish her independence on the field. Very well then, says the Historian, draw your sword and *come on!* This is a curiously happy sarcasm, addressed to a nation carefully disarmed by law, and whose houses are at all times subject to search for any kind of weapon. A gang of robbers seize a traveller, tie him to a tree, disarm him, strip him, rob him of his money: he cries out and remonstrates; calls them a pack of rascals, demands to be let loose: but one of the brigands replies to him; "Friend, you have no right to liberty unless you fight for it. Your arguments are good, are unanswerable: therefore, will you fight us all, there as you stand, with your hands tied behind your back to that tree? If you cannot do this, stop your vain arguments and 'blatant' bawlings,—enough to disgust the very owls in the trees." As Dean Swift said, concerning the book of Molyneux: "In reason, all government, without the consent of the governed, is the very definition of slavery; but, *in fact*, eleven men, well armed, will certainly subdue one single man in his shirt."

Here, then, is the whole political theory and principle of

the Historian. We have you down, throttled, stripped, disarmed, garotted: our treatment of you and of your country has been stupid, and a scandal: it is going to be in the future what it has been in the past: and now, what are you going to do about it? I must confess that I like this Crusader of the Period for so honest an exposition of his principles; and feel inclined to take his part against the savage, word-catching critics who have been finding him guilty of misquotations, mistranslations, and even ignorant blunders, as they fondly dream.

And does a citizen of Brooklyn, indeed, or that keen Scotchman, Mr. Hosack, or the *Quarterly Review*, and "fifty others," do they, or does any of them, innocently imagine that they can corner the First Living Historian, by pointing out misquotations, falsified authorities and the like? The Historian defies them. He has composed his "History of England" from "perhaps two hundred thousand documents," and, with a calm irony, invites his critics to follow him through those two hundred thousand pigeon-holes, some in the British Museum, some in the State-Paper Office, some in Trinity College Library, or elsewhere; and he cannot think of replying to any special charge of fraud or forgery, unless his accusers go through all those references. "I have read everything myself," he observes in his last lecture. "I have made my own extracts from papers which I might never see a second time." And again—"It often happens that half a letter is in one collection and half in another. There will be two letters from the same person and the same place, on the same subject and on the same day. One may be among the State Papers, another in the British Museum. I will not say that passages from two such letters may not at times appear in my text as if they were one." But he has done his utmost, as he assures us, to tell the truth. And those who doubt it have only to go through his 200,000 pigeon-holes. Thus a rabbit squats at one of the burrows of his intricate warren, and invites the terriers to chase: they give chase: there are a thousand galleries, corridors, labyrinths: the rabbit's ears are seen for a moment peeping at one of the holes: the dog goes for him; but in the twinkling of an eye the rabbit's *fud* is seen at another hole forty yards off. No straightforward terrier can follow him up, though a well-trained ferret might. Thus, when the Historian brandishes before us the 200,000 authorities which we must master before we can "convict" him of even one error, he intimidates the simple mind. In vain the citizen of Brooklyn points out that the Historian has printed a letter as from Randolph, in Edinburgh, which was never written by said Randolph, attributing to Queen Mary of Scotland an atrocious and blood-thirsty saying, which she never said. He replies that, if Randolph, in Edinburgh, did not write that letter, yet another man somewhere in England did write another letter: and although that *other* letter does not attribute the blood-thirsty utterance to Queen Mary at all, yet the Historian denies that he has been *convicted:* no, only accused by the citizen of Brooklyn. If he answered the citizen he would have to answer "fifty others"—so many are the charges which have been made against him: and with a frank and noble candor he offers to submit the examination of his authorities to a commission of five Irish Judges (out of twelve), with the Irish Lord Chancellor to preside: they are to examine the 200,000 authorities, and if they find that he has been unfaithful in citing any one, he will expunge that passage: can a candid Historian do more?

Some persons may term this proposal an illusory kind of challenge: because the human mind is incapable of conceiving the Lord Chancellor of Ireland and four of the Judges quitting the bench, where they have their own business to mind, flinging off wigs and ermine, burying themselves for (let us say) seven years in the crypts of record-offices, museums and college libraries, closely following the Historian as he fits his references or parts of them to a MS. in London, then dives and re-appears in Dublin to find the other lines of the letter. Not seven years, but seventeen, would be needful for this labor: and the enemies of our First Historian will be sure to say that he never would have proposed such an inquiry but that he knows it to be impossible. I suggest, then, that he add to the list of Commissioners the name of General Grant.

In short, the Historian is too hard a nut for these word-catching critics to crack. Let them not imagine that they can impale such a man as this upon the horn of an inverted comma, or hang him at the tail of a semi-colon. It is in vain for the citizen of Brooklyn, or fifty others, to taunt him with misquotations; he smiles in front of his 200,000 pigeon-holes, and says to them, "Come on, then, gentlemen, follow! follow!—or send on the Lord Chancellor or the President: either do this, or forever hold your peace." It is in vain also that another small critic points out how the First Historian, having occasion to refer to the oil-bottle of Rheims, speaks of the bottle as a man, and calls him "Saint Ampoul." Do they think they have caught him here! Vain dreams! Mr. Froude *connait son Rabelais:* and knows that famous voyage which Pantagruel made to consult the Oracle of the *Holy Bottle*, whose name was Bac-Buc; and this is the very Saint, and the very bottle, which the learned person means.— Ah! critics, you are not going to trip up the First Living Historian in this flimsy kind of way!

I am now in good humor with the Crusader of the Period; and in the next chapter shall come closer to him.

CHAPTER II.

CONSPIRACY AGAINST THE "FIRST HISTORIAN"—JOHN P. PRENDERGAST—COLONEL MELINE—ATTITUDE OF THE "HISTORIAN"—HE MARCHES OFF—HIS BOOK—THE "NORMANS"—THE "MASSACRE" OF 1641—"PROTESTANTS," GOOD AND BAD.

FROUDE is really a man to be congratulated, or almost envied. He has stirred up hosts of vindictive enemies on both sides of the Atlantic. He is the Hero of Two Worlds, in another sense than the Lafayette sense. Like bloodhounds, they are upon his track in either hemisphere; his new book, *The English in Ireland in the Eighteenth Century*, will have a sale unexampled: and this—as they say in New England,—this is the calculation.

I said that the discussion raised by the Crusader is only beginning. Now it grows hotter and fiercer every day. Not only that fell critic, the bulldog "Citizen of Brooklyn," holds our Historian fast, with a grip like death, but I find that Mr. Prendergast, author of the "Cromwellian Settlement," has fallen upon Historian Froude with a fury even more ferocious than Mr. Meline's own; not counting the long array of his other enemies in England and Scotland. I have the honor to make him my compliment. Nothing could fall out more happily for him than this *view-hallo* and full cry of eager hunters. Mr. Prendergast, after having read the first volume of the new book, has addressed several letters to the Dublin press; one of which opens thus—

"Mr. Froude, I believe, is lighting a fire that he has little conception of. Deep as our hatred has hitherto been at our unparalleled historic wrongs, it is as nothing to the intense detestation we shall hereafter hold the English in. Though the vile English press are unwilling to commit themselves to the support of Mr. Froude's crusade against the exiled Irish, until they see the success of it, it is easy to perceive how they sympathize with it, and how gladly they would see the Americans hate us as deeply as they do themselves. For, in truth, the self-imposed mission of this friend and lover of Ireland (God save us from our English lovers!) is to turn the Americans against us."

Here Mr. Prendergast is quite wrong, on one point. Our Historian knew very well that he was lighting a fire; and intended it. Moreover, he will get out of it himself without singing a whisker, by means of a patent fire-escape which he has invented. But now, some one may ask *who* is Mr. Prendergast? He is an author of whom Mr. Froude has himself made honorable mention in this very book, the *English in Ireland*. He says (p. 134 *n*.) :—

"I cannot pass over this part of my narrative without making my acknowledgments to Mr. Prendergast, to whose personal courtesy I am deeply indebted, and to whose impartiality and candor in his volume on the Cromwellian Settlement I can offer no higher praise than by saying that the perusal of it has left on my mind an impression precisely opposite to that of Mr. Prendergast himself. He writes as an Irish patriot—I as an Englishman : but the difference between us is not on the facts, but on the opinion to be formed about them."

—Meaning that, in Prendergast's opinion, it was hard measure to compel all Irish land-owners, in three of the four provinces, on a certain day in Winter, by sound of trumpet and *beate of drumme*, to arise and transplant themselves, into the wilds of Connaught ;—but that in Froude's opinion it was a wholesome measure, intended for the good of the Irish themselves. But what I specially desire to call attention to, in this place, is the excessive discourtesy with which Mr. Prendergast repays that honorable mention by the First of Living Historians. After having, by his "personal courtesy" (and something more than that) earned so grateful and graceful an acknowledgment from so grand a prince of literature, this Irishman no sooner reads the book in which a flattering notice of himself is contained, than he suddenly turns rough and rude, and even brutally barbarous. He ignores entirely the compliment to himself; and is perhaps ashamed of it. "The twistings and wrigglings of this English viper" —such is about the best language he can find for his *quondam* acquaintance. Mr. Prendergast admits that he did guide the researches of our Historian, and did furnish him with authorities and references, sometimes directly, sometimes through others. But he soon had reason to doubt the good faith of this ardent historic investigator, and thought it needful to deal with him accordingly. In the first quarter of the eighteenth century, about the years 1719 and 1723, occurred certain legislative proceedings in the Colonial Parliament of Dublin, concerning which some doubts arose; and both Mr. Prendergast and Mr. Froude were at the same moment laboring in record offices to ascertain the facts, and discover the documents. Mr. Prendergast found what was wanted;—I do not enter here into the odious and indecent details; but must do so before I have done with Froude. Having lighted upon the documents, the laborious Irish scholar, in all good faith, thought he was bound to communicate them to Mr. Froude. Here is his own account of that matter in his late letter to the Irish journals:—

"Now for Mr. Froude's treatment of this event. He knew he could not avoid it, or mis-state it, as he has done so many other events. For, having met Mr. Froude shortly afterwards, making his searches in the State Paper Department at Dublin Castle, I thought it right to tell him of my discovery. But he was already aware, so he told me, of the fact, having seen the original letter in the Public Record Office, London. There was something, however, so extraordinary in the man's demeanor that I had my misgivings that he intended to *misdeal* with the transaction in some way; so I published it in the *Freeman's Journal* of the 28th April, 1871. I confess I had great curiosity to see how he would treat the matter in these circumstances."

The writer then reprints some words and phrases from this book; and continues:—

"Let it be remembered that I had bound him with such strong cords, by publishing the entire letter beforehand, that there was no possibility of his mis-stating the terms or the scope of it; and then observe the writhings and twistings of this English viper, that, nursed in his youthful sickness by the poor peasantry of Mayo, and since that day a frequent visitor to Ireland, seeks to spit his venom against us at home by publishing this book, and then immediately rushes to America to endeavor to instill into the English race abroad the same hatred he and his colleagues are filled with at home."

Words that burn!

I mean to tell something of the matter which was in question, before I have done: but in the meantime it is enough

to arouse the sympathies of all readers in favor of Mr.
Froude, by showing the shocking manner in which his
kindly overtures to Prendergast have been received. It is
true, no compliment from our Historian could elevate the
reputation of John P. Prendergast, the author of the most
perfect Monograph, of one special and cardinal point in our
Irish history: but still it seems hard that the recipient of
so pretty a compliment, should have no better return to
make than refusing the courtesy with both his hands, saying,
" Keep off, you English viper ! " Is the time indeed come
when these generous tributes from one literary man to
another, which give such a grace and charm to the intercourse of lofty intellects, are to become of no account? Is
a gentleman who has received so flattering an eulogy from a
great man justified in responding with a kick and a curse?
Let a discerning public judge.

In the midst of all this tumult of abuse, the First Historian
walks serene: he is altogether impassive, going calmly on
the even tenor of his way, answering all hostile critics with
disdain. Mr. Meline has vainly tried to worry him into
giving some sign, making some defence, in the matter of
Queen Mary of Scotland and her " latest Historian." Yet
the critic seems to have been aware from the first that he
would get nothing out of the man. Says that inevitable citizen of Brooklyn:—

" That Mr. Froude at this or at any other time would
answer the charges presented in ' Mary Queen of Scots and
her latest English Historian,' I have never expected. He
cannot do it and better his position, and I am, moreover,
sufficiently familiar with his ' manner of fence ' with critics
at home to know that he would not now attempt serious
responses in a case of any gravity. Mr. Froude cannot reply
to my allegations, because, he says, ' I am on one side of
the Atlantic, and my books and papers are on the other ; '
and he then repeats the plaintive wail, made several years
ago in the Pall Mall *Gazette*, touching his gigantic labors
with documents and MSS. ' in half a dozen languages.'
But during all the years Mr. Froude was at home among his
books and papers, his most aggressive critics and those of
bluntest speech succeeded no better than I have in obtaining answer, explanation, or apology from him. In reply
to the most damaging imputations, to the most offensive

accusations, he had nothing to say—and wisely, said nothing."

It is an attitude of grand disdain : but implacable Meline does not like it : he would prefer that the Historian would be good enough to explain some of those very numerous passages in which he has brought forward misquotations or palmed off mistranslations, and to expound how it has happened that *all* those "clerical errors," as Froude calls them, were on one side, always going to favor the scoundrel he intended to whitewash, and to blacken the unhappy Papist he meant to cover with obloquy.

Father Burke, I think, in his lectures, only ventured to call in question one citation of a documentary authority made by his opponent, purporting to be an Address to King George the Third, while the Americans were in revolt—an Address from the Irish Catholics represented by Lord Fingal and others, wherein the said Irish Catholics are shown in the act and attitude of crawling to the foot of the throne, praying to be led against the rebellious Americans. The great Dominican said he had searched for some such address, thinking very naturally that a document of so much importance would certainly have been printed; but he had not found any document answering the description, although he had found, in Curry's Collection, an address testifying general loyalty. It is servile enough, God knows—I have it now before me—and is signed, certainly, *Fingal, Gormanstown, Dillon, Kenmare,* and many others; but it says no word of America. Here is the Historian's proud rejoinder, in his last lecture :—

"I quoted a loyal address to George the Third, signed in the name of the whole body by the leading Irish Catholics. Father Burke says that, though fulsome in its tone, it contains no words about America. As he meets me with a contradiction, I can but insist that *I copied* the words which I read to you from the original in the State Paper Office, and I will read one or two sentences of it again. The address declares that the Catholics of Ireland abhorred the unnatural rebellion against his Majesty which had broken out among his American subjects; that they laid at his feet 2,000,000 loyal, faithful, and affectionate hearts and hands, ready to exert themselves against his Majesty's enemies in any part of the world; that their loyalty had been always as the dial to the sun, true though not shone upon."

This last line,—is the Historian very certain that it is not a quotation from Tom Moore? At any rate, he peremptorily shuts all mouths by saying, "I can but *insist* that I copied it in the State Paper Office." Now, the fact is, that nobody, by this time, believes one word that the First of Living Historians writes or utters, upon his own authority. There are, accordingly, many still who will not believe that such a document exists,—not, at least, until after the Lord Chancellor of Ireland and the Judges have exhibited a certified copy of it, in the Chancery Office, Four Courts, Dublin.

With his head high, and lofty disdain upon his countenance, this haughty creature thus finally brushes off the troublesome swarm of his assailants, and wraps himself nobly in his mantle of proof. Closing his last lecture, he says :—

"Here I must leave him" [namely, Father Burke]. "I leave untouched a large number of blots which I had marked for criticism; but if I have not done enough to him already, I shall waste my words with trying to do more; and for the future, as long as I remain in America, neither he, if he returns to the charge, nor any other assailant, must look for further answer from me. His own knowledge of his subject is wide and varied; but I can compare his workmanship to nothing so well as to one of the lives of his own Irish Saints, in which legend and reality are so strangely blended that the true aspects of things and character can no longer be discerned."

This sarcasm about the Irish Saints is in English good taste, being addressed to an Irish Dominican Friar! The Christian Young Men rub their hands with glee, over so neat and cunning a cut administered to those superstitious Romanists. Yet, after all, perhaps the Historian has not spent much of his time in studying the lives of the Irish Saints. He is more deeply read in the legend of that round-bellied French Saint, the jolly "St. Ampoul;" where, perhaps, Father Burke cannot follow him.

The main thing which we learn most explicitly from this last paragraph is, that the malignant critics of the Historian may now consider themselves safe from the effects of his resentment. There are fifty of them; and I am thus emboldened to become the fifty-first: he will not notice any of us; his sole reply to one and all being "*dixi.*" Very well; although I should deem it a very high honor indeed, if I could anyhow goad and badger so illustrious a person into replying, even in the most damaging manner to *me*, I must not think of so flattering an encounter: and as I have the Book itself before me, I can only comment upon its text as my lights may enable me. So now for the book itself.

At the opening of a "section" of chapter third, the Historian, speaking of the situation of the country in the reign of James II., has this frank and satisfactory statement of the position of affairs:—

"The Irish believed *that Ireland was theirs:* that the English were invading tyrants who had stolen their land, broken up their laws and habits, and proscribed their creed. The English believed that Ireland was a country attached, inseparably, *by situation and circumstances*, to the English crown; that they were compelled to govern a people who were unable or unwilling to govern themselves; and that the spoliation with which they were reproached had been forced upon them by the treachery and insubordination of the native owners. Between these two views of the same facts no compromise was possible."

Certainly not; and, indeed, everybody who has any interest in the question ought to feel obliged to the English Historian for stating the issue so clearly, and for arguing it so steadily and consistently throughout his work. Mr. Prendergast expresses the hope that *The English in Ireland* may be translated and published in France and in Germany, as we may be very sure it will be. In the meantime, we have it in very plain English: so that Americans (if they care) have the best opportunity of learning the whole case of our nation in its relation to England, upon excellent authority. I call it excellent authority *for this special purpose*, namely, for ascertaining the genuine sentiment of the English people, because all the author's historical books have an enormous currency in that country; and this one, above all, is sure to be devoured, by the multitudinous readers of England, with a greedy delight. I beg leave to commend it to them. I give my modest aid to the advertising of it. In truth, if some Irishman, possessed of the grim humor of

Dean Swift, had written these chapters with the intention of presenting the English case in the most grotesquely horrible and offensive point of view, he could scarcely go beyond our Historian. One might be almost inclined to suspect him of this malignant design, if the man were a wit, like the Dean of St. Patrick's. But there is not a ray of humor in his intellect: and when he gravely propounds that, to term the "abolishing" of the religion of a people, by fines, whipping, transportation, and the gallows, a case of religious persecution, is "a mere abuse of words;" and when he mentions, as a wholly untenable theory, the belief prevalent among the Irish, *that Ireland was theirs,* he means no sarcasm: it is the most serious and stolid British insolence: not intended to be laughed at by any means, nor a fit subject for amusement at all. The thing has an odor of blood. Such words call up the ghosts of many generations of murdered men; and they are intended, and calculated, to make more such ghosts for ages yet to come. If I have heretofore spoken of this man's performances in a tone somewhat like levity, I drop that tone from the present moment, and proceed to expose the Historian in all his naked horror.

There is no need, for the present purpose, to examine this writer's account of the "occupation of Ireland," at the end of the twelfth century, by people whom he calls Normans, "whose peculiar mission was to govern men." The conquerors of England, and the invaders of Ireland, were, according to the Historian, not only Normans but Norman aristocrats. In this, as in everything else, he carefully consults and flatters the prevailing sentiment of his own people at the present day. The English cannot endure to say, or to hear, that their island was conquered in one battle by a mob of *Frenchmen,*—Frenchmen pure and simple, including those who lived in Normandy. They cannot endure to be told that one whole wing, and one-third of William's army, consisted of Bretons; another wing of Gascons and other people of the south and centre of France. And as for the "Normans," who came over, afterwards, to "take charge" of Ireland, it seems to our English friends invidious to dwell upon the fact that they were not Normans at all;—you might as well call them Auvergnats or Savoyards. The Fitzstephens and Fitzmaurices who preceded Henry II., were Geraldines, the Italian Gherardini; and their mother was the notorious Nesta, a Welsh lady of no uneasy virtue. Out of the same nest of Nesta came also Giraldus Cambrensis, the very first of the "carpet-bag" school of writers upon Ireland. And when Henry himself came over with his Knights, he also had no title to be called a Norman aristocrat, nor a Norman at all; —for in fact he was born in Anjou, where his father before him was born, and his children after him. He became indeed Duke of Normandy, as he became King of England; yet he never called himself a Norman; and if any one had affronted him by calling him an *Englishman*, he would have had the insulter lashed with dog-whips.

I notice this rubbish about "Norman rulers of men," only to point out how sedulously the Historian has consulted the national vanity of his public: but I shall now apply myself to his treatment of that which he calls "the gravest event in all Irish history, the turning-point on which all later controversies between England and Ireland hinge"—

"Those who see in that massacre the explanation and the defence of the subsequent treatment of Ireland, however unwilling to revive the memory of scenes which rivalled in carnage the horrors of St. Bartholomew, are compelled to repeat the evidence once held to be unanswerable.". In these words (p. 83) the Historian commits himself to the whole ghastly story. He will not, indeed, insist that two hundred thousand Protestants were assassinated in six months. But, if there was a certain exaggeration in the estimate of the numbers, he assures us that—"for these enormous figures the Catholic priests were responsible. They returned the numbers of the killed in their several parishes, up to March, 1642, as 154,000." Also, "Sir John Temple considered that 150,000 perished in two months, or 300,000 in two years." But as our learned Historian knows well enough that there were not so many Protestants in all Ireland, counting women and children, he thinks it best to take the cooler and calmer estimate of Lord Clarendon, who reduced the estimate to 40,000; or he is willing even to take Sir William Petty's numbers, namely 37,000. And even these figures, he says, may "seem too large." But that there was, in fact, a most frightful massacre perpetrated in Ulster, he feels it his duty to re-affirm; and for proof of it, in all its details, he refers to the folio volumes of sworn depositions now to be read in the library of Trinity College, "whose evidence is the eternal witness of blood which the Irish Catholics have, from that time to this, been vainly trying to wash away."

Now, I propose to show—

First, that there was no massacre at all.

Second, that the Historian knows there was no massacre.

Third, that he intentionally and advisedly cites "authorities" which prove nothing and shed not a ray of light.

Fourth, that in producing Temple, Petty, Dean Maxwell and others, as witnesses, he is producing those carpet-baggers who had need of establishing a "massacre," because it was their title-deed to the great estates afterwards confiscated:—that in short there was *money in the massacre*.

Fifth, that he has woven together this tissue of sanguinary falsehood for the purpose of blackening and scandalizing a whole people before the civilized world, or, as he expresses it, making that gory fable "the explanation and defence of the subsequent treatment of Ireland," meaning Penal Laws, and the whipping-post and the gallows and universal plunder of all persons who went to Mass.

Sir William Petty gathered together, out of the confiscated estates, those vast domains which his descendant, Lord Lansdowne, now possesses in Ireland. Sir John Temple was the founder of the Irish fortunes of the Temples Lords Palmerston. Dr. Maxwell was made Bishop of Kilmore, in reward for one affidavit: to be sure it was a hard one, as we shall see; but he swallowed it, and it agreed with him. Sir John Borlase, an Englishman, but a carpet-bag Judge on the Irish bench, had a share out of the spoil of the Papists. And these men, and many others like them, and their dependants, could not afford to let the "massacre" be questioned at all: it was on the massacre they lived and were providing for their little families: if any man at that time doubted the massacre they would have his blood.

Indeed, in the last Lecture of the Historian, he refers to the Rev. Ferdinando Warner, a very respectable clergyman of the Church of England, and author of a History of Ireland, who made a most careful examination into the alleged murders of Protestants, and reduced them to two thousand one hundred people—a heavy hecatomb enough, one might think: but it will not answer our Historian's purpose at all: he cannot come down to so low a figure: he does not know but that the next Protestant may whittle it down to nothing.

So he treats Mr. Warner's estimate with a *pooh-pooh*, and actually says: "I am sorry to say I have known many Protestants entirely unable to distinguish truth from falsehood." The Historian is utterly disgusted at such a "Protestant" as this, who tries to cut and lop away the whole foundation on which the treatment of Ireland is grounded and justified. Such a Protestant is no better than that Papist keeper of records in London who actually answered Mr. Meline's inquiry by giving him such information as convicted the Historian of fraud.

I am about to prove myself a very poor sort of Protestant, according to the Historian's religious test: for the task I have undertaken and the end I have set before me are to demonstrate, to all rational and fair-minded people, that this individual, purporting to be a Historian, has, both by his Lectures and his Book, deliberately falsified the very History which he undertook to elucidate; that he has used his researches of years with the cold malignity of a spider, to involve his intended victim in an inextricable network of black falsehood; referring for his "facts" to authorities he knew to be worse than worthless; presenting those pretended authorities to his readers as trustworthy and undeniable; suppressing, in general, or else disparaging (as of no consequence), all evidence which bore against his bloody plan; and that he has done all this with a certain "purpose fixed as the stars"—to use a fine expression of his own; but in fact I prefer my illustration to his, my own spider to his star:—and that this settled purpose was, to cover with execration and to overwhelm with a load of calumny, a generation of men, all dead two or three hundred years ago, in such sort as to cast a shadow of horror over their children and their children's children, even to the ninth and tenth generation. I know it may be suggested that the motive of his labor was perhaps no worse than to insure a vast circulation for his Book, by flattering the conceit of his own people and feeding their bitterest and dearest national passion:—let those who find this a good excuse give to the Historian all the benefit of it.

CHAPTER III.

MAKING THE ISSUE — THE PRETENDED MASSACRE — FROUDE'S "CHAMBER OF HORRORS."

I SHALL have little or nothing to say touching the cruel oppressions inflicted, for so many ages, upon my countrymen; and absolutely nothing at all in the way of complaint or vituperation on account of those sad events. Let it be granted, for the present, that the English, or the Normans, or whoever the Historian pleases, were "forced by circumstances to take charge" of Ireland, and that, having so taken charge, they were forced to take all the lands of the island for their own people; forced to proscribe the religion of the country, and transport priests for saying Mass; forced to stir up continual insurrections in order to help the good work of confiscation: let all this theory stand admitted; but whatever may be thought of all that, the present point which I shall make is, that the Historian bears false witness at any rate;—Historian and History being all one huge fraud together. If I do not prove this, I prove nothing.

Taking up, then, the said History at the "turning-point" of the famous "Masacre," I shall first give some account of the array of witnesses brought forward to establish it; and especially of Temple, Borlase, and Petty, and of the "forty folios" of depositions: testimonies, indeed, which I did not expect that any Englishman, or any Orangeman, would ever have the audacity to cite again. As the First of Living Historians, however, has thought proper to drag to light the whole hideous romance, and has actually come over to America to pour it into the horrified ears of this people,—both by Lectures and through the medium of a Book,—I shall now follow him into the revolting details at least of the one period of a few years which he has selected as the turning-point in the History of my native country.

It is very observable indeed, and somewhat entertaining, that from his very dark portraiture of the Irish people in general, he kindly excepts us *Protestants*. "When I call them a generation of riotous and treacherous cut-throats," he says, "I don't mean *you*. You Protestants, on the contrary, are the noble and godly element, which we, the English, have introduced, to bring some order out of this bloody chaos:—you are the missioned race—as Macaulay (the predecessor of Froude) calls you—the *imperial race* that we have planted, enabling you to help yourselves to all the lands and goods of the irreclaimable Popish savages, that you might hold the fair island in trust for us,—for *us*, Ireland's masters, and yours. You are our own 'Protestant Boys:' I pat you on the back, and exhort you not to do the work of the Lord negligently." But I am not myself acquainted with any Irish Protestant gentleman who is likely to accept graciously this considerate exception in our favor. My own friends in Ireland, from boyhood,—at school,—at the University, and in after life,—have been generally of opinion that it would be a blessed and glorious deed to sweep into the sea the last remnants of English domination in their country. I never was taught in my youth that the man of Two Sacraments has a natural right and title to take all the possessions, and to take the lives of the men of Seven Sacraments. My father was not only a Protestant, but a Protestant clergyman; and he, in the year '98, when only a student in college, was sworn in as an United Irishman; and then proceeded to swear in his friends; and the noble object of that society was to abolish the English power in Ireland. Grattan was a Protestant, and he declared that he despised the pretended liberty of half a million of his countrymen, based upon the serfdom and slavery of two millions more: and it was this Protestant who penned the Declaration of Irish Independence, and created a Volunteer army to make good his words. And Tone was a Protestant, who brought on two invasions of the French, to free his native island from the English. And Tandy was a Protestant, who commanded the artillery of the Volunteer army. I fear that the Historian will find, in our Protestants, an ungrateful set of clients. We will not have his advocacy upon any terms. I can imagine that I see William Smith O'Brien receiving the courtesies of our Historian, as a Protestant, and therefore, a sort of deputy Briton. This revered name of O'Brien I cannot mention without bowing in homage to so grand a memory. For years we broke the bitter bread of exile together, and drank of the same cup of captivity. He lived for the cause of his country's independence; and never, till his latest breath, repented of his gallant though fruitless effort to destroy, with armed hand, the tyranny that was gnawing away his people's life. It would be easy to name many other Protestants of the same principles; but at present let us content ourselves with Mr. Prendergast, who has so fiercely declined the special compliment offered him by this Historian. And, in truth, the very best book upon the subject of the turning-point of Irish history is this very "Cromwellian Settlement," by Prendergast. Let nobody take Froude's poison without taking Prendergast's antidote.

That there was an insurrection is certain. It began on the 23d of October, in the year 1641; and the whole plan and purpose of it were to retake and possess the farms and houses which had been forcibly taken away from the Irish of Ulster, only a few years before. From twenty years to thirty years had elapsed since most of the people of six counties had been driven to the mountains and bogs, that their pleasant fields might be occupied by Scotch and English settlers. The remnant of those Ulster clans had been reduced to the condition of laborers, or very small cottiers. Many men of high name, with the culture and associations of the gentry of that day, were tilling, as ploughmen, and reaping as harvest men, for the stranger, fields that had been their own. Others, with their shivering families, could look down from the brow of Tyrone hills upon those smiling valleys of the Blackwater and the Foyle, whence their own fathers had trooped, forty years before, to join their clans on the Blackwater, and to ride beside the bridle-rein of Hugh O'Neill, at the Yellow Ford. Of this sad and plundered people many of the young and high-spirited had emigrated to France or Spain, to take service in the armies of those countries. The rest lingered sorrowfully, in the hope that some alteration might be brought about, in their doleful lot, by a change of kings. For example, when King Charles the First came to the throne of England, there seemed to them a prospect of some share of relief or reparation: in the meantime, they endured life, hiding their clergy in woods and caves, concealing themselves, with their wives and little ones, as much as possible, from the notice of the insolent intruders. And when, at last, that King Charles and his Parliament were on the very point of open war, the leaders of the Northern Irish thought they might give counsel to their people,—disarmed and scattered as they were,—that the time was come to strike a blow. Of the long series of exasperating provocations which now at last made them ready to try this desperate remedy, I need not here speak. It is enough that the turning-point was reached.

The Historian here cannot bring himself to specify names and dates; nor even to indicate, save in a general way, the authorities for his fearful story. His sensibilities will not permit him to dwell upon scenes so sanguinary; but he gives this general account of the situation:—

"Savage creatures of both sexes, yelping in chorus, and brandishing their skenes; boys practising their young hands in stabbing and torturing the English children;—these were the scenes which were witnessed daily through all parts of Ulster. The fury extended even to the farm-stock, and sheep and oxen were slaughtered, not for food, but in the blindness of rage. The distinction between Scots and English soon vanished. Religion was made the new dividing line, and the one crime was to be a Protestant. The escorts proved in most cases but gangs of assassins. In the wildest of remembered winters, the shivering fugitives were goaded along the highways stark naked and foodless. If some, happier than the rest, found a few rags to throw about them, they were torn instantly away. If others, in natural modesty, twisted straw ropes round their waists, the straw was set on fire. When the tired little ones dropped behind, the escort lashed the parents forward, and the children were left to die. One witness, Adam Clover, of Slonory, in Cavan, swore that he saw a woman who had been thus deserted, set upon by three Irish women, who stripped her naked in frost and snow. She fell in labor under their hands, and she and her child died. Many were buried alive. Those who died first were never buried, but were left to be devoured by dogs, and rats, and swine. Some were driven into rivers and drowned, some hanged, some mutilated, some ripped with knives. The priests told the people 'that the Protestants were worse than dogs; they were devils and served the devil; and the killing of them was a meritorious act.' One wretch stabbed a woman with a baby in her arms, and left the infant in mockery on its dead mother's breast, bidding it 'Suck, English bastard.' The insurgents swore in their madness they would not leave English man, woman, or child alive in Ireland. They flung babies into boiling pots, or tossed them into the ditches to the pigs. They put out grown men's eyes, turned them adrift to wander, and starved them to death. Two cowboys boasted of having murdered thirty women and children; and a lad was heard swearing that his arm was so tired with killing, that he could scarce lift his hand above his head."

The main authority for all this is Sir John Temple, whose story is founded upon the famous folios of Depositions; but the Historian does not cite the depositions themselves, merely saying that they are the "eternal witness of blood." To those who have made Irish history a study, these wonderful affidavits are familiar; and I should be ashamed to take up space with them, but that to most readers they will be something new, and will besides show the exact sources from which the Historian has drawn his bloody marvels. Here, for example, are several specimens:—

"The examination of Dame Butler, who, being duly sworn, deposeth that

"*She was credibly informed by Dorothy Renals*, who had been several times an eye-witness of these lamentable spectacles, that she had seen to the number of five-and-thirty English going to execution; and that she had seen them when they were executed, their bodies exposed to devouring ravens, and not afforded as much as burial.

"And this deponent saith, That *Sir Edward Butler did credibly inform her*, that James Butler, of Finyhinch, had hanged and put to death *all the English that were at Goran and Wells, and all thereabouts!!!*

"Jane Jones, servant to the deponent, did see the English formerly specified going to their execution; and, as she conceived, they were about the number of thirty-five; *and was told by Elizabeth Home*, that there were forty gone to execution. Jurat, Sept. 7, 1642.

"ANNE BUTLER."

"Thomas Fleetwood, late curate of Kilbeggan, in the county of Westmeath, deposeth, That *he hath heard from the mouths of the rebels themselves of great cruelties acted by them*. And, for one instance, that they stabbed the mother, one Jane Addis by name, and left her little suckling child, not a quarter old, by the corpse, and then they put the breast of its dead mother into its mouth, and bid it '*suck, English Bastard,*' and so left it there to perish."

"Richard Bourk, bachelor in divinity, of the county of Fermanagh, deposeth, That *he heard, and verily believeth*, the burning and killing of one hundred, at least, in the castle of Tullah ; and that the same was done after fair quarter promised. Jurat, July 12, 1643."

In looking through the monstrous farrago of swearing, it is remarkable, first, that scarcely any one saw the horrid deeds he or she swears to, but only tells what somebody told somebody else, who told this deponent : also, that in most cases the authorities for the statements are called, in general terms, "the rebels." For example :—

"Katherine, the relict of William Coke, of the county of Armagh, deposeth, That many of her neighbors, who had been prisoners among the rebels, *said and affirmed, that divers of the rebels would confess, brag and boast,* how they took an English Protestant, one Robert Wilkinson, at Kilmore, and held his feet in the fire until they burned him to death."

To do the Historian justice, there is not one of the fearful scenes he has above described that he did not find in evidence duly sworn to upon the Holy Evangelists. The babies flung into boiling pots, or left to be devoured by swine ; the men and women stripped naked, and driven out under the wild winter weather. Nay, more, he is too modest, and does not cite by any means the most revolting cases, fearing, perhaps, to give a certain grotesque air to his pages. I can supply him, for his second edition, with more and better horrors. Stripping, for instance, is but a trifle : why not give us the case of Margaret Fermeney, an old woman of seventy-five, who swears that on her way up to Dublin, "She was stripped naked by the Irish *seven times* in one day." He will find this in the famous folios, and also in Temple. Or why not tell us what Elizabeth Baskerville swears she heard a murderer's wife say to the murderer, her husband :—

"Elizabeth Baskerville deposeth, That *she heard the wife of Florence Fitz-Patrick find much fault with her husband's soldiers,* because they did not bring along with them the grease of Mrs. Nicholson, whom they had slain, for her to make candles withal. Jurat, April 26, 1643."

Indeed, several of the affidavits make express mention of the strong desire those Irish had to collect Protestant grease. And it is all set forth in those volumes which are the "eternal witness of blood!"

I observe that the Historian has avoided the many miracles and ghost stories which are found in the same repertory of facts. Yet these would greatly heighten the sensational charm of his work; and here is one which might probably suit him:—

"Arthur Culm, of Cloughwater, in the county of Cavan, esquire, deposeth, That *he was credibly informed*, by some that were present there, that there were thirty women and young children, and seven men, flung into the river of Belturbert; and when some of them offered to swim for their lives, they were, by the rebels, followed in boats, and knocked on the head with poles; the same day they hanged two women at Turbert; and *this deponent doth verily believe*, that Mulmore O'Rely, the then sheriff, had a hand in the commanding the murder of those said persons, *for that he saw him write two notes*, which he sent to Turbert, by Brien O'Rely, upon whose coming these murders were committed: and those persons who were present also affirmed, that the bodies of *those thirty persons drowned did not appear upon the water till about six weeks after, past; as the said O'Rely came to the town, all the bodies came floating up to the very bridge;* those persons were all formerly stayed in the town by his protection, when the rest of their neighbors in the town went away."

There are many other very miraculous facts sworn to, which are quite accessible to the Historian: also many other and still more savage cruelties, which he does his readers positive wrong in suppressing. In the next chapter, I shall present still another *spicilegium* culled from the "eternal witness of blood;" and afterwards explain *why* these depositions were called for, *how* they were obtained, and how they were paid for. All which the learned Historian knew very well, but preferred to suppress for the honor of Protestant human nature.

CHAPTER IV.

THE SWEARERS—THE "GHOSTS OF THE BANN"—DEAN MAXWELL—MORE "MURDERS BY PAPISTS"—FROUDE'S TREATMENT OF THE EVIDENCE.

THE seventeenth century was the period of our most thriving Protestant trade in swearing. It was the time of Popish *Plots*, and of multitudinous "depositions." As for the thirty-four folio volumes of oaths, to which Historian Froude calmly refers us, as an "eternal witness," that learned person must know that many of them were paid for, in money, most of them in confiscated land and lucrative office: that many of them were never sworn at all, appearing with the pen drawn across the words "being first duly sworn:" that the Lords of the Council of Ireland, and the heads of the "English interest" in the island, absolutely needed these oaths for procuring the indictment of all Irish Catholics who owned anything; and that they bought the said oaths as in market overt. Carte, author of the Life of Ormonde, is a Protestant authority; and Mr. Froude has read his work, for he often cites it where it suits him: but he takes care not to give us this passage from Carte's first volume:—

"The Roman Catholics complained that *there were strange practices used with the jurors, menaces to some, promises of rewards, and parts of the forfeited estates;* and though great numbers of the indicted persons might be really guilty, *there was too much reason given to suspect the evidence.* I am the more inclined to suspect there was *a good deal of corruption and iniquity in the methods of gaining the indictments,* because I find a very remarkable memorandum made by the Marquis of Ormonde, in his own writing, of a passage in the Council, on April 23, 1643. There was then a letter read at the Board, from a person who claimed great merit to himself, in getting some hundreds of gentlemen indicted, and the rather for that he had laid out sums of money to procure witnesses to give evidence to a jury, for the finding those indictments. This was an intimate friend of Sir William Parsons, and might very well know that such methods would be approved by him."

The trade in affidavits had begun in 1642, a few months after the insurrection broke out; in the following year, when Ormonde read this letter, there was a perfect deluge of oaths; and the business went on very briskly for several years, until Sir William Petty, who longed to get at the Ormonde estates themselves, used a remarkable expression, as we read in the same Carte:—

"Sir William Petty bragged, that he had got witnesses who would have sworn through a three-inch board to evict the Duke."

It may perhaps be thought very harsh to blame too much these poor, hard-working swearers, if our good Protestants, driven out of house and home by "the rebels," and, finding that there was a demand for oaths, put their imaginations to the rack to invent the most horrible tales,—the more ghastly the higher price,—and hawked them in Dublin to noble lords and honorable gentlemen who would buy. Is a forlorn Protestant, who has been stripped bare, to be grudged even the chance of selling his naked soul?

Many of the swearers, indeed, received no cash in hand, but were sure of higher reward; which was the case of Dean Maxwell and other parsons. But, in dealing with the whole mass of evidence, it is curious to observe what caution and discrimination the Historian has shown. He names but two of the swearers, Dean Maxwell and one Adam Clover, and in constructing his general narrative of the atrocities, never hints that most of them are related on hearsay; and he omits altogether those which contain manifest impossibilities, and true Protestant miracles, and especially the *ghosts*.

In the last chapter, I mentioned the miracle of the floating corpses on the river at Belturbet, that, after lying drowned six weeks, came up and swam against the stream, up to the very bridge, at the moment when Maelmorra O'Reilly entered the village by that bridge. They came up to confront and accuse him of their murder—as a certain person was "credibly informed:" for, in fact, O'Reilly had still an estate in Cavan; and it was this estate which was guilty of the murder. But these swimming corpses did not speak, in which respect they fall short of the spectres of the Bann. It was said, and repeated several times in depositions, that, "about the 20th of December," (for they seldom give us dates at all, and then in a very loose way,) "the rebels" drowned one hundred and eighty Protestants in the Bann, at Portadown bridge; that this was followed by other *noyades* at the same place, week after week, until, as Dean Maxwell computes, there were over a thousand Protestants drowned there. The widow Catherine Cooke, not only swears to this, but adds in her affidavit this ghastly fact:—

"And that, *about nine days afterwards, she saw a vision or spirit, in the shape of a man*, as she apprehended, that appeared in that river, in the place of the drowning, *bolt upright, breast-high, with hands lifted up, and stood in that posture there until the latter end of Lent next following:* about which time, some of the English army marching in those parts, whereof her husband was one, (*as he and they confidently told this deponent*,) saw that spirit or vision standing upright, and in the posture aforementioned: but after that time, the said spirit or vision vanished, and appeared no more, that she knoweth."

This was not sworn until the 24th of February, 1643, when there was a most urgent demand, and good price, for the most frightful oaths. Other witnesses had a still more inventive imagination: and Elizabeth Price, of Armagh, swears that, on a certain day—

"She went unto the bridge aforesaid, *about twilight in the evening; then and there, upon a sudden, appeared unto them a vision or spirit, assuming the shape of a woman waist-high, upright in the water, often repeating the word Revenge! Revenge! Revenge!* whereat this deponent, and the rest, being put into an amazement and affright, walked from the place."

There are five or six other deponents who swear to these shrieking apparitions: but it is time to come to Dean Maxwell, afterwards bishop, that consecrated, anointed, and mitred perjurer, whose long affidavit is relied upon with the greatest confidence by Borlase and Temple, and is, therefore, cited by Froude, as a main part of his authorities, but without giving any of the Dean's very words. So it is now necessary to state *what* this reverend divine swore to.

This affidavit was sworn on August 22d, 1642, ten months after the insurrection began. The first notable thing in it is the extraordinary habit which "the rebels" had, whenever they had cut a good many throats anywhere, to come running to this Protestant divine to tell him their exploits:—

"Deponent saith, That *the rebels themselves told him*, this deponent, that they murdered nine hundred and fifty-four in one morning, in the county of Antrim; and that, besides them, *they supposed* they killed above eleven or twelve hundred more in that county; *they told him likewise*, that Colonel Brian O'Neill killed about a thousand in the county of Down, besides three hundred killed near Killeleigh, and many hundreds, both before and after, in both these counties."

It is even more strange to find that Sir Phelim O'Neill himself, the very head and front of the "Massacre," whenever he had slaughtered a good herd of Protestants, always made a confidant of our amiable Dean:—

"That *he heard Sir Phelim likewise report*, that he killed six hundred English at Garvagh, in the county of Derry; and that he had left neither man, woman, nor child alive in the barony of Munterlony, in the county of Tyrone, and betwixt Armagh and the Newry, in the several plantations and lands of Sir Archibald Atcheson, John Hamilton, Esq., the Lord Caulfield, and the Lord Mountnorris: and saith also, that there were above two thousand of the British murdered for the most part in their own houses, *whereof he was informed by a Scotsman*, who was in those parts with Sir Phelim, and saw their houses filled with their dead bodies. In the Glenwood, towards Dromore, there were slaughtered, *as the rebels told the deponent, upwards of twelve thousand in all*, who were all killed in their flight to the county of Down. The numbers of the people drowned at the bridge of Portnadown are diversely reported, according as men staid among the rebels. This deponent, who staid as long as any and *had better intelligence* than most of the English amongst them, and best reason to know the truth, saith, There were (*by their own report*) one hundred and ninety drowned with Mr. Fullerton; at another time, they threw one hundred and forty over the said bridge; at another time, thirty-six or thirty-seven; and so continued drowning more or fewer, for seven or eight weeks, so as the fewest which can be supposed there to have perished must needs be above one thousand, besides as many more drowned, between that bridge and the great lough of Montjoy, besides those that perished by the sword, fire, and famine, in Coubrasil (Clanbrassil), and the English plantations adjacent; which, in regard there escaped not three hundred out of all these quarters, must needs amount to many thousands.

"And further saith, that he knew one boy, that dwelt near unto himself, and not exceeding fourteen years of age, who killed at Kinnard, in one night, fifteen able strong men with his skein, they being disarmed, and most of their feet in the stocks."

The reader must remark that this hard-swearing divine does not affirm any of the above matters as of his own knowledge, until he comes to the wicked boy. About this there can be no mistake: for he knew the boy: not that he actually saw the bad boy kill those fifteen able strong men; but perhaps some frightened woman told some other woman, who told the Dean. Or probably some of the "rebels" themselves narrated the story to him; for these rebels appear to have had a certain malicious pleasure in "taking a rise out of" the Dean, if I may use a colloquial Irish expression.

But the reader is not to imagine that the Dean was not himself an eye-witness of anything at all: indeed he was so; for he saw, like Moses and the Israelites, a *pillar of fire;* and he remarked the disloyal silence of the dogs and cocks; as follows:—

"And the deponent further saith, That the first three days and nights of this present rebellion, viz., October 23, 24, and 25, *it was generally observed that no cock crew, or any dog was heard to bark, no not when the rebels came in great multitudes unto the Protestants' houses by night to rob and murder them;* and about three or four nights before the six-and-fifty persons were taken out of the deponent's house and drowned, and amongst those the deponent's brother, Lieutenant James Maxwell, in the dark of the moon, about one of the clock at night, *a light was observed, in manner of a long pillar, to shine for a long way through the air, and refracted upon the north gable of the house. It gave so great a light, about an hour together,* that *divers of the watch read both letters and books of a very small character thereby.* The former the deponent knoweth to be most true, both by his own experience, and the general observation of as many as the deponent met with in the county Armagh. The latter was seen by all those of the deponent's family, and besides by many of his Irish guard."

The zealous divine is next happily enabled to expose a most cunning device of "the rebels," for the purpose of concealing the extent of the carnage they had committed, and to make people believe that, after all, they had only assassinated one hundred and fifty-four thousand (out of 20,000 Protestants in Ulster,) within three or four months.

"And further saith, that it was credibly told him, that the rebels, *least they should hereafter be charged with more murders than they had committed*, commanded their priests to bring in a true account of them; and that the persons so slaughtered, whether in Ulster or the whole kingdom, the deponent durst not inquire, in March last, amounted unto one hundred and fifty-four thousand."

We shall see this monstrous fable repeated by others, adopted without scruple by Sir John Temple, and embodied in a letter to the King from the Lords of the Council at Dublin; as follows:—

"They murdered, up to the end of March last, of men, women, and children, 154,000, as is acknowledged by the priests appointed to collect their numbers."

Of course, Mr. Froude eagerly repeats this story, and dares to say that, if there was any exaggeration in the numbers, "the Catholic priests were responsible" (p. 111). But the most singular circumstance is, that nobody ever saw these "returns" made by the priests: nobody even knows to whom the returns were made, nor where they were preserved. They were important documents decidedly, and deserved to be kept in some safe place of deposit; yet, even this diligent Historian, with all his painstaking researches, could never get a glimpse of them. There never were any such returns: and it is beyond measure impudent, at this day, to cite such a tale; but it served its calumnious purpose then, and is reproduced as fresh as ever to serve the same purpose now.

It would be a pity to dismiss so soon the testimony of the devout Dean: his affidavit continues:—

"He might add to these many thousands more: but the diary which he the deponent wrote, among the rebels, being burned with his house, books, and all his papers, *he referreth himself to the number in gross*, which the rebels themselves have, upon inquiry, found out and acknowledge, which notwithstanding will come short of all that have been murdered in Ireland, there being above one hundred and fifty and four thousand now wanting of the British within the very precinct of Ulster. And the deponent further saith, that it was common table-talk amongst the rebels, that the ghosts of Mr. William Fullerton, Timothy Jephes, and the most of those who were thrown over Portnadown bridge, were daily and nightly seen to walk upon the river, sometimes singing of psalms, sometimes brandishing of naked swords, and sometimes screeching in the most hideous and fearful manner. The deponent did not believe the same at first, and yet is doubtful whether to believe it or not; but saith that divers of the rebels assured him that they themselves did dwell near to the said river, and being daily frighted with these apparitions (but especially with their horrible screeching,) were in conclusion forced to remove further into the country. Their own priests and friars could not deny the truth thereof; but as oft as it was by deponent objected unto them, they said, that it was but a cunning sleight of the devil to hinder this great work of propagating the Catholic religion, and killing of heretics; or that it was wrought by witchcraft. The deponent himself lived within thirteen miles of the bridge, and never heard any man so much as doubt of the truth thereof; howsoever the deponent obligeth no man's faith, in regard he saw it not with his own eyes; otherwise he had as much certainty as morally could be required of such a matter."

The Dean, you observe, "obligeth no man's faith," except in such cases as the pillar of fire, and the silent Papist dogs and cocks, and the bad boy, whom *he knew.*

Many readers may now begin to be of opinion, that they have had enough of Froude's forty folios of abominations: but I must give those readers still another dose of the "eternal witness of blood:"—for let it not be forgotten, that these documents form the whole foundation for the superstructure raised by Temple, Borlase, Leland, and Froude, and the whole justification for the policy of England in Ireland during these last two hundred years. The record must not be dismissed too lightly, in justice to the First Living Historian. I had thought it was exploded long ago; but now that this illustrious person has taken his stand upon it, and not only rested upon it his own credit as a historian, but also the whole subsequent policy of *his* country in relation to *my* country, there is a real necessity of probing it to the bottom and letting the light through it. Dean Maxwell's discourse—the most fructifying sermon that divine ever preached in his life, for it placed upon his head a bloody mitre, encircled by a black *aureole* of perjury,—has now been sufficiently exposed, though far from completely. Nothing would be easier, if the task were not so revolting, than to disgust all decent people with minute narratives of most grotesque obscenity, and cruelty more ingeniously horrible than ever entered into the head of an Iroquois; but the reader must be content with a few samples of the tamer sort. It will be observed that the deponents who swear to the horrid facts were in general mercifully dispensed from the pain of seeing them with their own eyes. Here is a hideous matter which somebody in Kilkenny told Mr. William Lucas—" taking a rise " out of William, as Kilkenny fellows are too apt to do:—

"William Lucas, of the city of Kilkenny, deposeth, That although he lived in the town till about five or six weeks past, in which time, he is assured, divers murders and cruel acts were committed, yet he durst not go abroad to see any of them; but he doth confidently believe, that the rebels having brought seven Protestants' heads, whereof one was the head of Mr. Bingham, a minister, they did then and there, as triumphs of their victories, set them upon the market-cross, on a market day; and that the rebels slashed, stabbed, and mangled those heads; put a gag, or carrot, in the said Mr. Bingham's mouth; slit up his cheeks to his ears, laying a leaf of a Bible before him, and bid him preach, for his mouth was wide enough; and after they had so laced themselves, threw those heads into a hole, in St. James's Green. Jurat, August 16, 1643."

Some of Mr. Froude's general statements, as I have before shown, are accurately confirmed by affidavit upon affidavit. If anybody doubts that "the wicked rebels" did really burn women and children in a house, and cut them to pieces if they tried to come out, let that doubter only read what an unknown woman, without a name, did *absolutely* tell the Widow Stanhaw:—

"Christian Stanhaw, the relict of Henry Stanhaw, late of the county of Armagh, Esquire, deposeth, That a woman that formerly lived near Laugale, absolutely informed this deponent, that the rebels enforced a great number of Protestants, men, women, and children, into a house, which they set on fire, purposely to burn them; as they did: and still as any of them offered to come out, to shun the fire, the wicked rebels, with scythes, which they had in their hands, cut them to pieces, and cast them into the fire, and burned them with the rest. Jurat, July 23, 1642."

Poor Mrs. Jane Stewart, residing in the town of Sligo, had, on a certain day, the good luck to be confined to her bed by sickness; and a piece of rare good fortune it was for Jane, seeing she was thus saved from the fate decreed to all the Protestants of that quiet town, and preserved alive to contribute her chapter to the "eternal witness of blood." She deposeth and saith:—

"All the men, women, and children of the British that then could be found within the same town (saving this deponent, *who was so sick that she could not stir*) were summoned to go into the gaol, as many as could be met with, all were carried and put into the gaol, where, about twelve o'clock in the night, they were stripped stark naked, and after most of them were cruelly and barbarously murdered with swords, axes, and skeins, and particularly by two butchers named James Buts and Robert Buts, of Sligo, who murdered many of them; wherein also were actors, Charles O'Connor, the friar, and Hugh O'Connor, afore-named, brother to the said Teigue O'Connor, Kedagh O'Hart, laborer, Richard Walsh and Thomas Walsh, the one the jailor, the other a butcher, and divers others whom she cannot name: and saith, that above thirty of the British which were so put into the gaol, were then and there murdered: besides Robert Gumble, then Provost of the said town of Sligo, Edward Nusham, and Edward Mercer, who were wounded and left for dead amongst the rest, and Joe Stewart, this deponent's son, which four being the next day found alive, yet all besmeared with blood, were spared to live. All which particulars the deponent was credibly told by those that escaped, and by her

Irish servants and others of the town: and further saith, that on the said sixth day of January, there were murdered in the streets of the town of Sligo, these British Protestants following, viz.: William Shiels and John Shiels, his son, etc.: and that they of the Irish, that came to bury them, stood up to the mid-leg in the blood and brains of those that were so murdered: who were carried out, and cast into a pit digged for that purpose, in the garden of Mr. Ricrofts, minister of Sligo."

Poor Jane Stewart, lying on her sick bed, did not see anything of it herself; but I think she had bad dreams.

Why should I wade any more through all this blood and brains? The reader must be weary of it, if not sick. Let it be sufficient to say that folio after folio, with *Jurat, Jurat* upon the pages, is full charged and reeking with the same kind of abomination. By far the greater part of the depositions are sworn upon hearsay: yet now and then a man comes boldly up and swears that he saw dreadful things with his own eyes. For example:

"James Geare, of the county of Monaghan, deposeth, That the rebels at Clownes murdered one James Netterville, proctor to the minister there, who although he was diversely wounded, his belly ripped up, and his entrails taken out, and laid above a yard from him, yet he bled not at all, until they lifted him up, and carried him away; at which this deponent being an eye-witness, much wondered; and thus barbarously they used him, after they had drawn him to go to Mass with them."

Another saw an "Irish rebel" make three passes with his drawn sword point-blank into the body of a woman, she with hands clasped defying him to hurt her unless God permitted him; and accordingly the sword never grazed her skin; and the wicked rebel walked off much discomfited, and all the onlookers mightily marvelled. Yet another swearer tells how the "rebels" took a Scotchman (they seldom have any names, neither the rebels nor victims); and having cut open his body to get at his "small guts," they did nail the end of said small guts to a tree, and then whipped the Scotchman round and round the tree, until all that intestine was drawn out and wound neatly round the trunk;—then whipped him back again, till it was unwound: and all this, as they said, to find out whether a Scotchman's gut or a dog's is the longer.

We have seen that the Historian scarcely names one of the swearers, except Dean Maxwell, whose testimony is the rock and strong tower to our Protestant interest; that he never gives any of the words of the swearers, and carefully omits any allusion to ghosts and miracles: but in one instance he has actually named another witness, Adam Clover, of the county Cavan, and gives him as authority for an act of cruelty perpetrated by three Irishwomen, who stripped a Protestant woman naked at the time of her childbirth, and left her and her child to die. I am delighted to find that he knows Adam Clover: but why not give us a little more of what Adam saw with his own eyes—for Adam was a good swearer. Why does our Historian withhold from his admiring readers such a choice horror as that which follows. Now Adam Clover deposeth and saith—

"That he *observed* thirty persons to be barbarously murdered, and about one hundred and fifty more cruelly wounded, so that traces of blood, issuing from them, lay upon the high road for twelve miles together: and many very young children were left and perished by the way, to the number of sixty or thereabouts."

Mr. Froude's friend Adam does not say where he *observed* all this, nor on what road, nor between what towns, nor by whom, nor upon whom, the murders and other cruelties were committed. At any rate we see here an example of the manner in which this great Historian manipulates his authorities, presenting only those particulars which he thinks may go down, with credulous people, and suppressing the rest.

One blunder, however, he has made, in calling attention at all to the atrocious cruelties charged in these oaths against Irishmen and Irishwomen, as perpetrated upon helpless women and children of another nationality. At no time in their history have the Irish,—our proud, fierce, generous Irish,—been capable of cruelty to women and children; no, nor to defenceless men. If Froude wants to tell of massacres, let him consult the annals of his own country: let him go back to St. Brice's day, 1002, at cock-crow in the morning, and feed full on horrors; or let him tell how the same Saxon slaves, who massacred their Danish masters on St. Brice's day, afterwards formed a plot to massacre their

French masters in the time of William the Conqueror: or let him turn his eyes a moment to the wild valley of Glencoe, and tell how King William's Protestant soldiers knew how to deal with women and infants.

Mr. Froude is right in saying that England and Ireland will never arrive at a good understanding until the business of the "massacre" (that turning-point in history) shall have been fully cleared up. It is true: but *he* has not cleared it up; nor was that his intention. The man's idea has been that the public would take his very general account of the matter, and rest upon his authority for those *other* authorities which ought to support him. He never was more mistaken in his life; and I shall be much deceived if the examination of that portion of Irish history, an examination which is now sure to go on, does not end in the gibbeting of Froude on high, as the most immoral of historic impostors.

My next chapter will finish his delinquencies as to the "Massacres;" and I shall afterwards have to show that in compiling the history subsequent to that, he has proved himself even more recklessly and desperately depraved.

CHAPTER V.

TOO MUCH FROUDE—THE "CLOUD OF WITNESSES"—SIR JOHN TEMPLE—DOCTOR PETTY—WHO "PARED THE FORESTS."

SOME readers, by this time, may be disposed to say, we have had enough of Froude: he is already a notoriously convicted Impostor, and no historian: and it is making too much of him to keep pursuing him in this way. Certainly, it is making too much of *Froude*, himself, whose literary pretensions I estimate very low, and whose historic merits are far less than nothing. He composes fiction in a picturesque style: and ought to have confined himself to that species of composition. He could match Mrs. Emma Southworth, or our graphic fellow-countryman Captain Mayne Reid. If he would contribute a striking tale of horror to the New York *Weekly Fee-Faw*, he could command more *per* column than ever did Sylvanus Cobb; but he had no call to the writing of history. However, it still seems needful to expose a little more of his "misdealing," as Prendergast mildly terms it, in the matter of the great "Massacre" of 1641.

"You who would form an independent opinion on the matter, I would advise you to read (*whatever else you read*) Sir John Temple's History of the Rebellion, and Dr. Borlase's History of it. Temple was, as I said, an eye-witness. Borlase's book contains, in the appendix, large selections from the evidence taken on oath before the Commissioners at Dublin."

This is from the Impostor's last lecture, in reply to Father Burke. His main authority for the whole story is still Temple, whom he calls an "eye-witness;" though in fact Temple was never out of Dublin all that time, and the alleged "Massacre" was seventy or eighty miles off: for Borlase is but a reproduction of Temple's History, and they are both founded wholly upon the famous Depositions. In this passage, then, as well as in his new Book, Froude commits himself and his readers entirely to the testimony of the eloquent Master of the Rolls: and he does not whisper one hint of the fact, that Sir John Temple himself, a few years later, tried to suppress that Book. Froude knows of course (for what is there that he does not know!)—but thinks his readers may not have met with, the published "Letters of his Excellency Arthur Capel, Earl of Essex, Lord Lieutenant of Ireland." It is no abstruse State-paper pigeon-hole I refer him to: the book was printed in London, 1770, a fair quarto; and it stands upon the shelves of all historic libraries; and we learn from it, that, in the year 1674, Lord Essex was soliciting from the English Government a considerable grant for Temple—five hundred pounds a-year, "on the forfeited estates." And the Ministry seems to have made the republication of Temple's History an objection against the grant, which objection Lord Essex, on the part of his friend, thus endeavors to remove:—

EXTRACT OF A LETTER FROM THE EARL OF ESSEX, LORD LIEUTENANT OF IRELAND, TO MR. SECRETARY COVENTRY:—

"I am to acknowledge the receipt of yours of the 22d of December, wherein you mention a book that was newly published, concerning the cruelties committed in Ireland, at the beginning of the late war. Upon further inquiry, I find Sir J. Temple, Master of the Rolls here, author of that book, was this last year sent to by several stationers of London, to have his consent to the printing thereof. But he assures me that he utterly denies it; and whoever printed it, did it without his knowledge. Thus much I thought fit to add to what I formerly said upon this occasion, that I might do this gentleman right, in case it was suspected he had any share in publishing this new edition."

"He utterly *denied* it;" that is, did not absolutely deny that he had written and published the book, but only denied that he had given permission to any stationers to reprint the offensive thing; and his friend Lord Essex pleads this in order "to do the gentleman right." In fact the grant of an annuity was made: poor Sir John Temple never had enough. He was already an "Adventurer" under the Parliamentary arrangement for dividing the confiscated lands: he had invested money in the "Massacre," and I find his name amongst the subscribers to the fund of the "gentlemen adventurers;" but he always wanted *more, more,* being the son of a horse-leech's daughter; and he got more and more. Now, some innocent reader, greener than the rest, will say, well at least the poor man was ashamed at last of his naughty book, and endeavored to make people forget it. Alas! no: he was not ashamed; but the *Restoration* had occurred in the meantime: the Stuarts were come back: Charles II. was King; about the court there was supposed to be much Papistry; and a hard-working Protestant feared that his former zealous labors in doing "the work of the Lord" might not meet with such recognition and encouragement as they were assured of under the godly government of the Lord Protector.

But Temple's abandonment and repudiation of his nasty work does not suit Froude at all. Froude has no idea of permitting a man who has laid such a fine cockatrice egg, to fling it aside to rot: no; he, Froude, will pick up that egg, warm it, *sit on* it, hoping to hatch it into a venomous brood. It is true the egg is long ago rotten; and even we, Protestants, have noses, which we must hold, when things grow too fœtid.

So much for Temple. "Read Temple," says Froude— "whatever else you read, you who would form an independent opinion."

Doctor Petty is, perhaps, next after Temple, the favorite authority relied upon by our Impostor-Historian: although in citing the Doctor at all, Froude feels that he is making a too great concession to Irish susceptibilities. From Temple's account of 154,000 Protestants, whose throats were cut, in Ulster alone, the Doctor, in his estimate, subtracts 116,000: and Petty is mentioned by Froude as an authority not likely to be unfavorable to the Irish: so much he claims for him in one of his lectures: and in his book he terms that clever Doctor "a cool-headed, sceptical sort of man," whose computation is surely not excessive! Cool-headed! Well, this is true: a cooler head, a cooler hand, did not appear in those days, within the four seas of Ireland, than Doctor Petty. The value of him as an "authority" might, perhaps, be questioned; for at the time of the alleged "Massacre" he was a boy; had never been in Ireland at all; was at that time learning his trade, that of a carpenter, in the city of Caen, in France; and it was only in the track of Cromwell's army that he took up his empty carpet-bag, and went to make his fortune in Ireland. A biographical sketch of this extraordinary person was written and published, about six months ago—before there was any word of Froude's Lectures or History,—by a citizen of Brooklyn—not Mr. Meline, but another citizen, whose name is Major Muskerry,—from which sketch I may venture to give an extract or two altogether appropriate in this place: and let the reader be assured that the career of Doctor Sir William is worth some study, as that of the most successful land-pirate (for a private adventurer) and most voracious land-shark who ever appeared in Western Europe. The Doctor is authority for most of his story himself; but here I cite the words of Major Muskerry:—

"Quitting Caen in 1643, when he was twenty years old, he spent a little time in England, and then as the war had checked the industries of the country, he voyaged again and spent three years in France and the Netherlands. Here he studied medicine and helped his younger brother, Anthony, in his schooling, their father being now dead. He was not fond of explaining how he managed to get along during these years. But he mentions that when he returned to England with his brother, he had saved seventy pounds beyond his expenses. He must have carried on some kind of pedlery, or perhaps acted as agent in the sale of English cloth. He was a man of shifts and must have had severe experiences, for he told his friend Aubrey that he once lived for a week in Paris on two pence worth of walnuts—'bread at discretion' being beyond his means. Aubrey used to say he suspected Petty had been put into a French prison for something. And it is very likely the young trafficker ran into somebody's debt, and so lost his liberty for a time, in the good old feudal fashion.

"While he was in Paris, Petty became acquainted with Hobbes, the philosopher, and studied the 'Anatomy of Vesalius' along with him, at the same time drawing the diagrams of a treatise on optics, which that old 'Leviathan' was then writing. In 1646, Petty returned to England. He then carried his French learning to Oxford, where it was recognized; and in three years he got his degree of M.D. at that College. He was also admitted into the London College of Physicians."

There was nothing that Petty could not learn, if there was money in it; and he spent some years, as a projector and an inventor; but without distinguished success, until, in a happy hour, he bethought him of the mighty spoils in Ireland, which the "Massacre" had placed within the reach of every God-fearing Englishman who would invest a little money in it, and "seek the Lord" with his whole heart. Here follows some more from his Brooklyn biographer:—

"But there was another great field of effort and enterprise now opened before the eyes of Dr. Petty—the field of Ireland. Cromwell had beaten down the Irish Confederation, and the English Parliament was arranging the plan of driving the native Irish out of three provinces of Ireland into Connaught. Ten thousand English adventurers seized their carpet-bags, and swarmed into the confiscated island. Among these was Dr. Petty, one of the ablest brains ever exercised over the area of a conquered country. He got himself appointed at once to an Irish office of high character—that of Physician to the Army in Ireland. He landed at Waterford in September, 1652. He himself records that he was worth about £500 when he came to Ireland. His biography is composed in a great measure from notices left by himself, and he repeatedly mentions the sums in his possession at the several crises of his life, as if they were the chief points of interest. But the most remarkable part of the business is that these notices occur in his will, written at the end of his life. He mixes biography and bequests together, as if he meant to save space and time, and show himself an economist to the last. It is certainly one of the most singular wills on record, exhibiting some of the most enlightened ideas of social polity, jumbled with the penurious apologies of a genuine mammon-scraper familiar with much of the sharp practice of his time. But his intimations are very brief, and the story of his acquisitions was one he would not care to tell at any length, very probably. He slurs things over, like Richard Boyle, first Earl of Cork.

"He tells enough, however, to show that his gatherings of Irish property were large and rapid. He says he was appointed to survey the Irish estates, and in this way made £9,000; which sum, with other smaller items, including salaries as Doctor and as Clerk of the Council of Dublin, enabled him to purchase land at a time ' when men bought as much land for ten shillings as in 1685 yielded the same amount per annum.' Aubrey says his lands brought in a rental of £18,000 ; which would be about £40,000, and over, at the present day."

The Doctor was returned to Parliament (Richard Cromwell's Parliament) in 1658. A certain Jerome Sankey was a member of the same Parliament, who was a large "adventurer" in Ireland upon the confiscated estates, as well as Petty, but who had been overreached by the smart Doctor and his "Ring" in the matter of land-grabbing. This is not wonderful: the Doctor, as Surveyor, had many chances: and as he was relied upon for "setting out" lands for whole regiments and brigades, he had endless opportunities of buying up for little or nothing estates of great value. The Doctor had surveys made, and all the field-work done by private soldiers instructed by himself; "hardy men," says Prendergast, "nttest to ruffle with the rude spirits they were like to encounter, who might not see without a grudge their ancient inheritance, the only support of their wives and children, measured out before their eyes for strangers to occupy; and they must often, when at work, be in danger of a surprise from Tories." In fact, many of them were surprised and captured, and lost their ears, as tithe-proctors and bailiffs did in late years: but, on the whole, Doctor Sir William and his friends had not only the large discretion which the survey gave them, but could very often, when some Cromwellian officer or soldier came to see his lot, gravely show him a few leagues of quaking black bog; and the poor fellow instantly offered to sell his estate for a horse to ride away upon; so that the county Meath tradition about the "White Horse of the Peppers" was not only true in fact, but was only a sample of many bargains in landed estate which took place in those days, under the prudent administration of the Doctor. In short, he had so many advantages over his brethren of the carpet-bag, that Sir Jerome Sankey could stand it no longer. Especially there was the case of some very fine lands, the Liberties of Limerick. One Captain Winkworth, a prayerful officer of the Protector's army, had obtained an order for this coveted district: at least the Captain thought his order covered that place, and so he presented his credentials to the Doctor, as Surveyor-general, who told him those lands were "reserved." This forms one of the many charges brought by Sir Jerome against the Doctor in his speech in Parliament. "Why, then, Mr. Speaker (said Sir Jerome), there's Captain Winkworth: Captain Winkworth came with an order for the Liberties of Limerick; but *the Doctor said:* 'Captain, will you sell? Will you sell?' 'No,' said the Captain, 'it is the price of my blood.' Then, said the Doctor, ''tis bravely said. Why, then, my noble Captain, the Liberties of Limerick are meat for your master, meaning the Lord Deputy,'" and so forth. In short, the Doctor was bound to give the best things within his own "Ring." But Petty says that Sankey's real cause of quarrel with him was that he, Petty, "had stopped Sankey's unrighteous order for rejecting 3,000 acres fallen to him by lot, and enabling him arbitrarily to elect the same quantity in its stead, thus rejecting at his pleasure what God had predetermined for his lot." The Doctor retorted upon Sir Jerome with much bad language, for he had a rough and rasping tongue; and the other carpet-bagger challenged him. Petty accepted, and being the challenged party, and having choice of weapons, and being somewhat short-sighted, but a skilful carpenter, he chose *adzes*, in a dark cellar. This proposal was thought too professional by the "friends" of the other carpet-bagger. It was as if you quarrelled with the first mate of a whaling-ship, and challenged him, and he selected for weapons *harpoons*, stipulating that the duel should be fought from two boats in the open sea. The duel never in fact took place. But such a storm of inquiry was raised, that Sir Richard Cromwell, the Lord Lieutenant, could not protect his Physician, and the latter was dismissed from his public employments.

I resume the narrative of Major Muskerry, citizen of Brooklyn No. 2—

"Then came the flurry of 1660, when Charles II. came back again. Petty did not grieve much for the Cromwells. He went to see his Majesty soon after his arrival at Whitehall, and his Majesty 'was mightily pleased with his discourse'—the discourse of a richer man than himself. Petty could lend the King money; and perhaps he did. At any rate that menace of Parliamentary 'inquiry' went off with the Roundheads, and in 1662 Petty was made one of a Court of Commissioners for Irish estates, and Surveyor-general of Ireland. He was also knighted, and, on his arrival in Ireland, returned to the Irish Parliament for Enniscorthy. Still he did not escape entirely scot-free. The 'Court of Innocents,' which sat in the Irish capital, found that he had got much ground that belonged to 'innocent Papists;' and so he disgorged some of his acquisitions—'great part,' he says himself. But he still retained an enormous property. From one hill in Kerry, it was said, he could look round and see no ground that did not belong to himself. That was the hill of Mangerto, now spelled Mangerton—the rude old peak of the Devil's Punch Bowl, on which, perhaps, some of my readers have stood and looked down on the Lake of Killarney.

"Sir William Petty goes on to explain the swift rise of his fortunes. He says he lived within his income, set up iron-works and pilchard fishing, opened lead mines, and sold timber. But of course he did not tell everything, nor mention half the advantages which his position brought to his hands. His fortunes grew from the ruins of a thousand old Irish families ejected from the county of Kerry; and time has only quadrupled the value of the territory he won for his descendants."

I need not follow the fortunes of that smart Doctor any further. Enough to say that when he grew rich, he bribed one of the poor high-born but beggared Geraldine Fitzmaurices to marry his daughter, and also to take his paltry name of Petty. The great estate afterwards came to the present Lansdownes, whose surname is Petty-Fitzmaurice, at the reader's service. This last affair is a matter of no consequence: the thing that I specially note here is, that Doctor Sir William Petty, the man in all Ireland who had most money invested in the "massacre," who made most profit on his investment, who had the largest interest in establishing the grand fact of the "massacre,"—that this land-pirate is palmed off upon us by the Impostor Froude, as a witness for the said grand fact; nay, as the most moderate witness and most favorable to the Irish people. He cannot see more in it—this moderate and friendly Sir William—than, (say) 38,000 throats cut in the massacre; a pretty fair and handsome massacre, a valid and substantial massacre for history to make a turning-point of, and for the Lansdowne estates to derive title from.

Indeed, our bold Doctor was the great administrator of

the whole Transplantation: he ran the Transplantation; and he ran the massacre into the ground, but in the most pious and God-fearing spirit. His own candid autobiographical notes let us perceive that for himself he believed neither in a God nor in anything else, except in the value of acres of ground: yet when he had contracted with the government and the army to make an accurate survey, and maps of the confiscated lands, he did not dare to begin this mighty work for the glory of God without,—but here I call in the aid of Prendergast—

"This great step in perfecting the scheme of Plantation was consecrated with all the forms of religion, the articles being signed by Doctor Petty in the Council Chamber of Dublin Castle, on the 11th of December, 1654, in the presence of many of the chief officers of the army, after a solemn seeking of God performed by Colonel Thomlinson, for a blessing upon the conclusion of so great a business."

It will be remembered that, in the first chapter, I cited from Froude that passage in which he says that the Irish were endowed by Providence with a lovely land; but that "they had pared its forests to the stump, and left it shivering in dampness and desolation;" and I requested the reader to bear that in mind. Now, the chief parer of the forests was Froude's friend, Doctor Sir William. He knew the use of an axe right well; and if he was disappointed in his wish to hew down Sir Jerome Sankey in the cellar, he could, at least, fell oaks and beeches in Kerry. Students of Irish history know, that the Irish were never very solicitous to clear away their fine forests; and that it was the English commanders in Elizabeth's reign who made the first serious inroads upon those waving woods, when they had occasion to open up passes into the Irish enemy's "fastnesses." Froude knows particularly well, that the successive occupiers of "forfeited estates," who were always sensible, in those days, of the precariousness of their tenure, always aware that a new settlement, unsettlement, resettlement, a new "resumption," confiscation, revolution, or general bedevilment of all things, might come upon them any day, thought they could do no better than realize the value, at least, of the woods while they had them. To get a crop of wheat a man must plough, and sow, and wait for the season; but he can cut down and sell a tree at any time, or a hundred thousand trees. The reason why I say "Froude knows" all this, is that the whole process is very clearly set forth in the "Report of the Commissioners appointed by the Parliament of England to take cognizance of the properties that were confiscated upon the Irish who were concerned in the rebellion of 1688, etc." Froude knows this Report, because it is not abstruse nor recondite; and if it were abstruse or recondite he would then know it still better; for he admits that he knows everything. The Commissioners, in section 77 of their Report, say, "that dreadful havoc had been committed upon the woods of the proscribed;" and they further say, "Those upon whom the confiscated lands have been bestowed, or their agents, have been so greedy to seize upon the most trifling profits, that large trees have been cut down and sold for sixpence each." They say, also, "this destruction is still carried on in many parts of the country." And so it continued to be carried on, not by the Irish, but by holders of forfeited estates, until Dean Swift, some years later, lamented that in the once well-wooded island there was not left timber enough for house-building or for shipbuilding, and that the land had a naked and dreary appearance for want of trees. Now, it was bad enough in these rascals to pare our forests to the stump; but this British historical being, coming forward at the present day to complain to the civilized world that *we*, the Irish, pared our forests to the stump, might be thought to add insult to injury: and if he means so, it is his mission.

It is in the county of Kerry chiefly that the Parliamentary Commissioners specify the cruel havoc made in Irish woods; and it was in the county of Kerry that Dr. Sir William Petty had his principal estates. For years the vales of Dunkerron and Iveragh rung with the continual fall of giant oaks. There was a good market; Spain and France were searching the world for pipe-staves: in English dockyards, there was steady demand for ship-knees; and Sir William knew exactly where there was the best market for everything. In Ireland, itself, also, he set on foot iron-works, and fed the fires from his own woods; that is woods which were not his own, and from which the right owners might expel him some day. There was no source of profit, known to the commerce and traffic of that day, in which Sir

William did not bear a hand: he "took hold" of everything that was available and saleable, after first seeking the Lord in the midst of his Ring of saints: for Sir William was truly one of the elect. When he went to his "Down Survey," along with some faithful officers of the Army of the Saints, I find an affecting narrative of a truly touching scene, Doctor Sir William and his swaddling "Ring" upon their marrow-bones, wrestling with the Lord, with strong crying and tears, calling upon the Lord ("stand and deliver, O Lord!") to bless the great work! Bravo! Doctor Sir William: go forward boldly, and seize and divide this mighty spoil! You never had such a chance in all your varied life before: there were no such prizes in the carpenters' shops of Caen: profits upon pills in London suburbs were nothing in comparison with the victorious sharing of these wide vales of Munster. Yea, the gleaning of the grapes of Ephraim is better than the clusters of Manasses. Go ahead, then, prosperously, and ride victorious, O Doctor: for behold the earth and the fulness thereof is thine; and thy name shall be called, not Petty, but Maher-shalal-hash-baz; "for he hasteth unto the dividing of the spoil."

CHAPTER VI.

THE PRETENDED AND THE REAL MASSACRE—ISLAND-MAGEE—OWEN ROE O'NEILL.—THE BATTLE OF BENBURB.

The reader can now estimate the value of the evidence for the "Massacre" of 1641. The Reverend Ferdinando Warner, a Protestant clergyman, pronounces this damaging sentence:

"It is easy enough to demonstrate the falsehood of the relation of every Protestant historian of this rebellion."

It would be hard, indeed, upon us Protestants, if we were compelled to support and maintain those raw-head-and-bloody-bones histories; but fortunately there is no such compulsion upon us. Mr. Warner was not one of the "gentlemen adventurers:" he expected no lands, nor money, out of the "Massacre:" he wrote his history with the single desire to report the truth; and although he had a horror of the "rebellion," and of Popery and priests, we see that he felt himself free to denounce that gory falsehood. It is true that his researches did lead him to conclude that there were murders of Protestants within the three or four months, to the number of two thousand and upward; but this estimate is liable to be more than questioned. In fact, all writers on the subject, including even Temple and Froude, agree that the slaughter of Protestant colonists did not enter into the plan of the insurrection at all, the sole object being to drive away the intruders and resume possession of the lands so lately confiscated. Sir John Temple himself says—

"It was resolved *not to kill any*, but where of necessity they should be forced thereunto by opposition."

And Warner says:—

"Their first intention went no farther than to strip the English and the Protestants of their power and possessions; and, unless forced to it by opposition, *not to shed any blood.*"

"Resistance," (says Leland,) "produced some bloodshed;

and, in some instances, private revenge, religious hatred, and the suspicion of some valuable concealment, enraged the triumphant rebels to insolence, cruelty, and murder. So far, however, was the *original scheme* of the conspiracy at first pursued, that *few fell by the sword, except in open war and assault.*"

A volume was published by another Protestant clergyman, and a contemporary of the event; which Froude notices in this cavalier style:—

"At that time there was a Protestant parson in Ireland who called himself a minister of the word of God. He gives his account of the whole transaction in a letter to the people of England, begging of them to help their fellow-Protestants of Ireland. Here are his words:

"'It was the intention of the Irish to massacre all the English. On Saturday they were to disarm them, on Sunday to seize all their cattle and goods, and on Monday they were to cut all the English throats. The former they executed; the third—that is the massacre—they failed in.'"

It would surely be a curious circumstance, that they "failed in" the massacre, if massacre had been their intention, seeing that the Ulster Protestants were entirely at their mercy. But this Historian cannot endure Protestants, like Mr. Warner and this other "parson," who cast a doubt over the grand fact. A pretty "Protestant" indeed! who tries to make the "turning-point in history" turn the wrong way! A horrible cool-blooded massacre there was,—there must have been, or else our Protestant interest is surrendered; so the Historian still stands upon his thirty-eight thousand mangled corpses. Yet he tries to uphold the story by some other evidence than that of the Adventurers who had money in it. He craves an admission from some Papist. So he gives us, in a note, a passage from Richard Beling's *Vindiciæ Catholicorum Hiberniæ.* Beling was a Catholic; and the fraudulent Historian tells us that he "half confirms, in shame, Sir Phelim O'Neill's barbarities." Froude gives the passage in Beling's Latin; and it states that O'Neill, for the sake of revenge (or retaliation) did raise tumults and enact tragic scenes in some parts of Ulster, which are the less to be commended—*if the stories are true*—on the part of a man who is a Catholic. If the stories are true, we would all say that, and without "half-confirming" the truth of them. If Sir Phelim, or his people, did really slaughter defenceless people, with their women and infants, unless it were in retaliation for the like outrages committed by the other side, every one would admit that such conduct cannot be commended, if, as Beling says, "*si vera referuntur.*" In short, the Historian of the turning-point fails entirely to produce evidence of any massacre at all, except the evidence of men notoriously living by the said massacre.

But there was *retaliation*, in the course of the war. Certainly, when the sword is once drawn, retaliation *in kind*, for outrage committed contrary to the laws of war is not only a right but a duty. It would have been cruelty on the part of Sir Phelim and the other Irish leaders,—cruelty towards their own people,—if they had failed in such a case to repay slaughter with slaughter. Even this was done with great moderation, and to a trifling extent: nor is there to be found, I think, in history, another example of an insurrection, by an oppressed and despoiled people, commenced and carried on so bloodlessly for at least two months. Here, then, it becomes of vital interest to the truth of history to ascertain which side began the murdering calling for retaliation. And this carries us at once to Island-Magee.

Irish writers, as well as the constant tradition of the country, have represented the slaughter of the peaceful, unarmed people of Island-Magee, by the Scotch garrison of Carrickfergus, as the first unprovoked act of butchery. Island-Magee is a peninsula, six miles long, by one and a half in breadth, attached to the coast of Antrim, and running northward parallel to that coast, from the entrance to Carrickfergus Bay. It is a very fertile district and has always been thickly peopled. In November, 1641, it held not only its own permanent inhabitants, but also some hundreds more who had betaken themselves to that remote place, to live for a while with their kindred, and avoid the troubles of the time. The peninsula rises gradually from west to east, and its eastern side sinks down perpendicularly to the sea in a wall of cliff four hundred feet high. On one fatal night, when the people were all in their beds, a force of Munroe's soldiers, from the garrison of Carrickfergus, issued forth in silence, and traversed the whole peninsula, gathering the people as they went, and goading them forward, unarmed men and half-naked women, with children in their arms or at their knees; and so drove them to the brink of the steep, where a pebble dislodged from the edge will fall into deep water; and then, Hurrah for the Protestant Interest! One volley and one bayonet charge, and the shrieking multitude was forced *over*. They were all dead before they reached the water. Ferguson, himself an Antrim Protestant, tells the tale in some verses, describing the escape of a man and woman to Scotland in an open boat, upon that same night:

> The midnight moon is wading deep;
>   The land sends off the gale;
> The boat beneath the sheltering steep
>   Hangs on a seaward sail:
> And leaning o'er the weather-rail,
>   The lovers, hand in hand,
> Take their last look of Innisfail:—
>   "Farewell, doomed Ireland!
>
> "And art thou doomed to discord still?
>   And shall thy sons ne'er cease
> To search and struggle for thine ill?
>   Ne'er share thy good in peace?
> Already do thy mountains feel
>   Avenging Heaven's ire?
> Hark—hark!—this is no thunder peal!
>   That was no lightning fire!"
>
> It was no fire from heaven he saw,
>   For, far, from hill and dell,
> O'er Gobbin's brow the mountain flaw
>   Bears musquet-shot and yell,
> And shouts of brutal glee, that tell
>   A foul and fearful tale,
> While, over blast and breaker, swell
>   Thin shrieks and woman's wail.
>
> Now fill they far the upper sky,
>   Now down 'mid air they go,
> The frantic scream, the piteous cry,
>   The groan of rage and woe;
> And wilder in their agony
>   And shriller still they grow—
> Now cease they, choking suddenly;—
>   The waves boom on below.

This is the massacre of Island-Magee, and the first real butchery of the war, as the Irish have always steadily insisted. Whether it befell in November, 1641, or in the ensuing January ; whether three thousand people were there murdered, as Irish authorities allege, or only " thirty families," as Dr. Leland declares, or thirty persons, as Mr. Froude tells us, upon his own authority ; on all these points there is a controversy, and, no doubt, will continue to be. Froude, following Leland, places the incident in January, that it may appear to be an act of retaliation for other outrages which, he says, the Irish had been guilty of on their side. Now, Dr. Leland is no authority at all, because he was not yet born a hundred years after. But our Historian quite complacently cites the authority of a Dr. Reid, author of a History of the Irish Presbyterians, who cannot allow that his Scotch clients that night tumbled over the cliff more than " thirty persons," counting only the heads of Leland's thirty families. "Every detail of that business," says Froude, "has been preserved, and can be traced to the minutest fibre of it: " and in a note, " The particulars are given exactly by Dr. Reid." Now, I know this decent clergyman, a country minister dwelling in the village of Rathmelton, Donegal county, —if he still lives. If he were to narrate to me a fact which he saw with his own eyes, I should believe him : but who will accept him as authority for what happened about a hundred and fifty years before he was born? If he said he had dreamed it, or that " the spirits" told him, I should suspect his reverence of being crazy ; if he cited anything from the folios of the swearers, I should more than suspect his good faith. And is it not too audacious in Froude to pretend to stop the mouth of all authority and all tradition, with his Doctor of Donegal?

There is no compiler of Irish history more perfectly trustworthy than Dr. John Curry : and he has devoted a considerable space to an investigation of the affair of Island-Magee. I cannot hope to improve upon his remarks, nor effectively to condense them. He says:—

"The report that his Majesty's Protestant subjects first fell upon, and murdered the Roman Catholics, got credit and reputation, and was openly and frequently asserted," says Jones, Bishop of Meath, in a letter to Dr. Borlase, in 1679. And Sir Audley Mervin, Speaker of the House of Commons, in a public speech to the Duke of Ormonde, in 1662, confesses, ' that several pamphlets then swarmed to fasten the rise of this rebellion upon the Protestants; and that they drew the first blood.' And, indeed, whatever cruelties may be charged upon the Irish in the prosecution of this war, 'their first intention, we see,' says another Protestant voucher, 'went no further than to strip the English and the Protestants of their power and possessions, and, unless forced to it by opposition, not to shed any blood.' Even Temple confesses the same; for mentioning what mischiefs were done in the beginning of this insurrection, 'certainly,' says he, 'that which these rebels mainly intended, at first, and most busily employed themselves about, was the driving away the Englishmen's cattle, and possessing themselves of their goods.'

"In a MS. journal of an officer in the King's service, quoted by Mr. Carte, wherein there is a minute and daily account of everything that happened in the North of Ireland, during the first weeks of the insurrection, there is not even an insinuation of any cruelties committed by the insurgents on the English or Protestants; although it is computed by the journalist, 'that the Protestants of that Province had killed near a thousand of the rebels in the first week or two of the rebellion.' And on the 16th of November, 1641, 'Mr. Robert Walbank came from the North, and informed the Irish House of Commons, that two hundred of the people of Coleraine, fought with one thousand of the rebels, slew six of them, and not one of themselves hurt. That in another battle, sixty of the rebels were slain, and only two of the others hurt, none slain.' Nor do we find, in this account, the least mention of cruelties then committed by the Irish; but much of the success and victory of his Majesty's Protestants subjects, as often as they encountered them.

"It is worthy of particular notice, that a Commission of the Lords Justices, Parsons and Borlase, dated so late as December 23d, 1641, was sent down to several gentlemen in Ulster (where it is agreed on all hands that these cruelties and outrages were chiefly committed), in virtue of which Commission Temple and Borlase confess, 'several examinations were afterwards taken of murders committed by the rebels, and the perpetrators of many of these murders were discovered.' Yet the Commission itself, though it authorizes these gentlemen 'to call upon all those who had then suffered in the rebellion, and all the witnesses of these sufferings, to give in examinations of the nature of them, and of every minute circumstance relating to them, expressly and particularly specifying every other crime usual in insurrections, and, then committed, in this, viz., plunder, robbery, and even traitorous words, actions, and speeches: yet I say there is not a syllable mentioned of any murders, then committed, in this Commission, nor any express power given by it to make inquiry into them. From whence it seems necessarily to follow, either that few or no such cruelties had been committed by the insurgents before the 23d of December, 1641, or that these Lords Justices deemed murders and massacres less worthy of their notice, of being strictly inquired after, than even traitorous words and speeches.

"That a great number of unoffending Irish were massacred in Island-Magee, by Scottish Puritans, about the beginning of this insurrection, is not denied by any adverse writer that I have met with. An apology, however, is made for it by them all, which even if it were grounded on fact, as I shall presently show it is not, would be a very bad one, and seems at least to imply a confession of the charge. These writers pretend that this massacre was perpetrated on those harmless people in revenge of some cruelties before committed by the rebels on the Scots in other parts of Ulster. * * * *

"A late learned and ingenious author of an history of Ireland (Leland) has shifted off this shocking incident from November, 1641, (in which month it has been generally placed), to January following, many weeks after horrible cruelties (as he tells us) had been committed by the insurgents on the Scots in the North. 'The Scottish soldiers,' says he, 'who had reinforced the garrison of Carrickfergus, were possessed of an habitual hatred of Popery, and inflamed to an implacable detestation of the Irish, by multiplied accounts of their cruelties. In one fatal night they issued from Carrickfergus into an adjacent district called Island-Magee, where a number of the poorer Irish resided, unoffending and untainted with the rebellion. If we may believe one of the leaders *of this party*, thirty families were assailed by them in their beds, and massacred with calm and deliberate cruelty. As if,' proceeds the historian, 'the incident were not sufficiently hideous, Popish writers have represented it with shocking aggravation.'"

An angry man was Sir Phelim O'Neill when he heard of the drowning at Island-Magee; but his duty to his own people called for stern retaliation; and that some acts of this nature were done, cannot and need not be denied. Sir Phelim was not naturally disposed to cruelty, and had anxiously sought to keep his men,—wild as they were with their wrongs and sufferings,—within the limits prescribed at the beginning. Yet he had to give way to some extent; and it must be true that some Protestants were flung into the Bann river at Portadown, just as Catholics had been flung over the Gobbins cliffs.

I am bound to maintain, after all the examination I have been able to give to the ghastly story, that the Irish insurrection of 1641 was notable amongst insurrections for its mildness and humanity; and that, if the Irish were not the most gentle, patient, and good-natured people in the whole world, their island would long since have been a smoking wilderness of cinders soaked in blood.

Sir William Petty, looking calmly into the whole business, shortly after, says, with his usual coolness, that, at any rate:

"Upon the playing of this game, or match, the English won, and had, amongst other pretenses, a gamester's right at least to their estates. As for the blood shed in the contest for these lands, God best knows who did occasion it!"

Ah! yes; God knows; and Petty knew; but could not afford to tell; for the title to those confiscated estates was at stake; not legally indeed, but morally, in the estimation of civilized mankind; and the prosperous Doctor, having a gloriously winning hand in that "match or game," was content to enjoy his good luck, and leave the rest to God. The English did, indeed, win the game, after ten years of painful struggle and carnage; for Ireland did not sink under one blow, as Scotland did, at Dunbar: and this philosophic Doctor was the principal carver at the mighty feast of spoil. The insurrection was followed by a general war throughout the island, a war which the Lords of the Council took care to *make* general, because then the confiscations would be general also.

In the course of the war there were some bright days for Ireland, and especially the day of Benburb; for the same covenanting rascal, Munroe, who slew the poor people of Island-Magee, had the ill-luck, six years later, on a bright June day, to look in the face the greatest of all the O'Neills, the magnificent Owen Roe. It is one of the shining points in our history, gleaming through the general darkness, on whose brightness Irish eyes love to dwell. Therefore, in this large History of Ireland, Mr. Froude takes care never to mention how, on that bright summer day, General Munroe marched along the northern bank of the Blackwater with a formidable army, making no doubt that he would dislodge and disperse the Irish chiefs and their clansmen. But he knew little of the soldier opposed to him,—an officer trained in the French and Spanish wars; the defender of Arras against a Marshal of France; and an O'Neill of Ulster, full of vindictive loathing against the Covenanting leader who had shed the innocent blood of the clansmen of Tyrowen, at Newry and at Island-Magee. The whole forenoon of that memorable day was spent in repeated attacks by Munroe's troops, which were always steadily repulsed. O'Neill kept his men well in hand, and especially restrained his impetuous commander of horse, MacNeney, who burned to launch his riders upon the squadrons of Scottish cavalry. "Wait for the sun," O'Neill said: "when the sun begins to sink towards the west, then will the Lord have delivered those Covenanting scoundrels into our hands." Still the assaults continued, with loss and exhaustion on the part of the enemy; until the prudent Irish chief, who observed the sun that day, like an astronomer, saw that its rays were beginning to dart into the faces of the Scots. Now, steady, rapid, advance all along the line! And, *now*, MacNeney, the spur in your horse's side, and the bridle upon his mane! In a few moments down went horse and foot, and there was no Covenanting army any more, only a howling rabble rout, flying for their lives. They had need; for O'Neill, when he did move, "was hot upon the spur;" and Munroe and a party of officers betook themselves to ignominious flight. The General lost his hat and wig; but eastward still he urged his horse, splashing through the marshes of the Montiaghs, by the southern shore of Lough Neagh, across the Bann, about the place where the ghosts were still shrieking;

and before morning, Protestant burghers of Lisburn were disturbed by the gallop of horses ready to founder. They looked out of window: it was only General Munroe and staff making their entry; but the frightened shopkeepers almost thought they heard at the town's end the thundering hoofs of Owen Roe's riders. Three thousand Scottish and English men fell on that day of Benburb; and the Irish nation felt that they had got a leader able to cope with the Lord General Cromwell.

As this affair of Benburb is creditable to Irish soldiership, therefore, Froude never alludes to it. The miserable " Historian" is always anxiously on the watch, rather to find some pretext for goading our people with a taunt; and it is really wonderful to observe how low down, and how far out of his way, he will go to contrive a cutting and stinging gibe. For example, by way of enforcing his favorite theory, that Irishmen require to be used with severity, and that the more you scourge them the more they love you, he quotes what he calls a Hibernian proverb, in Latin, to the effect that, if you soothe and flatter an Irishman, he will stab you, but if you kick him he will be your affectionate servant. Froude knows perfectly well, that this is a French proverb, which the proud *seigneurs* applied to their serfs, and that it had no reference to Ireland at all:—"*Oignez vilain; il vous poindra: poignez vilain; il vous oindra.*" But our kind Historian, finding the proverb turned into a Latin hexameter, and perceiving that *Hibernicus* fits the measure, cannot resist the temptation. The Irish, according to him, made a proverb on themselves, proclaiming their own dastard servility. They say to all mankind in this proverb—Do us the pleasure, good sirs, to kick us, that we may have the gratification of kissing your honors' boots! True, this is a small matter: so is the omission of all mention of Benburb: so is the taunt about the Irish paring their forests; yet these things show the vicious *animus* of the creature. If he cannot be always bombarding the Irish with cannon, he, at least, can occupy himself in pricking them with needles.

CHAPTER VII.

"CLAN OLIVER"—FROUDE'S "WERE WOLVES"—THE IRISH TRANSPORTED TO BARBADOES—PERILS OF THE IRISH EPISCOPATE—SECRET OF ENGLISH TOLERATION—FROUDE'S FEARS FOR THE FUTURE.

Now came in the deluge of Cromwellians, who were termed by the Irish *Clan Oliver,* as the invaders of Elizabeth's day had been called sometimes Clan London, or Clan Sacsanagh. It is not my purpose to follow Froude through all his details relating to the Cromwellian Settlement; because this is rendered unnecessary by the admirable work of Mr. Prendergast; and Froude has himself fully admitted in one place the accuracy of Prendergast's facts and authorities, at the same time that, in many other passages, he makes statements of his own utterly at variance with those facts and authorities. What is material to point out here is, that the Historian most warmly approves of the *régime* established by Cromwell in Ireland, only lamenting that "he died too soon." Speaking of that General and his indiscriminate slaughters of soldiers and civilians, of men, women, and children at Drogheda and Wexford, he says, pathetically: "Happier far would it have been for Ireland, if, forty years later, there had been a second Cromwell before Limerick!" (p. 125.) It had been better, he thinks, if Sarsfield and his men, and all the peaceful traders, and all the heroic women of Limerick city had had their throats cut, instead of being admitted to a Treaty. Perhaps he is right, seeing that the Treaty was to be instantly violated. This Historian does not mind being charged with bloodthirstiness: on the contrary, he is flattered by it: he loves to write of blood, and to urge on other people the duty of shedding it: the odor of gore is grateful to his nostrils; and he despises "rose-water," which is Carlyle's phrase to designate any kind of gentleness or mercy, or even ordinary good faith observed towards Papists. Cromwell, he says with delight, did not assuredly come to Ireland "to make war with rose-water." No, it was the genuine red liquid, venous and arterial. There is no part of the Cromwellian system which seems to give him such heartfelt pleasure as the treatment of the priests. Only it was too mild, and was applied for too short a time: if the great Statesman had but lived, there would soon have been not a single priest left to "work mischief;"—for this is his way of describing the saying of Mass.

The good Father Burke, who is so amiable towards Froude, must be all the while aware of how it would have fared with himself if he had lived in the time of Froude's hero. Doubtless it is the duty of a Christian divine to love all men, even his enemies; and it was in this sense that he said he loved Froude. But he knows very well that in Froude's political economy, his (Father Burke's) head is exactly of the same value as the head of a bitch-wolf; namely, six pounds sterling of the money of that day, equal, we may say, to eighteen pounds of to-day. And it will not do to say that Froude estimates the goods at that price, only in the case that Father Burke had lived in the latter part of the eighteenth century; for he regrets, passionately, the too-early relaxation of that system; wishes there had been a Cromwell before Limerick; wishes that there were a Cromwell for Ireland's sake *now:* for, while the wolves were cleared off entirely, there are priests in Ireland still. Evidently, while the wolf-price was enough, the priest's head-money ought to have been raised. My own estimate of the value of Father Burke's head, differs from Froude's, and is based upon another sort of tariff; for I hold it to be worth at least five hundred heads of the Froudes. Let nobody deceive himself, however, by assuming that this Historian discusses these matters in a historic spirit, as matters whose interest is long past and gone with the changing current of events. By no means: he treats them in the spirit of a party pamphleteer, and with an obvious intention to act upon the present politics and passions of men. Thus, instead of giving a word of praise to the devoted clergy who persisted in hearing confessions and administering Sacraments, under the imminent penalty of transportation and of death, he never mentions those wonderful men without ribald abuse and calumny. "Priests and dispossessed proprietors," he says, "were hiding in disguise among the tribes, *making mischief* when they were able." He never alludes to the deadly risks those clergy ran in staying by their flocks. Close as has been his inspection of documents, in public-record offices, he never found the bills duly furnished by and paid to god-fearing troopers for their captives—" To five priests captured in the county of Cavan and sent in "—" To two priests *with their appurtenances* [namely books and cups and stoles] sent in by Lieutenant Wood," and so-forth, to great length: for which see Prendergast and Curry;—you need not look to the Historian of "The English in Ireland." He cannot help, indeed, mentioning some of the severe measures used against the clergy; he only affirms that not *so many* were transported as those who were arrested; but nobody had said there were.

As to the people actually transported from Ireland to Barbadoes or other colonies or plantations, he, in his last lecture, questions Father Burke's estimate of the numbers so exiled within a few years. He says:—

"Father Burke says that Cromwell meant to exterminate the Irish. I distinguish again between the industrious Irish and the idle, fighting Irish. He showed his intention towards the peasantry a few days after his landing; for he hung two of his own troopers for stealing a hen from an old woman. Cromwell, says the Father, wound up the war by taking 80,000 men and shipping them to the sugar plantations of Barbadoes. In six years, such was the cruelty, that not twenty of them were left. Eighty thousand men, Father Burke! and in six years not twenty left! I have read the Thurlow Papers, where the account will be found of these shipments to Barbadoes. I can find nothing about 80,000 men there. When were they sent out, and how, and in what ships?"

I think, however, that Father Burke's estimate is not far from correct; though, to be sure, 80,000 is a large round number. But it is well known that the deportation, both of priests and of laymen, of young men and maidens, was on a very large scale. In consequence of the great increase of priests towards the close of the year 1665, a general arrest by the justices of the peace was ordered: it was the sporting-season for priests, and even wolves were left comparatively at peace for a time. "On the 3d of May," says Prendergast, "the Governors of the respective precincts were ordered to send them with sufficient guards from garrison to garrison to Carrickfergus, to be there put on board such ships as should sail with the first opportunity for the Barbadoes." Poor old Father Paul Cashin, a very ancient and frail man, being apprehended at Maryborough, and sent on to Philipstown, on the way to Carrickfergus, there fell desperately sick, and was in danger of perishing in a dungeon from want and hardship. After months the Commissioners ordered him an allowance of sixpence a day; and when he should be well enough to move, this allowance was to be continued to him during his journey to Carrickfergus "in order to his transportation to the Barbadoes." It would not be much sugar Father Paul would make, after being set down there and bidden to take up the shovel and the hoe; but the authorities thought that under a Barbadoes planter he would at least be kept from "mischief," that is, from Mass and Confession. The difficulty suggested by Froude in the paragraph above cited,—How, and in what ships were these 80,000 sent to Barbadoes? is not so very serious a difficulty. The operation extended over several years, and shipping was not so very scarce then, either in England or in Ireland. Besides, Doctor Sir William Petty and other adventurers were piling up all the shipyards in the kingdom with the best of Irish timber. Still there was some shortcoming in the tonnage available for this service, and it cost too much; so that, on the 27th of February, 1657, the government referred it to the Lord Lieutenant to consider where the priests, then crammed into the prisons of Dublin, might be most safely disposed of. And so they were carried across the island, placed in boats, and flung out upon the bare islands of Arran, in the Atlantic, and Innisbofin, off the coast of Connemara, there to consider themselves, upon an allowance of sixpence *per* day. It was when private enterprise came in aid of the government that no want of shiping was experienced. The merchants of Bristol contracted with the Commissioners, not for cargoes of priests, but for young men and marriageable girls, who would be more useful, these merchants thought, upon their West India plantations. Ostensibly, all these were to be persons having no visible means of support; but practically, it was a slave-hunt. Says Prendergast:—

"Messrs. Sellick and Leader, Mr. Robert Yeomans, Mr. Joseph Lawrence, and others, all of Bristol, were active agents. As one instance out of many:—Captain John Vernon was employed by the Commissioners for Ireland into England, and contracted in their behalf with Mr. David Sellick and Mr. Leader, under his hand, bearing date the 14th of September, 1653, to supply them with two hundred and fifty women of the Irish nation above twelve years, and under the age of forty-five; also three hundred men above twelve years of age, and under fifty, to be found in the country within twenty miles of Cork, Youghal, and Kinsale, Waterford, and Wexford, to transport them into New England. Messrs. Sellick and Leader appointed their shipping to repair to Kinsale; but Roger Boyle, Lord Broghill (afterwards Earl of Orrery), whose name, like that of Sir C. Coote, seems ever the prelude of woe to the Irish, suggested that the required number of men and women might be had from among the wanderers and persons who had no means to get their livelihood in the county of Cork alone. Accordingly, on the 23d of October, 1653, he was empowered to search for them and arrest them, and to deliver them to Messrs. Sellick and Leader, who were to be at the charge of conducting them to the water side, and maintaining them from the time they received them; and no person, being once apprehended, was to be released, but by special order in writing under the hand of Lord Broghill."

Many such operations took place in various parts of the country; until this Bristol firm alone had shipped above 6,400 young strong people within the desirable ages. Many a girl of gentle birth and delicate nurture must have been seized by those slave-dealers and hurried to the private prisons. Daniel Connery, a gentleman of Clare County, was sentenced to banishment for harboring a priest in 1657. " This gentleman had a wife and twelve children: his wife fell sick, and died in poverty. Three of his daughters, most beautiful girls, were transported to the West Indies, to an island called the Barbadoes; and there, if they are alive, they are in miserable slavery." (*Morison's Threnodia:* cited by Prendergast.) On the whole, taking priests and laymen together, men and women, girls and boys, and allowing some years for the operation, I think we may allow Father Burke's estimate to be a fair and probable one.

But the matter, and perhaps the only matter, which disquiets and perplexes the mind of the " Historian," is the fact, that in the midst of all these horrors, Catholic priests were not only ministering all over the country, but coming in from France and Spain and Rome; not only supplying the *vacuum* made by transportation and by death, but keeping up steadily the needful communication between the Irish Church and its head : and not only coming, but going, (both times incurring the risk of capital punishment,) and not in commodious steamships, which did not then exist, but in small fishing luggers or schooners; not as first-class passengers, but as men before the mast. Archbishops worked their passage. The whole of this strange phenomenon, which continued more than a century, belongs to an order of facts which never entered into the Historian's theory of human nature. It is a factor in the account that he can find no place for: he gives it up. Yet Edmund Spenser, long before this day, as good a Protestant as Froude, and an undertaker, too, upon Irish confiscated estates, had at least somewhat of the poetic vision and poetic soul. There were moods of his undertaking mind in which he could look upon such strange beings as Irish priests with a species of awe, if not with full comprehension. He much marvels at the zeal of these men, " which is a greate wonder to see how they spare not to come out of Spain, from Rome and from Remes, by long toyle and daungerous travayling hither, where they know perill of death awayteth them and no reward or richesse." Mr Froude, indeed, speaks of them as engaged in nothing else but keeping up treasonable alliances with countries at war with England, and recruiting for foreign armies. As for their expecting " no reward or richesse " for such laborious service, he would bid you tell that to Judæus Apella, or to " the horse marines ! "

" Reward and richesse ! " I know the spots, within my own part of Ireland, where venerable Archbishops hid themselves as it were in a hole of the rock. In a remote part of Louth County, near the base of the Fews mountains, is a retired nook called Ballymascanlon. There dwelt for years, in a farm-house which would attract no attention, the Primate of Ireland and successor of St. Patrick, Bernard McMahon, a prelate accomplished in all the learning of his time, and assiduous in the government of his archdiocese; but he moved in secret, with danger, if not with fear, and often encountered hardships in travelling by day and by night.

His assumed name was Bernard Ennis; his coat was frieze; and he paid his half-yearly rent with much punctuality. His next successor, but one, was Michael O'Reilly: and he dwelt in a cabin at Termonfeckin, near Clogher Head, a very wild place, and greatly out of the way, as it lay between the great Northern road and the sea, and could only be found by those who searched for it. Here he died. And if such were the toils, hardships, and dangers of the highest ecclesiastics, we may conjecture what kind of life awaited the simple priests who devoted themselves to the mission. Yet it was, with full knowledge of all this, with full resolution to brave all this, that many hundreds of educated Irishmen, fresh from the Colleges of Belgium or of Spain, came to the French seacoast at Brest or St. Malo, bent on finding some way of crossing to where their work lay. Imagine a priest ordained at Seville or Salamanca, a gentleman of high old name, a man of eloquence and genius, who has sustained disputations in the college halls on questions of literature or theology, and carried off prizes and crowns;—imagine him on the quays of Brest, treating with the skipper of some vessel to let him work his passage: he wears tarry breeches and a tarpaulin hat (for disguise was generally needful)—he flings himself on board, takes his full part in all hard work, scarce feels the cold spray and the fierce tempest. And he knows, too, that the end of it all, for him, may be a row of sugar-canes to hoe, under the blazing sun of Barbadoes, overlooked by a broad-hatted agent of a Bristol planter: yet he goes eagerly to meet his fate; for, he carries in his hand a sacred desposit, bears in his heart a sacred message, and must deliver it or die. Imagine him then springing ashore, and repairing to seek the Bishop of the diocese in some cave, or behind some hedge, but proceeding with caution by reason of the priest-catchers and their wolf-dogs. But, Froude would say, this is the *ideal* priest you have been portraying. *No:* it is the real priest, as he existed and acted at that day, and as he would again in the like emergency. And is there nothing admirable in all this? Is there not something superhuman and sublime? Ah! we Protestants are certainly most enlightened creatures. Mr. Froude says we are the salt of the earth. West and, each of us, with triumphant conceit, upon the sacred and inalienable right of private stupidity; but I should wish to see our excellent Protestantism produce some fruit like this.

And not only has our Crusader no word of admiration or commendation for the more than chivalrous bravery of the priests who dared and defied the toil and the peril, humiliation, transportation, and death, for the sake of feeding those flocks which the English were shearing;—not only does he pass over in silence, or make light of, or attempt to deny, the frightful persecutions continually inflicted upon those clergy, or hanging over their heads, but the great leading theme of his whole book, the thing which he most earnestly repeats is *this*— the priests were never persecuted enough except only in Cromwell's time! Ah! "if Oliver Cromwell had but left a son like himself," he pathetically exclaims, Ireland's lot at this day had been happier; and it would be now as easy to find a wolf in the island as a priest. He is very hard, indeed, to satisfy in the matter of persecution; for, although the laws for making Ireland too hot to hold a priest, were constantly elaborated, and made more atrocious, nearly every year, for the next century after Cromwell, still there was occasional *connivance ;* and those obnoxious pastors were often left unpunished, and even their saying of Mass was often winked at, provided they committed the offence in some very obscure place. This does not suit the Historian at all: he wants their heart's blood all the time; and it was such "mistaken leniency" on the part of the government that made Papists so insolent that they continually rose in new insurrections, and even at one time, (when James the Second came to the throne,) their presumption mounted to such a pitch, that he tells us with disgust, "the Irish thought *Ireland was theirs.*" It is to be feared that the Historian, after all his researches, fails to comprehend the exact purpose and extent of those occasional connivances or tolerations: the purpose was to keep up an efficient machinery for getting a hold of more and more of the lands which were still remaining in the hands of Papists, under secret trusts or illegal leases. The Protestant interest could not afford to suppress the Mass, so long as any Catholic possessed an acre of land or a good horse. If there had been no priests, and no Catholic service could anywhere be celebrated, it was feared that nearly all the Catholics would conform; and then, where would our Protestant interest be! Our good Protestants could no more afford to do without the Mass than without the "massacre." So, successive Viceroys and Lords of Council changed their policy from time to time, either suspending the operation of the most ferocious of the penal laws, or enforcing them in all their horror, as political exigencies for the time being might seem to require. Mr. Froude, with all his unbending Protestant honesty, must really have some indulgence for people who, after doing the work of the Lord so well, felt that they had not yet received their full reward: for certain Papist Hittites, Edomites, and Amalekites, could still be found, by means of earnest and prayerful diligence, who were fraudulently receiving the rents and profits of their own estates, and thus cheating honest colonists. For these Amalekites it was needful to keep up a kind of secret hole-and-corner Mass; and the army of informers who were kept in pay might be trusted to find out who attended those useful ministrations. Here is the true key to the Penal Laws and to their administration.

Yes: evil must come of it, as this honest being truly apprehends. In his last lecture, by way of reply to Father Burke, he cannot conceal his uneasiness. He says:—

"England is afraid, however, and deeply afraid. She is afraid of being ever driven to use again those measures of coercion against Ireland which have been the shame of her history."

The shame of her history, inasmuch as they were not duly executed! But what is England afraid of now? Ireland is very quiet, and so free from disturbance, and every sort of crime, that many a single county in England exhibits more murders, poisonings, burglaries, and waylayings with intent to murder, in one year, than the whole of Ireland can show. What, then, thinks the Historian, is the provocation which is likely to drive his countrymen to new penal laws against Ireland? Can it be the Home Rule agitation,—an agitation which is not only perfectly legal and constitutional, but also entirely harmless and useless? No; certainly not this. As for the outcry some Irishmen are making, claiming that they ought to be governed according to "Irish Ideas,"— governed *by England*,—neither can this disquiet their English masters much. Their English owners know how to deal with such matters as these; by seizing on such newspapers

as offend them, and by trying the most noisy of the agitators
before packed juries. What then, precisely, does the Historian's ominous threat portend? What does he wish his
countrymen to do to us more? It may be that the learned
and eloquent gentleman, having lived a good deal in Ireland
of late, has observed that many industrious Irish people,—
grandsons and descendants of those who were once so
thoroughly stripped bare,—have gradually worked themselves
into possession again of broad estates, often in the very
tribe-lands of their own clans. Those estates were taken
from their ancestors and given to the " saints " without money
and without price: the present owners have won some of
them back in the sweat of brow and brain. Catholics, too,
having been plundered of their own cathedrals, churches
and abbey-lands, are now found in possession of new and
splendid churches, and of great and beneficent religious
houses. Here is a matter which is evidently worthy of the
serious consideration of us, the enlightened Protestants: for,
if the earth is not ours and the fulness thereof, we should
like to know to whom it does belong? Would not a good,
prudent system of penal laws, jockey those idolatrous Papists
out of all they own, even as before? And is it any wonder
that Historian Froude begins really to *fear* that England
may be forced to resort to the old system of coercion once
more?

Is this the explanation of his ominous menace? or is it
(merely, as one of his English critics has insisted) a general craving on his part " to burn or boil somebody, if only
he could make up his mind whom to boil or burn? " On this
last question I do not really think the Historian labors under any doubt or difficulty. I know whom he wishes to cook.
At any rate, it really seems that this Crusader, like many
another great man, is in advance of his age, or else behind
it. He is either above the general level of human conscience and morals, or else below it. Either way, whether
he is behind or before, whether too high or too low, his shot
has failed to strike right between wind and water: and his
Crusade is a failure.

In one other chapter I shall wash my hands of our Historian; and, having washed, shall slightly perfume them.

CHAPTER VIII.

RELIGIOUS LIBERTY IN IRELAND—KING JAMES'S PARLIAMENT—THE KING'S "ARTFUL LANGUAGE"—THE IRISH GOVERNOR OF NEW YORK—RELIGIOUS LIBERTY IN AMERICA—FAREWELL TO FROUDE.

THE only period—and it was a very short period—in which Liberty of Conscience was recognized in Ireland by express law, from the time of Henry VIII., until the reign of Queen Victoria—the *only* bright moment of respite—was that in which the Parliament of King James II. sat in Dublin. And this was the only Parliament that ever represented the Irish nation even unto this day. For the Parliament elected after "Emancipation," upon the basis of wholesale disfranchisement, certainly did not represent Ireland; and neither has any one of the Parliaments from that time to the present moment. The famous Assembly convened by King James, was composed indifferently of Catholics and Protestants, but Catholics in the great majority. Some exclusive Protestant boroughs, whose Corporate authorities did not admit a Catholic to live within their bounds, did not, indeed, send any members. There was no representative from Derry, from Coleraine, from Enniskillen, nor from Carrickfergus. But Bandon sent two gentlemen of the MacCarthy clan; Dublin, City and County, and the University were represented,—the County by Simon Luttrell and Patrick Sarsfield; the City by Sir Michael Creagh, Lord Mayor; and by Terence Dermot, Alderman; the College by Sir John Meade and Michael Coghlan; the Borough of Belfast by Marcus Talbot and Daniel O'Neill; Newry by Rowland White and Rowland Savage; Down County by two of the MacGennises. On the whole, I find in the roll of that famous Parliament,—the only genuine Parliament Ireland ever saw—a large and liberal admixture of gentlemen of English race and of Irish families; a list which it does one good to read: Fitzgeralds and O'Reillys, O'Briens and Nugents, Aylmers, Eustaces, and Archbolds. The borough of Wicklow was represented by an O'Byrne and an O'Toole—very proper members for that constituency. Naas, in Meath, returned Charles

White and Walter, Lord Dongan, a near relative of that Thomas Dongan (properly O'Donegan), who had been obliged, a year before, to resign his office as Governor of New York; and he was the best Governor New York ever had. There were but six or seven Protestants in the House of Commons; but in the House of Peers we find, besides the temporal Lords, four Protestant Bishops—Meath, Ossory, Limerick and Cork. Mr. Froude counts amongst them the Bishop "of Munster;" (I quote Scribner's edition); but there never was any Bishop of Munster: and the Historian must mean Dr. Dopping, Bishop of Meath, who is his especial favorite amongst all the Irish episcopacy, being in fact the very Bishop who shortly afterwards, on the conclusion of the Treaty of Peace, preached before the Court, in Christ Church Cathedral, on the sinfulness of observing any compacts or treaties with Papists. The greater number of the Protestant Peers absented themselves, as they were generally devoted adherents to the usurper, the Prince of Orange. Substantially, however, there was a good and respectable representation of the Irish nation at that day.

This is a matter perplexing, and even disgusting, to the Impostor Historian: so he passes it over very lightly. Yet the acts of that Assembly deserve to be held in remembrance a little. One of its earliest enactments was "an Act for securing Liberty of Conscience, and repealing such acts or clauses in any act of Parliament which are inconsistent with the same." I need not here dwell upon the other measures passed by that excellent Parliament,—an Act declaring the Parliament of England incapable of binding Ireland; an Act repealing the unjust Navigation Laws; an Act for attainder of rebels; that is, of persons who had borne arms against their Sovereign, King James; an Act for removing all incapacities and disabilities of the natives of this Kingdom; etc. For the present, it is enough to attend to the Act for Liberty of Conscience, and to see how the English Historian deals with that:—

"We hereby decree that it is the law of this land of Ireland, that neither now, nor ever again, shall any man be prosecuted for his religion."

This looks plain enough; sounds fair and straightforward: but the British Historian has found out the secret and malign intention: he says in his book (p. 191)—and it is the only notice he takes of the Act for Liberty of Conscience:—

"In harmony with the *language* which James had ingeniously used to advance Romanism behind principles which were abjured in every Catholic country of Europe, laws interfering with liberty of conscience were declared repealed."

What an artful tyrant! Not only to invent such *ingenious language*, declaring that no man should be punished for his religion, but also to impress this cunning artifice of speech upon 'his Parliament in Ireland! There are some persons who might wish that Oliver Cromwell could have learned this sort of ingenious language, instead of saying to General Taaffe, who attempted to stipulate for Liberty of Conscience before surrendering Ross:—"I meddle," said Cromwell, "with no man's conscience; but if, by liberty of conscience, you mean liberty to exercise the Mass, I judge it best to use plain dealing, and let you know that where the Parliament of England has power, *that* will not be allowed." And what a blessing it would have been if the grandfather of this same James the Second had learned, in his day, the use of that "language" (for there was nothing in it, Mr. Froude assures us, but empty words) instead of issuing his famous proclamation of the 4th of July, 1605, wherein he "declared to his beloved subjects of Ireland that he would not admit any such liberty of conscience as they were made to expect!"

Froude's account of the matter is that King James had committed to memory certain vile, hypocritical phrases about freedom of conscience,—probably under the tuition of some Jesuit—in order "to advance Romanism *behind* those principles." What advancing of Romanism did he ever seek, either in England or in Ireland? He did wish to be at liberty to go to church himself, *behind those principles:* he wished such of his subjects as chose to be Catholics to be free to hear Mass, and make Confession without being fined, whipped, pilloried, or transported. But, neither he, nor any government official in his reign, whether in England or in Ireland, *ever* sought to injure, punish, or disfranchise any Protestant for *not* going to Mass.

In fact, the thing which offends our English Historian the most, and admonishes him to touch lightly on that whole subject, and drop it like a hot potato, is the fact that King

James' own actions, and the measures of the Parliament which he called, and the administration of law in the High Courts of the Kingdom, were all guided and governed by the very same ingenious "language." Here was the infernal cunning of it. That Jesuit who tutored the King, I dare say, thought himself a deep schemer; but no Romish devices can escape the searching probe of Froude. In his last New York lecture he says of King James:—

"He was meditating the restoration of Popery in England, and he *took up* with toleration that he might introduce Catholics, under cover of it, into high offices of state, and bribe the Protestant Nonconformists to support him."

And so he advanced the treacherous declaration for liberty of conscience only to advance Romanism behind that principle! And what did James the First, what did Oliver Cromwell, then wish to advance behind those opposite principles of *no liberty of conscience?* It must have been Protestantism they wanted to advance; or, at any rate, the Protestant interest. But, after all, what was this insidious form of words which the Jesuits had invented for King James? Mr. Froude does not give it; but here it is:—

"KING JAMES'S SPEECH TO BOTH HOUSES OF PARLIAMENT IN IRELAND, PUBLISHED BY HIS MAJESTY'S ORDER, MAY 10TH, 1689.

"MY LORDS AND GENTLEMEN,—The exemplary loyalty which this nation express to me, at a time when others of my subjects so undutifully behaved themselves to me, or so basely betrayed me; and your seconding my deputy as you did, in his bold and resolute asserting my right, and preserving this kingdom for me, and putting it in a posture of defence, made me resolve to come to you, and to venture my life with you, in the defence of your liberty, and my right; and to my great satisfaction I have not only found you ready and willing to serve me, but that your courage has equalled your zeal. *I have always been for liberty of conscience*, and against invading any man's property; having still in my mind the saying of holy writ, 'Do as you would be done by; for that is the law and the prophets.' It was this liberty of conscience I gave, which my enemies both at home and abroad dreaded, especially when they saw that I was resolved to have it established by law in all my dominions, and made them set themselves up against me, though for different reasons; seeing that if I had once settled it, my people in the opinion of the one would have been too happy, and in the opinion of the other too great. This argument was made use of to persuade their own people to join with them, and too many of my own subjects to use me as they have done; but nothing shall ever persuade me to change my mind as to that: and wheresoever I am master, I design, God willing, to establish it by law, and to have no other test or distinction, but that of loyalty. I expect your concurrence in so Christian a work, and in making effectual laws against profanings and debauchery. I shall also most readily consent to the making such good and wholesome laws as may be for the general good of the nation, the improvement of trade, and the relieving such as have been injured by the late acts of settlement, as far forth as may be consistent with reason, justice, and the public good of my people. And as I shall do my part to make you happy and rich, so I make no doubt of your assistance, by enabling me to oppose the unjust designs of my enemies, and to make this nation flourish. And to encourage you the more to it, you know with how great generosity and kindness the Most Christian King gave a secure retreat to the Queen, my son, and self, when we were forced out of England, and came to seek protection and safety in his dominions; how he embraced my interest, and gave supplies of all sorts, as enabled me to come to you, which, without his obliging assistance, I could not have done: this he did at a time when he had so many and so considerable enemies to deal with; and so still continues to do. I shall conclude as I began, and assure you, I am as sensible as you can desire me, of the signal loyalty you have exprest to me, and shall make it my chief study, as it always has been, to make you and all my subjects happy."

Here the designing creature actually says that he had been, at all times, for liberty of conscience; and the puzzling matter to the Froudes, is, that he had been so in fact; of which one illustration was seen, even here on Manhattan Island,—such was the malign cunning of that artful tyrant, in spreading far and wide over the dependencies of the British Crown, that same shocking delusion of liberty of conscience.

When King James was Duke of York, in the reign of his brother, Charles, he was "Proprietary Governor" of the Province of New York; and, in the year 1682, he commissioned Colonel Thomas Dongan, of an ancient Irish family, who had commanded a regiment in the French service, to proceed to New York as his Lieutenant, or Resident Governor. He proceeded at once, according to his instructions, to issue his warrants for the election of a General Assembly. This was an auspicious beginning of his administration, as it was a concession from the Duke of York for which the people had long struggled. This illustrious body, consisting of the Governor, ten Councillors, and seventeen Representatives elected by the people, assembled in the City of New York, on the 17th of October, 1683. As he was the first, so he was the most liberal and friendly Royal Governor that presided over the popular legislatures of New York; and the contests between arbitrary power and popular rights, which distinguished the administration of future Governors, down to the Revolution, did not have their origin under his administration. The first act of this General Assembly was the framing of a charter of liberties—the first guaranty of popular government in the province. This noble charter ordained:

"That supreme legislative power should forever reside in the Governor, Council, and people, met in General Assembly; that every freeholder and freeman might vote for Representatives without restraint; that no freeman should suffer but by the judgment of his peers, and that all trials should be by a jury of twelve men; that no tax should be assessed, on any pretext whatever, but by the consent of the Assembly; that no seaman or soldier should be quartered on the inhabitants against their will; that no martial law should exist; that no person, professing faith in God, by Jesus Christ, should, at any time, be in any way *disquieted or questioned for any difference of opinion in matters of religion.*"

So Colonel Dongan also had learned the ingenious language which King James had been taught by that "Jesuit!"

There had been penal laws in force against Catholics in all these provinces; and seeing that Governor Dongan was, himself, a Catholic, and desired the liberty of going to church without penal consequences, just as James himself always wished; he thought it would be no harm if the people of New York could be prevailed upon to let one another alone on that one matter, at least. He had a great amount of popular prejudice and ignorance to encounter; and there was plenty of jealousy and ill-will against him as a " Papist : " yet as he was, in fact, not only a very good and honorable gentleman, but also a most zealous and efficient Governor, as all authorities agree, he did succeed in procuring the adoption of that famous charter. The clause assuring religious liberty was found to hurt nobody; and people lived peaceably enough under it, until what is called the abdication of King James, in England, and the invasion by William of Orange. Then the Governor retired from office. He perceived that the days of " Ascendancy " and the Protestant interest were returning; and he went to live quietly on Staten Island, where he had a cottage and a mill. But he was not to be allowed to escape observation in this retreat. A revolutionary government, called a " Committee of Safety," was established in the city; Catholics were hunted down in every direction; and orders were issued for the arrest of Governor Dongan. He took refuge on board a vessel in the harbor, where he remained in concealment many weeks. In the meantime, his servants were arrested, and his effects seized at his residence. The " Charter of Liberties," passed in 1683, under a Catholic governor, was repealed, with all other laws passed by the late General Assembly of New York, in 1691, and a so-called " Bill of Rights " passed, which expressly deprived Catholics of all their political and religious *rights*. In 1697 this " Bill of Rights " was repealed, " probably as being too liberal," says Bishop Bayley; and, in 1700, an act was passed which recited that " Whereas, divers Jesuits, priests, and Popish missionaries have, of late, come, and for some time have had their residence in the remote parts of this province, and others of his Majesty's adjacent colonies, who, by their wicked and subtle insinuations, industriously labored to debauch, seduce, and withdraw the Indians from their due obedience to his most sacred Majesty, and to excite and stir them up to sedition, rebellion, and open hostility against his Majesty's government; " and enacted that every priest, etc., remaining in or coming into the province, after November

1st, 1700, should be "deemed and accounted an incendiary and disturber of the public peace and safety, and an enemy of the true Christian religion, and shall be adjudged to suffer *perpetual imprisonment;*" that, in case of escape and capture, they should suffer *death;* and that harborers of priests should pay a fine of two hundred pounds, and stand three days in the pillory.

In short, the Penal Laws of England and Ireland were carefully copied by the Colonists on this side the Atlantic. Even in Maryland, whose Catholic founders had made liberty of conscience an organic law, the same scenes of persecution were now enacted; and it need not be said that New England was ready to go all lengths against Papists, and against Protestants, too, if they were not the right kind of Protestants.

It may not be so generally known as it ought to be, how zealously and steadily our worthy Protestant Colonists followed the examples set them across the ocean, for the greater part of a century. Many persons vainly suppose that the series of Penal Laws in Ireland, with which we are all so familiar, were invented for the sole sake of our countrymen. Let such persons read the following, from the Statute Books of Virginia:—

"1753.—An Act for reducing the several laws made for establishing the General Court, and for regulating and setting the proceedings therein into one Act of Assembly.

"*Recusant Convict, disabled to be a Witness.*

"XXIV. That Popish recusant convicts, (that is, convicted of recusancy,) shall be incapable to be witnesses in any cause whatsoever."

"1756.—An Act for disarming Papists and reputed Papists, refusing to take the oaths to the government.

"*No Papist to keep Arms, etc.*

"III. And for the better securing the lives and properties of his Majesty's faithful subjects, Be it further enacted and declared, That no Papist or reputed Papist, so refusing or making default as aforesaid, shall or may have or keep in house or elsewhere, or in the possession of any other person to his use, or at his disposition, any arms, weapons, gunpowder, or ammunition, other than such necessary weapons as shall be allowed to him, by order of the Justices of the Peace, at their court, for the defence of his house or person."

"*No Papist to keep any Horse above the Value of £5.*

" VIII. And be it further enacted, That no Papist or reputed Papist, so refusing or making default as aforesaid, at any time after the first day of July, in the year of our Lord one thousand seven hundred and fifty-six, shall or may have, or keep in his own possession, or in the possession of any other person to his use or at his disposition, any horse or horses which shall be above the value of five pounds, to be sold; and that any two or more Justices of the Peace, from time to time, by warrant under their hands and seals, may and shall authorize any person or persons, with the assistance of the constable where the search shall be (who is hereby required to be aiding and assisting herein), to search for, and seize for his Majesty and his successors, all such horses, which horses are hereby declared to be forfeited to his Majesty and his successors." The Acts of Assembly now in force in the Colony of Virginia, *Williamsburg*, 1769, pp. 300, 332, 333.

" Negroes, mulattoes, and Indians not to be sworn as witnesses against whites." Pp. 202, 260.

But Catholics could not be witnesses, even against negroes.

But all this is a mere disgression, scarcely worth dwelling upon in this place, but that we happen to be here, in the State of New York; which is now happily under the fair *régime* imagined by the Catholic Governor, Dongan; and also that the story of this estimable Governor, coinciding, as it does, with the efforts made for freedom by King James at home, may help to illustrate a truth which is an ugly one to have to admit—namely, that religious persecution is of the very essence of Protestantism. Perhaps this is natural, and all right: for we, being the enlightened portion of Christendom, must feel ourselves authorized, and indeed *called*, to make others think our thoughts, and go our way, or else " to burn them and to boil them."

It is time to drop this offensive and irritating subject. Nothing would be easier than to demonstrate the excessive bad faith and malign intention which the " Historian " has brought to the narration of the reign of King James the Second, and the measures of his excellent Parliament. Of course the principal witness to all the cruelties alleged to have been inflicted upon "the Protestants," in that reign, is Archbishop King ("State of the Protestants of Ireland"). According to his usual system, Mr. Froude palms off upon his readers a bad and discredited authority, suppressing all others. It need not be said that the author who cited Sir John Temple without telling how that wretch afterwards attempted to suppress his own book, should a little further on give us the frightful fables of King, without telling that the man had composed his book, after King James's fall, to help the confiscations, to stimulate the penal laws, and to win his mitre; and without mentioning that Dr. Leslie, a worthy clergyman of King's own church, who dwelt in Ireland and had full knowledge of passing events, was seized with a sacred wrath on reading that bad book of the Archbishop, and demonstrated (to use his own words) that it contained "scarcely a true word." The Archbishop never replied to, nor noticed Leslie's scorching book for thirty years,—that is as long as he lived: he was content with the service it had done: he had his mitre; the Protestant interest was thriving; and, like Sir John Temple, he did not care to stand by his book any more. Such is precisely the species of authority that Froude chooses to rely upon: and, therefore, when his next, and last, volume comes forth, his readers may expect that he will dose them with plenty of Sir Richard Musgrave.

Perhaps I should never have undertaken to expose any of the delinquencies of Froude, but that the excellent Father Burke, in his most admirable course of lectures, dealt so gently with the Impostor, and even admitted his honesty and good faith. Father Burke's lectures, as I read them now in their collected form, appear to me a most complete answer, and most scathing rebuke; a work, indeed, which will live while the Irish race lives. If I have ventured to come forward into the same field, it has been mainly with a view of exhibiting not the honesty and good faith, but the determined dishonesty and treachery of that pretended "Historian;" and to show that all this has been perpetrated with the odious intention of affronting and scandalizing a whole race and nation. I am not so good a Christian as

Father Burke; and it gives me pleasure to think that I may have contributed a little to destroy such remnant of credit as Froude had, whether at home or abroad.

He has done evil as he could: he has sought grievously to injure a people that had done him no wrong; and I would now counsel him—after the example of his Cromwellian heroes—to fall down upon his knees, and "seek the Lord," and wrestle nightly with the Lord, so that, peradventure, grace might be given him to repent, and confess, and receive absolution of his sin.

THE LAST CONQUEST OF IRELAND,

(PERHAPS.)

CHAPTER I.

INTRODUCTION—ADDRESS OF THE AMERICAN CONGRESS "TO THE PEOPLE OF IRELAND," IN 1775—STATISTICS AND CONDITION OF IRELAND—IRELAND IN 1843—O'CONNELL—THE REPEAL DEBATE IN THE CORPORATION OF DUBLIN—THE "MONSTER MEETINGS" IN 1843—OPINION IN THE ENGLISH PARLIAMENT —SIR ROBERT PEEL'S DECLARATION IN ANSWER TO MR. BERNAL [OSBORNE].

"*We are desirous of possessing the good opinion of the virtuous and humane. We are peculiarly desirous of furnishing you with the true state of our motives and objects; the better to enable you to judge of our conduct with accuracy and determine the merits of the controversy with impartiality and precision.*"

These sentences are taken from the "Address to the People of Ireland," by the Continental Congress of America, adopted July, 1775. They fit the other side at present. The Irish People are now the pleaders and appellants. Americans are the virtuous and humane.

In the same Address, Congress was pleased to say to the People of Ireland:

"*Your* Parliament had done us no wrong. You had ever been friendly to the rights of mankind; and we acknowledge with pleasure and gratitude that your nation has produced patriots who have nobly distinguished themselves in the cause of humanity and America."

Ireland, at that time, had a Parliament, and national existence; and her voice counted for something among civilized nations. And Americans, at that time, would have been very unwilling that the civilized world should form its ideas of their rights, wrongs, and resistance from the British Press; but their eventual success set them quite above that apprehension; for the civilized world "sympathizes" with success. Ireland, on the contrary, having been, since that day, *twice* broken, conquered, and utterly ruined, it may seem that the English have a patent-right in our history, as well as in everything else of ours, and must not be interrupted or controverted.

Yet there are some circumstances which perplex an inquirer who derives his information from the English periodical press. That an island which is said to be an integral part of the richest empire on the globe—and the most fertile portion of that empire;—with British Constitution, *Habeas Corpus*, Members of Parliament, and Trial by Jury—should in five years lose two and a half millions of its people (more than one-fourth) by hunger, and fever the consequence of hunger, and flight beyond sea to escape from hunger,—while that empire of which it is said to be a part, was all the while advancing in wealth, prosperity, and comfort, at a faster pace than ever before,—is a matter that seems to ask elucidation.

In the year 1841, Ireland, a country precisely half the size of the State of Georgia, had a population of 8,175,124. The natural rate of increase of population in Ireland, through all her former troubles, would have given upwards of nine millions in 1851; but in 1851 the Census Commissioners find in Ireland but 6,515,794 living souls. (*Thom's Official Directory.*)

Another thing, which to a spectator must appear anomalous, is that during each of those five years of "famine," from '46 to '51—that famine-struck land produced more than double the needful sustenance for all her own people; and of the best and choicest kind. Governor Wise, of Virginia, was in Brazil while the ends of the earth were resounding with the cry of Irish starvation; and was surprised to see unloaded at Rio abundance of the best quality of packed beef from Ireland. That the people who were dying of hunger did, in each year of their agony, produce upon Irish ground, of wheat and other grain, and of cattle and poultry, more than double the amount that they could all by any gluttony devour, is a fact that must be not only asserted, but proved beyond doubt.

That with one hundred and five members in the Parliament of the "United Kingdom," the Irish people (supposing them to suffer any grievance or injustice) could get no redress; that with the British Constitution, *Habeas Corpus*, and Trial by Jury, as aforesaid, most Irishmen you meet with in America tell you there is no Law or Justice to be had in Ireland;—that to the benevolent exertions on a vast scale, which English periodicals assure us were made by the Imperial Government to rescue the perishing Irish from their sufferings, that people, though "warm-hearted" to a proverb, respond not only with ingratitude, but with imprecations,—that even now, when the country is, we are assured, prosperous and wealthy, there is still an eager, multitudinous emigration, to fly from such prosperity,—that all this time, be the island hungry or well fed, prosperous or insolvent, more than one-half of Queen Victoria's army consists of Irishmen, of all ranks and creeds, who fight as zealously for their Queen, (or at least for their pay,) in Russia, India, and China, as any other of her troops;—all these phenomena together, present a case not paralleled in any other country or any other age.

A plain narrative of events may throw some light on it. My authorities shall be principally the Parliamentary Reports, as given in the newspapers of the time; Official Returns and Blue Books, as abstracted in the Government Statistical Directories; Speeches of O'Connell and O'Brien, as well as of Palmerston and Russell; Pamphlets and Memoirs which shall be cited hereafter; and my own personal knowledge.

So much by way of preface and programme.

The Spring of the year One thousand eight hundred and forty-three opened brightly on Ireland. For years the seasons had been favorable and abundant; and although there had been, as usual, much ejectment and extermination of tenants, and the ordinary and normal amount of distress and hunger; although of the greater products there were greater exports to England, and a larger resort of landlords to England to spend the improved rentals; although every

Winter was a Winter of misery which in any other land of white men would be intolerable;—still there had been no desolating and sweeping "famine" for twenty years.

O'Connell was at the height of his popularity and power. He had wrung from a hostile English ministry Catholic Emancipation, and was now representative in Parliament for the county of Cork, the greatest county in Ireland. He had, further, forced from England a measure of municipal reform, which opened the city corporations to Catholics; and had been, himself, first Catholic Lord Mayor of Dublin. The people believed he could do anything; and he almost believed it himself. In the beginning of this year he announced that it was the "Repeal year;" asked for three millions of enrolled Repealers in the Repeal Association; and confidently promised, and fully believed, that no English administration would venture to resist that great measure so enforced. The more thoroughly to arouse the people, he declined to go over to London to take his seat in Parliament, (many other members following his example,) and resolved to hold multitudinous meetings in every corner of the island.

First, he moved in the Dublin Corporation a resolution, for the adoption of a petition to Parliament, demanding a Repeal of the Union with England—that is to say, demanding back the Irish Parliament which had been extinguished in 1800; so that Ireland should once more have her own House of Peers and House of Commons; the Sovereign of England to be also Sovereign of Ireland. His speech was masterly, and covered the whole case. He cited the ablest jurists to show that the so-called Union was in law a nullity; reminded his audience of what was at any rate notorious and never denied—that supposing the two Parliaments competent to pass such an act, it had been obtained by fraud and open bribery; an open market of bribery, of which the accounts are extant: £1,275,000 paid to proprietors for the purchase of nomination boroughs, at £15,000 per borough (which seats were immediately filled by English officers and clerks);—more than one million sterling expended on mere bribes; the tariff being quite familiar, £8,000 for an Union vote, or an office worth £2,000 a-year, if the Member did not like to touch the ready money; twenty peerages, ten bishoprics, one chief-justiceship, six puisne judgeships; not to count regiments and ships given to officers in the army and navy; all dispensed as direct payment for their votes. He reminded them that the right of holding public meetings to protest against all this was taken away during the time the Union was in agitation; that county meetings convened by High-sheriffs of counties, as in Tipperary and Queen's county, were dispersed by troops; that martial law was in force and the Habeas Corpus suspended; that, in 1800, the number of soldiers concentrated in that island (half the size of Georgia) was 129,000, as "good lookers-on;" that, notwithstanding all intimidation, seven hundred thousand persons had petitioned against the measure; and, notwithstanding all enticements, only three thousand had petitioned for it, most of these being government officials and prisoners in the gaols. If he had stopped here, most persons would think it enough: *that* was a deed which at the earliest possible moment must be undone and punished.

But he did not stop here: he went into all the details of ruined trade and manufactures since the Union—immensely increased drains in the shape of absentee rents and surplus taxation—frauds in subjecting Ireland to a charge for the *English* national debt, and even charging to Ireland's special account the very moneys expended in bribes and military expenses for carrying the Union; which he said was about as fair as "making Ireland pay for the knife with which Lord Castlereagh cut his throat;"—injustice in giving Ireland but 100 members in the House of Commons while her population and revenue entitled her to 175; and above all the injustice of fixing the qualification of *electors* of these members much higher in Ireland, the poorer country, than in England.

This is a sketch only of the case for Repeal of the Union; —the necessity for some remedy or other was only too apparent in the poverty and wretchedness which moved and scandalized all Europe—in the increasing beggary, notwithstanding the new Poor law,—a measure which had been forced on the country against its will, and was totally unsuited to it.

The petition for Repeal was adopted by a vote of forty-one to fifteen in the Dublin Corporation; and a similar petition shortly after by the Corporation of Cork. Hitherto the English press, and the Irish press in the English interest, looked on with affected or real indifference and contempt.

5

The Spring opened; and O'Connell left Dublin for the provinces. Then began the series of vast open-air meetings, to which the peasantry, accompanied by their priests, Repeal Wardens, and "Temperance bands," flocked in numbers varying from 50,000 to 250,000,—(I take the reduced and disparaging estimate of enemies; but the Repeal newspapers put up the Tara meeting to 400,000.) Of course the orator always addressed these multitudes; but though his voice was the most powerful of his day, he could not be heard by a tenth of them. Neither did they come to hear; they were all well indoctrinated by local Repeal Wardens; had their minds made up; and came to convince their leader that they were with him, and would be ready at any time when called upon.

But all was to be peaceable. They were to demand their rights imperatively; they were, he assured them, tall men and strong; at every monster meeting he had around him, as he often said, the materials of a greater army than both the armies combined that fought at Waterloo. But, he said—

"But take heed not to misconceive me. Is it by force or violence, bloodshed, or turbulence that I shall achieve this victory, dear above all earthly considerations to my heart? No! perish the thought forever. I will do it by legal, peaceable, and constitutional means alone,—by the electricity of public opinion, by the moral combination of good men, and by the enrolment of four millions of Repealers. I am a disciple of that sect of politicians who believe that *the greatest of all sublunary blessings is too dearly purchased at the expense of a single drop of human blood.*"

Many persons did not understand this sort of language; and what is worse, did not believe him sincere in using it. The prevailing impression was that while the Repeal Association was a peaceful body, contemplating only " constitutional agitation," yet the parade of such immense masses of physical force had an ulterior meaning, and indicated that if the British Parliament remained absolutely insensible to the reasonable demands of the people, the Association must be dissolved; and the next question would be how best and soonest to exterminate the British forces. I say of my own knowledge that many who were close to O'Connell expected all along that the English Parliament and government never would yield; and these would have taken small interest in the movement if it was never to go beyond speeches and cheers.

Meanwhile, nothing could be more peaceful, orderly, and good-humored than the meetings. Father Mathew's temperance reformation had lately been working its wonders; and all the people were sober and quiet. Repeal Wardens everywhere organized an "O'Connell Police," with wands, and any person of the whole immense multitude who was even noisy was instantly and quietly removed. The government, indeed, soon took alarm, or affected to do so, for the peace of the country; and they sent large forces of armed constabulary to bivouac on the ground; but there never was the slightest excuse for interference.

The movement of the people, throughout this whole Summer, was profound and sweeping: it carried along with it irresistibly the Catholic clergy, though in many cases against their will: but they were of the people, bound up with the people, dependent on the people, and found it their best policy to move not only with the people, but at their head. The Catholic Bishops and Archbishops gave in their adhesion, and began to take the chair at meetings; the French and German Press began to notice the struggle, and eagerly watch how England would deal with it. At last, on April 27th, Mr. Lane Fox, a Tory member of Parliament, gave notice, "That it is the duty of her Majesty's Government to take immediate steps to put an end to the agitation for Repeal"—and on the same day Lord Eliot, Chief Secretary for Ireland, gave notice of a Bill "for the regulation of *arms* in Ireland." At the same moment the Funds fell one and a half per cent.

The first threat of coercion brought important accessions to the ranks of the Repealers; and the monster meetings became now more monstrous than ever; but, if possible, even gayer and more good-humored. O'Connell appeared in the Repeal Association on the Monday after Mr. Lane Fox's notice of motion; and on the proceedings being interrupted for a moment by the braying of a donkey on Burgh-quay, he said gently: "Maybe that's Lane Fox:" whereupon the braying was in turn drowned by roars of laughter. Mr. Lane Fox wrote a newspaper letter to O'Connell, inquiring when he would be in his place in Parliament, that the motion to put down Repeal might be proceeded with. O'Connell replied by a card, recommending the friends of that gentleman "to obtain for him that protection which the court in matter of lunacy is enabled to give," etc. At another meeting he exclaimed :—

"That man is one of the legislators for Ireland ; and though I went to Parliament as the representative of 700,000 Irishmen in the county of Cork, the individual who can talk such nonsense is equal to me there. If I had no other reason for looking for a repeal of the Union than that Mr. Lane Fox is a legislator for Ireland, I never cheered my beagles upon a drag with one half the voice that I would hunt this foolish fox."

His sarcasm was bitter, his reasoning irrefragable, his array multitudinous in its peaceful might ; but in the meantime Lord Eliot was preparing his Arms Bill (an invention which I shall presently describe) ; and on the ninth of May, the Duke of Wellington, in the Lords, and Sir Robert Peel, in the Commons, declared that all the resources of the empire should be exerted to preserve the Union ; and Sir Robert Peel added, quoting Lord Althorp, that, deprecating civil war as he did, he should hold civil war preferable to the "dismemberment of the Empire." Mr. Bernal [Osborne] instantly asked Sir Robert, as he cited Lord Althorp's words, "whether he would abide by another declaration of that noble lord, namely, that if all the members for Ireland should be in favor of Repeal, he would consider it his duty to grant it." And Sir Robert Peel replied—" I do not recollect that Lord Althorp ever made any such declaration; but if he did, *I am not prepared to abide by it.*"

At this point issue was joined. The majority of the Irish nation desired to undo the union with England; but England declared that if all Ireland demanded that measure, England would rather drown the demand in blood.

In the next chapter, I shall endeavor to give an idea of the *personnel* of the Repeal Association, and of its enemies.

CHAPTER II.

THE "REPEAL YEAR" (1843)—RESOURCES OF O'CONNELL—CLARE ELECTION AND CATHOLIC EMANCIPATION—SHIEL—"YOUNG IRELAND"—DAVIS, DILLON, DUFFY—THE "NATION"—RESOURCES OF THE ENGLISH—DISARMING LAWS.

The "Repeal Year," then, had only advanced as far as the month of April. O'Connell was collecting the suffrages of an unarmed people by millions for the restoration of Irish nationhood; England had already announced, through the mouth of her Premier and her commander-in-chief, that though all Ireland should demand Repeal, England's will was to keep her as a province.

We are to see what were the resources and relative strength of the two islands for the struggle which seemed impending. On the Irish side was O'Connell, with his miraculous power over the vast Catholic population of Ireland, which he wielded absolutely at his will. No country had ever seen so potent a popular leader. When he began his career, the Catholics of Ireland were a degraded race. After the defeat of the Stuarts, the capitulation of Limerick, and the breach of the Treaty concluded at that city, by imposing a code of penal laws upon Catholics, they had sunk into a state of abject submission and impotence under the operation of those laws, from which it seemed impossible ever to arise. Denied the privilege of bearing arms—forbidden education—prohibited to exercise trade or commerce in any corporate town—excluded from all professions,—disqualified from holding a lease of land for a longer term than thirty-one years—and forbidden to own a horse of more than five pounds value; it was no wonder they had become impoverished in spirit as well as in means.

The immense increase in their numbers towards the end of the last century; the success of the American Revolution, and the disasters of the British arms in the Netherlands, had made it necessary to conciliate them by a relaxation of that infamous code; and when O'Connell first undertook their cause, they had been relieved from most of those restrictions; but were still excluded from Parliament, the Corporations, and the Judicial Bench. At first he had devoted himself to their service in his own profession of the law. He was the great Catholic Barrister. If any tyrannical scheme of the Orange Corporation of Dublin was to be exposed and baffled; if, in any prosecution of a Catholic newspaper, the Orange Judges were to be bearded on the Bench, and the Orange jurors shamed in their jury-box, O'Connell was the champion to whom the labor and the honor fell. It would be long to tell the series of legal battles he fought in the Four Courts and at county assizes. His tone and manner were always defiant and contemptuous. If he knew the Judges were predetermined, and the jury well and truly packed, he condescended to argue no points of law; but launched out into denunciation of the whole system of law and government in Ireland; informed the jurors that they knew they were packed; charged the Judges with having advised and urged on the prosecution which they pretended to try; in short, set his client and his client's case at one side as a minor and collateral affair; took all Ireland for his client; and often made Judges, Sheriffs, and juries feel that they were the real criminals on trial.

It is easy to understand that this conduct, if it did not save his clients, inspirited the people. All Ireland was proud of him, and felt that he had been sent as their deliverer. At length he renounced the general practice of law (which brought him in £8,000 per annum) and became a professional Agitator. He established the Catholic Association, expressly to promote the emancipation of the Catholics from all remaining penal laws; and finding that his agitation produced small impression in England, he at length suddenly left Dublin on the eve of an election for Clare County; travelled day and night to Ennis; announced himself, though a proscribed Catholic, as a candidate against Mr. Vesey Fitzgerald; and easily carried the election. He then went to London, proceeded to the House of Commons, and demanded to take his seat without the oaths which excluded Catholics. Of course he was refused; and a new writ was issued for a new election in Clare. He returned to Ireland, resolved to be returned again for the same county; but, before the new election, Parliament was dissolved; and Sir

Robert Peel and the Duke of Wellington announced their Bill for emancipation of the Catholics—expressly, as the Duke avowed, to avert civil war.

Undoubtedly this was a daring achievement and a noble triumph: and O'Connell thought the same system of agitation might at any time coerce the British Government to yield all the rest. Catholic Emancipation, however, it must be remembered, was a measure for the consolidation of the "British Empire;" it opened high official position to the wealthier Catholics and educated Catholic gentlemen; and thus separated their interest from that of the peasantry. But it was of the peasantry mainly that the government had any apprehension; and British Ministers felt that Catholic Emancipation would place this peasantry more completely in their power than ever.

Besides, Emancipation had a strong party in its favor both amongst Irish Protestants and in England: and in yielding to it England made no sacrifice, except of her ancient grudge. To her it was positive gain. O'Connell did not bethink him that, when his agitation should be directly aimed at the "integrity of the empire," and the supremacy of the British in Ireland, it would be a different matter.

Such, however, had been his achievements. The door of Parliament once opened, he made brilliant use of his privilege. At the next election he looked round the island to see where he could strike the most telling blow at the "Ascendancy." He pitched on Waterford. That county had been hitherto under the complete control of the great Orange family of Beresford, to which belongs the Marquis of Waterford. They were of the wealthiest and haughtiest of the British landlord garrison of Ireland, and predominated over the people like Pachas. O'Connell at once entered the lists against the nominee of the Beresfords, to the astonishment both of friends and foes. To the Catholic electors of Waterford themselves it seemed an act of almost godlike audacity; the long nightmare of oppression still lay upon their breasts; but his voice rung amongst them, and the proud defiance of an Irish Catholic flung down to the mighty house of Waterford, awoke them from their dreaming. By an overwhelming majority he trampled on the pride of Beresford; and old men embraced him with tears of joy, and women would have spread their hair beneath his feet.

This Emancipation was carried in 1829. Thence till the "Repeal Year," the people had greatly multiplied in numbers, and improved in education and spirit.

Hitherto I have spoken of all movements in Ireland as created, moved, and appropriated by this giant O'Connell. It was so: there was no man equal to him, and none second to him. His most effective aid during the Emancipation struggle was Richard Lalor Shiel, another Catholic barrister, and a man of great genius and accomplishments: but Shiel desisted from agitation after that was won. Up to the time of the Ministerial declaration against Repeal in April, very few members of Parliament were actual members of the Association; but among them was Henry Grattan, member for Meath, who brought to its ranks an illustrious name, if nothing else of great value. O'Brien still stood aloof. The working staff of the Association in Dublin consisted of obscure people, generally very humble servants of O'Connell.

But within this same Association there was a certain smaller Association, composed of very different men. Its head and heart was Thomas Davis, a young Protestant lawyer of Cork County, who had been previously known only as a scholar and antiquarian; a zealous member of the Royal Irish Academy, and of the Archæological Society. In the Autumn of '42, he and his friend John B. Dillon (then a Roscommon lawyer and afterwards a New York lawyer) had projected the publication of a weekly literary and political journal of the highest class, to sustain the cause of Irish nationhood, to give it a historic and literary interest which would win and inspire the youth of the country, and above all, to conciliate the Protestants, by stripping the agitation of a certain suspicion of sectarianism, which, though disavowed by O'Connell, was naturally connected with it by reason of the antecedents of its chief.

Mr. Duffy, the editor of a provincial newspaper in Belfast, happened to be then in Dublin, on the occasion of a State prosecution against his journal, and Davis and Dillon proposed that he should undertake the ostensible editorship of the new paper; of which, however, Davis was to be the principal writer. So commenced the *Nation* newspaper; and for three years it was, next to O'Connell, the strongest power in Ireland on the national side. Its editor, Mr. Duffy, had good literary talent, great ambition, abundant vanity, but defective education. He had been connected with the Press from his boyhood, had most excellent ideas about the arrangement and organization of a newspaper, and great zeal and earnestness in the cause of Repeal. Dillon was a man of higher mark and greater acquirement: but both these were indolent; and in fact Davis took upon him the burden of the labor. Writing was a small part of his duty. He was indefatigable in searching out efficient recruits amongst the young men of his acquaintance, kindling their ambition, and filling them with the same generous spirit of mutual forgiveness for the past, and a common hope for the future, by which he designed to obliterate the religious feuds of ages and raise up a new Irish nation. Whatever was done, throughout the whole movement, to win Protestant support, was the work of Davis. His genius, his perfect unselfishness, his accomplishments, his cordial manner, his high and chivalrous character, and the dash and impetus of his writings, soon brought around him a gifted circle of young Irishmen of all religions and of none, who afterwards received the nick-name of "Young Ireland." Their head-quarters was the *Nation* office; and their bond of union was their proud attachment to their friend.

O'Connell knew well, and could count, this small circle of literary privateer Repealers; he felt that he was receiving, for the present, a powerful support from them—the *Nation* being by far the ablest organ of the movement; but he knew also, that they were outside of his influence, and did not implicitly believe his confident promises that Repeal would be yielded to "agitation"—nor believe that he believed it; that they were continually seeking, by their writings, to arouse a military spirit among the people; and had most diligently promoted the formation of Temperance Bands with military uniforms, the practice of marching to monster meetings in ranks and squadrons, with banners, and the like; showing plainly, that while they helped the Repeal Association, they fully expected that the liberties of the country must be *fought* for at last. O'Connell, therefore, suspected and disliked them; but could not well quarrel with them. Apparently, they worked in perfect harmony; and during all this "Repeal Year" few were aware how certainly that alliance must end. Personally, they sought no notoriety; and the *Nation* was as careful to swell O'Connell's praise, and make him the sole figure to which all eyes should turn, as any of his own creatures could be. O'Connell accepted their services to convert the "gentry," and the Protestants;—they could not dispense with O'Connell, to stir and wield the multitudinous people.

Here, then, was the array and the whole force at one side. When Ministers came down to Parliament, and pledged themselves to maintain the Union, even by civil war, they had on *their* side these following powers and agencies:

First.—A million and a half of Protestants, most of them English or Scottish by descent; and bound to England by having been for ages maintained in a position of superiority over the Catholics. Five hundred thousand of these were Presbyterians, nearly all in the northern province of Ulster. The rest belonged to the Established Church; and in the hands of these last was almost all the landed property of the island. This gave them the power of life and death over the tenantry.

Second.—A regular army of between thirty and forty thousand men, disposed in barracks and fortresses, at the principal strategic positions in the island.

Third.—Another regular force of eleven thousand armed and drilled police, cantoned in small police-barracks all over the country, in parties of from four to twelve. These were all picked men, well paid, partly by assessments on the counties, and partly by the Treasury. A portion of them were mounted and trained to act as cavalry; and they had a complete code of signals, for communicating from station to station, by day and by night; with blue lights, red lights, and other apparatus. To this service was also attached a numerous corps of detective police, whose functions will be mentioned more fully hereafter.

Fourth.—A Revenue Police, and Coast-guard Service with a large fleet of armed revenue cruisers.

Fifth.—The Church Establishment—which is, in truth, nothing but an apanage of the aristocracy, supplying lucrative situations to many younger sons. Catholics and Presbyterians are both obliged to pay for the support of this Church —not now by tithes, but in a way much more effectual, and impossible to resist or evade; namely, by a tithe rent-charge, payable in the first instance by the proprietor, and then levied by distraining on the tenant. This system, together with the land laws, placed all the peasantry in the power of their landlords—that is of the government.

Sixth.—The Presbyterian Church must also be counted amongst the forces of the government. During the insurrection of 1798 the northern insurgents had been Presbyterians, all at that time zealous Republicans. After the "Union" the English government had taken the precaution to make a large grant for payment of the Presbyterian clergymen; after which, that body of divines was counted on as part of the general police of the island.

Seventh.—A Poor Law had been forced upon the country a few years before. The island was now studded with Union Workhouses, built like fortresses; and in each Union was a gang of well-paid officers; all humble servants of the government.

Eighth.—The system of making all education penal had been discontinued; but very carefully. There was now "National Education," under the management of a board of Commissioners appointed by government, the Chairman of which board was Dr. Whately, Archbishop of Dublin—an Englishman. He took charge of preparing and revising the school-books which were to be used; and he took care to keep out of them any, even the remotest, allusion to the history of the country, and even such extracts from well-known authors as illustrate or celebrate the virtue of patriotism in *any* country. The 3,000 national school-teachers, paid by the government, were 3,000 *more* servants of the government; and the system required in the schools was, as we see, carefully calculated to crush every spark of national feeling.

Ninth.—The only investment of their small savings which industrious people could make was in the Savings Banks (land being unpurchaseable in small lots);—and the Savings Banks are government institutions. The law requires them to invest the money deposited with them in the public funds; and so every depositor, feeling that his little all is in the power of the English government, is to that extent interested in maintaining its credit and stability.

Tenth.—The Sheriffs are nominees of the Crown; and the Sheriffs arrange the Juries. In England, every corporate city elects its own Sheriff; but in the "Municipal Reform Bill" for Ireland, this power was reserved to the Crown. It is in the city of Dublin that State prosecutions are usually tried; and the Sheriff of Dublin is always a creature of the government. The use of this is too obvious.

Eleventh.—And best of all—for even the other ten arrangements, though you may think they give England a tolerably strong grasp of the little island, could not have been relied upon without *this*—a system of Disarming Acts. I have mentioned that on the same day the Ministers declared in the Queen's name that the Union must at all hazards be maintained, Lord Eliot introduced a new "Arms Bill" for Ireland. Ever since the Union it had been thought necessary by the British Government to have stringent laws in force to prevent "improper persons" from possessing arms,—that is, persons supposed to be disaffected,—that is, the great majority of the population. I shall not detail the long series of acts for this purpose, with their continual amendments; but simply describe the provisions of this new one, which Lord Eliot recommended in the House of Commons, by the remark: "that it was substantially similar to what had been the law in Ireland for half a century," (June 15th,) and again, (June 26th,) "He would ask the noble lord to compare it with the bill of 1838, and to point out the difference. In fact, this was milder." This mild act, then, provided: that no man could keep arms of any sort, without first having a certificate from two householders, "rated to the poor" at above £20, and then producing that certificate to the Justices at Sessions (said Justices being all appointed by the Crown, and all "sure" men); and then—if the Justices permitted the applicant to keep arms at all—they were to be registered and *branded* by the police. After that they could not be removed, sold, or inherited, without new registry. And every conversation respecting these arms in which a man should not tell truly whatever he might be asked by any policeman, subjected the delinquent to penalties. To have a pike or spear, "or instrument serving for a pike or spear," was an offence punishable by transportation for seven years. Domiciliary visits by the police might be ordered by any Magistrate "on suspicion;" whereupon any man's house might be broken into by day or night, and his very bed searched for concealed arms. Blacksmiths were required to take out licenses, similar to those for keeping arms, and under the same penalties; in order that the workers in so dangerous a metal as iron might be known and approved persons. And to crown the code, if any weapon should be found in any house, or out-house or stack-yard, the occupier was to be convicted, unless he could prove that it was there without his knowledge.

Such had been " substantially the law of Ireland for half a century." The idea of arms had come to be associated in the people's minds with handcuffs, jails, petty sessions, and transportation; a good device for killing the manly spirit of a nation.

There is, however, one precedent for the Arms Bill in history. The Israelites were forty years under the dominion of the Philistines; and we read in 1st Samuel, c. 13: "Now there was no smith found throughout all the land of Israel; for the Philistines said, Lest the Hebrews make them swords and spears."

Review, now, those eleven arms of British power; and say whether it was an easy enterprise to tear Ireland out of their iron grip.

Biblical analogies

CHAPTER III.

"THE REPEAL YEAR" STILL—O'BRIEN'S MOTION—ARMS BILL—SIR EDWARD SUGDEN—DISMISSED MAGISTRATES—ARBITRATORS—MORE MONSTER MEETINGS.

The Disarming Act passed into a law, of course, by large majorities. It was in vain that some Irish members resisted; in vain Mr. Smith O'Brien moved that instead of meeting the discontent of Ireland with a new "Arms Bill," the House should resolve itself into a committee " to consider the causes of the discontent with a view to the redress of grievances." O'Brien, who was afterwards to play so conspicuous a part, was not yet a Repealer; he had been for twenty years one of the most industrious Members of Parliament, and was attached, on most questions, to the Whig party. His speech, however, on this motion, showed that he regarded it as a last effort to obtain any approach to justice in a British Parliament; and that if they still resolutely adhered to the policy of coercion, and nothing but coercion, he would very shortly be found by O'Connell's side. He pointed out the facts which justified discontent;—that the Union made Ireland poor, and kept her poor;—that it encouraged the absenteeism of landlords and so caused a great rental to be spent in England;—that nearly a million sterling of "surplus revenue," over what was expended in the government of Ireland, was annually remitted from the Irish to the English exchequer; that Irish manufactures had ceased, and the profits on all the manufactured articles consumed in that island, came to England;—that the tenantry had no permanent tenure or security that they would derive benefit by any improvements they might make;—that Ireland had but 105 members of Parliament, whereas her population and revenue together entitled her to 175;—that the municipal laws of the two countries were not the same: —that the new "Poor Law" was a failure, and was increasing the wretchedness and hunger of the people;—and the right honorable gentleman (Sir R. Peel) had now declared his *ultimatum ;* he declared that "conciliation had reached its limits; and that the Irish should have an Arms Bill, and nothing but an Arms Bill." (Speech of July 4th, 1843.)

His facts were not disputed. Nobody in Parliament pretended to say that anything in this long catalogue was overstated; but the House refused the committee of inquiry; would discuss no grievances; and proceeded with their Arms Bill.

It may be said that these excessive precautions to keep arms out of the hands of the Irish people, testified the high esteem in which the military spirit of that people was held in England; and in that point of view the long series of Arms Acts may be regarded as a compliment. In truth the English had some occasion to know that the Irish make good soldiers. In this very month of July, 1843, for example, a British General fought the decisive battle of Meeanee, by which the Ameers of Scinde were crushed. While the Bill for disarming Ireland was pending in London, far off on the banks of the Indus, Napier went into action with less than 3,000 troops against 25,000; only four hundred of his men being "British" soldiers; but those four hundred were a Tipperary regiment,—the 22d,—and they did their work in such style as made the gray old warrior shout with delight: "Magnificent Tipperary!" In some distant latitude or longitude arms are thought to fit Irish hands; but not at home.

In the meantime, some additional regiments, mostly of English or Scotch troops, were landed in Ireland; and several war-steamers, with a fleet of gun-brigs, were sent to cruise around the coast. Barracks began to be fortified and loop-holed; and police-stations were furnished with iron-grated windows. It was quite plain that the English Government intended, on the first pretext of provocation, to make a salutary slaughter.

The vast monster meetings continued, and with even intenser enthusiasm; but always with perfect peace and order. The speeches of O'Connell at these meetings, though not heard by a fourth of the multitudes, were carefully reported, and flew over all Ireland and England too, in hundreds of newspapers. So that probably no speeches ever delivered in the world had so wide an audience. The people began to neglect altogether the proceedings of Parliament, and felt that their cause was to be tried at home. More and more of the Irish Members of Parliament discontinued their attendance in London, and gathered around O'Connell. Many of those who still went to London were called on by their constituents to come home or resign.

Sir Edward Sugden was then Lord Chancellor of Ireland; and he began offensive operations on the British side by depriving of the Commission of the Peace all magistrates who joined the Repeal Association, or took the chair at a Repeal meeting. He had dismissed in this way about twenty, including O'Connell and Lord French, usually accompanying the announcement of the *supersedeas* with an insolent letter; when Smith O'Brien wrote to him that *he* had been a magistrate for many years, that he was not a Repealer, but could not consent to hold his commission on such humiliating terms. Instantly his example was followed by many gentlemen; who flung their commissions in the Chancellor's face, sometimes with letters as insulting as his own. And now O'Connell brought forward one of his grand schemes. It was to have all the dismissed magistrates appointed "arbitrators," who should hold regular courts of arbitration in their respective districts,—all the people pledging themselves to make no resort to the Queen's magistrates, but to settle all questions by the award of their "arbitrators." This was put into operation in many places and worked very well.

In reply to questions in Parliament, as to what they were concentrating troops in Ireland for, Peel and Wellington had said they did not mean to make war or attack anybody, but only to maintain the peace of the country. Shortly after, there was a monster meeting in Kilkenny; the Trades of the city marched in procession with their banners; thirty or forty Temperance bands in military array, and playing Irish music; vast bodies of horsemen, amounting probably to twenty thousand ranked in deep masses around the outskirts of the meeting. Now I shall give you a specimen of the Agitator's oratory. After having called for "three cheers for the Queen"—

"I suppose you have heard," he said, "of the Duke of Wellington and Sir Robert Peel having come down to Parliament one fine evening to declare they would prevent the Repeal of the Union even by civil war. We will not go to war with them; but let them not dare to go to war with us! The great Duke and the crafty Sir Robert have pulled in their horns a little; and said they did not mean to attack us. Very well; there is peace, then, for we will not attack them. . . .

"What is the next step? Up comes Chancellor Sugden,—what an ugly name the fellow has! Why, there is not one of you would call a decent-looking pig *Sugden*. This Chancellor issues a letter, striking us from the Commission of the Peace. . . The Commission of the Peace was also taken from Colonel Butler, from Lord French, from Sir Michael Dillon Bellew, and from Daniel O'Connell, and other vagabonds. This Sugden, who took away the Commission of the Peace from us, is a lawyer, and has made an enormous fortune by the law; yet he does not understand the law; for he says it is unconstitutional to attend meetings, while he himself publishes an alleged speech of the Queen, and attributes to her the unconstitutional speech uttered by a Prime Minister. But they have sent over 36,000 men here, cavalry, infantry, artillery, and marines. . . Do you know what they are going to do? The Admiral is coming down the Grand Canal to examine all the turf-boats, and look into their potato-lockers to try if they have any hidden cannon on board. . . . And a lieutenant of the navy has been sent by the fly-boat on the Royal Canal to find out what became of the army of 15,000 men that the Rev. Mr. O'Higgins had hid in his back parlor!"

The Kilkenny meeting, like all the other meetings, dispersed in perfect order and tranquillity; but O'Connell pledged them to come back to that spot whenever he might want them.

Undoubtedly this sort of procedure from week to week, and O'Connell's ridicule and vituperation, poured out upon every one who opposed " the repeal," was extremely provoking to the government and their party; yet no great progress was made. O'Connell, indeed, knew the law: he knew how far he could go with safety; and the people had full confidence that he would accomplish all he promised, " without the shedding of a drop of blood; " but all the while the enemy was in actual occupation and full possession of the whole country, its revenues and resources; and intended so to continue. Some of our friends about the *Nation* office began to ask themselves how long this was to go on. When all Ireland shall have paraded itself at monster meetings, they said, what then? What next?

Notwithstanding the very resolute countenance shown by the government, however, O'Connell still believed that they must yield at last, as they had done upon the Catholic Emancipation question; and, certainly, the impetus and volume which his movement was daily acquiring, would have seemed to make almost anything possible to him who wielded such a wondrous machine. He moved to tears, or convulsed with laughter, or excited to suppressed rage, hundreds of thousands of people every week ; and his loud defiance to the Saxon made men's hearts burn within them as they prayed that he would only give them *the word.*

One of his great meetings was at Baltinglass, in Wicklow county. The proprietor of most of the land thereabouts was Lord Wicklow: and his lordship had posted over his estate a placard exhorting, or almost commanding, his tenants to stay home at their work, and not to be flocking to a meeting "only to minister to the vanity of an individual." They all disobeyed; and O'Connell, when he rose up to address them, opened a copy of the placard. He read it, and the hills re-echoed the laughter of a hundred and fifty thousand throats. "I know whom he means by *an individual*," he exclaimed. "He means *me*. Individual in his teeth! I'm no more an individual than Lord Wicklow's mother!"

Lord Beaumont, an English Catholic peer, who owed his seat in the House to O'Connell, thought himself called on to denounce the Repeal agitation. "Do you know who this Beaumont is?" asked O'Connell, at his next meeting. "Why, the man's name is Martin Bree, though he calls himself Stapleton. His grandfather married a Stapleton for her fortune, and then changed the name. He was a Stapleton when I emancipated him. I beg your pardon for having emancipated such a fellow."

Sir Edward Sugden, as Lord Chancellor, had the control over all lunatic asylums; and frequently visited those near Dublin. After he had dismissed about a dozen magistrates, and others were pouring in their resignations, and getting appointed arbitrators in consequence—and his act of vigor was manifestly and admittedly a failure, O'Connell, at one of the meetings of the Repeal Association in Dublin, said:—

"If these men are not mad, they give some signs of madness; and a most ludicrous instance of a thing of the kind occurred on Saturday last. The Lord Chancellor, in the intervals of making out writs of *supersedeas*, was fond of investigating the management of lunatic asylums, and made an appointment with the Surgeon-General to visit, without any previous intimation, an asylum kept by a Dr. Duncan in this city. Somebody sent word to the asylum that a patient was to be sent there in a carriage that day who was a smart little man, that thought himself one of the Judges, or some great person of that sort. Sir Edward came there, and on knocking at the door, he was admitted and received by the keeper. He appeared to be very talkative, but the attendants humored him and answered all his questions. He asked if the Surgeon-General had arrived, and the keeper assured him he was not yet come, but would be there immediately. 'Well,' said he, 'I will inspect some of the rooms until he arrives.' 'Oh! no, sir,' said the keeper; 'we could not permit that at all.' 'Then I will walk awhile in the garden,' said his Lordship, 'while I am waiting for him.' 'We can't let you go there either, sir,' said the keeper. 'What?' shouted Sir Edward, 'don't you know that I am Lord Chancellor?'—'Sir,' said the keeper, 'we have four more Lord Chancellors here already' (roars of laughter). He got into a great fury, and they were thinking of a strait waistcoat for him, when fortunately the Surgeon-General drove up. 'Has the Lord Chancellor arrived yet?' said he. 'Yes, sir, we have him safe; but he is far the most outrageous patient we have' (renewed laughter)."

Since that day the English Press has mocked at the whole Repeal movement; and in Parliament it was never mentioned, save with a jeer. In the Summer of 1843, they neither laughed nor jeered. Sir James Graham, earnestly appealing to the House to refuse O'Brien's motion of inquiry, exclaimed :—

"*Any hesitation* now, *any delay* and *irresolution*, will multiply the danger an hundredfold (hear, hear). If Parliament expresses its sense in favor of the course pursued by Government, Ministers have every *hope* that with the confidence of the House, they will be enabled to triumph over all difficulties (*cries of oh, oh*, and loud cheers). I appeal, then, to both sides—not to one, but to both—I appeal to both sides, and say, if you falter now, if you hesitate now in repressing the rebellious spirit which is at work in the struggle of Repeal, *the glory of the country is departed*—the days of its power are numbered; and England, this all-conquering England, must be classed with those countries *from whom power has dwindled away*, and present the melancholy aspect of a falling nation (oh, oh, and cheers)."

To refuse a Committee of Inquiry was reasonable enough; because Parliament, and all the people—men, women, and children—already knew all. The sole and avowed idea of the Government was that to admit the idea of *anything* being wrong, would make the Repeal movement altogether irresistible. The various projects now brought forward in England showed the perplexity of that country. Lord John Russell made an elaborate speech for conciliation; but the meaning of it seemed to be merely that it was no wonder Ireland was unquiet, seeing *he* was out of power. The grievance of Ireland, said he, in effect, is a Tory Ministry. Let her be ruled by us, Whigs, and all will be well. Lord Brougham also gave it as his opinion, that "you must purchase, not prosecute Repeal." The *Morning Chronicle* (Whig organ), in quite a friendly spirit, said, " Let us have a *perfect* Union; let us know each other; let the Irish Judges come circuit in England; and let the English Judges occasionally take the same round in Ireland," and so forth. " Is it absolutely certain," asked the *Westminster Review*, " that we can beat this people?" And the *Naval and Military Gazette*, a high military authority, thus expressed its apprehensions:—

"There are now stationed in Ireland 35,000 men of all arms, but widely scattered over the island. In the event of a rebellion—and who can say that we are not on the eve of one?—we feel great solicitude for the numerous small detachments of our gallant soldiers. . . . It is time to be up and doing. We have heard that the order and regularity of movement displayed by the divisions which passed before Mr. O'Connell, in review order, en route to Donnybrook lately, surprised many veteran officers, and led them to think that some *personal* training, in private and in small parties, must be practised. The ready obedience to the word of command, the silence while moving, and the general combinations, all prove organization to have gone a considerable length. In these trained bands, our soldiers, split up into detached parties, would find no ordinary opponents; and we therefore hope soon to learn that all small parties have been called in, and that our regiments in Ireland are kept together and complete. That day, we fear, is near, when '*quite peaceably*,' every Repealer will come armed to a meeting to be held simultaneously as to day and hour all over the island, and then try to cut off quite peaceably every detachment of her Majesty's loyal army."

What contributed to disquiet the British exceedingly, was, that great and excited Repeal meetings were held every week in American cities; meetings not only of Irish-born citizens, but of natives also; and considerable funds were remitted from hence to O'Connell's Repeal Exchequer.

" If something is not done (said Colonel Thomson in the *Westminster*) a fleet of steamboats from the United States will some fine morning be the Euthanasia of the Irish struggle."

I might cite many extracts from the Press of France, exhibiting a powerful interest in what the French conceived to be an impending military struggle. Take one, from the *Constitutionnel:—*

" When Ireland is agitated—when, at the sound of the powerful voice of O'Connell, four hundred thousand Irish assemble together in their meetings, and pronounce, as if it were by a single man, the same cry and the same word, it is a grand spectacle, which fills the soul, and which, even at this distance, moves the very strongest feelings of the heart, for it is the spectacle of an entire people who demand justice—of a people who have been despoiled of everything, even of the means of sustenance, and yet who require with calmness and with firmness the untrammelled exercise of their religion, and some of the privileges of their ancient nationality."

Now, nobody, either in France or the United States, would have given himself the trouble to watch that movement with interest, if they had not all believed that O'Connell and the Irish people meant to fight. Neither in America nor in France had men learned to appreciate " the ethical experiment of moral force." Clearly, also, the English expected a fight, and were preparing for it, and greatly preferred that mode of settling the difficulty (having a powerful army and navy ready) to O'Brien's method, inquiry, discussion, and redress—seeing that they were wholly unprovided with arguments, and had no idea of giving redress.

It is also quite as clear that the Irish people then expected, and longed, and burned for battle; and never believed that O'Connell would adhere to his " peace policy " even in the last extremity. Still, as he rose in apparent confidence, and became more defiant in his tone, the people rallied more ardently around him; and thousands of quiet, resolute men flocked into the Repeal cause, who had hitherto held back from all the agitations, merely because they had always believed O'Connell insincere. They thought that the mighty movement which now surged up around him had whirled him into its own tempest at last; and that " the time was come."

No speech he ever uttered roused such a stormy tumult of applause as when, at Mallow "monster meeting," referring to the threats of coercion, and to an anxious Cabinet Council which had just been held, he said :—

"They spent Thursday in consulting whether they would deprive us of our rights, and I know not what the result of that council may be ; but this I know, there was not an Irishman in this council. I may be told that the Duke of Wellington was there (oh, oh, and groans). Who calls him an Irishman (hisses and groans) ? If a tiger's cub was dropped in a fold, would it be a lamb (hear, and cheers) ? But perhaps I am wrong in anticipating, perhaps I am mistaken in warning you (no, no). But is there reason to caution you ? The council sat for an entire day, and even then did not conclude its deliberations, but adjourned to the next day, while the business of the country was allowed to stand still (hear, hear, hear). What had they to deliberate about ? The Repealers were peaceable, loyal, and attached—affectionately attached—to the Queen, and determined to stand between her and her enemies. If they assailed us to-morrow, and that we conquered them—as conquer them we will one day (cheering)—the first use of that victory which we would make would be, to place the sceptre in the hands of her who has ever shown us favor, and whose conduct has ever been full of sympathy and emotion for our sufferings (hear, hear, and loud cheers). Suppose, then, for a moment, that England found the act of Union to operate not for her benefit—if, instead of decreasing her debt, it added to her taxation and liabilities, and made her burthen more onerous—and if she felt herself entitled to call for a repeal of that act, I ask Peel and Wellington, and let them deny it if they dare, and if they did they would be the scorn and byeword of the world, would she not have the right to call for a repeal of that act (loud cheers)? And what are Irishmen that they should be denied the same privilege? Have we not the ordinary courage of Englishmen? Are we to be trampled under foot? Oh, they shall never trample me at least (tremendous cheering, which lasted several minutes). I was wrong—they may trample me under foot (cries of no, no, they never shall)—I say they may trample me, but it will be my dead body they will trample on, *not the living man.*"

—And a roar, two hundred thousand strong, rent the clouds. From that day, the meetings went on increasing, in numbers, in regularity of training, and in highly-wrought excitement; until at Tara, and at Mullaghmast, the Agitator shook with the passion of the scene, as the fiery eyes of three hundred thousand upturned faces seemed to crave *the word.*

If it be asked whether I now believe, looking calmly back over the gulf of many years, that O'Connell's voice could indeed have made a revolution in Ireland, I answer, beyond all doubt, *Yes.* One word of his mouth, and there would not, in a month, have been one English epaulette in the island. He had that power; we shall see what he did with it.

CHAPTER IV.

O'CONNELL'S ORATORY—ITS THEMES—THE WHIGS—DAVIS AND THE ".NATION"—THE YOUNG AGITATORS—TARA MEETING—COUNCIL OF THREE HUNDRED—THE "QUEEN'S SPEECH" AGAINST REPEAL—GREAT MEETING AT MULLAGHMAST—MEETING AT CLONTARF FORBIDDEN.

I HAVE sought to give somewhat like a correct idea of Daniel O'Connell; yet feel that an extract here and there from speeches is but a brick from Babylon. This orator was no maker of sentences; and when he attempted now and then to perorate, the thing was a failure. His power lay in his perfect knowledge of the people he addressed, their ways of life, wants and aspirations; and his intensely human sympathy with all. Thus it needed but a small joke from him to convulse a large meeting, because his lip and eye quivered with inexpressible fun. His pathos had no occasion for modulated periods, because when he told in simplest words some tale of sorrow and oppression (and many a sorrow and oppression was close at hand to point the moral),—and when the deep music of his voice grew husky, and clenched hand and swelling chest revealed the wrath and pity that burned and melted within him,—the passions of mighty multitudes rose and swayed and sunk again beneath his hand, as tides heave beneath the moon.

Every day's history gave him his theme and his illustrations.

From a Londonderry newspaper, I cut an advertisement, signed by one M'Mullin, "Emigration Agent," which will show what was going on throughout Ireland in the Spring of this year, better than particular details could do:—

"NOTICE.—A favorable opportunity presents itself, in the course of the present month, for Quebec, to gentlemen residing in the counties of Londonderry, Donegal, Tyrone, or Fermanagh, who wish to send to the Canadas *the overstock tenantry* belonging to their estates—as a moderate rate of passage will be taken, and six months' credit given for a lump sum to any gentleman requiring such accommodations," &c.

The mode in which the "overstock tenantry" are persuaded in Ireland to embark for America, is ejecting them, and pulling down their houses. And in 1843, and many years before and since, this process has been going on so extensively and notoriously, that I shall have no further occasion to refer to it, until we arrive at what the British call the "Famine." This treatment of the peasantry, though continued ever since O'Neill and O'Donnell fell, early in the 17th century, seemed yet new and strange to the Irish peasant, and to him more intolerable than to any other in Europe, except the Highland Scots;—for the reason that, in the social polity of the Gael, no such thing as a "tenant" was known: every man being as free as his Chief, and by virtue of the clanship, owning as clear a title in the tribe-lands. Upon this ancient social system the new feudal tenures were forced in by English power; and the struggle between them lasts to this day. O'Connell, then, was sure of a sympathetic audience, when he thus addressed a vast meeting in Connaught:—

"When struggling for Catholic emancipation, they were only looking for the rights of a class, but they were at present struggling to bring back nine millions a year to their country, which would give comfort and riches to Protestant, Presbyterian, and Catholic (hear, hear). They were struggling to give Fixity of Tenure to the landholder, and safety to the landlord: and, oh! he would call upon the landlords of Ireland to unite with him in the attainment of a measure that would ultimately be of the greatest benefit to themselves, whilst it would put a stop to the horrible clearance system, with all its frightful crimes and evils upon one side, and the dreadful assassinations, on the other, which were prompted by deep despair and vengeance (hear, hear, hear). He often heard the poor woman say, when about to be turned out of the cabin, that it was there she lighted the first fire in her own house,—it was there her children were born and brought up about her,—there her husband reposed after the hard toil of the day,—there where all her affections centred, because they called to her mind all the pleasing reminiscences of early life; but her tears were disregarded, her feelings scoffed at; and the tyrant mandate was heard to issue— 'Pull down the house!' (Very great sensation.) Yes, wholesale murders were committed, on the one side, by a slow but not less certain process;—sudden individual assassinations were committed on the other;—both bringing down upon the perpetrators the wrath of the Divine Being! With the blessing of heaven they would put an end to these crimes, and he called upon the good and virtuous to unite with him in the attainment of so holy a purpose."

So, when he would suddenly ask: "Did you ever hear of

the *tithes?*" he knew what long and bitter memories of blood and horror the question would call up.

"Did you ever hear of the Tithes? They call them Rent-charge now; do you like them any better since they have been newly christened?"

And when the murmur of execration had subsided:

"Well; repeal the Union, and you get rid of that curse: no widow woman's stack-yard will ever more be plundered by the police and red-coats, to pay a clergyman whom she never saw, and whose ministration she would not attend. Repeal the Union, and every man will pay the pastor of his choice. I don't want Protestants to pay our Catholic clergy;—why should we be compelled to pay theirs?"

Language, this, which generally seemed to his audience perfectly fair.

Whig newspapers and politicians in England (the Whigs being then in opposition) began now to suggest various conciliatory measures—talked of the anomaly of the "Established Church"—and generally gave it to be understood, that if *they* were in power, they would know how to deal with the Repeal agitation. At every meeting, O'Connell turned these professions into ridicule. It was too late now, he said, to offer to buy up Repeal by concessions, or good measures. An Irish Parliament in College Green; this was his ultimatum. He "once knew an *omadhaun* (idiot) in Kerry—where, by the bye, there were not many of them—who used to watch till the hen was out, and then slip to the nest and suck her eggs. One day he went to the nest and found some eggs—bored a hole in the end of one with his finger, and just as he turned the whole contents of it over his tongue, the chicken that was in it *squeaked.* 'Ha! lad,' said he, '*you spoke late.*' He would say the same to Lord John Russell and the Whigs, when they talked of offering *justice* instead of Repeal : 'Ha! lads, you spoke late.'"

Again, at another meeting, referring to the same matter:—

"It had also been said by another paper that he had always preferred the Whigs to the Tories; but let them always recollect that it had been a familiar jest of his, that Paddy supported the Whigs for the same reason that he stuffed his hat in a broken pane,—not to let in the light, but to keep out the cold (laughter)."

There was not the least fear, however, of either Whig or

Tory killing Repeal by too much kindness. If the whole unbroken mass of grievances was necessary to keep up the agitation in full force, he was likely to be left in clear possession of it all. For example, when Mr. Ward, Whig member for Sheffield, on the first of August in this year, brought forward a motion directed against the Irish Church Establishment, the principal Whig leaders were absent; all the Ministers were absent except Lord Eliot; and nearly all the Members of Parliament rose and left the House. On motion of Mr. Escott, the House was "counted out," and there was an end of the subject.

It was clear enough that the mind of England was made up. Any faltering—any admission, even that there was anything in Ireland to be complained of, and everything might follow. Repeal was to be crushed, said the Tories; was to be bought, said the Whigs. And still, as England grew more resolute on the one side, Ireland became more ardent on the other.

I have already mentioned Thomas Davis, and his circle of friends. Through the *Nation*, they had now the ear of the people almost as completely as O'Connell himself; and while they carefully reported and circulated all his speeches, they were at the same time infusing into the agitation a proud and defiant military spirit—by essays on Irish history, and national ballads, presenting, with the symmetry and polish of a cut gem, the most striking events and personages of our story; from Clontarf, where "King Brian smote down the Dane," to Benburb, where Owen Roe O'Neill trampled the blue banner of the Covenanting army, and Limerick, from whose old towers and moats the sword of Sarsfield bore back King William. In any account of the movement which then stirred the Irish people, it would be a blunder to omit this silent band of literary revolutionists with their exciting appeals to history, their popular essays, full of accurate knowledge, and instinct with genial fire, and their impassioned and hopeful songs. The enemy appreciated them well; and O'Connell feared them hardly less; for they threatened to precipitate a species of struggle for which he was by no means prepared. The *Morning Post*, one of the Ministerial organs, in July, described these young revolutionists in no complimentary terms, thus:—

"We have reason to believe that the younger part of the Irish agitators are a far more serious set of men than their fathers. They think more, and drink and joke a great deal less. They are full of the dark vices of Jacobinism. They worship revenge as a virtue. It suits the gloomy habit of their souls. They look forward to the slaughter of those they hate as the greatest enjoyment they could experience. Our correspondent tells us that the example of Belgium is much in the heads of these agitators, but that, in his opinion, if these people had their way, the upshot would be a Republic, and not a Monarchy. We have every reason to believe that this opinion is a correct one. The young men of the movement are Jacobin Republicans. They are full of vanity and of bad passions, and they want to be themselves the government; and they have an enthusiasm, which, once brought into action, may perhaps almost convert dreams into realities, and make short work with our placid, patient, unmovable lookers-on, who think they are discharging the functions of government."

The presence, and vehement activity, and growing influence of these men—namely, Dillon, Barry, Doheny, MacNevin, Duffy, and, above all, Davis—had the effect of urging and goading O'Connell forward. He could not ignore, nor combat, the spirit they were arousing in the masses; he saw and appreciated their power in kindling the fine enthusiasm of our cultivated youth; and felt himself obliged to raise his own tone in accord with them. Yet he loved them not. Such men are dangerous; and he would have been much better content to have around him only his own humble dependants, expectant barristers, paid inspectors of Repeal Wardens, and poor Tom Steele, once a noble gentleman and soldier, then a ruined wreck, solemn sesquipedalian buffoon, and "Head Pacificator" to the Liberator.

We approach the end of the monster meetings. Neither England nor Ireland could bear this excitement much longer. The two grandest and most imposing of these parades were at Tara and Mullaghmast; both in the province of Leinster, within a short distance of Dublin; both conspicuous, the one in glory, the other in gloom, through past centuries, and haunted by ghosts of kings and chiefs.

On the great plain of Meath, not far from the Boyne river, rises a gentle eminence, in the midst of a luxuriant farming country. On and around its summit are still certain mouldering remains of earthen mounds and moats, the ruins of the "House of Cormac" and the "Mound of the Hostages," and the Stone of Destiny. It is Temora of the Kings. On Tuesday morning, the 15th of August, most of the population of Meath, with many thousands from the four counties round, were pouring along every road leading to the hill. Numerous bands, banners, and green boughs, enlivened their march, or divided their ordered squadrons. Vehicles of all descriptions, from the handsome private chariot to the Irish jaunting-car, were continually arriving, and by the Wardens duly disposed around the hill. In Dublin, the "Liberator," after a public breakfast, set forth at the head of a *cortége*, and his progress to Tara was a procession and a triumph. Under triumphal arches, and amidst a storm of music and acclamations, his carriage passed through the several little towns that lay in his way. At Tara the multitudes assembled were estimated in the *Nation* at 750,000; an exaggeration, certainly. But they were at least 350,000. Their numbers were not so impressive as their order and discipline; nor these so wonderful as the stifled enthusiasm that uplifted them above the earth. They came, indeed, with naked hands; but the Agitator knew well that if he had invited them they would have come still more gladly with extemporaneous pikes and spears, " or instruments serving for pikes and spears." He had been proclaiming from every hill-top in Ireland for six months that *something was coming*—that Repeal was " on the wild winds of heaven." Expectation had grown intense, painful, almost intolerable. He knew it; and those who were close to him as he mounted the platform, noticed that his lip and hand visibly trembled, as he gazed over the boundless human ocean, and heard its thundering roar of welcome. He knew that every soul in that host demanded its enfranchisement at *his* hand.

O'Connell called this meeting "an august and triumphant meeting;" and as if conscious that he must at least seem to make another step in advance, he brought up at the next meeting of the Repeal Association, a detailed "plan for the renewed action of the Irish Parliament," which, he said, it only needed the Queen's writs to put in operation. The new House of Commons was to consist of three hundred members, quite fairly apportioned to the several constituencies; and in the meantime, he announced that he would invite three hundred gentlemen to assemble in Dublin early in December, who were to come from every part of Ireland, and virtually represent their respective localities. This was the "Council of Three Hundred," about which he had often talked before in a vague manner; but had evidently great difficulty in bringing to pass *legally*. For it would be a "Convention of Delegates,"—and such an assembly, though legal enough in England, is illegal in Ireland. Conventions (like arms and ammunition) are held to be unsuitable to the Irish character. For, in fact, it had been a Convention which proclaimed the independence of Ireland in Dungannon; and the arms and ammunition of the Volunteer army had made it good, in 1782; good, for eighteen years.

The plan of this Council of three hundred was hailed with great joy by the *Nation* party. They felt that if boldly carried into effect, it must bring on the crisis one way or another. "The hour is approaching," they wrote, "that will test the leaders of the people, and try the souls of the millions. The curtain has risen on the fifth act of the drama."

Two weeks after, the London Parliament was prorogued; and the Queen's speech (composed by Sir Robert Peel) was occupied almost entirely by two subjects,—the disturbances in Wales, and the Repeal Agitation in Ireland. There had been some rioting and bloodshed in Wales, in resistance to oppressive turnpike dues, and the like;—there was a quiet and legal expression of opinion in Ireland, unattended by the slightest outrage, demanding back the Parliament of the country. The Queen first dealt with Wales. She had taken measures, she said, for the repression of violence—*and* at the same time, directed an inquiry to be made into the circumstances which led to it. As to Ireland, her Majesty said, there was discontent and disaffection, but uttered not a word about any inquiry into the causes of that. "It had ever been her earnest desire," her Majesty said, "to administer the government of that country in a spirit of strict justice and impartiality"—and "she was firmly determined, under the blessing of Divine Providence," to maintain the Union. The little principality of Wales was in open revolt; *there* ministers would institute inquiry. Ireland was quiet, and standing upon the law; *there* they would meet the case with horse, foot, and artillery: for we all knew that was what the Queen meant by "the blessing of Divine Providence."

Again the Agitator mustered all Connaught at three great monster meetings—in Roscommon, Clifden, and Loughrea.

Again he asked them if they were for the Repeal; and again the mountains and the sea-cliffs resounded with their acclaim. Yes; they were for the Repeal; they had said so before. What next?

Leinster, too, was summoned again to meet on the 1st of October, at Mullaghmast, in Kildare county, near the road from Dublin to Carlow, and close on the borders of the Wicklow highlands. Every device was used to make this the most imposing and effective of all the meetings. The spot was noted as the scene of a massacre of some chiefs of Offaly and Leix, with hundreds of their clansmen, in 1577, by the English of the Pale, who had invited them to a great feast, but had troops silently drawn around the banqueting-hall, who, at a signal, attacked the place and cut the throat of every wassailer. The hill of Mullaghmast, like that of Tara, is crowned by a Rath, or ancient earthen rampart, enclosing about three acres.

To this meeting it was supposed that additional importance would be given, if the members of the town corporations of Leinster should repair thither in their corporate robes. O'Connell took the chair in the scarlet cloak of Alderman. There had lately been invented a "national cap," modelled after the form of an ancient Irish crown. One of these was prepared, splendidly embroidered, wherewith to crown O'Connell on the Rath of Mullaghmast; and it was with great ceremony placed on his head by John Hogan, the first of Irish sculptors. We read in the papers of the day how the Liberator's face beamed with pleasure when Hogan placed the cap upon his head, saying—"*Sir, I only regret that this cap is not of gold.*"

And again there was a vast assemblage; and again the numerous bands discoursed Irish music, and the air was fanned by a thousand banners, and rent by the acclamations of hundreds of thousands of human beings; and again O'Connell assured them that England could not long resist these demonstrations of their peaceful resolve that the Union was a nullity—that he had already arranged his plan for the new Irish Parliaments—and that this was the Repeal year.

In truth, it was time for England either to yield with good grace, or to find or make some law applicable to this novel "political offence," or to provoke a fight and blow away Repeal with cannon. Many of the Protestants were joining O'Connell; and even the troops in some Irish regiments had been known to throw up their caps with "Hurrah for Repeal!" It was high time to grapple with the "Sedition."

Accordingly, the government was all this time watching for an occasion on which it could come to issue with the Agitation, where all advantages were on its side. The next week that occasion arose. A great metropolitan meeting was appointed to be held on the historic shore of Clontarf, —two miles from Dublin, along the Bay,—on Sunday, the 8th of October. The garrison of Dublin amounted then to about 4,000 men, besides the 1,000 police, with abundance of field artillery.

Late in the afternoon of Saturday, when it was already almost dusk, a *Proclamation* was posted on the walls of Dublin, signed by the Irish Secretary and Privy Councillors and the Commander of the Forces, forbidding the meeting; and charging all magistrates and officers, "and others whom it might concern, to be aiding and assisting in the execution of the Law, in preventing said meeting."

"Let them not dare," O'Connell had often said, " to attack us!" The challenge was now to be accepted. The curtain rises on the fifth act.

CHAPTER V.

DETERMINATION OF THE ENEMY—CLONTARF—THE "PROJECTED MASSACRE"—ARREST OF O'CONNELL AND THE "CONSPIRATORS"—OPENING OF "CONCILIATION HALL"—O'BRIEN JOINS THE REPEALERS—PREPARATION FOR THE TRIALS.

BRITISH GOVERNMENT, then, closed with Repeal; and one or the other, it was plain, must go down.

The British Empire, as it stands, looks vast and strong; but none know so well as the statesmen of that country how intrinsically feeble it is: and how entirely it depends for its existence upon *prestige*, that is, upon a superstitious belief in its power. England, in short, could by no means afford to part with her "sister island:" both in money and in credit the cost would be too much. In this same Repeal year, for example, there was an export of provisions from Ireland to England of the value of seventy-five million dollars.* And between surplus revenue remitted to England, and absentee rents spent in England, Mr. O'Connell's frequent statement that £9,000,000 of Irish money was annually spent in England, is not over the truth. These were substantial advantages, not to be yielded up lightly.

In point of national *prestige*, England could still less afford to repeal the Union, because all the world would know the concession had been wrung from her against her will. Both parties in England, Whigs and Tories, were of one mind upon *this ;* and nothing can be more bitter than the language of all sections of the English Press, after it was once determined to crush the agitation by force. The *Times* said:—

"Repeal is not a matter to be argued on; it is a blow which despoils the Queen's domestic territory—splinters her crown—undermines, and then crushes her throne—exposes her to insults and outrage from all quarters of the earth and ocean; a Repeal of the

---

* Official Reports of the amount of this Export ceased to be kept after 1826. Up to that date, the food export from Ireland had been rapidly increasing; and the act which was then passed, placing it on the footing of a coasting-trade, prevented accounts from being kept of it, and thus concealed its amount. The estimate given above is perhaps too low; certainly not too high.

Union leaves England stripped of her vitality. Whatever might be the inconvenience or disadvantage, therefore, or even unwholesome restraint upon Ireland—although the Union secures the reverse of all these—*but even were it gall to Ireland*, England must guard her own life's blood, and sternly tell the disaffected Irish: 'you shall have me for a sister or a subjugatrix; that is my *ultimatum*.'"

And the *Morning Chronicle*, speaking of the Act of "Union," said:—

"True, it was coarsely and badly done; but stand it must. A Cromwell's violence, with Machiavelli's perfidy, may have been at work; but the treaty, after all, is more than parchment."

The first bolt launched, then, was the Proclamation to prevent the meeting at Clontarf. I have mentioned that the Proclamation was posted in Dublin shortly before dusk on Saturday. But long before that time thousands of people from Meath, Kildare, and Dublin counties were already on their way to Clontarf. They all had confidence in O'Connell's knowledge of law; and he had often told them (and it was true) that the meetings, and all the proceedings at them, were perfectly legal: and that a proclamation could not make them illegal. They would, therefore, have most certainly flocked to the rendezvous in the usual numbers, even if they had seen the Proclamation.

Readers may not fully understand the object of the Privy Council in keeping back their Proclamation to so late an hour on Saturday, seeing that the meeting had been many days announced; and they might as well have issued their command earlier in the week. Some may also be at a loss to understand why the Proclamation called not only upon all Magistrates and civil and military officers to assist in preventing the assembly; but also "all others whom it might concern." They meant to take O'Connell by surprise —so that he might be unable to prevent the assembly entirely, or to organize it (if such were his policy) for defence —and thus they would create confusion and a pretext for an onslaught, or "salutary lesson." Besides, they had already made up their minds to arrest O'Connell and several others, and subject them to a State Prosecution; and the Crown lawyers were already hard at work getting up a case against him. It is quite possible that they intended (should O'Connell go to Clontarf in the midst of such confusion and excitement) to arrest him then and there; which would have been certainly resisted by the people; and so there would

have been a riot; and everything would have been lawful
then. As to the "others whom it might concern," that
meant the Orange Associations of Dublin, and everybody
else who might take the invitation to himself. "Others
whom it may concern! Why this is intended for, and addressed to, Tresham Gregg and his auditory!" [said O'Connell.] Thus the enemy had well provided for confusion,
collision, and "a salutary lesson."

O'Connell and the Committee, did, perhaps, the best
thing possible in that exigency; except *one*. He issued
another proclamation, and sent it off by parties of gentlemen known to the people and on whom they would rely, to
turn back the crowds upon all the roads by which they were
likely to come in. All that Saturday night their exertions
were unremitting; and the good Father Tyrrell, whose pa-
rishioners, swarming in from Fingal, would have made a
large part of the meeting, by his exertions and fatigue that
night fell sick, and died. The meeting was prevented. The
troops were marched out, and drawn up on the beach and on
the hill; the artillery was placed in a position to rake the
place of meeting, and the cavalry ready to sweep it; but
they met no enemy.

Within a week, O'Connell and eight others were held to
bail to take their trial for "conspiracy and other misde-
meanors."

If I am asked what would have been the very *best* thing
O'Connell could do on that day of Clontarf—I answer: To
let the people of the country come to Clontarf,—to meet
them there himself, as he had invited them,—but, the
troops being almost all drawn out of the city, to keep the
Dublin Repealers at home, and to give them a commission
to take the Castle and all the barracks, and to break down
the canal bridge and barricade the streets leading to Clontarf.
The whole garrison and police were 5,000. The city had a
population of 250,000. The multitudes coming in from the
country would, probably, have amounted to almost as many;
and that handful of men between——! There would have
been a horrible slaughter of the unarmed people without, if the
troops would fire on them,—a very doubtful matter,—and
O'Connell himself might have fallen. It were well for his
fame if he had; and the deaths of five or ten thousand that
day might have saved Ireland the slaughter, by famine, of an

hundred times as many; a carnage of which I have yet to give the history.

The "Government," as they called themselves,—but, as I choose to call them, the enemy,—were much delighted with the success, even so far as it was a success, of their first blow. They had prevented the meeting, and that by a display of force. Next, they proceeded with great ostentation to prepare for the State Trials of the "Conspirators."

O'Connell, on his side, laughed both at the "Clontarf War" and at the State Trials. He seemed well pleased with them both. The one proved how entirely under discipline were the virtuous, and sober, and loyal people, as he called them. The other would show how wisely he had steered the agitation through the rocks and shoals of Law. In this he would have been perfectly right, his legal position would have been impregnable, but for two circumstances. First, "Conspiracy," in Ireland, means anything the Castle Judges wish: second, the Castle Sheriff was quite sure to pack a Castle jury;—so that whatever the Castle might desire, the jury would affirm on oath, "so help them God!" The Jury System in Ireland I shall have occasion more than once to expound hereafter.

For the next eight months, that is, until the end of May, 1844, the State Prosecution was the grand concern around which all public interest in Ireland concentrated itself. The prosecuted "Conspirators" were nine in number—Daniel O'Connell; his son, John O'Connell, M.P., for Kilkenny; Charles Gavan Duffy, Editor of the *Nation;* the Rev. Mr. Tyrrell, of Lusk, county Dublin (he died while the prosecution was pending); the Rev. Mr. Tierney, of Clontibret, county Monaghan; Richard Barret, Editor of the *Pilot*, Dublin; Thomas Steele, "Head Pacificator of Ireland;" Thomas M. Ray, Secretary of the Repeal Association; and Dr. Gray, Editor of the *Freeman's Journal*, Dublin. All these gentlemen were waited upon by the Inspector of Police, and requested to give bail for their appearance.

While the proceedings were pending, the agitation seemed to gather strength and acquire impetus. There was general indignation even among anti-Repealers at the transaction of Clontarf; and Lord Cloncurry made no scruple to term it "a projected massacre." In every corner of the island there was new and multitudinous enrolment of Repealers; and large sums were forwarded to the Association under the title of "Proclamation Money." Every Monday, as usual, O'Connell attended the weekly meeting of the Association, and treated the legal proceedings as a new and powerful agency placed in his hands for working out "the Repeal." He poured ridicule on the Law-officers, the Ministers, the Lord Lieutenant, the Privy Council; and promised that he would put them all to shame, and come triumphantly out of the prosecution (which he did); and that he would thereafter hold the Clontarf meeting, and call together the Council of Three Hundred;—neither of which he ever did.

The specific charge in the indictment (which was the longest indictment ever seen in any court) was "conspiracy" (conspiracy hatched in public meetings!) to bring the laws and administration of the laws into contempt, and to excite hatred and dissension between various classes of her Majesty's subjects; and the overt acts were O'Connell's speeches;—the appointment of Repeal Arbitration Courts, in contempt and derogation of the regular tribunals held under royal commission;—and articles in the several newspapers whose editors were included in the prosecution.

All these "overt acts" continued to be transacted with even greater activity than ever. The open air monster meetings, indeed, ceased; as Clontarf was to have been the last of them, at all events, owing to the approach of winter; but in no other respect was there any change in the system of agitation. The new Hall, which had been built as a place of meeting for the Association, was just finished; and O'Connell, who had a peculiar taste in nomenclature, christened it "Conciliation Hall;" intending to indicate the necessity for uniting all classes and religions in Ireland, in a common struggle for the independence of their common country.

This "Conciliation Hall" was a large oblong building on Burgh Quay, next door to the Corn Exchange, the scene of O'Connell's agitation for many years. The new Hall was not a beautiful building, externally, presenting to the street a front ornamented with pilasters,—the Harp and Irish Crown, cut in stone—and over all a balustrade. Internally, it was spacious, handsome, and convenient. On the 22d of October it was opened in great form and amidst high enthusiasm. The chair was taken by John Augustus O'Neill, of Bunowen Castle, a Protestant gentleman, who had been early in life a cavalry officer and Member of Parliament for Hull, in England. Letters from Lord French, Sir Charles Wolesley, Sir Richard Musgrave, and Mr. Caleb Powell, one of the Members for Limerick county, were read and placed on the minutes,—all breathing vehement indignation against the "government," and pledging the warmest support. But this first meeting in the New Hall was specially notable for the adhesion of Mr. Smith O'Brien. Nothing encouraged the people, nothing provoked and perplexed the enemy, so much as this. O'Brien was of the great and ancient house of Thomond, in Munster; his father was Sir Edward O'Brien, an extensive proprietor in Clare county, and regarded as the chief of his clan. His eldest brother was Sir Lucius O'Brien, then a Baronet, but afterwards Lord Inchiquin. The family had been Protestant for some generations; and Smith O'Brien, though always zealous in promoting everything which might be useful to Ireland in Parliament, had remained attached to the Whig party, and was hardly expected to throw himself into the national cause so warmly, and at so dangerous a time. His Whig associates, not having been accustomed to meet with men of his stamp, confessed their surprise.

As Mr. O'Brien afterwards became a conspicuous figure in Irish politics, I here present the greater part of the letter in which he sought admission into the national association:—

"CAHERMOYLE, RATHKEALE, Oct. 20, 1843.

"DEAR SIR,—I beg to transmit herewith an order for £5, my first subscription to the treasury of the Loyal Repeal Association of Ireland.

"As it is due to those who have hitherto honored me with their confidence that I should state the reasons which induce me to take this step, I shall feel obliged if the Association will allow the following remarks to appear in the next report of their proceedings:

"When the proposal to seek for a Repeal of the act of Union was first seriously entertained by a large portion of the Irish people, I used all the influence which I possessed to discountenance the attempt. I did not consider that the circumstances and prospects of Ireland then justified the agitation of this question. Catholic Emancipation had been recently achieved, and I sincerely believed that from that epoch a new course of policy would be adopted towards Ireland. I persuaded myself that thenceforth the statesmen of Great Britain would spare no effort to repair the evils produced by centuries of misgovernment—that the Catholic and Protestant would be admitted to share, on equal terms, in all the advantages resulting from our constitutional form of government—that all traces of an ascendancy of race or creed would be effaced—that the institutions of Ireland would be gradually moulded so as to harmonize with the opinions of its inhabitants—that in regard to political rights, legislation for both kingdoms would be based upon the principle of perfect equality—that an improvement in the social condition of our people would become an object of the deepest interest to the British Parliament—that the disadvantages resulting to Ireland from the loss of her legislature, and from the transfer of her public establishments to London, would be compensated by equivalents such as would enable every friend of the Union to point to numberless benefits as consequent upon that measure—and that in interest and feeling the two nations would be for ever identified as one people.

"Fourteen years have elapsed since that event, and the experience of each succeeding year has tended to show the fallacy of these expectations, and to dissipate these hopes. I have elsewhere taken an opportunity of illustrating in detail the progress of misgovernment. Recapitulation is almost unnecessary. We have seen that the anti-Catholic prejudices of the English people are still as strong as when they brought these countries to the verge of a civil war by protracted resistance to Emancipation. The feelings of the Irish nation have been exasperated by every species of irritation and insult; political equality has been denied to us. Every proposal tending to develop the sources of our industry,—to raise the character and improve the condition of our population,—has been discountenanced, distorted, or rejected. Ireland, instead of taking its place as an integral part of the great empire which the valor of her sons has contributed to win, has been treated as a dependent, tributary province; and at this moment, after forty-three years of nominal union, the affections of the two nations are so entirely alienated from each other, that England trusts for the maintenance of their connection, not to the attachment of the Irish people, but to the bayonets which menace our bosoms, and to the cannon which she has planted on all our strongholds. . . . . . .

"For myself, I have not been able to witness this course of events without feeling that the conduct of the British Parliament has fully justified the endeavor to obtain the restitution of our national legislature; but a strong sense of the difficulties which obstruct the accomplishment of that measure—a thankless apprehension of inconveniences which it might possibly cause to England—a lingering hope that a nobler or wiser spirit would still exhibit itself in the policy to be adopted towards Ireland—perhaps also personal considerations connected with my own education and individual position, have hitherto restrained me from engaging in pursuit of the remedy proposed by my fellow-countrymen for wrongs which, equally with them, I resent. I resolved, before I should throw myself into your ranks, to leave no effort untried to obtain redress by other means. Of our labors in Parliament, during the last session, you know the result. We condescended to address to the government entreaties and expostulations, humiliating to ourselves and to the country whose interests we represent;—all was in vain. We made a last appeal to the British people ; our warning—the friendly remonstrance of men averse to agitation, and for the most part favorable to the Union,—was treated with neglect, ridicule, or defiance. Still a hope remained on my mind that the government, alive to the evils to which Ireland is exposed from the continuance of national discontent, would call Parliament together in the Autumn, and submit some general system of conciliatory measures for its tranquillization. Lest I should be led to form a precipitate decision, I availed myself of the interval which followed the close of the session to examine whether, among the governments of central Europe, there are any so indifferent to the interests of their subjects as England has been to the welfare and happiness of our population. After visiting Belgium, and all the principal capitals of Germany, I returned home impressed with the sad conviction that there is more human misery in one county in Ireland than throughout all the populous cities and districts which I had visited. On landing in England, I learn that the Ministry, instead of applying themselves to remove the causes of complaint, have resolved to deprive us even of the liberty of discontent,—that public meetings are to be suppressed,—and that state prosecutions are to be carried on against Mr. O'Connell and others, on some frivolous charges of sedition and conspiracy.

"I should be unworthy to belong to a nation which may claim at least as a characteristic virtue that it exhibits increased fidelity in the hour of danger, if I were to delay any longer to dedicate myself to the cause of my country. Slowly, reluctantly convinced that Ireland has nothing to hope from the sagacity, the justice, or the generosity of the English Parliament, my reliance shall henceforth be placed upon our own native energy and patriotism."

The example of a man so universally esteemed as O'Brien, of course induced many other Protestants to follow his example. The weekly contributions to the revenue of the Association became so great as to place in the hands of the Committee a large treasury to be used in spreading and organizing the movement; arbitration courts decided the people's complaints with general acceptation : and great meetings in American cities sent, by every steamship, their words of sympathy and bills of exchange.

It is not very certain that the "Government" was at first resolutely bent on pressing their prosecution to extremity. Probably they rather hoped that the show of a determination to put down the agitation somehow would cool the ardor both of demagogues and people. Plainly it had no such effect; and it was, therefore, resolved to pursue the "Conspirators" to conviction and imprisonment, at any cost and by any means.

By what means they sought to secure this result—and how juries and verdicts are manufactured in Ireland—I shall narrate in the next chapter.

CHAPTER VI.

THE TRIAL—SYSTEM OF "SELECTING" A JURY IN IRELAND—VERDICT AGAINST O'CONNELL—DEBATE IN PARLIAMENT ON THE STATE OF IRELAND—OPERATION OF THE ARMS ACT—SENTENCE AND IMPRISONMENT OF O'CONNELL.

On the 2d of November, 1843, in the Court of Queen's Bench, Dublin, began one of the most remarkable comedies of modern times—the trial of the Repeal " Conspirators." To spectators from other lands, it was, doubtless, highly entertaining; and, indeed, Irishmen themselves, being naturally prone to merriment, could not but laugh. Yet, to thoughtful minds in that country, there was somewhat tragic in the comedy—seeing that it was enacted in the high courts of law, with aged and venerable Judges for actors; and many deemed it an irreverent and demoralizing species of play.

To begin with the " Jury "—(a word which I enclose by inverted commas purposely),—the Sheriff of Dublin was of course a nominee of the Crown, instead of being elected, as in England, like other municipal officers. The inhabitants of Dublin qualified to serve on juries were in the proportion of three Catholics to one Protestant. And it was the business of the Sheriff to take care that not one of these Catholics should be on this jury, or any other jury, to try what is called a " political offence." But, further, there were large numbers of the Protestant residents of Dublin favorable to the Repeal of the Union; as, in fact, over and above the general interest of the whole country in that measure, Dublin had a special interest, as the metropolis. The Sheriff's function, then, was to make it sure that none of those Protestant residents should be on the jury. This limited his range of selection to a small number—Orangemen, Englishmen, and tradesmen, " by special appointment," to the Lord Lieutenant: in short, to men whose vote (which was, however, to be called a " verdict ") might be counted upon with the utmost certainty. It was to be a part of the performance that these men, being so well and truly packed, should make oath on the holy Bible to give a true verdict according to the evidence—so help them God!

A revisal of the special jury-list took place before Mr. Shaw, Recorder of Dublin, with a special view to these trials. The names, when passed by the Recorder from day to day, were then sent to the Sheriff's Office, to be placed on his book. Counsel were employed before the Recorder to oppose by every means the admission of every Catholic gentleman against whom any color of objection could be thought of; yet, with all this care, a large number of Catholics were placed on the list. As the names were transferred to the Sheriff's office, it happened that the slip which contained the largest proportion of Catholic names missed its way, or was mislaid; and the sixty-seven names it contained never appeared on the Sheriff's book. This became immediately notorious, and excited what one of the Judges called "grave suspicion."

In striking a special jury in Ireland, forty-eight names are taken by ballot out of the jurors' book in the Crown Office. Then each party, the Crown and the traverser, has the privilege of striking off twelve; leaving twenty-four names. On the day of trial, the first twelve, out of these twenty-four, who answer when called, are sworn as jurors. Now, so well had the Sheriff discharged his duty in this case, that of the forty-eight names there were eleven Catholics. They were all struck off by the Crown; and a "Jury" was secured on whose patriotic vote her Majesty could fully rely.

Of course, the "Conspirators," through their counsel, challenged the array on the express ground of fraud in the matter of the list of names which missed its way as aforesaid; and of the four judges, one, Perrin, gave his voice for quashing the whole proceeding and letting the Crown begin anew; —but the other three held the jury panel to be good enough; and the drama was to proceed.

The indictment covered, with close print, the skins of a flock of sheep; the parchment monster measured thirty-three yards in length, and gave a history of the whole agitation, including speeches at Monster Meetings and ballads from the *Nation*. The most eminent counsel in Ireland were employed at either side, with hosts of juniors; and the ingenuity of every one of them was exerted for many weeks to devise motions, affidavits, demurrers, pleas in abatement, and the other incidents of a highly-developed and full-blown State Prosecution. The trial proceeded; and both inside and outside the courts, there was a strange mixture of jest and earnest. The Attorney-General was T. B. C. Smith (afterwards Master of the Rolls), a very small, withered gentleman, of great legal learning, but most peevish temper, and very sensitive to taunt and ridicule. Of taunt and ridicule, therefore, he had plenty, both in the court and the newspapers. Stung to madness, he at last slipped to Fitzgibbon, in open court, a pencilled note, requiring that gentleman to name a friend and meet him next morning in mortal combat. Fitzgibbon read the note to the Judges; and they mildly rebuked the rancorous little public prosecutor. Day after day passed, and week after week;—O'Connell and the traversers all the time attending public festivals and Repeal meetings, and organizing the Repeal Wardens in a more compact and steady power. All the world soon perceived that the cause of the country in no way depended on what was passing in the Queen's Bench; and the trials would have been absolutely devoid of interest, but for the brilliant speeches of Shiel, Whiteside, and MacDonagh, and the occasional jokes which enlivened the galleries and awaked the Judges.

Early in February the Trials ended: and when the Chief Justice, in his charge to the jury, argued the case like one of the counsel for the prosecution, and so far forgot himself as to term the traversers' counsel "the gentlemen on the other side," there was more laughter than indignation throughout the country. The jury brought in their verdict of GUILTY,—of course. O'Connell addressed a letter to the People of Ireland, informing them that "the Repeal" was now sure; that all he wanted was peace, patience, and perseverance; and that if they would only "keep the peace for six, or at most, for twelve months more," he would promise Repeal. Having published this letter, he went straight to London, and strode into Parliament, where he was received with a tumult of acclamation by the Whigs, then out of place, who saw in his whole movement nothing more than a machinery to raise *them* to power. It was while they were engaged in a debate on the state of Ireland, that O'Connell stalked into the House. *He* had got somewhat to say on the state of Ireland. But before going farther, take two extracts from the speeches of Lord John Russell and of Mr. Macaulay, in that debate,—both of them, being then out of place, zealous for "Justice to Ireland," and highly indignant at the packing of juries. Said Lord John Russell:—

"Nominally, indeed, the two countries have the same laws. Trial by jury, for instance, exists in both countries; but is it administered alike in both? Sir, I remember on one occasion when an honorable gentleman, Mr. Brougham, on bringing forward a motion, in 1823, on the administration of the law in Ireland, made use of these words: —'The law of England esteemed all men equal. It was sufficient to be born within the King's allegiance, to be entitled to all the rights the loftiest subject of the land enjoyed. None were disqualified, and the only distinction was between natural-born subjects and aliens. Such, indeed, was the liberality of our system in times which we called barbarous, but from which in these enlightened days it might be as well to take a hint, that if a man were even an alien-born, he was not deprived of the protection of the law. In Ireland, however, the law held a directly opposite doctrine. The sect to which a man belonged, the cast of his religious opinions, the form in which he worshipped his Creator, were grounds on which the law separated him from his fellows, and bound him to the endurance of a system of the most cruel injustice.' Such was the statement of Mr. Brougham, when Mr. Brougham was the advocate of the oppressed (hear, hear). But, sir, let me ask, was what I have just now read the statement of a man who was ignorant of the country of which he spoke? No; the same language, or to the same effect, was used by Sir Michael O'Loghlen in his evidence before the House of Lords. That gentleman stated, that he had been in the habit of going the Munster circuit for nineteen years; and on that circuit it was the general practice for the Crown in criminal prosecutions to set aside all Catholics and all the liberal Protestants; and he added, that he had been informed that on other circuits the practice was carried on in a more strict manner. Sir Michael O'Loghlen also mentioned one case of this kind which took place in 1834, during the Lord Lieutenancy of the Marquis of Wellesley, and the Attorney-Generalship of Mr. Blackburne, the present Master of the Rolls, and in which, out of forty-three persons set aside (in a cause, too, which was not a politic alone), there were thirty-six Catholics and seven Protestants, and all of them respectable men. This practice is so well known, and carried out so generally, that men known to be Liberals, whether Catholics or Protestants, have ceased to attend assizes, that they might not be exposed to these public insults. Now, I would ask, are these proofs of equal laws, or laws equally administered? Could the same or similar cases have happened in Yorkshire, or Sussex, or Kent? Are these the fulfilment of the promises made and engagements entered into at the Union?"

This sounds extremely fair. Who would think that Lord John Russell was Prime Minister in '48! Mr. Macaulay said, in the same debate (Feb. 19th, 1844):—

"I must say, too, in the spirit of truth, that the position which Mr. O'Connell holds in the eyes of his fellow-countrymen, is a position such as no popular leader in the whole history of mankind ever occupied (loud cheers). You are mistaken if you imagine that the interest with which he is regarded is confined only to the island. Go where you will upon the Continent, dine at any *table d'hôte*, tread upon any steamboat, enter any conveyance, from the moment your speech betrays you an Englishman, the very first question asked— whether by the merchants or manufacturers in the towns in the heart of France, or by the peasants, or by the class who are like our yeomen in this country—is, what has become of Mr. O'Connell (cheers, and cries of oh, oh)? Let those who deny this assertion take the trouble to turn over the French journals (cheers). *It is a most unfortunate, it is a most unhappy fact,—but it is impossible to dispute it,—that there is throughout the Continent a feeling respecting the connection between England and Ireland not very much unlike that which exists with respect to the connection between Russia and Poland.*

. . . .

"I do say that on this question it is of the greatest importance that the proceedings which the government have taken should be beyond impeachment, and that they should have obtained a victory in such a way that that victory should not be to them a greater disaster than a defeat. Has that been the result (cheers)? First, is it denied that Mr. O'Connell has suffered wrong? Is it denied that if the law had been carried into effect without those irregularities and that negligence which has attended the Irish trials, Mr. O'Connell's chance of acquittal would have been better?—no person denied that. The affidavit which has been produced, and which has not been contradicted, states that twenty-seven Catholics were excluded from the jury-list (hear, hear, from Mr. Sheil). I know that all the technicalities of the law were on the side of the Crown; but my great charge against the government, is, that they have merely regarded this question in a technical point of view. We know what the principle of the law is in cases where prejudice is likely to arise against an alien, and who is to be tried *de medietate linguæ*. Is he to be tried by twelve Englishmen? No; our ancestors knew that that was not the way in which justice could be obtained;—they knew that the only proper way was to have one-half of the jurymen of the country in which the crime was committed, and the other half of the country to which the prisoner belonged. If any alien had been in the situation of Mr. O'Connell, that law would have been observed. You are ready enough to call the Catholics of Ireland 'aliens,' when it suits your purpose; you are ready enough to treat them as aliens when it suits your purpose; but the first privilege, the only advantage, of alienage, you practically deny them (hear, hear, and loud cheers)."

This orator also was a member of the Administration in 1848; and he did not utter any of his fine indignation at what was done *then :* of which I shall hereafter give some account.

Bear in mind these fair and liberal protestations of Russell and Macaulay, until we come down four years later in this history.

The debate lasted more than a week. O'Connell listened to it; and, at last, amidst breathless silence, arose. He did not confine himself to the narrow ground of the prosecution, but reviewed the whole career of British power in Ireland, with bitter and taunting comments. As to the prosecution, he treated it slightly and contemptuously:—

"I have at greater length than I intended, gone through the crimes of England since the Union—I will say the follies of England. I have but little more to say; but I have in the name of the people of Ireland,—and I do it in their name,—to protest against the late prosecution (loud cries of hear, hear, hear). And I protest, first against the nature of that prosecution. Forty-three public meetings were held, and every one of them was admitted to be legal; not one was impeached as being against the law, and every one of them making on the calendar of crime a cypher; but by multiplying cyphers, you come, by a species of legal witchcraft, to make a number that shall be fatal. *One meeting is legal, another meeting is legal, a third is the same; and three legal meetings, you say, make one illegal meeting.* The people of Ireland understand that you may oppress them, but not laugh at them. That, sir, is my first objection. The second is the striking out all the Catholics from the jury panel. There is no doubt of the fact. Eleven Catholics were upon the jury panel, and every one of them was struck out."

All the world knew it. Nobody pretended to deny it, or publicly to excuse it: but what availed all this? The *ultimatum* of England was, that the Union must be maintained at any cost, and by all means. And O'Connell was to return to Dublin by a certain day for judgment and sentence. It may have been some satisfaction to him—or it may not—to expose and turn inside out the whole procedure of that trial before English audiences; the loud laughter of all Liverpool may have pleased him, when he described, with exuberant merriment, the nature of the cumulative crime, contained in his Monster Meetings—one meeting legal, another meeting legal, but forty-three illegal. Said he, in Liverpool:—

"What would a merchant of this city say if a fellow, just escaped from some Lunatic Asylum, were to come into his office and request him to tot up forty-three *noughts?* Would he not turn the mad fellow out of his office? This is what I want done to the present Ministry;—I want them turned out of office."

This was extremely gratifying and amusing to Liverpool

Whigs, who looked only at the chances of their friends coming into power. But no man in all England ever, for one moment, suffered the idea to enter his head, that Ireland was to be in any case permitted to govern herself.

In truth, it was apparent, both to Englishmen and Irishmen, that the real struggle between the two islands did not lie in the Court of Queen's Bench, but in the country—and that it would be decided, not by the learned Judges with their packed jury, but by the Repeal Wardens on the one side, and the troops and police on the other. And British Whigs could well afford to let O'Connell have a legal triumph, to the damage of British Tories, so long as the real and substantial policy of England in Ireland was pursued without interruption. As to this point, there must be no mistake: no British Whig or British Tory regarded the Irish question in any other point of view than as a question on which might occur a change of Ministry.

An army of fifty thousand men, including police, was all this while in full military occupation of the island; the Arms Bill had become law; and in the registration of arms before magistrates, under that act, those who were in favor of their country's independence were usually refused the privilege of keeping so much as an old musket in their houses for the purposes of self-defence. This same registration made manifest the fact that the Protestant " gentry " of the country were providing themselves with a sufficient armament. For example, Mrs. Charlotte Stawell, of Kilbritton Castle, registers " six guns and six pistols; " and Richard Quinn, of Skivanish, " nine guns, one pair pistols, two dirks, two bayonets, and one sword." No objection was offered against these persons keeping as many fire-arms as they chose! So worked the disarming act.

The police-barracks were strengthened; the detectives were multiplied; the regular troops were kept almost constantly under arms, and marched to and fro with a view of striking terror; improved codes of signals were furnished to the police, for use by day and by night—to give warning of everything they might conceive suspicious; and, above all, the Post-office was used systematically as a bureau of espionage. During the progress of the trials, Mr. Gartlan, one of the attorneys for the traversers, and Mr. O'Mahony were surprised to see their private letters printed in the government newspapers of Dublin. Sir Edward Sugden and the Secretary of State for Ireland had issued warrants under which the correspondence of any suspected person was to be carried to the Castle, opened by a government clerk, copied, resealed, and forwarded as if nothing had happened. The extent to which this system operated was hardly appreciated, until the discovery, during this same year, 1844, of Sir James Graham's behavior with respect to the correspondence of Mazzini, the Italian. By diligent inspection of the letters to and from Mazzini, the British Minister was enabled (in the interest of good order, tranquillity, and civilization,) to give notice to the King of Naples of all the movements and designs of the brothers Bandiera; and thereby had the satisfaction of putting it in that monarch's power to entrap, capture, and kill those rash young men.

It has been the custom, ever since the "Union," for either the Lord Lieutenant, or Secretary, or any of the Lords Justices or Privy Councillors, to order the detention in the post-office of letters to and from any person whomsoever they might think fit to suspect, or pretend to suspect. The mode of opening the letters was by softening the seals or wafers by means of steam; and the government kept workmen cunning in re-sealing; so that the parties might not conceive suspicion, and thus be put on their guard. After the Mazzini case was exposed, the British Public affected to be indignant; and the House of Commons appointed a committee to investigate. That committee very coolly informed the British Public and the rest of mankind that the practice was not new,—was common,—was needful; and gave the public names and dates to make the most of. Confining myself to Irish cases alone, it appears by this report that warrants were issued at the following times by the following persons, for opening and copying the letters of various individuals:—

"Year 1832—Marquis of Anglesey.
    1834—E. J. Littleton (Secretary).
    " —Marquis Wellesley.
    1835—Earl of Mulgrave [afterwards Marquis of Normanby].
    1836—Ditto.
    " —T. Drummond (Secretary).
    1837—Ditto.
    " —Lord Plunket (one of the Lords Justices).
    " —Archbishop of Dublin (ditto).

1838—Lord Morpeth (Secretary) [afterwards Earl of Carlisle].
1839—Marquis of Normanby.
   "   —Lord Viscount Ebrington.
   "   —Gen. Sir T. Blakeney (one of the Lords Justices).
1840—Lord Viscount Ebrington.
1841—Chief Justice Bushe (one of the Lords Justices).
   "   —Earl De Grey.
1842—Ditto.
   "   —Sir E. Sugden (one of the Lords Justices).
1843—Earl De Grey."

The British Public, seeing the thing to be "necessary," said no more about it; and the practice has continued in full activity from that day to this.

With so firm a hold upon the Island, the British Ministers might have thought themselves in a condition to abandon their questionable prosecution; but they had the idea that O'Connell's power lay very much in the received opinion of his legal infallibility; so they were resolved to imprison him, at any rate for a short time—even though he should finally trample on their prosecution and come forth in triumph;—as in fact he did.

On the 30th of May, the "Conspirators" were called up for sentence; and were imprisoned in Richmond Penitentiary,—a suburban prison at the south side of Dublin, with splendid gardens and handsome accommodations. Here they rusticated for three months, holding *levées* in an elegant *marquée* in the garden; addressed by bishops; complimented by Americans; bored by deputations; serenaded by bands; comforted by ladies; half smothered with roses; half drowned in champagne.

The great multitudinous People looked on in some amaze. "Peace" was still the order; and they obeyed: but they much marvelled what it meant, and when it would end.

7

CHAPTER VII.

O'CONNELL IN PRISON—DAVIS, HIS MISGIVINGS—REVERSAL OF THE JUDGMENT—WHIG LAW-LORDS—REJOICINGS IN DUBLIN—THE PEOPLE DISAPPOINTED—FEDERALISM—O'BRIEN.

The Repeal year had conducted not to a Parliament in College Green, but to a Penitentiary at Richmond. Yet the people believed in O'Connell's power, wisdom, and truth. From his prison he sent weekly messages to the Repeal Association (which continued to meet as usual), announcing that the independence of the country was never so certain;—that he rejoiced to be imprisoned for Ireland;—above all, that he implored the people to be peaceful and patient. Peaceful and patient they were; and the Wardens and clergy labored more zealously than ever to keep up the agitation and swell its funds. Corporations, bishops, "dismissed magistrates," and mayors of cities, thronged the courts and gardens of the prison, bringing their addresses of confidence and assurances of co-operation. Very considerable indignation had been excited, even amongst the Protestants, by the means which had been used to snatch this conviction. The agitation had rather gained than lost: and many gentlemen who had held back till now, sent in their names and subscriptions. O'Brien was a constant attendant at the Association; and by his boldness and purity of character, and his extensive knowledge of public affairs, gave it both impetus and steadiness.

Yet O'Connell and his friends were in a prison, sentenced to an incarceration of one year; and it would be vain to deny that there was humiliation in the fact. True, the jury had been notoriously packed; the trial had been but a sham; and the sentence would probably be reversed by the House of Lords. Still, there was Ireland, represented by her chosen men, suffering the penalties of crime in a gaol. The island was still fully and effectively occupied by troops, as a hostile country; and all its resources were in clear possession of the enemy. Many began to doubt whether the

"Moral-Force principle" of O'Connell would be found sufficient.

In an elegant tent, with a green flag flying over it, O'Connell, with his green Mullaghmast cap on, received the deputations, and made them gracious answers, not without a seasoning of merry jest. Through the trees, and amongst parterres of flowers, one might see the "martyrs" and their friends sauntering about; the tall form of Mr. Steele, the "Head Pacificator," strode alone and apart; pretending to read "Kane's Industrial Resources of Ireland." John O'Connell, with a smile ready for all comers, but an air somewhat pre-occupied, as if intent on weighty business, remained generally near to his father. He was then about thirty-two years of age, small of stature, but rather corpulent, and extremely unlike in every respect to the "Liberator." He was then member of Parliament for Kilkenny. Duffy might have been seen on a rustic bench, surrounded by certain young poets, his pale face illuminated with a glow that looked very like the light of enthusiasm, and almost of genius; and he seemed to be rather too nervously anxious that the "*Nation* party" should be forward and conspicuous at this crisis of the cause. Davis was still making the columns of the *Nation* flash with proud hope and defiance; but did not affect to conceal a certain despondency. "No," he said; "O'Connell will run no more risks. Even when this judgment shall be set aside, and he will come out in triumph, he will content himself with 'imposing demonstrations.' He will *not* call the Clontarf meeting again—he will *not* summon the Council of Three Hundred; and from the day of his release the cause will be going back and going down. What care the government," he exclaimed, with bitterness, "how many thousands of people may meet peacefully and legally, or in what trappings they dress themselves, or to what tunes they march, or what banners they may flaunt,—while there are fifty thousand bayonets in all our garrisons, besides the Orange Yeomanry!" In truth, the Repeal Agitation, as a living and formidable power, was over from the day of imprisonment; and I shall not dwell on the details of it any farther.

The judgment of the Irish Court of Queen's Bench was brought up to the British House of Peers on a Writ of Error; and on the 2d and 4th of September, the opinions of nine English Judges were delivered, and the decision pronounced. Eight of the Judges gave their opinion that the jury was a good jury, the verdict good, and the judgment good. It appeared, however, that Mr. Justice Coleridge dissented. Lord Lyndhurst, the Lord Chancellor, then delivered his decision; he agreed with the majority of the judges, and thought the judgment should stand, packing of the jury being immaterial. He was followed by Lord Brougham,—and nobody could doubt what would be the decision of that learned person;—the jury was a good enough jury; some of the counts in the indictment might be bad; but, bad or good, the judgment of the Irish court was to stand; and O'Connell was to remain in prison.

Lord Denman, Chief Justice of England, then arose. I have already mentioned that the whole Irish question was regarded in the British Parliament solely with reference to its affording a chance for turning out the Tory ministry, and conducting the Whigs into power and place. We have seen, accordingly, the virtuous indignation of Lord John Russell, and of Mr. Macaulay, against the packing of the juries. It seems an atrocious charge to make upon Judges and Lawlords—that they could be influenced by any other considerations than the plain law and justice of the case. But the mere matter of fact, is, that the majority of the English Judges were of the Tory party. Lord Chancellor Lyndhurst was a violent Tory, and moreover, an avowed enemy to Ireland. Lord Brougham was at that time a Tory, and also a personal foe to O'Connell, having been often stung by the vicious taunts and ridicule of that gentleman. But Lord Denman, Lord Cottenham, and Lord Campbell were Whigs; and Denman, Cottenham, and Campbell gave it as their opinion that the jury had been unfair and fraudulent—that no fair trial had taken place—and, therefore, that the judgment against the Repeal Conspirators should be reversed.

Some circumstances attending this transaction deserve to be stated. After the delivery of the opinions of the Lawlords, the Chancellor put the question, "Is it your lordships' pleasure that the judgment be reversed?"—and several lay-lords, who knew no more of law than of anything else, shouted in chorus to Lord Brougham, "Not Content." This was too much: Lord Wharncliffe, President of the Council, himself rebuked the indecency; and even Lord

Brougham declared that it was better not to go out of the usual course, even for the sake of doing justice in so important a case; as it would diminish the respect and confidence of mankind towards that most illustrious tribunal. The noisy lay-lords, therefore, took their hats and went out; and the votes only of the law-lords were taken. Lyndhurst and Brougham were for sustaining the judgment; and three others against it. The Chancellor, therefore, announced —"the judgment is reversed."

The State Trials, then, were at an end. It has been beside my present purpose to detail the complicated incidents of that procedure—the motion for a new trial, motion for amendment in the *postea*, and so forth,—which served to protract the affair, month after month. Proof of the "overt acts," also, has been omitted, as being of no consequence at the time, nor at any time since. The thing was indeed no criminal trial at all;—it was a *de facto* government making use of its courts of justice and officials, of its executive power to try and convict a whole people for the crime of demanding their independence. Thus considered, it was deemed by all high-spirited Irishmen, as an outrage and public affront before the world; and the reversal of the judgment by Whig law-lords in London, and consequent liberation of the prisoners, was by no means regarded as atoning the outrage or wiping out the insult. We tried hard, indeed, to feel triumphant: it needed no trouble to feel indignant and humiliated. The *Nation* exclaims:—

"What—what—what! is the decision of the Queen's Bench of Ireland reversed? So they have kept us for three months from our freedom without law, or right, or justice? Out upon their constitution!

"And was the Trial by Jury made a 'mockery, a delusion, and a snare,' for this opening of the prison-gates? Were the names omitted, the list fraudulent, and did all the attendant circumstances of a Government conspiracy take place only that the unwilling hands which closed the doors of Richmond prison should open them to-day?

"And so the 'convicted conspirators,' the 'hoary criminal,' and his 'suffering dupes,' were *robbed* of their liberty by the Government of England! With hot, indecent haste—with furious hurry—they drove them from the Court-house to the Gaol. The men who stood convicted appealed to a higher, and, as it appears, a luckier court, from the inferior tribunal; yet, contrary to all the dictates of true justice, they were forced to endure the punishment without their crime being proved. The Government were warned not to inflict this wrong. They were warned to abide the issue of the appeal—to stay their vengeance—to balk their appetite for punishment. Yet that sleek tyrant at their head would not have it so. He would have O'Connell in the prison. He would wreak malignant vengeance on his 'difficulty';—he did so. He inflicted three months' false imprisonment."

Yes, it was true; the "sleek tyrant" had done it; and we might make the most and say our worst of it. He had shown that he dared inflict three months' false imprisonment:—and the very appeal to a British House of Lords, from an Irish law Court, was felt to be degradation, because it was an *attornment* to the jurisdiction of the enemy.

Before quitting the subject, one or two matters deserve commemoration. The British Government, by openly and ostentatiously striking off from the jury panel all Catholics without exception, and all Protestants of moderate and liberal opinions, made proclamation that they knew the great mass of the people to be averse to them and their rule,— avowed that they accounted that small remainder, out of whom they selected their jurors, to be the only "good and lawful men." This, to be sure, amounted to an admission that nine-tenths of Irishmen, desired the freedom of their country;—but then it also amounted to a declaration that England meant to hold the country, whether Irishmen would or not.

One other noteworthy matter: after the verdict, but before the sentence, it was well known that the traversers would bring the whole matter up to the House of Lords by Writ of Error; but it was also known that Ministers would insist upon imprisonment, pending the Writ of Error, and that the Judges would refuse all bail; for the sole policy of "government" seemed to be that O'Connell must see the inside of a gaol, guilty or not guilty, law or no law. Accordingly it was conceived by certain Whig statesmen in London (then out of place, as aforesaid, and eager to "make capital" by their friendship for Ireland), that a Bill might be introduced into Parliament, authorizing bail to be received in criminal cases, pending a Writ of Error, in order that persons might not suffer imprisonment as criminals, who might turn out to be innocent. Lord Campbell introduced the Bill. On the second of May, he moved that it should be referred to a committee. Lord Lyndhurst, the Chancellor, opposed it on the part of the government. He said not a word against the fairness and justice of the measure; but boldly founded his opposition on the ground *that it was brought in to answer a particular case.* Lord Brougham, of course, opposed it too; and was so foolish as to say that—

"*Though approving of the general principles of the measure, he had at the first stated that it was most objectionable to introduce a measure so important pending the proceedings now going on in Dublin.*"

Lord Clanricarde observed that the opposition of their Lordships to the measure amounted to this: that if it were passed they might be unable wrongly to imprison six or seven gentlemen then in Dublin. Without so much as a division, the motion was negatived; and, on the 30th of the same month of May, O'Connell and his friends were carried to prison.

It was easy to expose and denounce all these proceedings; and they were triumphantly denounced in prose and verse. But the more thoroughly they were exposed and dwelt upon, and the more ostentatious and audacious they were, just the more stinging and deadly was the insult to our people. It was a kind and amount of outrage which if any people endure, without battle, virtue has gone out of them. Under that insult I do not pretend to deny that our national honor still lies a-bleeding.

But in Dublin there was the show of high rejoicing; and the Prisoners were escorted from the Penitentiary, through the city, by a vast and orderly procession, to O'Connell's house in Merrion Square. In deep and ordered ranks, the "Trades" of Dublin marched, preceded by bands; and innumerable banners fanned the air; and splendid carriages, with four horses and with six, conveyed committees, attorneys for the traversers, aldermen, and other notabilities. The procession marched through College Green; and just as O'Connell's carriage came in front of the Irish Parliament House (the most superb building in Dublin), the carriage stopped; the whole procession stopped; and there was a deep silence as O'Connell rose to his full height, and pointing with his finger to the portico, turned slowly around and gazed into the faces of the people, without a word. Again and again, he stretched forth his arm and pointed; and a succession of pealing cheers rent the air and "shook the banners like a storm," until, say the reporters, "Echo herself was hoarse."

All the country, friends and enemies, Ireland and England, were now looking eagerly and earnestly for O'Connell's first movement, as an indication of his future course. Never, at any moment in his life, did he hold the people so wholly in his hand. During the imprisonment, both clergy and Repeal Wardens had labored diligently in extending and confirming the organization; and the poor people proved their faith and trust by sending greater and greater contributions to the Repeal Treasury. They kept the " peace " as their Liberator bade them; and the land was never so free from crime— lest they should "give strength to the enemy."

I am proud of my people; and have always regarded with profound admiration the steady faith, patient zeal, self-denial, and disciplined enthusiasm they displayed for these two years. To many thousands of those peasants the struggle had been more severe than any war; for they were expected to set at naught potent landlords, who had over them and their children power of life and death,—with troops of insolent bailiffs, and ejecting attorneys, and the omnipresent police: and they did set them at naught. Every vote they gave at an election might cost them house and home, land and life. They were naturally ardent, impulsive, and impatient; but their attitude was calm and steadfast. They were an essentially military people; but the great " Liberator " told them that "no political amelioration was worth one drop of human blood." They did not believe the formula, and in assenting to it often winked their eyes; yet steadily and trustfully, this one good time, they sought to liberate their country peacefully, legally, under the advice of counsel. They loyally obeyed that man, and would obey no other. And when he walked in triumph out of his prison, at one word from his mouth they would have marched upon Dublin from all the five ends of Ireland, and made short work with police and military barracks.

But what shall I say of *him?* He knew that millions of his countrymen were hanging upon his lips, and secretly praying that he would bring this long agony to the arbitrament of manhood;—and his soul sank within him. For years he had been promising them freedom or his head upon the block: he had taken the starving peasant's mite, and " the priceless trust of youth ; " and, now, let me not say he betrayed, but he disappointed that trust. Let there be such excuses for him as the nature of the case admits: he was old; the disease of which he died (softening of the brain) had already begun to work upon his energies ; the thought of bloodshed was horrible to him ; for he was haunted by the ghost of D'Esterre, whom he had slain in the pride of life. Yet, after all, what a poor comfort, what a poor excuse is all this !

Almost the first thing he proposed after his release, in a secret conclave of the Repeal Association, was the dissolution of the Association, in order to construct another body on a little more legal and safe basis. He knew that the Association now contained thousands who eagerly demanded some decisive step in advance ; and though he constantly flattered Smith O'Brien in public, yet he already feared that man's well-known inflexibility of character, and knew that he had not thrown himself into the cause without stern purpose. The proposal to disband was combated, and was given up. He occupied his weekly speeches with collateral issues upon parliamentary questions which were often arising,—the "Bequests Act," the "Colleges Bill," the Papal Rescript negotiation, and the like ;—all matters which would have been of moment in any self-governing nation, but were of next to no account in the circumstances ;—or he poured forth his fiery floods of eloquence in denunciation, not of the British Government, but of *American Slavery*, with which he had nothing on earth to do.

Very shortly after his release, he went so far as to declare in a' published letter (2d October,) that he preferred *Federalism* to Repeal—that is, a local Parliament for local purposes: but here again he was met. Duffy published a letter, very respectfully but firmly declaring that the cause we were all enlisted in was the national independence of Ireland. From other quarters also came symptoms of discontent; and at the next meeting of the Association he exclaimed : " Federalism !—I would not give *that* for Federalism ; " and he snapped his fingers. And still his entreaties for "peace, law, and order," became more nervously anxious, day by day; and he often declared that his "Head Pacificator" was now the most important person in the Association.

He said no more of his plan for a Council of Three Hundred, or adjourned it to a distant contingency. He praised too much, as many thought, the sublime integrity and justice of the three Whig law-lords who had voted for reversing the judgment against him. But the most significant change in his behavior was in the querulous captiousness he showed towards the *Nation* and those connected with it. He had much to say in deprecation of rash young men; and hinted that the youngsters in question were no better than infidels.

All these symptoms of retreating from his position, these good words to British Whiggery, and censure on "rash young men," appearing from week to week, fell upon the highly wrought excitement of the people with the effect of a repeated shower-bath; and the patient perceptibly cooled.

The Association all this time was becoming more powerful for good than ever. O'Brien had instituted a "Parliamentary Committee," and worked on it continually himself; which, at all events, furnished the nation with careful and authentic memoirs on all Irish questions and interests, filled with accurate statistical details. Many Protestant gentlemen, also, of high rank, joined the Association in '44 and '45—being evidently unconscious how certainly and speedily that body was going to destruction. The meetings were constant and crowded; and to a casual observer the agitation was as formidable and active as ever. "Our position," said the *Nation*, "is as good as the Duke's at Torres Vedras." Perhaps; but then the enemy was inside our position, not outside; which makes a great difference. In short, the British government set its back to the wall, loaded and primed, and let the Repealers *talk*.

The history of Ireland must now be sought elsewhere than in the Repeal Association; and I have next to mention the movements on the other side. The situation was uneasy, was intolerable, and had to be brought to an end somehow or other.

CHAPTER VIII.

APPROACH OF THE FAMINE, IN 1845—REPEAL PROSPECTS AFTER THE LIBERATION OF O'CONNELL—IRISH PRODUCE EXPORTED TO ENGLAND IN 1844—ARMS AND DETECTIVES IN RETURN FOR IT—"LANDLORD AND TENANT" COMMISSION—EJECTMENT LEGISLATION—CONDITION OF IRELAND IN 1845—THE DEVON COMMISSION—THE "TENANT-RIGHT OF ULSTER"—CONSPIRACY OF LANDLORDS AND LEGISLATORS—SIR ROBERT PEEL.

The Fall of the year 1845 brought the first shadow of "Famine." But before coming to that dreadful time, some preliminary information will be useful.

After the liberation of O'Connell, there was apparently greater zeal and diligence than ever in working the cause of Repeal. But the English, being now quite sure there would be no fighting, at least while O'Connell lived, paid it much less regard. There was no more terror of the monster; which indeed had proved itself a harmless monster, and boasted that it was toothless and fangless. They could even afford to dally with it in a playful manner, or to reprove it gently and good-humoredly. The *Times*, for example, which was then accounted the most influential organ of British opinion, published some articles, immediately after the liberation, advocating some sort of *federal* Union. Said the *Times:*

"The idea of a Congress has occurred to other minds before this as a solution of many existing difficulties. We are becoming less of a nation and more of an empire. The conduct of an empire and the government of one's own people seem quite different and incongruous operations. The very ethical qualities necessary, perhaps, for keeping a barbaric continent in subjection don't do at home. One is shocked to see either Irish peasants or English laborers ruled with the same rod of iron as Mahrattas or Belochees—with the same suspicious discipline as a mutinous man-of-war crew, or a black regiment at the Cape. There is, too, something absolutely ridiculous in the present mixture of parliamentary subjects. An hour's talk on the balance of power between the Continental empires is followed by three days' animated discussion on a personal squabble."

Did this indicate that the English mind was becoming

reconciled to the thought of a distinct legislature for Ireland? Not at all; every real movement was the other way, tending to consolidation and centralization,—not of the legislature only, but of the very law-courts, and stamp-office, and other public departments. It indicated only that the *Times* thought it might be politic to throw out this federal idea as an apple of discord amongst Repealers: and it had some effect. Again, said the same *Times*, remarking on the high rank of some of those Irishmen, who were now (not in masses, but in units,) joining Repeal:—

"No, the movement is not essentially a democratic one. It is no more democratic than the American Revolution was in its onset. That was a revolution of which the most earnest leaders and the most respectable were, in the first instance, men of birth and family, representatives of some of the oldest families in the colony. The course of events changed with time, and swept the Virginian gentleman into the same gulf of equality as the grocer of Boston or the drab-colored draper of Pennsylvania. But the principles from which that revolution sprung were the same as those which are now operating in Ireland—impatience of control, private ambition—and, we must add, a poetical patriotism, which is charmed by the sound and enchanted by the vision of 'The Kingdom and Parliament of Ireland.'"

It is evident, then, that there was no more shrieking and howling in England over the phenomenon. For, in fact, all this time, the steady policy of England towards her "sister island" was proceeding on the even tenor of its way quite undisturbed. Four millions sterling of the rental of Ireland, was, as usual, carried over every year, to be spent in England; and the few remaining manufactures which our island had struggled to retain were growing gradually less and less. The very "frieze" (rough, home-made woollen cloth,) was driven out of the market by a far cheaper and far worse Yorkshire imitation of it. Some Repeal artist had devised a "Repeal button," displaying the ancient Irish Crown: the very Repeal button was mimicked in Birmingham; and hogsheads of ancient Irish Crowns were poured into the market, to the utter ruin of the Dublin manufacturer. True, they were of the basest of metal and handiwork; but they lasted as long as "the Repeal" lasted.

All great public expenditures were still confined to England; and, in the year 1844, there was, quite as usual, Irish produce to the value of about fifteen millions sterling exported to England. We cried out that our trade was ruined, and our fine harbors empty: the "Cyclops" and "Rhadamanthus" war-steamers came to us, with 25,000 stands of arms for distribution among the garrisons. We complained that nothing was done in their Parliament for Ireland: straightway we got an Arms Bill. We represented that our factories had stopped work, and our citizens were starving: without delay the Government powder-mill near Cork was set to work. While Irishmen were talking and passing resolutions, the Parliament and Government were steadily confirming, extending, strengthening their grip upon all things Irish. We all lived, at all times, in the full sight and full power of the enemy, and lay down to rest under the shadow of his wings. If it was desirable to know the movements of any suspected person, detectives dogged his footsteps in ever-changing disguises; if he was supposed to be in communication with others, the letters of both correspondents were carefully opened and copied in the Post-office. Much care had been used during the past year, in strengthening police-stations, to resist any sudden attack of peasantry; in fortifying barracks, and disposing garrisons still more and more cunningly, so as to be in full military occupation of every strategic point and road in the island. The Arms Act, too, was administered with much care at Petty Sessions; and it was made certain that any Repealer who had a gun in his house should be at least well known to the police.

I recapitulate all this, that readers may bear in mind, throughout the remainder of the story, what a powerful and cunning tyranny it was which pressed upon that people at every point, and by means of which British Ministers believed they might safely pledge themselves to maintain the Union, at all hazards, "under the blessing of Divine Providence." It was the British Government, not we, who held the position of "Torres Vedras."

In 1843, the Government sent forth one of their endless "Commissions"—the famous "Landlord and Tenant Commission"—to travel through Ireland, collect evidence, and report on the relations of landlord and tenant in Ireland. In '44 it travelled and investigated; and the next year its Report came out, in four great volumes. The true function and object of this Commission was to devise the best means of getting rid of what Englishmen called "the surplus population" of Ireland. Ever since the year 1829, the year of

Catholic Emancipation, British policy had been directing itself to this end. We shall see how it worked.

As a condition of Catholic Emancipation, the "forty shilling franchise" had been abolished; so that the privilege of voting for members of Parliament should be taken away from the great mass of the Catholic peasantry. This low franchise had theretofore induced landlords (for the sake of securing political power,) to subdivide farms and create voters. The franchise abolished, there was no longer any political use for the people; and it happened about the same time that new theories of farming became fashionable. "High farming" was the word. There was to be more grazing, more green cropping; there were to be larger farms; and more labor was to be done by horses and by steam. But consolidation of many small farms into one large one could not be effected without clearing off the "surplus population;" and then, as there would be fewer mouths to be fed, so there would be more produce for export to England. The clearance system, then, had begun in 1829, and had proceeded with great activity ever since; and as the tenants were almost all tenants-at-will, there was no difficulty in this, except the expense.

The Code of Cheap Ejectment was therefore improved for the use of Irish landlords. As the laws of England and of Ireland are extremely different in regard to franchise and to land-tenure; and as the Ejectment-laws were invented exclusively for Ireland, to clear off the "surplus population," I shall give a short account of them.

There had been an act of George the Third (1815) providing that in all cases of holdings, the rent of which was under £20—this included the whole class of small farms—the Assistant-Barrister at Sessions (the County Judge) could make a decree at the cost of a few shillings, to eject any man from house and farm. Two years after, the proceedings in ejectment were still further simplified and facilitated, by an act making the sole evidence of a landlord or his agent sufficient testimony to ascertain the amount of rent due.

By another act of the first year of George the Fourth, it was declared that the provisions of the cheap Ejectment Act "had been found highly beneficial" (that is to say, thousands of farms had been cleared off)—"and it was desirable that same should be extended." Thereupon it was enacted that the power of summary ejectment at Quarter Sessions should apply to all holdings at less than £50 rent; and by the same statute, the cost of procuring ejectments was still farther reduced. In the reigns of George the Fourth and Victoria, other acts were made for the same purpose, so that the cost and trouble of laying waste a townland and levelling all its houses had come to be very trifling. It must be admitted that there is cheap justice in Ireland, at least for some people.

In many parts of the island, extermination of the people had been sweeping. At every quarter sessions, in every county, there were always many ejectments; and I have seen them signed by Assistant-Barristers by hundreds in one sheaf. They were then placed in the hands of bailiffs and police, and came down upon some devoted townland with more terrible destruction than an enemy's sword and torch. Whole neighborhoods were often thrown out upon the highways, in Winter, and the homeless creatures lived for awhile upon the charity of neighbors; but this was dangerous; for the neighbors were often themselves ejected for harboring them. Some landlords contracted with Emigration companies to carry them to America "for a lump sum," according to the advertisements I cited before. Others did not care what became of them; and hundreds and thousands perished every year, of mere hardship.

All this seems a tale of incredible horror. But there are in these United States, this moment, at least one million of persons, each of whom knows the truth of every word I have written, and could add to my general statement, circumstances of horror and atrocity, that might make one tremble with rage as he reads.

The Irish are peculiarly attached to their homesteads; and, like all people of poetic temperament, surround their homes and hearths with more tender associations than a race of duller perception could understand. Take, from a volume published in '44, one *ejectment tableau*—

"Having swept from every corner towards the door, she now took the gatherings by handfuls, and flung them high into the air to be scattered by the winds. Having next procured some salt upon a plate, she went again through every part of the dwelling, turning the salt over and over with her fingers as she went. This lustral visit finished, she divided the salt into separate parcels, which she handed to those without, with directions for its farther distribution.

"She now wrenched from the threshold the horseshoe which the Irish peasantry generally nail upon it, imputing to it some mystic influence; after which, standing erect, with one foot within the house, and the other outside, she signed the sign of the Cross on her brow and on her breast. This strange ceremony was concluded by a sweeping motion of the hand towards the open air, and a similar one in the contrary direction, attended by a rapid movement of the lips, as though she muttered some conjuration. A reverent inclination of her body followed, and again she made the holy sign; then drawing herself up to her full stature, she took her place among the children, and, without casting a look upon the desecrated cabin, she departed from the place."

It is but fair to tell, that sometimes an ejecting landlord or agent was shot by desperate, houseless men. What wonder? There were not half enough of them shot. If the people had not been too gentle, forgiving, and submissive, their island could never have become a horror and scandal to the earth.

There was a "Poor Law" in Ireland since 1842,—a law which had been forced on the country against its will, on the recommendation of an English tourist, one Nicholls; and work-houses, erected under that law, received many of the exterminated people. But it is a strangely significant fact, that the *deaths by starvation* increased rapidly from the first year of the poor-law. The Report of the Census Commissioners, for 1851, declares, that, while in 1842 the deaths registered as deaths by famine amounted to 187, they increased every year, until the registered deaths in 1845 were 516. The "registered" deaths were, perhaps, one-tenth of the unregistered deaths by mere hunger.

Such, then, was the condition of Ireland in 1844–5: and all this before the "Famine."

Now, the "Landlord and Tenant Commission" began its labors in '44. The people were told to expect great benefits from it. The Commissioners, it was diligently given out, would inquire into the various acknowledged evils that were becoming proverbial throughout Europe and America;—and there were to be parliamentary "ameliorations." This Commission looked like a deliberate fraud from the first. It was composed entirely of landlords; the chairman, Lord Devon, being one of the Irish absentee landlords. It was at all times quite certain that they would see no evidence of any evils to be redressed on the part of the tenants; and that, if they recommended any measures, those measures would be such as should promote and make more sweeping the depopulation of the country. "You might as well," said O'Connell, "consult butchers about keeping Lent, as consult these men about the rights of farmers."

The Report of this set of Commissioners would deserve no more especial notice than any of the other Reports of innumerable Commissions which the British Parliament was in the habit of issuing, when they pretended to inquire into any Irish "grievance"—and which were usually printed in vast volumes, bound in blue paper, and never read by any human eye,—but that the Report of this particular "Devon Commission" has become the very creed and gospel of British statesmen with regard to the Irish People from that day to this. It is the programme and scheme upon which the Last Conquest of Ireland was undertaken in a business-like manner years ago; and the completeness of that conquest is due to the exactitude with which the programme was observed.

The problem to be solved, was, how to get rid of the people. There was a "surplus population" in Ireland—this had long been admitted in political circles—and the alarming masses of powerful men who had trooped to the summons of O'Connell, and had been by him paraded "in their moral might," as he said, at so many points of the island, brought home to the bosoms of Englishmen a stern conviction of the absolute necessity that existed to thin out these multitudinous *Celts.*

One of the strongest demands and most urgent needs of these people, had always been permanence of tenure in their lands;—O'Connell called it "fixity of tenure," and presented it prominently in his speeches, as one of the greatest benefits to be gained by repealing the Union. It was indeed the grand necessity of the nation—that men should have some security—that they who sowed should reap—that labor and capital expended in improving farms should in part, at least, profit those who expended it. This would at once prevent pauperism, put an end to the necessity of emigration, supersede poor-laws, and prevent the periodical famines which had desolated the island ever since the Union. It is a measure which would have been sure to be recommended as the first, or indeed the only measure for Ireland, by any other Commission than a Commission of Irish landlords.

In the northern province of Ulster, there was, as before mentioned, a kind of unwritten law, or established custom, which, in some counties, gave the tenant such needful security. The "Tenant-Right of Ulster" was the name of it. By virtue of that Tenant-Right, a farmer, though his tenure might be nominally "at will," could not be ejected so long as he paid his rent; and if he desired to move to another part of the country, he could sell his "good-will" in the farm to an incoming tenant. Of course the greater had been his improvements, the larger price would his Tenant-Right command; in other words, the improvements created by his own or his father's industry were his. The same custom prevented rents from being arbitrarily raised in proportion to the improved value; so that in many cases which came within my own knowledge, in my profession, lands held "at will" in Ulster, and subject to an ample rent, were sold by one tenant-at-will to another tenant-at-will at full half the fee-simple value of the land. Conveyances were made of it. It was a valuable property, and any violent invasion of it, as a witness told Lord Devon's Commission, would have "made Down another Tipperary."

The custom was almost confined to Ulster. It was by no means (though this has often been stated,) created or commenced by the terms of the Plantation of Ulster in the time of King James the First; but was a relic of the ancient free social polity of the nation, and had continued in Ulster longer than in the other three provinces, simply because Ulster had been the last part of the island brought under British dominion, and forced to exchange the ancient system of tribe-lands for feudal tenures. Neither is the custom peculiar to Ireland. It prevails in Italy, in Spain, in Hungary, in all Austria. In France and Prussia it has ripened into full peasant proprietorship; and nowhere, perhaps, in all Europe, is it denied or disallowed to the tillers of the soil, except in Galicia (the Austrian part of Poland), and in the three Southern provinces of Ireland.

Surely it was fair, it was not unnatural, that Tipperary should seek to become another Down; and if, throughout all Munster, Leinster, and Connaught, there was idleness and indifference to improvement of farms, who could expect it to be otherwise, seeing that if a man was so insane as to improve, to drain, to fence, to build a better cabin, his landlord was quite sure to serve him with a "notice to quit." In fact, on many estates, those notices were always served regularly from six months to six months,—so that at every Quarter Sessions the whole population of such estates was liable to instant extermination.

The people of Ireland are not *idle.* They anxiously sought opportunities of exertion on fields where their landlords could not sweep off all their earnings; and many thousands of small farmers annually went to England and Scotland to reap the harvest, lived all the time on food that would sustain no other working men, and hoarded their earnings for their wives and children. If they had had Tenant-Right they would have labored for themselves, and Tipperary would have been a peaceful and blooming garden.

Is the American mind able to conceive it possible that noble lords and gentlemen, the landlords and legislators of an ancient and noble people, should deliberately conspire to slay one out of every four—men, women, and little children, —to strip the remainder barer than they were,—to uproot them from the soil where their mothers bore them,—to force them to flee to all the ends of the earth,—to destroy that Tenant-Right of Ulster, where it was, and to cut off all hope and chance of it where it was not? No; I can hardly suppose that an American is able to grasp the idea: his education has not fitted him for it: and I hesitate to make the assertion of this deliberate conspiracy. Take the facts and documents; and draw such inferences as they will bear.

First, then, for the Report of the Devon Commission. As first printed, it fills four stupendous "Blue Books." But it contained too much valuable matter to be buried, like other Reports, in the catacombs which yawn for that species of literature. The Secretary of the Commission, therefore, was employed to abstract and condense, and present the cream of it in two or three octavo volumes. This had the advantage, not only of condensation, but of selection; the Commissioners could then give the pieces of evidence which they liked the best, together with their own recommendations. Now, those volumes have been the Bible of British legislators and Irish landlords;—the death-warrant of one million and a half of human beings, and the sentence of pauper banishment against full a million and a half more. It is worth while to examine so portentous a volume. It is called a "Digest of the Evidence, &c."—is published by authority; and has a preface signed "Devon."

Much of the volume is occupied with dissertations and evidence respecting "Tenant-Right," which the North had, and the South demanded. The Commissioners are clearly against it in every shape. They term it "unphilosophical;" and in the preface they state that the Ulster landlords and tenants look upon it in the light of a life-insurance;—that is, the landlord allows the sale of Tenant-Right, and the incoming tenant buys it, lest they should both be murdered by the outgoing tenant. The following passage treats this Tenant-Right as injurious to the tenant himself:—

"It is even questionable whether this growing practice of Tenant-Right, which would *at the first view* appear to be a *valuable assumption* on the part of the tenant, be so in reality; as it gives to him without any exertion on his own part an *apparent property* or security, by means of which he is enabled to incur future incumbrance in order to avoid present inconvenience—a practice which frequently terminates in the utter destitution of his family, and in the sale of his farm, when the debts thus created at usurious interest amount to what its sale would produce."

It appears, then, that it is injurious to the tenant to let him have anything on the security of which he can borrow money;—a theory which the landlords would not relish if applied to themselves. Further, the Commisioners declare that this Tenant-Right is enjoyed without any exertion on the part of tenants. Yet they have, in all cases, either created the whole value of it in the sweat of their brows, or bought it from those who did so create it.

The Commissioners "foresee some danger to the just *rights of property*, from the unlimited allowance of this Tenant-Right." But they suggest a substitute: "Compensation for future improvements;" surrounding, however, that suggestion with difficulties which have prevented it from ever being realized.

Speaking of the *consolidation* of farms, they say:—

"When it is seen in the evidence, and in the return of the size of the farms, how small those holdings are, it cannot be denied that such a step is absolutely *neccessary*."

And then, as to the people whom it is thus "necessary" to eject, they say:—

"*Emigration* is considered by the Committee to be peculiarly applicable as a remedial measure."

They refer to one of their Tables (No. 95, p. 564), where—

"The calculation is put forward, showing that the consolidation of the small holdings up to eight acres* would require the removal of about one hundred and ninety-two thousand three hundred and sixty-eight families."

That is, the removal of about one million of persons.

Such was the Devon programme:—Tenant-Right to be disallowed;—one million of people to be *removed*,—that is, swept out on the highways, where their choice would be America, the poorhouse, or the grave. We shall see with what accuracy the details were carried out in practice.

The "Integrity of the Empire" was to be menaced no more by half-million Tara meetings: those ordered masses of the "Irish Enemy," with their growing enthusiasm, their rising spirit, and their yet more dangerous discipline, were to be thinned, to be cleared off: but all in the way of "amelioration." They were to be ameliorated out of their lives: there was to be a *battue* of benevolence. Both government and landlords had been thoroughly frightened by that vast parade of a nation: and they knew they had only been saved by O'Connell and his Peace-principle: and O'Connell was not immortal.

When I say there was a conspiracy of landlords and legislators to destroy the people, it would be unjust, as it is unnecessary, to charge all members of the Queen's Government, or all or any of the Devon Commissioners, with a privity to that design. Sir Robert Peel knew how Irish landlords would inquire,—and what report they would make,—just as well as he knew what verdict a jury of Dublin Orangemen would give. Sir Robert Peel had been Irish Secretary. He knew Ireland well: he had been Prime Minister at the time of Catholic Emancipation: and he had taken care to accompany that measure with another, *disfranchising* all the small farmers in Ireland. This disfranchisement, as before explained, had given a stimulus and impetus to the clearance system. He had helped it by cheap Ejectment Acts. But it had not worked fast enough.

---

* An Irish acre is to an English one in the proportion of eight to five, nearly.

CHAPTER IX.

LAND-TENURE REPORT—O'BRIEN—EIGHTY-TWO CLUB—GREY PORTER—A NATIONAL MILITIA—PRESIDENT POLK AND OREGON TERRITORY—ROBERT TYLER—COLLEGES BILL—MACNEVIN—JAMES HAUGHTON—JOHN O'CONNELL AND GENERAL JACKSON—LORD STANLEY'S BILL—"SURPLUS POPULATION"—DEATH OF DAVIS—FAMINE.

IT was in the month of February, 1845, that the first of the four voluminous Reports was published by the Land Tenure Commission. Sir Robert Peel was Prime Minister; Lord Stanley (afterwards Lord Derby) was Colonial Secretary. In England, the Repeal Agitation was still regarded as formidable. Twenty-six of the hundred and five Irish Members of Parliament were declared and enrolled Repealers; and these, despairing of influencing the course of Imperial legislation by attending the London Parliament, gave their attendance in "Conciliation Hall," along with O'Connell and O'Brien, or else stayed at home. O'Brien, zealously aided by Davis and his friends in the *Nation* Office, and by John O'Connell, was laboring on the Committee of the Association; whose reports and pamphlets, widely circulated amongst the people, were diffusing sound information upon the national resources of the Island, and the state of the account lying open between Ireland and England. Mainly through the exertions of Davis, "Repeal Reading Rooms" sprang up in every town; and a Club was formed, which called itself the "Eighty-two Club," in honor of the era of Ireland's Independence (1782). The members of the Club attended public meetings and festivals in a dark-green uniform, adorned with gold lace; and the uniform cap resembled the forage-cap of an officer of hussars. Mr. Grey Porter, a gentleman of large property in Fermanagh, and son to the Bishop of Clogher, joined the Association; and forthwith published a pamphlet, propounding, amongst other things, that Ireland ought to have a *national militia* of 100,000 men. Men's thoughts were tending towards battle: the agitation was beginning, notwithstanding all the Head Pacificator's labors, to assume a semi-military look; and this hardly alarmed the English more than it alarmed O'Connell. He loved not that "Eighty-two Club," with its forage cap; but seeing he could not prevent its formation, he accepted—that is, assumed—the presidency of it; and soon took care to swamp it with his own peaceful and constitutional creatures.

Grey Porter's pamphlets were stirring and bold: and his ideas about the militia were welcomed warmly and passionately by Davis. "Honor to Mr. Porter," he wrote, "for having had the manliness to propose what thousands thought but spoke not." His appeals to his fellow Protestants were strong and warm. His first pamphlet says:—

"At present the Irish Protestants have a great deal of smothered national feeling. They may be distinct from their Catholic countrymen—they are equally so from the natives of England. Their psychology is national, though their politics are imperial. They have more self-control, more self-reliance, than their Catholic countrymen; but who that is familiar with their minds but knows that they are full of Irish ardor,—of Irish love of whatever is dashing and splendid; and that in favorable circumstances they are just the body who, backed by the Catholic multitudes, would achieve a revolution in Ireland, whose vibrations would be felt wherever a single foundation of British empire has been laid? It would certainly be a most magnificent consummation of Irish history, if that proud and fiery body, the Protestants of Ireland, should, inflamed by a generous nationality, marshal in the ranks of their Catholic countrymen—unfurl the standard of Orange and Green, and casting off the shackles of England, display their hereditary valor in fields that would eclipse the glories of Derry and the Boyne."

All this talk about unfurling standards, and the like, was highly distasteful to O'Connell; and the "Head Pacificator" snuffed carnage. But O'Brien hailed with a calm smile the evident progress of the true gospel of manhood; and the *Nation* busied itself in pointing out and enumerating the militia force of all the countries of Europe; and telling how even the British Colonies, Canada, and the West India islands, were guarded by that indispensable kind of force. To exhibit and prove all this was easy; but all the while there was the *Disarming Act;* and the crime of training or drilling in Ireland was felony, punishable by transportation.

Still the enemy looked on not without uneasiness. It was to them very evident that they held Ireland only by the tenure of O'Connell's life: and therefore it became highly necessary to break up the organization before the Agitator's death.

The extermination of tenantry, which was expected to follow Lord Devon's Report, might be too slow for their purposes, though it was quite sure. The "Report" was in the mouths of all; and was precisely such as Sir Robert Peel had expected, and intended to get, from Irish landlords. It was a report of foxes upon a flock of geese; and it clearly appeared in its pages that the geese had nothing to say for themselves why judgment should not be passed upon them, to be devoured whole, with the feathers. Upon that "Report" Sir Robert was determined, indeed, to act, and did act with sweeping effect. But in the meantime, something must be done to divide and distract the Repeal cause. The people were becoming perilously organized; and any accident might in a moment shiver to atoms the "ethical experiment of moral force."

Danger threatened from the side of America. President Polk had declared that the American title to the Oregon territory, up to a certain line of latitude, was "clear and unquestionable." Sir Robert Peel had declared that a great portion of what was so claimed belonged to England, and England would defend it. Now, there had sprung up, within two or three years, a close correspondence and alliance between the Irish in America and the Irish at home; and encouraging and inspiring addresses were regularly sent over, accompanied by large remittances of money. The addresses were generally written by Robert Tyler, who was then, as he is yet, a warm and disinterested friend of the Irish race. O'Connell was glad to get the money; but the tone of the addresses sometimes made his old brown wig stand on end; and the poor "Head Pacificator" snorted with alarm for the "ethereal and balmy principle." The *Nation* gave unmistakable notification that in case of war about Oregon, the Americans might count upon a diversion in Ireland.

Suddenly, Sir Robert Peel's Ministerial organs announced that there were "good measures," or what the English call "ameliorations," in store for Ireland. And in truth three measures, having much show of liberality, were soon brought forward. They were all cunningly calculated to the great end—the breaking up of our Repeal Organization. On the

2d of April, then, Sir Robert " sent a Message of Peace to Ireland ":—it was a proposed Bill to give some additional thousands *per annum* to the Catholic College of Maynooth; and in the House of Commons the Premier thus urged his measure :—

" I say this without hesitation, and recollect that we have been responsible for the peace of Ireland : you must, in some way or other, break up that formidable confederacy which exists against the British government and British connection (hear, hear). I do not believe you can break it up by force. You can do much to break it up by acting in a spirit of kindness, and forbearance, and generosity (cheers)."

It was novel to hear these good words; and we knew they meant fraud. But the Premier continued :—

" There rises in the far western horizon a cloud [Oregon], small indeed, but threatening future storms. It became my duty on the part of the government, on that day, in temperate but significant language, to depart so far from the caution which is usually observed by a Minister, as to declare publicly, that while we were most anxious for the amicable adjustment of the differences—while we would leave nothing undone to effect that amicable adjustment, —yet, if our rights were invaded, we were prepared and determined to maintain them (loud cheers.) I own to you, that when I was called upon to make that declaration, I did recollect with satisfaction and consolation, that the day before *I had sent a message of peace to Ireland.*"

The object of the bill was to provide more largely for the endowment of Catholic Professors, and the education of young men for the Catholic Church; and the Minister prudently calculated that it would cool the ardor of a portion of the Catholic clergy for Repeal of the Union. It was forced through both Lords and Commons as a party question, though vehemently opposed by the intense bigotry and ignorance of the English nation. But the Premier put it to them in that irresistible form—Vote for our measure or we will not answer for the Union!

Another of the Premier's ameliorations was the Colleges Bill, for creating and endowing three purely secular colleges in Ireland, to give a good course of education without references to religious belief. This also was sure to be regarded as a great boon by a portion of the Catholic clergy,—while another portion was just as sure to object violently to the whole scheme; some because it would place education too much under the control of the English Government; and others because the education was to be "mixed,"—strict Catholics being much in favor of educating Catholic youth separately. Here then was a fruitful source of quarrel among Repealers; and in fact it arrayed bishop against bishop, and O'Connell against "Young Ireland." The walls of Conciliation Hall rung with denunciations, not of the Union but of "Godless Colleges," and of "the young infidel party."

But the Premier had another plot in operation. For ages, Protestant England had refused to recognize the Pope as a Sovereign, or to send a Minister to the Vatican. It was still illegal to send an avowed Minister; but Sir Robert sent a secret one. He was to induce his Holiness to take some order with the Catholic bishops and priests of Ireland, to draw them off in some degree from the Repeal agitation. By what motives and inducements that agent operated upon the Pope, one can only conjecture; and my conjecture is this: Italy was then in continual danger of revolution;—if Sardinia and Naples should whip out their kings, the Pope would not be safe. Within the year that had passed, England had demonstrated that she held in her hand the clue to all those Republican conspiracies, by her post-office espionage; and it was evident that the same Sir James Graham, who had copied the private correspondence of Mazzini and the Bandieras, and laid it all before the King of Naples, could as easily have kept it all to himself. Highly desirable, surely, that "peace, law, and order" in Italy should secure so useful a friend.

In short, the Sacred College sent a Rescript to the Irish clergy, declaring that whereas it had been reported to His Holiness that many of them devoted themselves too much to politics, and spoke too rashly in public concerning affairs of State,—they were thereafter to attend to their religious duties. It was carefully given out, in the English Press, that the Pope had denounced the Repeal: if he had done so, nobody would have minded it, because Catholics do not admit his jurisdiction in temporal affairs. Hear how MacNevin, a young Catholic lawyer, spoke of this fulmination on its first appearance, and while yet it was generally believed to be directly aimed against the Repeal Agitation :—

"By whom was the Holy Father informed that certain prelates were 'nimium addicti politicis negotiis et minus prudentes de republica,' which I translate Repeal (cheers)? By whose whisperings did he learn that the Bishop of Ardagh or the Priest of Clontibret were too prominent or too imprudent? We are informed, sir, that there is an English emissary,—shall I say spy? it is now an established English functionary,—at Rome (loud cheers). Is his the discretion which guides the Cardinal Prefect of the Propaganda? Do not suppose, for a moment, that I question the supremacy of the Pope in religious matters. Surely nothing is farther from my mind. But, sir, I do question his right to dictate to an Irish clergyman the degree of prominence or prudence with which he shall serve his country. I hope I am not irreverent in doing so. I shall continue to hold my opinion until I am authoritatively informed that he has the right,—then I shall be silent. But I never heard before, and it will be a singular doctrine, in my view of the case, that his Holiness can take cognizance of the political movements of the Irish people, and use his influence to disarrange the powers we bring to bear in favor of our liberty (cheers). Now, mark who will applaud this repressive movement the most:—why, the men who for centuries have denounced you, and falsely denounced you, as being under the influence of the temporal power of Rome. They made it high treason to communicate with Rome; they sank to the mean vulgarity of withholding the usual diplomatic relations between European courts; they invented a præmunire to keep out the corruption of the Seven-hilled City; but they are now moving every engine to induce the Pope to lend a hand at suppressing Repeal. I beg to tell them, neither he nor they can do it (tremendous applause). If our liberty depended on a monarch or a mob—if it waited on the dictum of a prelate or a Pope—if it could be wrested from us by intrigue—if it were not a thing to be won and kept by honor, and courage, and fidelity,—I would prefer to see the country remain the comfortable servant of England, with a little better food, and a degree of higher wages (cheers)."

It was soon settled, however, that the Rescript had no such power, and presumed that it had no such intention, on the part of the Pope; yet a certain prudent reserve began to be observable in the Repeal speeches of the clergy. So far, the Premier's Roman policy had succeeded.

Mr. Grey Porter, the dangerous pamphleteer, who wanted 100,000 militia-men, was soon disgusted out of the Repeal Association. In fact, he found that no accounts of the money transactions of that body were ever published; although they were always open to any member who might go to the offices to examine them. He suddenly washed his hands of the whole affair, went to Rome, and hunted all the next season in the Campagna,—thinking on accounts.

One word on these accounts. O'Brien, Davis, and all the circle denominated "Young Ireland," were always in favor of a publication of the accounts, because it would take out of the mouth of the enemy a very common taunt against Mr. O'Connell—that he was taking the people's money and not telling what he did with it. They knew also that much of it was employed in paying unnecessary salaries, and to very unworthy persons,—for it was one singular fatality of O'Connell, that his creatures, dependants, and employés, were always of the rascal species. Yet none of us ever suspected that O'Connell used one farthing of the money for any other purpose than furthering the Repeal cause, according to his best judgment. The man did not care for money, save as a political engine; and I have no doubt, for my own part, that, when he died, Ireland was in his debt. It was a point gained, however, for the English, to send Grey Porter to hunt in the Campagna of Rome. To create a grudge between Irish Repealers and the Americans was the next point.

There dwelt in Dublin a benevolent-looking, elderly gentleman of the name of James Haughton; a Protestant of some sect or other; Quaker, perhaps. He joined all benevolent enterprises; interested himself for plundered Indian Rajahs—made temperance speeches—was against "flogging in the army," capital punishments, and in general everything that was strong, harsh, or unpleasant; and being a wealthy man, in a good position in society, his sayings were generally treated with respect. Such a character, of course, was desperately excited about *negro slavery*. But he was also a zealous Repealer; and he even seemed to have associated together in his mind (by some logical process which I have not learned) the cause of "Abolition" with the cause of Irish Independence. Mr. Haughton, accordingly, was sorely scandalized by Robert Tyler's sympathy, and even by the money which authenticated it. And he wrote a public letter, from which I extract a few sentences:—

"I believe in my soul that Robert Tyler is one of the greatest enemies of Irishmen and of Irish liberty on the face of the earth. He knows that our countrymen have much political power in America; he is anxious to gain their suffrages for his party; these are cheaply purchased by a few hollow-hearted and fiery speeches in favor of Irish independence, and by a willingness to contribute to our Repeal fund. I unite with the Liberator in repudiating all such unhallowed sympathy and assistance."

O'Connell afterwards followed up this by rejecting and

sending back, with contumelious words, some money remitted from a Southern State in aid of his Repeal Exchequer. In the September of this year, '45, John O'Connell, in Conciliation Hall, thus deals with the subject,—and it will doubtless be mortifying to American readers to learn that this gentleman felt it his duty to pass a censure upon General Jackson:—

"No one could admire all that was worthy of imitation in General Jackson's character more sincerely than he (Mr. J. O'Connell). He was unquestionably a man of great firmness, and of undaunted courage in carrying out his views; and there was this feature in the history of his life which it was not likely many in that Hall would revere his memory the less for—namely, that he had given a capital good licking to England (loud and vehement applause). That seemed to cover a multitude of sins (hear, hear). He would not—the more particularly as the man was dead—be found to indulge in any lengthened attack upon him. He spoke only to vindicate himself, and to vindicate those— and he believed they were a majority of the Irish people—who abhorred negro slavery, and who could not allow any palliation for those who tolerated it (cheers). It was for this reason he adverted to the subject, and no matter how high General Jackson might have stood in the estimation of the world, he would not for a moment have it supposed that the Irish people were admirers of all parts of his character (hear). It was a blot upon General Jackson's otherwise bright name, that he was a steadfast and inveterate supporter of the accursed system of slavery."

So far, the Premier's plans were successful in breaking up the Repeal movement. Religious disputes were introduced by the Colleges Bill; and this held the Protestants aloof, and produced bitter altercation throughout the country. By the discussion on slavery, American alliance and co-operation were checked; a great gain to the Premier; for the Americans, and the Irish in America, all looked forward to something stronger than "moral force."

The Minister thought he might proceed, under cover of this tumult of senseless debate, to take the first step in his plan for the depopulation of Ireland in pursuance of the "Devon Commission" Report. Accordingly, his third measure for the "amelioration" of Ireland was a bill ostensibly providing for "Compensation of Tenants in Ireland," but really calculated for the destruction of the last relics of Tenant-Right. In introducing this bill, Lord Stanley said:—

"Now, my Lords, I apprehend there is no man who knows aught of the state of Ireland who will not concur in this statement of the report—that between the population and the means of employing the population there is a great and alarming disproportion (hear, hear); and that that disproportion can be met and conquered only by one of two modes; either by reducing the population to the limits of the means of giving employment, or by increasing the employment in proportion to the population."

I need not go through the details of the proposed measure: it is enough to observe that Lord Stanley admitted that he contemplated the " removal of a vast mass of labor" from its present field. "In justice to the colonies," he would not recommend, as the Devon Commissioners did, merely that the whole of this vast mass should be shot out naked and destitute upon their shores; and his bill proposed the employment of a part of it on the *waste lands* of Ireland,—of which waste lands there were four millions of acres capable of improvement. A portion of the " vast mass of labor" removed from other places was to be set to work under certain conditions to reclaim these lands for the landlords.

The bill, though framed entirely for the landlords, did yet propose to interfere, in some degree, with their absolute rights of property. They did not choose that tenants should be presumed to have any right to " compensation," even nominally; or any other right whatever; and as for the waste lands, they wanted them for snipe-shooting. Accordingly they resisted the bill with all their power; and English landlords, on principle, supported them in that resistance. On the other hand, the Irish Tenants, with one consent, exclaimed against the bill as a bill for open robbery and slaughter. A meeting of county Down tenants resolved that it would rob their class (in one province, Ulster, alone,) of £1,500,000 sterling. The *Nation* commented upon it under the title of " Robbery of Tenants (Ireland) Bill." The opposition of the tenant class, and of the Repeal newspapers, would have been of small avail, but for the resistance—upon other grounds—of the landlords. The bill was defeated; Sir Robert Peel had to devise some other method of getting rid of the " surplus population."

Reflect one moment on the established idea of there being a " surplus population" in Ireland;—an idea and phrase which were at that time unquestioned and axiomatic in political circles; while, at the same time, there were four millions of improvable waste-lands; and Ireland was still, this very year, exporting food enough to feed eight millions of people in England. Ireland, perhaps, was the only country in the world which had both surplus produce for export and surplus population for export;—too much food for her people, and too many people for her food.

It was with bitter disappointment and gloomy foreboding, that Davis and his friends witnessed the progress of disorganization and discomfiture in that Repeal movement which had so many elements of power at first. O'Brien, indeed, still labored on the Committees, preparing Reports and the like, with the same calm and imperturbable cheerfulness. If he felt discouragement he did not show it, and the agitation proceeded much as usual, with occasional interruptions, discussions about Catholic faith and Negro Slavery.

But towards the close of this year, two events befell, which gave the enemy most material aid. One was the potato blight, which threatened to cut off almost the whole supply of food on which the great mass of the people had been reduced to subsist.

The other was the sudden death of Thomas Davis. Of him, his peerless character, his work, and his loss, never to be repaired, I shall endeavor to give a more specific idea in my next chapter. That of all the band of friends and comrades who used to be called "Young Ireland," Davis was the foremost and best, the gentlest and bravest—the most accomplished and the most devoted—there is not one amongst us who is not glad and proud to proclaim;—the more readily, perhaps, seeing that Davis is dead.

But the potato blight, and consequent famine, placed in the hands of the British government an engine of State by which they were eventually enabled to clear off, not a million, but two millions and a half, of the "surplus population"—to "preserve law and order" in Ireland, (what they call law and order,) and to maintain the "integrity of the Empire" for this time. It was in the Winter of 1846-7 that proceedings began to be taken in a business-like manner—(and in a business-like manner I shall relate them)—for the Last Conquest of Ireland, (Perhaps.)

CHAPTER X.

DAVIS; HIS INFLUENCE, AIMS, AND LABORS—HIS OPINION OF "IMPOSING DEMONSTRATIONS"—HIS LETTERS—HIS DEATH—FATE OF MACNEVIN.

On the 16th of September, 1845, Thomas Davis died, and the cause of Ireland's independence lost its very heart and soul. He it was, and the lofty and generous impulse which his character and writings gave the movement, that won to its side such a man as William Smith O'Brien, and others of his high order of intellect, accomplishments, and honest purpose: and this was what redeemed the Repeal Association from brawling vulgarity and inanity. But for him, O'Connell's Agitation would have been all along, as it began (and as, indeed, it ended), a Catholic concern only. Educated and high-spirited Catholics themselves would have held aloof from it; and the most prominent persons, next to the "Liberator," would have been Mr. Arkins, Liberator's tailor, and a few Connaught members of Parliament who held their seats by virtue of the fiat of Catholic clergymen.

It is very safe to say, that to the personal influence of Davis, to the grandeur of his aims, to his noble tolerance, to his impassioned zeal, and the loving trust which all generous natures were constrained to place in him, the Association was indebted, not for O'Brien only, but for Dillon, MacNevin, Meagher, O'Gorman, Martin, and Reilly; and to the same influence *they* were indebted for their fate; pining captivity, long exile, death in mad-houses, or foreign graves. Yes, to them and hundreds more, he was indeed a Fate; and there is not one amongst them, still alive, but blesses the memory of the friend who first filled their souls with the passion of a great ambition and a lofty purpose. In the estimation of the British he was, of course, a Nena Sahib.

One may well perceive that this was no common being. Yet I cannot refer for proof of it to any masterpiece of literary or rhetorical effort. He was not a speaker at all; and "literature," for the mere sake of literature, he almost despised. He never wrote anything but for some immediate or remote effect which he sought to produce: every sentence was a lever or a wedge. His writing was the writing of a journalist, and was always done in a hurry. "As for writing," says his friend Wallis, "there is enough to make men love him, and guess at him—and what more can the best of readers do with the supremest writer, though he lived to the age of Sophocles or Goethe. The true loss is of the oak's timber, not of its own acorns or of the flowers at its base. The loss of its immediate influence on the events of his time, and on the souls of his cotemporaries, by guidance and example: that is the true bereavement; one which possibly many generations to come will be suffering from and expiating, consciously or unconsciously."

Davis is not an Irish name, but Welsh; and in fact his father was a Welsh gentleman who had settled in Cork county, where, at Mallow, on the banks of the Blackwater, Thomas Davis was born. He always boasted that he was of the Celtic race of the Cymry; he would rather have been a Cherokee than English; his *nom-de-plume* was ever "The Celt;" and his best loved study from boyhood, had been the language and literature, the traditions and antiquities, of the two branches of the great Western European family, the Gael and the Cymry. Though by profession a barrister, Davis had been a mere silent student till his twenty-fifth year; and his studies had ranged from poetry to statistics, and back again. Of history, in several languages, he was a voracious reader. He had thoroughly mastered the economic and political questions involved in the connexion of Ireland with England; and thought it shame and sin (which, indeed, it was and is,) that our old island should be devoured by strangers; that the people of the ancient clans, who had once taught half the schools and won half the battles in Europe, should send tribute of corn and cattle; nay, (as Athens did of old to Crete,) tribute of her choicest youth also, of her genius and her energy, to swell the pride and power of an inferior race. He longed to see Ireland standing on her own feet, using her own resources for her own behoof, living her own genial life, with her own flag floating above her,—a free and sovereign State among the nations of Europe. And he knew that all this might be achieved, if only the hereditary religious feuds of ages could be healed: and by inculcation

of mutual tolerance and respect, by kindling a common love
for our own land, by education, by the promotion of Irish
art, and re-awakening of Irish military spirit, he hoped to effect it all. It gave him intense pleasure when the Dublin
Evening Mail, the greatest organ of Irish Orangeism, came
out (for example) with such hints as this :—

"If a British Union cannot be formed, perhaps an Irish one
might. What could Repeal take from Irish Protestants that they
are not gradually losing '*in due course?*'

"However improbable, it is not impossible, that better terms
might be made with the Repealers than the government seems disposed to give. A hundred thousand Orangemen, with their colors
flying, might yet meet a hundred thousand Repealers on the banks
of the Boyne; and, on a field presenting so many solemn reminiscences to all, sign the Magna Charta of Ireland's independence.
The Repeal banner might then be Orange and Green, flying from
the Giant's Causeway to the Cove of Cork, and proudly look down
from the walls of Derry upon a new-born Nation."

Eagerly he thus hailed the overture in the *Nation*—

"Here it is at last—the dawning. Here, in the very sanctuary
of the Orange heart, is a visible angel of Nationality."

He was too sanguine, as we can now all see. He knew
not that such threats from Orangeism were meant only to
frighten the British Government into "better terms," for
Orangeism, for the Established Church, for the "Ascendancy." In the sanctuary of the Orange heart no Angel
dwells,—of the better species.

For a year before his death, Davis had been busy in
furthering the preparation of a series of small volumes,
called the "Library of Ireland;" each of which was to narrate some important period of Irish history, or to present
gems of Irish literature, or give a biography of some Irishman of whom we could all be proud. His friends had
eagerly responded to his suggestions. MacNevin had written
a "History of the Volunteers of 1782;" and Duffy had compiled a volume of National Ballads. He had undertaken,
himself, to write a Memoir of Wolfe Tone; but his other
multifarious labors had delayed its preparation, and death
cut short the task.

From the last chapter it is apparent that Sir Robert Peel
had skillfully thrown elements of discord amongst us; his
Colleges Bill, his Papal Rescript, his "message of peace to
Ireland," and the like; and that O'Connell and his creatures,

as if prompt to aid the Minister, had made Conciliation Hall (and, of course, a thousand minor Conciliation Halls throughout the country) a theatre of angry discussion and recrimination. Davis would gladly have accepted the new Colleges Bill, as he would accept almost any facilities for education. O'Connell and a portion of the clergy denounced it, not because it was an English invention, but because the colleges were to be "godless colleges." John O'Connell, the "Liberator's" son, who had most unaccountably gained much ascendancy over his father's mind since his imprisonment, was especially prominent and energetic in his opposition to the colleges, and to all who favored them. The question was perpetually dragged into discussion; and the grand national movement seemed to have become an organization for settling or guarding Catholic faith or morals. Davis saw too well that his dreams of years were to be dissipated; and though he never relaxed his exertions, the disappointment preyed upon him.

On the 30th of May, there was a great "demonstration" in Dublin. It was the anniversary of the imprisonment of the Conspirators, and it was determined by the Repealers to make an imposing show. A *pledge* was to be duly registered—not to give up the Repeal. It all came off according to programme. Mayors and aldermen from most of the towns in Ireland—the "Eighty Two Club," in their green and gold—the Trades of Dublin, with their bands and banners,—thronged the Rotundo, where O'Connell, surrounded by the other "conspirators," held levée. The pledge was read, adopted, cheered (some meaning to stand by it, and some not); and then there was a vast and brilliant procession; and the splendid streets of Dublin were once more thronged with marching men and waving banners.

The next morning, I sat with Davis in his study in Baggot street. The very Monday before, there had been a painful and acrimonious discussion in Conciliation Hall, about "godless colleges" and other trash. We were intent on some exquisite German engravings which he had just received. He was, or appeared to be, in the gayest humor— "Did you hear," he said, "Tom MacNevin's principle of action, which he lays down for the Mayo electors?"—(there had long been an anxious wish amongst decent people to get rid of Dillon Browne, member for Mayo, a great Repealer, but a bloated *bon vivant* and insolvent debtor):—"Tom says no man ought to be member for May-*owe*, but the man who can't pay!" We walked out—to the library of the Royal Irish Academy—to the studio of Moore, the sculptor, who was engaged on a bust of our friend Hudson. All the while, not a word of the demonstration of yesterday. At length I said—"Davis, yesterday was a great day for Ireland—'the Pacificator never was in greater force.'" He became serious instantly. "These demonstrations," he said, "are ruining us; they are *parading* the soul out of us. Why, the Mayor and Corporation of Kilkenny have gone home, satisfied that Kilkenny at least has done its *duty;* that if Ireland do not gain her independence this year, it is not Kilkenny's fault; for what could scarlet robes and gold chains do more?"

On returning to his house, he showed me a long row of small volumes,—copies of "The Artillerists' Manual,"—gave me one of them, and told me *that* was what we must all study now. I never saw him more.

This chapter I dedicate to the memories of that most royal creature; and thousands who read it will thank me for the minutest anecdote of him. For which reason I shall select, out of many of his letters to myself, two or three. His letters were always short; and he had no time to write long ones. The following note refers to his proposed Memoir of Wolfe Tone; but he was so busy in supplying information and suggestions to his fellow-laborers, that he had no leisure to apply himself to regular literary labor; and as for his editorial articles, he often wrote them with a pencil, using for a desk the top of his hat.

No. I.—(Postmark, July 7, 1845.)

"MY DEAR MITCHEL:—James Duffy's advertisement is wrong I cannot have the *Tone* then; and what between the *Nation*, and the bigots, and the quantity of exercise needed to keep me in health, there is small chance of my writing at all for the series, though I would greatly like to do so.

"MacNevin's 'Volunteers' has succeeded, though I wish it were more narrative and less speculative;—two thousand copies sold. The series will do whatever we like with Ireland. When printing your 'Aodh O'Neill,' reconsider the passage on the Reformation. I have not leisure to be accurate, much less infallible.

"The aspect of affairs were better without its sacerdotal Press; but we must bear it. O'C., under Johnny's culture, promises to throw up more bigotry.

"Yours, "T. D."

I was then living in the County Down, about seventy miles (English), from Dublin, and like many others, had frequent recourse to Davis for everything I wanted. I ought to have mentioned that I was engaged at that time on one volume of the series in which he took so deep an interest—a Memoir of Aodh O'Neill; and his next letter refers to some inquiries about that, and to an article of mine in the *Nation* newspaper.

"June 17th, 1845.

"My Dear Mitchel:—I have written to Petrie for answers to your queries. Meantime borrow (if from no nearer person, from Charles Duffy) the Battle of Magh Rath—*vulgo Moira*—and you will find a valuable essay on Irish Flags, etc., in the Appendix.

"I entirely agree in your view of Lord Stanley's Bill, and had written to that effect for last *Nation*—but a thick-skulled printer left my article out. I wish your contributions were more frequent. . . . . .

"Yours, "Thomas Davis."

I find another short but very singular note, referring to my antipathy against the new colleges, which, indeed, I detested as much as the Archbishop of Tuam, but for a different reason,—not that they were "godless," but that they were British:—

"67 Baggot-street.

"My Dear M.:—I think your title perfect in all ways. The prefatory remarks will *do good.*

"We are not likely to agree on Education, or Religion. I have deep faith in mere Truth, and in informal humanity; and moreover, I feel that an artificial education prevents that faith from being still deeper and more practical. This is a very abstract way of suggesting my religious position; but 'tis enough.

" Most truly yours,

"Thomas Davis."

One more letter, written on the very day that he was struck by his fatal sickness.

"Baggot-street, Sept. 6th.

"My Dear Mitchel:—C. G. D. told me you had heard many particulars as to Wolfe Tone from the Rev. Mr. Thackeray, of Dundalk. Would you spare an hour to put them down;—especially anything as to his manner and views of future events in Ireland. Mr. Thackeray kindly answered my note, but seems to distrust his memory.

" Truly yours,

"Thomas Davis."

"N.B.—The sooner I hear the better."

Three years' incessant labor and excitement, operating on

an ardent temperament and unresting brain, had done their work; and he died in his harness. Disappointment and despondency, too, had their share in wearing down his frame. He saw the powerful organization wherein he had trusted, gradually weakening, lowering its tone, and eating its words, until its heart died within it: and through the gloom, even his eye of faith could hardly discern an outlook to a brighter future: the Green Flag of sovereign Irish nationhood, that had streamed so proudly through the day-dreams of his youth, was fading into distance like the glories of Hy Brasil.

I cannot expect the ordinary reader to fully appreciate the character I have been describing, or the labors of his life; because, to the eye of a distant observer, his life was a defeat, and his labor was utterly lost. I do not believe so. I would not have dwelt upon it thus, but for a strong faith that the seeds he planted in that kindly soil will bear ripe fruit yet.

He was thirty-one years of age when he died. His figure was not tall, but compact and active. He walked fast, and with his head held slightly forward, as is the wont of eager and impulsive characters. But he was no mere revolutionist. In the antiquarian re-unions at the Academy, none was heard with more respect; in the gay drawing-rooms of Dublin, none was a more welcome guest. He laughed seldom, but heartily. He had not time to marry; but he loved passionately, as such men must; and over his early grave a fair woman shed bitter tears.

How felt O'Connell? Davis had been much in his way; and O'Connell was somewhat of a despot. Davis had been independent of him and his opinions while he gave impetus to his movement; and O'Connell saw no use in independence, and abhorred impetus, unless when he could bridle it himself. "Young Ireland" had been a thorn in his side, had applied fire to his back, and singed his beard. Yet, withal, the heart of Daniel O'Connell was large and loving: Davis had ever treated him with the most reverential respect; and he, on his side, could not but do homage to the imperial genius, nor fail to be won by such a gallant and gentle nature. He was, that month of September, at his house of Derrynane Abbey, far in the wilds of Kerry, among the cliffs of the Atlantic coast, trying to freshen his worn life in the vital air of his mountains, and persuading himself that he could still, when the fox broke cover, listen to the ringing music of his hounds with a hunter's joy. But the massive and iron frame was bent; the bright blue eyes had grown dim; and on that overwearied brain lay the shadow of death. And his heart was heavy; for, surely, the phantom of " Repeal " haunted him among the mountains; and to his inner ear pierced a cry that the ocean roar could not drown,—the passionate cry of his nine million People,— *Where is our Freedom?*

One morning, comes news of the death of Davis—and the old man is shaken by a sudden tempest of wildest grief. Well might he cry out, " Would God that I had died for thee, my son!" From Derrynane his habit was to send a long weekly letter, to be read at the meeting of the Association. This week his letter was very short—nothing but a burst of lamentation :—

. . . .

" As I stand alone in the solitude of my mountains, many a tear shall I shed in the memory of the noble youth. Oh! how vain are words or tears when such a national calamity afflicts the country!

" Put me down among the foremost contributors to whatever monument or tribute to his memory may be voted by the National Association. Never did they perform a more imperative, or, alas! so sad a duty.

" I can write no more—my tears blind me—and—after all, ' Fungar inani munere.' "

O'Brien's sorrow was less demonstrative, but not less deep, and much more lasting. Duffy, who almost idolized Thomas Davis, seemed for a time bewildered and stunned by the blow. The *Nation* was as a fortress ungarrisoned. " The Party " had lost its centre; and those young men who had been held in their sphere by the strong attraction of their chief, though they still remained friends, comrades, and zealous nationalists, were no longer a compact body informed by a single soul. To me it seemed that every survivor of that band lost a part of himself, of his power, purpose, capacity; part of him was buried; and in some cases the better part.

Before quitting this personal topic, I shall tell you how it fared with MacNevin. Brilliant, accomplished, and vivacious, with a pungent dash of sarcasm, he would probably never have been anything but a wit, of the sneering species, if he had not known Davis. Not one of our company was more devotedly attached to Davis, nor so entirely dependent on him, possessed by him. Though assuredly MacNevin was no intellectual pauper, and with strong literary ambition; yet he took his literary tasks submissively at the hand of his friend; and almost saw and felt as the more potent nature willed that he should see and feel. To him Davis had assigned to write for the *Library* a narrative of the "Plantation of Ulster;" and he was far off at Rose Park, in Galway,—his father's house,—busy on his history when Davis died. A few days after, on October 2d, he wrote to me, inquiring about some authorities for his book; and suddenly remembering, he exclaims—

"Poor Davis! how his overflowing treasury would have opened to my importunacy! The more I think of this death—and day by day it grows even more terrible—the more I am afraid to look its effects on the country and ourselves in the face. How well we could have spared a million lives for that bright, pure, manly spirit!"

Thus, throughout the letter, he interrupts himself with outbreaks of despair. The book was written. MacNevin seemed to regard it as a sacred task, imposed on him by the dead: but almost immediately after its publication his intimates perceived that his tasks in this world were over. He was going mad. From the moment of his friend's death, he had been drifting like a ship without a helm; his compass was lost; his pole-star gone out. At last he whirled into the vortex, hopelessly insane, and died in a lunatic asylum.

So far I have lingered on memories both sad and proud. Here I wave to the Dead farewell and *requiescant*.

We are next to see what was destined for the living. Before the grave had yet closed on Thomas Davis, began to spread awful rumors of approaching famine. Within the next month, from all the counties of Ireland, came one cry of mortal terror. Blight had fallen on the crop of potatoes —the food on which five millions of the Irish people had been reduced to depend for subsistence; three millions of them wholly and exclusively. We are at the beginning of the first year of the six years' *Famine*.

To Sir Robert Peel it would have seemed an impious tempting of Providence to neglect this weapon thus graciously placed in his hand for the consummation of the conquest on which he was bent. If the "Repeal" could not be crushed out by coercion, nor bought out by corruption, it might now be starved out by Famine. The thing was done by a process of "relieving" and "ameliorating;"—for, in the nineteenth century, civilized governments always proceed upon the most benevolent motives;—but it was done; and so effectually done for that time, that, a few years afterwards, the London *Times* (perhaps prematurely) thought it might announce—" The Celts are *gone*—gone *with a vengeance*. The Lord be praised."

CHAPTER XI.

DUTIES OF GOVERNMENT—ALMS—PLAYFAIR AND LINDLEY—MEMORIAL OF THE CORPORATION AND CITIZENS OF DUBLIN—LORD HEYTESBURY—O'CONNELL'S PROPOSALS—O'BRIEN'S—MEETING OF PARLIAMENT—COERCION BILL—REPEAL OF THE CORN LAWS—"RELIEF."

Lord Brougham, in his highflown, classical way, described the horrors of the Famine in Ireland, as "surpassing anything in the page of Thucydides,—on the canvas of Poussin,—in the dismal chant of Dante." Such a visitation, falling suddenly upon any land, certainly imposes onerous duties upon its *de-facto* government; and the very novelty of the circumstances, driving everything out of its routine course, might well excuse serious mistakes in applying a remedy to so monstrous a calamity. First, however, bear in mind that all the powers, revenues, and resources of Ireland had been transferred to London. The Imperial Parliament had dealt at its pleasure with the "sister island" for forty-six years, and had brought us to this. Second; remember that, now, for two years, a great majority of the Irish people had been earnestly demanding back those powers, revenues, and resources; and the English people, through their Executive, Parliament and Press, had unanimously vowed this must never be. They would govern us in spite of us, "under the blessing of Divine Providence," as the Queen said. "Were the Union *gall*," said the *Times*, "swallow it you must."

Well, then, whatsoever duties may be supposed to fall upon a government, in case of such a national calamity, rested on the English government. We had no legislature at home; in the Imperial legislature we had but a delusive semblance of representation; and so totally useless was it, that *national* Irish Members of Parliament preferred to stay at home. We had no authoritative mode of even suggesting what measures might (in mere Irish opinion) meet the case.

But we will see what was proposed by such public bodies in Ireland as still had power of meeting together in any capacity;—the city corporations, for example, and especially the Repeal Association. It has been carefully inculcated upon the world by the British Press, that the moment Ireland fell into distress, she became an abject beggar at England's gate;—nay, that she even craved alms from all mankind. Some readers may be surprised when I affirm that *neither Ireland, nor anybody in Ireland, ever asked alms or favors of any kind, either from England or any other nation or people;*—but on the contrary, that it was England herself that begged for us, that sent round the hat over all the globe, asking a penny for the love of God to relieve the poor Irish; —and further, that, constituting herself the almoner and agent of all that charity, *she*, England, took all the profit of it.

Before describing the actual process of the "Relief Measures," let us conjecture what would be the natural, obvious, and inevitable course of conduct in a nation which was indeed one undivided nation; France, for example. If blight and famine fell upon the South of France the whole common revenue of the kingdom would certainly be largely employed in setting the people to labor upon works of public utility; in purchasing and storing, for sale at a cheap rate, such quantities of foreign corn as might be needed, until the season of distress should pass over, and another harvest should come. If Yorkshire and Lancashire had sustained a like calamity in England, there is no doubt such measures as these would have been taken, promptly and liberally. And we know that the English Government is not slow to borrow money for great public objects, when it suits their policy so to do. They borrowed twenty millions sterling to give away to their slave-holding colonists for a mischievous whim. In truth, they are always glad of any occasion or excuse for borrowing money and adding it to the National Debt;— because, as they never intend to pay that debt, and as the stock and debentures of it are in the meantime their main safeguard against revolution, they would be well pleased to incur a hundred millions more at any moment. But the object must be popular in England; it must subserve some purpose of British policy;—as in the case of the twenty millions borrowed to turn negroes wild (set them "free" as it was called)—or the loans afterwards freely taken to crush the people of India, and preserve and extend the opium trade with China. To make an addition to the National Debt, in order to preserve the lives of a million or two of Celts, would have seemed in England a singular application of money. To *kill* so many would have been well worth a war that would cost forty millions.

On the first appearance of the blight, the enemy sent over two learned commissioners, Playfair and Lindley, to Ireland, who, in conjunction with Doctor [afterward Sir Robert] Kane, were to examine and report upon potatoes generally, their diseases, habits, etc. This passed over the time for some weeks. Parliament was prorogued and did not meet again till January.

In the meantime, the Corporation of Dublin sent a memorial to the Queen, praying her to call Parliament together at an early day, and to recommend the appropriation of some public money for public works, especially railways in Ireland. A deputation from the citizens of Dublin, including the Duke of Leinster, the Lord Mayor, Lord Cloncurry, and Daniel O'Connell, waited on the Lord Lieutenant (Lord Heytesbury), to offer suggestions as to opening the ports to foreign corn at least, for a time, stopping distillation from grain, providing public works, and the like; and to urge that there was not a moment to be lost, as millions of people would shortly be without a morsel of food. The reply of Lord Heytesbury is a model in that kind.. He told them they were premature; told them not to be alarmed; that learned men had been sent over *from England* to inquire into all those matters; that, in the meantime, the Inspectors of Constabulary and Stipendiary Magistrates were charged with making constant reports from their several districts; that there was "no immediate pressure on the market;"—finally, that the case was a very important one, and it was evident "no decision could be taken without a previous reference to the responsible advisers of the Crown." In truth, no other answer was possible, because the Viceroy knew nothing of Sir Robert Peel's intentions. To wait for the report of learned men,—to wait for Parliament,—in short, *to wait ;* that was the sole policy of the enemy for the present. He could wait; and he knew that hunger could not wait.

The Town Council of Belfast met and made suggestions similar to those of the Dublin Corporation; *but neither body asked charity.* They demanded that, if Ireland was indeed an integral part of the realm, the common exchequer of both islands should be used—not to give alms, but to provide employment on public works of general utility.

The plea of the enemy for not being ready with any remedy was the suddenness of the calamity. Now, it happened that, nearly eleven years before, a certain "Select Committee," composed principally of Irish members of Parliament, had been appointed by the House of Commons to inquire into the condition of the Irish poor. They had reported even then in favor of promoting the reclamation of waste lands; had given their opinion decidedly (being Irish) that there was no real surplus of population, seeing that the island could easily sustain much more than its actual population, and export immensely besides. Nevertheless, they warn the Government that—"If the potato crop were a failure, its produce would be consumed long before they could acquire new means of subsistence; and then a famine ensues."* Yet, when the Famine did ensue, it took "the Government" as much by surprise (or they pretended that it did) as if they had never been warned.

Not only the citizens of Cork and Belfast, but the Repeal Association also had suggestions to make. Indeed, this last-named body was the only one that could pretend especially to represent the very class of people whose lives were endangered by the dearth. Let us see what *they* had to propose :—

On the 8th of December, O'Connell, in the Repeal Association, said :—" If they ask me what are my propositions for relief of the distress, I answer, first, *Tenant-Right.* I would propose a law giving to every man his own. I would give the landlord his land and a fair rent for it : but I would give the tenant compensation for every shilling he might have laid out on the land in permanent improvements. And what next do I propose ? *Repeal of the Union.*" In the latter part of his speech, after detailing the means used by the Belgian legislature during the same season—shutting the ports against export of provisions, but opening them to import, and the like,—he goes on :—

"'If we had a domestic Parliament, would not the ports be thrown

---

* Report of the "Select Committee," 1836.

open—would not the abundant crops with which Heaven has blessed her be kept for the people of Ireland.—and would not the Irish Parliament be more active even than the Belgian Parliament to provide for the people food and employment (hear, hear)? The blessings that would result from Repeal—the necessity for Repeal—the impossibility of the country enduring the want of Repeal,—and the utter hopelessness of any other remedy—all those things powerfully urge you to join with me, and hurrah for the Repeal."

Still earlier, in November, O'Brien had used these words—

"I congratulate you, that *the universal sentiment hitherto exhibited upon this subject has been that we will accept no English charity* (loud cheers). The resources of this country are still abundantly adequate to maintain our population: and until those resources shall have been utterly exhausted, I hope there is no man in Ireland who will so degrade himself as to ask the aid of a subscription from England."

And the sentiment was received with "loud cheers." O'Brien's speech is an earnest and vehement adjuration not to suffer promises of " Relief," or vague hopes of English boons to divert the country one moment from the great business of putting an end to the Union. Take one other extract from a speech of O'Connell's :—

"If we had a paternal government, I should be first to counsel the appropriation of a portion of the revenues of Ireland to the wants of the people, and this, too, without very strictly considering whether the whole should be repaid or not. We have an abstract claim to such application of the Irish revenues ; but if we were to advocate such an arrangement now, we should be mocked and insulted (hear, hear). Therefore, I approach the government of England on equal terms. I say to the English people—You are the greatest moneylenders in Europe, and I will suppose you to be as determined as *Shylock* in the play (hear, hear, and cheers). During the last session of Parliament, an act was passed for the encouragement of drainage in England and Ireland. According to the provisions of that act, any money advanced for the purpose of draining estates takes priority over the other charges affecting those estates ; so that whatever amount of money may be so applied becomes the first charge on the estate of the proprietors of Ireland, and thus is its repayment secured beyond all hazard (hear, hear). The government can borrow as much money as they please on Exchequer bills, at not more than three per cent. If they lend it out for the purposes of drainage, they can charge such proprietors as may choose to borrow, interest at the rate of four per cent. They, therefore, will have a clear gain of one per cent., and we shall owe them nothing, but they will stand indebted to us for affording them an opportunity of obtaining an advantageous investment of the capital at their disposal."

All this while, until after the meeting of Parliament, there was no hint as to the intentions of government : and all this while the new Irish harvest of 1845, (which was particularly abundant,) with immense herds of cattle, sheep, and hogs, quite as usual, was floating off on every tide, out of every one of our thirteen seaports, bound for England; and the landlords were receiving their rents and going to England to spend them; and many hundreds of poor people had lain down and died on the roadsides for want of food, even before Christmas; and the Famine not yet begun, but expected shortly.*

All eyes were turned to Parliament. The Commission of learned naturalists—the inquiries and reports made by means of the constabulary—and various mysterious intimations in the Government newspapers—all tended to produce the belief that the Imperial "government" was about to charge itself with the whole care and administration of the Famine. And so it was—with a vengeance.

Late in January, Parliament assembled. From the Queen's (that is Sir Robert Peel's) speech, one thing only was clear—that Ireland was to have a new "Coercion Bill." Extermination of tenantry had been of late more extensive than ever, and therefore, there had been a few murders of landlords and agents—the most natural and inevitable thing in the world. The Queen says:—

"MY LORDS AND GENTLEMEN,

"I have observed with deep regret the very frequent instances in which the crime of deliberate assassination has been of late committed in Ireland.

"It will be your duty to consider whether any measure can be devised calculated to give increased protection to life, and to bring to justice the perpetrators of so dreadful a crime."

Whereupon the *Nation* commented as follows:—

"The only notice vouchsafed to this country is a hint that more gaols, more transportation, and more gibbets might be useful to us.

"Or, possibly, we wrong the Minister: perhaps, when her Majesty says that 'protection must be afforded to life,' she means that the people are not to be allowed to die of hunger during the ensuing Summer—or that the lives of tenants are to be protected against the extermination of clearing landlords—and that so 'deliberate assassination' may become less frequent. God knows what she means;—the use of royal language is to *conceal* ideas."

---

* The Census Commissioners admit only 516 "registered deaths" by starvation alone up to 1st January. There was, at that time, no *registry* for them at all; thousands perished, registered by none but the recording Angel. Besides, the Commissioners do not count the much greater numbers who died of typhus fever, the consequence of insufficient nourishment.

The idea, however, was clear enough. It meant more police, more police-taxes, police-surveillance, and a law that every one should keep at home after dark. The speech goes on to refer to the approaching Famine, and, declares that her Majesty had "adopted precautions" for its alleviation. This intimation served still further to make our people turn to "government" for counsel and for aid. Who can blame them? "Government" had seized upon all our means and resources. It was confidently believed they intended to let us have the use of some part of our own money in this deadly emergency. It was even fondly imagined by some sanguine persons that the government had it in contemplation to stop the export of provisions from Ireland—as the Belgian legislature had from Belgium, and the Portuguese from Portugal, until our own people should first be fed. It was not known, in short, what "government" intended to do, or how far they would go: all was mystery; and this very mystery paralyzed such private and local efforts, by charitable persons, as might otherwise have been attempted in Ireland.

The two great leading measures proposed in this Parliament by the Administration were, *first*, a Coercion Bill for Ireland, and *second*, Repeal of the Corn Laws. This Repeal of the duties on foreign corn had long been demanded by the manufacturing and trading interests of England, and had been steadily opposed by the great landed proprietors. Sir Robert Peel, as a Conservative statesman, had always hitherto vigorously opposed the measure; but early in this Parliament he suddenly announced himself a convert to free-trade in corn; and even used the pretext of the famine in Ireland to justify himself and carry his measure. He further proposed to abolish the duties on foreign beef and mutton and bacon. Shall we exclude any kind of food from our ports, he said, while the Irish are starving?

That is to say, the Premier proposed to cheapen those products which England bought, and which Ireland had to sell. Ireland imported no corn or beef—she exported those commodities. Hitherto she had an advantage over American and other corn-growers in the English market; because there was a duty on foreign, but not on Irish provisions. Henceforth, the agricultural produce of all the world was to be admitted on the same terms, duty-free; and precisely to the extent that this would cheapen provisions to the English consumer, it would impoverish the Irish producer. The great mass of the Irish people were almost unacquainted with the taste of bread and meat; they raised those articles, not to eat, but to sell and pay their rents with. Yet many of the Irish people, stupefied by the desolation they saw around them, had cried out for " opening the ports," instead of closing them. The Irish ports were open enough; much too open; and an Irish Parliament, if there had been one, would instantly have closed them in this emergency.

In looking over the melancholy records of those famine years, I find that usually the right view was seized, and the right word said, by William Smith O'Brien; and as he was always moderate in expression—never saying anything that he could not more than substantiate,—I am glad to perceive that he fully concurs in this view of Peel's measure. He said, in the Repeal Association :—

" With respect to the proposal before us, I have to remark that it professes to abrogate all protection. It is, in my opinion, a proposal manifestly framed with a view to English rather than Irish interests. About two-thirds of the population of England (that, I believe, is the proportion) are dependent on manufactures and commerce, directly or indirectly. In this country about nine-tenths of the population are dependent on agriculture, directly or indirectly. It is clearly the object of the English Minister to obtain the agricultural produce which the people of this country send to England, at the lowest possible price—that is to say, to give as little as possible of English manufactures and of foreign commodities in return for the agricultural produce of Ireland."

If this *was* the Minister's design, one can appreciate the spirit in which he addressed himself to the " relief measures " for Ireland. The measures were to commence by depreciating all our produce, say to the amount of two millions sterling per annum. And observe, that this did not give the slightest chance of the Irish people themselves being able to purchase and consume one grain of corn or one ounce of meat the more—because, except by the sale of those articles, Ireland had *no money*. So accurately the British legislation of half a century had arranged our affairs and fitted them to the hand of England.

Stupid and ignorant peers and landed men in England cried out bitterly against the Premier's desertion of their party, and declared that the " agricultural interest of *England* was betrayed." Blockheads! Their Minister was caring for them better than they could ask or think.

The other measure was the *Coercion Bill*. It authorized the Viceroy to *proclaim* any district in Ireland he might think proper, commanding the people to remain within doors (whether they had houses or not,) from sunset to sunrise; authorized him to quarter on such district any additional police force he might think needful—to pay rewards to informers and detectives—to pay compensation to the relatives of murdered or injured persons—and to levy the amount of all by *distress* upon the goods of the occupiers, as under the Poor Law; with this difference, that whereas, under the Poor Law, the occupier could deduct a portion of the rate from his rent, under the new law he could not; and with this further difference, that whereas, under the Poor Law, householders whose cabins were valued under £4 per annum were exempt from the rate, under this law, they were not exempt. Thus every man who had a house, no matter how wretched, was to pay the new tax; and every man was bound to *have* a house; for if found out of doors after sunset, and convicted of that offence, he was to be transported for fifteen years, or imprisoned for three—the Court to have the discretion of adding hard labor or solitary confinement.

Now, the first of these two laws, which abolished the preference of Irish grain in the English markets, would, as the Premier well knew, give a great additional stimulus to the consolidation of farms—that is, the ejectment of tenantry; because "High Farming,"—farming on a large scale, with the aid of horses and steam, and all the modern agricultural improvements—was what alone would enable Irish agriculturists to compete with all mankind.

The second law would drive the survivors of the ejected people (those who did not die of hunger,) into the poorhouses or to America; because being bound to be at *home* after sunset, and having neither house nor home, they would be all in the absolute power of the police, and in continual peril of transportation to the penal colonies.

By another act of this Parliament, the Police-force was increased, and taken more immediately into the service of the Crown; the Irish county cess was relieved from their pay; and they became in all senses a portion of the regular army. They amounted to 12,000 chosen men, well armed and drilled.

That readers may understand better the nature and duties

of this force, I shall give a few sentences out of a manual published in this same year, 1846, by David Duff, Esq., an active Police Magistrate. It is entitled "The Constable's Guide:"

"The great point towards efficiency, is, that every man should know his duty and do it, and should have a thorough and perfect knowledge of the neighborhood of his station; and men should make themselves not only acquainted with roads and passes, but the *characters of all*, which, with a little trouble, could be easily accomplished. A policeman cannot be considered *perfect* in his civil duty as a constable, who could not, when required, march direct to any house at night.

. . . .

"Independent of regular night patrols, whose hours should vary, men should by day take post on hills commanding the houses *of persons having registered arms*, or supposed to be *obnoxious*. The men so posted, will, if possible, be within view of other parties, so as to co-operate in pursuit of offenders.

. . . .

"Patrols hanging about ditches, plantations, and, above all, visiting the houses of suspicious characters, are most essential.

"The telescope to be taken always on day patrol, and rockets and blue lights used, as pointed out in the *confidential* memorandum."

The confidential memorandum I have not been privileged to see; but this will give an idea of the Irish Police, and the British method of relieving a famine. The Police were always at the command of Sheriffs for executing ejectments; and if they were not in sufficient force, troops of the Line could be had from the nearest garrison. No wonder that the London *Times*, within less than three years after, was enabled to say—"Law has ridden roughshod through Ireland: it has been taught with bayonets, and interpreted with ruin. Townships levelled with the ground, straggling columns of exiles, work-houses multiplied and still crowded, express the determination of the Legislature to rescue Ireland from its slovenly old barbarism, and to plant the institutions of this more civilized land"—*meaning England*.

These were the two principal measures for the prudent administration of the Famine; but there was also another, purporting to aim more directly at *Relief*. I approach the detail of these "Relief Acts" with great deliberation and caution. They have always appeared to me a machinery for the destruction of an enemy more fatal, by far, than batteries of grape-shot, chain-shot, shells, and rockets: but many persons

196 THE LAST CONQUEST, ETC.

who pass for intelligent, even in Ireland, do believe yet that they were in some sort measures of *Relief*, not contrivances for slaughter. In dealing with them, I shall endeavor to exaggerate nothing; as I shall certainly extenuate nothing.

"relief" aid was more deadly than grape-shot

~ very evocative language

CHAPTER XII.

LOSS OF THE IRISH CROPS—ACCOUNTS BETWEEN ENGLAND AND IRELAND—RAPID EXPORT OF IRISH HARVEST AND CATTLE—SIR ROBERT PEEL'S "REMEDIAL MEASURES"—O'BRIEN IN PARLIAMENT—ENGLISH PRESS ON "ALMS"—SIR ROBERT PEEL'S TWO WEAPONS—REPEAL ASSOCIATION—RESISTANCE TO THE COERCION BILL—EXTERMINATION IN CONNAUGHT—THE "NATION" AND YOUNG IRELAND—ANOTHER STATE PROSECUTION—CHANGE OF MINISTRY.

Mr. Labouchere, in Parliament, estimated the total money loss accruing by the potato-blight, at sixteen millions sterling. The people likely to be affected by it were always, in ordinary years, on the brink of destruction by famine—that is, most of them were always half-starved, for eight months in the year, and many always starved to death.

Now, to replace that lost food by foreign corn, and to pay the higher price of grain over roots (besides freight), would have required an appropriation of twenty millions sterling—the same amount which had been devoted, without scruple, to turning West Indian negroes wild.

England had, for so many years, drawn so vast a tribute from Ireland (probably eight millions *per annum* for forty-six years *), that now when the consequence of our intercourse with the sister island turned out to be that she grew richer every year, while Ireland on her side of the account had accumulated a famine, we claimed that there was something surely *due* to us. It is out of the question here to enter with me into these multifarious accounts. England beats all mankind in book-keeping by double entry; and as she has had the keeping of the books, as well as of everything else, it has been very difficult even to approximate to the truth. Yet one or two salient facts are easily stated.

In 1800, the year of the Union, Ireland owed twenty-one millions of national debt; England, four hundred and forty-six millions. Even of our debt of twenty-one millions, one large

---

* Mr. O'Brien, in his "Address," estimated the absentee rents alone at Five Millions sterling.

item was the charge for bribing members of Parliament, and buying up nomination boroughs, for the purpose of carrying that Union. Now the terms of the Union were that each country should remain liable to the annual charge upon her own debt. But England, as I said, kept the books; and, seventeen years after, she found a pretext for charging herself with our debt, and *charging us with hers.* It was called the " Consolidation Act." They made a fair exchange with us, as O'Connell said; they gave us half of their debt and took half of ours. Ever since, the annual charge upon the Irish Exchequer for interest on that consolidated debt, is nearly five millions.

Yet, with all this, Ireland remitted a *surplus* revenue to England over and above all that they could have the face to charge to her account, of about one million. Needless to say, it was all expended in public works in England. When the famine broke out, also, O'Connell pointed out the fact that the Quit and Crown Rents drawn from Ireland, under the head of "Woods and Forests," amounted to about £60,000, mostly expended in beautifying Trafalgar-square in London, and the Castle of Windsor.

Considering all these things, it was believed not unreasonable, that the common exchequer of the " three kingdoms " (so liberal when it was a question of turning negroes wild,) ought to devote at least as great a sum to the mitigation of so dreadful a calamity. Accordingly, our people demanded such an appropriation, not as alms, but as a right. The Committee of the Repeal Association, for example, said:

"Your committee beg distinctly to disclaim any participation in appeals to the bounty of England or of Englishmen. They demand as right that a portion of the revenue which Ireland contributes to the State, may be rendered available for the mitigation of a great public calamity."

Up to the meeting of Parliament, the enemy concealed their intentions in mystery; they consulted nobody in Ireland about this Irish emergency, but prepared their plans in silence.

In the meantime, the abundant and magnificent crops of grain and herds of cattle were going over to England both earlier in the season, and in greater quantities, than ever 'before; for speculators were anxious to realize, and the landlords were pressing for their rents; and agents and bailiffs were down upon the farmers' crops before they could even get them stacked. So the farmers sold them at a disadvantage, in a glutted market, or they were sold for them, by auction, and with costs. The great point was to put the English Channel between the people and the food which Providence had sent them, at the earliest possible moment.

By New Year's Day, it was almost all swept off. Up to that date, Ireland sent away and England received, of grain alone, of the crop of 1845, three millions two hundred and fifty thousand *quarters*,—besides innumerable cattle;—making a value of at least seventeen millions sterling.

Now, when Parliament met in January, the sole "remedial measure" proposed by Sir Robert Peel (besides the Coercion Bill, and the Corn Bill to cheapen bread in England), was a grant of £50,000 for Public Works, and another grant of as much for drainage of estates;—both these being grants, not to Ireland, but to the Commissioners of Public Works; and to be administered, not as Irishmen might suggest, but as to the said Commissioners might seem good. It was the two-hundredth part of what might probably have sufficed to stay the famine. It might have given sensible relief—if honestly administered—to the smallest of the thirty-two counties. How it *was* used, not for relief, but for aggravation of the misery, I have to tell hereafter. For that season's famine it was, at any rate, too late, and before any part of it became available, many thousands had died of hunger. The London newspapers complacently stated that the impression "in political circles" was, that two millions of the people must perish before the next harvest.

January, February, and part of March passed away. Nothing was done for relief; but much preparation was made in the way of appointing hosts of Commissioners and Commissioners' clerks, and preparing the voluminous stationery, schedules, specifications, and red-tape to tie them up neatly, which so greatly embarrass all British official action*—a very injurious sort of embarrassment in such a case as the Crimean war; but the very thing that did best service on the present occasion.

O'Connell, O'Brien, and some other Repeal members pro-

---

* In April of next year, Jones, Twistleton, &c., were enabled to report that they had sent to Ireland " Ten thousand books—besides fourteen tons of paper." They give no account of the tape.

ceeded to London in March, to endeavor to stir up Ministers, or at least discover what they were intending. In answer to Mr. O'Brien, Sir James Graham enumerated the grants and loans I have above mentioned; and added something about other public moneys, which, he said, were also available for relief of distress : adding :—

" Instructions have been given on the responsibility of the government to meet every emergency. It would not be expedient for me to detail those instructions; but I may state generally there is no portion of this distress, however wide-spread or lamentable, on which government have not endeavored on their own responsibility to take the best precautions, to give the best directions of which circumstances could admit."

O'Brien had just come from Ireland, where he had anxiously watched the progress of the "relief measures," and of the Famine; he had seen that while the latter was quick the former were slow—in fact, they had not then appeared in Ireland at all; but the very announcement that Government intended to interpose in some decisive manner, had greatly hastened collection of rents and ejectment of tenants: and both hunger and its sure attendant, the Typhus, were sweeping them off rapidly. British Ministers listened to all he could say with a calm, incredulous smile. Have we not told you, they said, we have sent persons, Englishmen, reliable men, to inquire into all those matters? Are we not going to meet every emergency?

"Mr. W. S. O'Brien was bound to say, with regard to the sums of money mentioned by the right hon. baronet as having been, on a former occasion, voted by the House for the relief of Ireland, that as far as his own information went, not one single guinea had ever been expended from those sources (hear, hear, from Mr. O'Connell). He was also bound to tell the right hon. baronet that 100,000 of his fellow-creatures in Ireland were famishing."

And here the report adds—the Hon. gentleman, who appeared to labor under deep emotion, paused for a short time. Doubtless it was bitter to that haughty spirit to plead for his plundered people, as it were, *in formâ pauperis*, before the plunderers; and their vulgar pride was soothed: but soon it was wounded again; for he added :—

" Under such circumstances, did it not become the House to consider of the way in which they could deal with the crisis? He would tell them frankly—and it was a feeling participated in by the majority of Irishmen—that he was not disposed to appeal to their generosity in the matter. They had taken, and they had tied, the purse-strings of the Irish purse!"

Whereupon the report records that there were cries of "Oh! Oh!" They were scandalized at the idea of Ireland having a purse.

Notwithstanding these repeated repudiations of alms, all the appropriations of Parliament, purporting to be for relief, but really calculated for aggravation of the Irish famine, were persistently called alms by the English Press. These Irish, they said, are never done craving alms. It is true they did not *answer* our statement that we only demanded a small part of what was due; they chose to assume that the Exchequer was *their* Exchequer:—neither did they think fit to remember that O'Brien and such as he were by no means suffering from famine themselves, but were retrenching the expenses of their households at home to relieve those who were suffering. To the common English intellect, it was enough to present this one idea:—here are these starving Irish coming over to beg from *you*. In the inculcation of this view of the case, the *Times*, of course, led the way:—

"There would be something highly ludicrous in the impudence with which Irish legislators claim English assistance, if the circumstances by which they enforce their claims were not of the most pitiable kind. The contrast between insolent menace and humble supplication reminds one forcibly of those types of Irish character so popular with the dramatists of the last century, who represent an O'Flanagan or an O'Shaughnessy hectoring through three acts of intermittent brogue—bullying the husband and making love to the wife," etc., etc.

From all this the reader may begin to appreciate the feeling that then prevailed in the two islands: in Ireland a vague and dim sense that they were somehow robbed—in England a still more vague and blundering idea that an impudent beggar was demanding their money with a scowl in his eye and a threat upon his tongue. In truth, only a few, either in England or in Ireland, fully understood the bloody game on the board. The two cardinal principles of the British policy in this business seem to have been these:— *first*, strict adherence to the principles of "political economy;" and *second*, making the whole administration of the Famine a government concern. "Political economy" became, about the time of the Repeal of the Corn Laws, a favorite study, or rather, indeed, the creed and gospel of

9*

England. Women and young boys were learned in its saving doctrines; one of the most fundamental of which was—"there must be no interference with the natural course of trade." It was seen that this maxim would ensure the transfer of the Irish wheat and beef to England; for that was what they called the natural course of trade. Moreover, this maxim would forbid the government or relief committees to sell provisions in Ireland any lower than the market price—for this is an interference with the enterprise of private speculators; it would forbid the employment of government ships—for this troubles individual ship-owners; and further, and lastly, it was found (this invaluable maxim) to require that the public works to be executed by laborers employed with borrowed public money should be unproductive works; that is, works which would create no fund to pay their own expenses. There were many railroad companies at that time in Ireland that had got their charters; their roads have been made since; but it was in vain they asked then for government advances, which they could have well secured and soon paid off; the thing could not be done. Lending money to Irish railroad companies would be a discrimination against English companies—flat interference with private enterprise.

The other great leading idea completed Sir Robert's policy. It was to make the Famine a strictly government concern. The Famine was to be administered strictly through officers of the government, from High Commissioners down to policemen. Even the Irish General Relief Committee, and other local committees of charitable persons who were exerting themselves to raise funds to give employment, were either induced to act in subordination to a Government Relief Committee, which sat in Dublin Castle, or else were deterred from importation of food by the announcement in Parliament that the *Government* had given orders somewhere for the purchase of foreign corn. For instance, the Mayor of Cork and some principal inhabitants of that city, hurried to Dublin and waited on the Lord Lieutenant, representing that the local committee had applied for some portion of the parliamentary loans, but " were refused assistance on some points of official form: that the people of that county were already famishing; and both food and labor were urgently needed. Lord Heytesbury simply recommended that they should communicate at once with the *Government* Relief Committee;"—as for the rest, that they should consult the Board of Works. Thus every possible delay and official difficulty was interposed against the efforts of local bodies—Government was to do all. These things, together with the new measure for an increase in the police force (who were their main administrative agents throughout the country), led many persons to the conclusion that the enemy had resolved to avail themselves of the famine in order to increase governmental supervision and espionage; so that every man, woman, and child in Ireland, with all their goings out and comings in, might be thoroughly known and registered—that when the mass of the people began to starve, their sole resource might be the police-barracks—that Government might be all in all;. omnipotent to give food or to withhold it, to relieve or to starve, according to their own ideas of policy and of good behavior in the people.

It is needless to point out that Government patronage also was much extended by this system; and by the middle of the next year, 1847, there were 10,000 men salaried out of the Parliamentary loans and grants for relief of the poor —as Commissioners, Inspectors, Clerks, and so forth; and some of them with salaries equal to an American Secretary of State. So many of the middle classes had been dragged down almost to insolvency by the ruin of the country, that they began to be eager for the smaller places as Clerks and Inspectors. For those 10,000 offices, then, it was estimated there were 100,000 applicants and canvassers;—so much clear gain from "Repeal."

The Repeal Association continued its regular meetings, and never ceased to represent that the true remedies for Irish Famine were Tenant-Right—the stoppage of export— and Repeal of the Union;—and as those were really the true and only remedies, it was clear they were the only expedients which an English Parliament would *not* try. The Repeal Members gained a kind of Parliamentary victory, however, this Spring:—they caused the defeat of the Coercion Bill, with the aid of the Whigs. Sir Robert Peel had very cunningly, as he thought, made this Bill precede the Corn Law Repeal Bill; and as the English Public was all now most eager for the cheapening of bread, he believed that all parties would make haste to pass his favorite measure first. The Irish Members went to London, and knowing they could not influence legislation otherwise, organized a sort of mere mechanical resistance against the Coercion Bill: that is, they opposed first reading, second reading, third reading, opposed its being referred to Committee, moved endless amendments, made endless speeches, and insisted upon dividing the House on every clause. In vain it was represented to them that this was only delaying the Corn Law Repeal, which would " cheapen bread." O'Brien replied that it would only cheapen bread to Englishmen, and enable them to devour more and more of the Irish bread and give less for it. In vain Ministers told them they were stopping public business: they answered that English business was no business of theirs. In vain their courtesy was invoked. They could not afford to be courteous in such a case; and their sole errand in London was to resist an atrocious and torturing tyranny threatened against their poor countrymen.

Just before this famous debate there had been very extensive clearing of tenantry in Connaught; and, in particular one case, in which a Mrs. Gerrard had, with the aid of the troops and police, destroyed a whole village, and thrown out two hundred and seventy persons on the high road. The *Nation* thus improved the circumstance with reference to the "Coercion Bill":—

"Some Irish Members, for instance, may point to the two hundred and seventy persons thrown out of house and home the other day in Galway, and in due form of law (for it was all perfectly legal,) turned adrift in their desperation upon the wide world—and may ask the Minister, if any of these two hundred and seventy commit a robbery on the highway—if any of them murder the bailiff, who (in exercise of his duty) flung out their naked children to perish in the winter's sleet—if any of them, maddened by wolfish famine, break into a dwelling-house, and forcibly take food to keep body and soul together, or arms for vengeance—what will you do? How will you treat that district? Will you indeed *proclaim* it? Will you mulct the house-holders (not yet ejected) in a heavy fine to compound for the crimes of those miserable outcasts, to afford food and shelter to whom they wrong their own children in this hard season? Besides sharing with those wretches his last potato, is the poor cottier to be told that he is to *pay* for policemen to watch them day and night—that he is to make atonement in money (though his spade and poor bedding should be auctioned to make it up) for any outrage that may be done in the neighborhood?—but that these GERRARDS are not to pay one farthing for all this—for, perhaps, their property is encumbered, and, it may be, they find it hard enough to pay their interest, and keep up such establishments in town and country as befit their rank? And will you, indeed, issue your commands that those houseless and famishing two hundred and seventy—after their roof-trees are torn down, and the ploughshare is run through the foundations of their miserable hovels —are to be *at home* from sunset to sunrise?—that if found straying, the gaols and the penal colonies are ready for their reception?"

It was precisely with a view to meet such cases that the Coercion Bill had been devised; and, were not our representatives well justified in resisting such a measure, courteously or otherwise? The English Whigs, and, at length, the indignant Protectionists, too, joined the Repealers in this resistance—not to spare Ireland, but to defeat Sir Robert Peel, and get into his place. And they did defeat Sir Robert Peel, and get into his place. Whereupon, it was not long before Lord John Russell and his Whigs devised a new and more murderous Coercion Bill for Ireland themselves.

The *Nation* still remained the most widely circulated and influential journal of the Irish Nationalists, and represented the extreme and most anti-English party. The "Young Ireland party" still stood, and was well known to the great enemy as its most unrelenting opponent. MacNevin and Doheny frequently contributed to the *Nation;* and the writings of Thomas Devin Reilly, in its columns, were greatly admired. Mr. Dillon went for the Winter to Madeira; but our fraternity began now to number among its members Thomas Francis Meagher and Richard O'Gorman, of whom (as they are well known in America,) I need not now speak. The English enemy heartily abhorred us, and in the Spring of this year aimed a blow at the *Nation* Office. It was a new State Prosecution. Mr. Duffy was indicted for an article of mine. I undertook to conduct his defence; and retained old Robert Holmes to make the speech to the jury; knowing that Holmes would repeat, improve, and redouble all the "sedition" which we were desirous to inculcate. He did so; and startled the Court and the Public by a stern and passionate denunciation of the whole course of British Government in Ireland. What was more wonderful, he dared this with safety to his client. The thing came too quick after the "slipped lists" and packed jury in O'Connell's case (which Lord Denman had said turned trial by jury in Ireland into a "fraud, a delusion, and a snare,") and they thought they could not repeat that game *so soon*. The Crown left on the panel of twenty-four *three* Repealers. Those three attended in court, were sworn on the jury, and refused to convict. Chief-Justice Blackburne kept them confined without food or drink for twenty-six hours, when they were discharged. This was the first State Trial in Irish history, so far as I know, in which the Crown had failed to pack the jury strictly; and the first in which a conviction was missed. It gave the *Nation*, probably, more popularity and larger influence amongst the people than it would otherwise have enjoyed; and thereafter it proceeded very diligently and inveterately, exposing, from week to week, the plots of the English enemy.*

I have mentioned that the Coercion Bill was defeated; this was on May 25th. Sir Robert Peel immediately resigned office, and left the responsibility of dealing with the Irish affair to the Whigs. He knew he might do so safely. His system was inaugurated. His two great ideas—Free Trade and Police Administration—were fully recognized by the Whigs; and Lord John Russell was even a blind bigot about what he imagined to be Political Economy. Sir Robert might retire to Tamworth, and "plant his cabbages."

* The prosecuted article was one in reply to a London Ministerial journal, which, in advocating Coercion for Ireland, had pointed out that the railroads then in progress of construction, would soon bring every part of the island within six hours of the garrison of Dublin. The *Nation* showed how effectually railroads could be made impassable to troops—how easily troops could be destroyed upon them, and how useful the iron of them would be in making pikes.

CHAPTER XIII.

"RELIEF OF FAMINE"—IMPORTATIONS OF GRAIN—IMPRISONMENT OF O'BRIEN—DESTRUCTION OF THE REPEAL ASSOCIATION—THE LABOR-RATE ACT—MORE POOR LAW—EXTERMINATION—RECRUITING.

SIR ROBERT PEEL and his Ministry resigned on the 29th of June, 1846; Lord John Russell formed a new Ministry, and went on without dissolving Parliament.

I must take care that I do no injustice to Sir Robert Peel, nor suppress any of his acts which might look like an attempt to stay the famine. It is true, then, that he advised and procured an appropriation of £100,000 by two several acts, to be laid out in giving employment in Ireland; but all this employment was to be given under the order and control of English officials: further, the professions of "Government,"—that *they* had taken all needful measures to guard against famine—had made people rely upon them for everything, and thus turned the minds of thousands upon thousands from work of their own, which they might have attempted if left to themselves. This sort of government spoon-feeding is highly demoralizing; and for *one* who derived any relief from it, one thousand neglected their own industry in the pursuit of it. In truth, the amount of relief offered by these grants was infinitesimally small, when you consider the magnitude of the calamity,* and had no other effect than to unsettle the minds of the peasantry, and make them more careless about holding on to their farms.

It is true, also, that the government did, to a certain small extent, speculate in Indian corn for Irish use, and did send a good many cargoes of it to Ireland, and form depots of it at several points; but as to this also, their mysterious

---

* Double the sum (£200,000) was by the same Parliament authorized to be borrowed on the security of the Crown revenue, to be laid out on Battersea Park, a suburban retreat for Londoners:—yet this was never spoken of as *alms* given by Ireland to England.

intimations had led all the world to believe they would provide very large quantities; whereas, in fact, the quantity imported by them was inadequate to supply the loss of the grain *exported* from any one county; and a government ship sailing into any harbor with Indian corn was sure to meet half a dozen sailing out with Irish wheat and cattle. The effect of this, therefore, was only to blind the people to the fact, that England was exacting her tribute as usual, famine or no famine. The effect of both combined was to engender a dependent and pauper spirit, and to free England from all anxiety about " Repeal." A landless, hungry *pauper* cannot afford to think of the honor of his country, and cares nothing about a national flag.

I may here mention that it was the English Government that invented *paupers* in Ireland, when they imposed on us their Poor Law. Before that time there had been plenty of poor men in Ireland, but "no able-bodied paupers." It is one of the very few English institutions in which they have made us full participants.

How powerfully the whole of this system and procedure contributed to accomplish the great end of uprooting the people from the soil, can be readily understood. The exhibition and profession of public "relief" for the destitute stifled compunction in the landlords; and agents, bailiffs, and police swept whole districts with the besom of destruction.

Another act had been done by Sir Robert Peel's Ministry, just before retiring, with a view of breaking up the Repeal Association. This was the imprisonment of Mr. Smith O'Brien several weeks in the cellar of the House of Commons. It grievously irritated the enemy that O'Connell, O'Brien, and the Repeal members still continued to absent themselves from Parliament. The House of Commons had tried various methods of persuading or coercing them to London. Mr. Hume had written them a friendly letter, imploring them to come over to their legislative duties, and *he* would aid them in obtaining justice for Ireland. A "call of the House" was proposed; but they declared beforehand, that if there were a call of the House they would not obey it, and the Sergeant-at-Arms must come to Ireland for them;—he would find them in Conciliation Hall. They were nominated on English Railroad

Committees, and the proper officer had intimated to them the fact. They replied that they were attending to more important business. Now, when they went over to oppose the Coercion Bill, it was understood that this was to be their sole errand, and they were not to engage themselves in the ordinary details of legislation. But they were not long in London before the opportunity was seized to place their names on Railway Committees. O'Connell and his son both obeyed the call. O'Brien, of course, refused, and was imprisoned in the cellar for "contempt." London and all England were highly pleased and entertained: *Punch* was brilliant upon the great "Brian Boru" in a cellar; and Mr. O'Brien was usually afterwards termed,—with that fine sarcasm so characteristic of English genius,—the "martyr of the cellar."

Instantly arose dissension in the Repeal Association. To approve and fully sustain O'Brien's action in refusing to serve, would be to censure O'Connell for serving. In that body a sort of unsatisfactory compromise was made; but the "Eighty-Two Club," where the *young* party was stronger, voted a warm Address of full approval to O'Brien (who was a member of the Club), and despatched several members to present it to him in his dungeon. I had the honor to be one of that deputation, and the "cellar" was the only part of the Houses of Parliament I ever visited.

The divisions in O'Connell's Association were soon brought to a crisis when the Whigs came in. O'Connell instantly gave up all agitation of the Repeal question, and took measures to separate himself from those "juvenile members" who, as Lord John Russell had asserted, were plotting not only to Repeal the Union, but to sever the connection with England ("the golden link of the crown")—and that by *physical force*. All this famous controversy seems to me now of marvellously small moment; but I find a very concise narrative of it in Mr. O'Brien's words, which will be enough:—

"Negotiations were opened between Mr. O'Connell and the Whigs at Chesham-place. 'Young Ireland' protested in the strongest terms against an alliance with the Whigs. Mr. O'Connell took offence at the language used by Mr. Meagher and others. When I arrived in Dublin, after the resignation of Sir Robert Peel, I learnt that he contemplated a rupture with the writers of the *Nation*. Before I went to the county of Clare, I communicated, through Mr.

Ray, a special message to Mr. O'Connell, who was then absent from Dublin, to the effect, that though I was most anxious to preserve a neutral position, I could not silently acquiesce in any attempt to expel the *Nation* or its party from the Association. Next came the Dungarvan election and the new 'moral force' resolutions. I felt it my duty to protest against both at the Kilrush dinner. Upon my return to Dublin, I found a public letter from Mr. O'Connell, formally denouncing the *Nation;* and no alternative was left me but to declare, that, if that letter were acted upon, I could not co-operate any longer with the Repeal Association. The celebrated two-day debate then took place. Mr. J. O'Connell opened an attack upon the *Nation* and upon its adherents. Mr. Mitchel and Mr. Meagher defended themselves in language which, it seemed to me, did not transgress the bounds of decorum or of legal safety. Mr. John O'Connell interrupted Mr. Meagher in his speech, and declared that he could not allow him to proceed with the line of argument necessary to sustain the principles which had been arraigned. I protested against this interruption. Mr. J. O'Connell then gave us to understand that unless Mr. Meagher desisted, he must leave the hall. I could not acquiesce in this attempt to stifle a fair discussion, and sooner than witness the departure of Mr. J. O'Connell from an association founded by his father, I preferred to leave the assembly."

When O'Brien left the Assembly, he was accompanied by his friends; and there was an end of the Repeal Association, save as a machinery of securing offices for O'Connell's dependants. Even for that purpose it was not efficient; because it had too clearly become impotent and hollow; there was no danger in it; and Ministers would not buy a patriot in that market unless at a very low figure.

In the meantime, the famine and the fever raged: many landlords regained possession without so much as an ejectment, because the tenants died of hunger; and the county Coroners, before the end of this year, were beginning to strike work—they were so often called to sit upon famine-slain corpses. The verdict,—" Death by Starvation,"—became so familiar that the county newspapers sometimes omitted to record it; and travellers were often appalled when they came upon some lonely village by the western coast, with the people all skeletons upon their own hearths. Irish landlords are not all monsters of cruelty. Thousands of them, indeed, kept far away from the scene, collected their rents through agents and bailiffs, and spent them in England or in Paris. But the resident landlords and their families did, in many cases, devote themselves to the task of saving their poor people alive. Many remitted their rents, or half their rents; and ladies kept their servants busy and their kitchens smoking with continual preparation of food for the poor. Local Committees soon purchased all the corn in the government depots (at market price, however,) and distributed it gratuitously. Clergymen, both Protestant and Catholic, I am glad to testify, generally did their duty; except those absentee clergymen, bishops, and wealthy rectors, who usually reside in England, their services being not needed in the places from whence they draw their wealth. But many a poor rector and his curate shared their crust with their suffering neighbors; and priests, after going round all day administering Extreme Unction to whole villages at once, all dying of mere starvation, often themselves went supperless to bed.

The Western and South-western coast, from Derry round to Cork, is surely the most varied and beautiful coast in all the world. Great harbors, backed by noble ranges of mountains, open all around the Western coast of Munster, till you come to the Shannon's mouth: there is a fine navigable river opening up the most bounteously fertile land in the island—Limerick and Tipperary. North of the Shannon, huge cliff-walls, rising eight hundred feet sheer out of deep water, broken by chasms and pierced by sea-caves, " with high embowed roof," like the choir of a cathedral; then the Bay of Galway, once thronged with Spanish and Irish ships, carrying wine and gold,—but now, it appears, dangerous and fatal (*statio mala fide carinis*) to steam-ships bound for America. Westward from Galway, and round the circuit of Connaught, the scene becomes savage and wild, with innumerable rocky islands,—deep inlets, narrow and gloomy, like Norwegian *fiords*,—and grim, steep mountains hanging over them. But the most desolate region of all is found in Ulster. As you travel northwards from Killybegs, by way of Ardara, Glenties, and Dunglow, you pass for nearly forty miles through the dreariest region of moor and mountain that is to be found within the five ends of Ireland;—wide tracts of quaking bog, interspersed with countless dismal lakes, intersected by rocky ridges, and traversed by mountain rivers roaring in tawny foam to the sea. The two or three wretched villages that lie along this road give to a traveller an impression of even more dreariness and desolation than the intervening country: a cluster of ragged-looking, windowless hovels, whose inhabitants seem to have gathered themselves from the wastes, and huddled together to keep some life and heat in them; a few patches of oats and potatoes surrounding the huts, and looking such a miserable provision for human beings against hunger in the midst of those great brown moors; hardly a slated building to be seen, save one or two constabulary and revenue police-stations, and a court-house in Glenties, for dealing out "justice," and close by that a certain new building—the grandest by far that those Rosses people ever saw—rearing its accursed gables and pinnacles of Tudor barbarism, and staring boldly with its detestable mullioned windows, as if to mock those wretches who still cling to liberty and mud cabins—seeming to them, in their perennial half-starvation, like a Temple erected to the Fates, or like the fortress of Giant Despair, whereinto he draws them one by one, and devours them there:—the Poorhouse.

This is the estate of a certain Marquis of Conyngham: and for him those desolate people, while health lasts, and they may still keep body and soul together, outside the Poorhouse, are for ever employed in making up a *subsidy*, called rent; which that district sends half-yearly to be consumed in England, or wherever else it may please their noble proprietor to devour their hearts' blood and the marrow of their bones.

So it is; and so it was, even before the Famine, with almost the whole of that coast region. The landlords were all absentees. All the grain and cattle the people could raise were never enough to make up the rent; it all went away, of course; it was all consumed in England; but Ireland received in exchange stamped rent receipts. Of course there were no improvements,—because *they* would have only raised the rent; and in ordinary years many thousands of those poor people lived mainly on sea-weed some months of every year. But this was trespass and robbery; for the sea-weed belonged to the lord of the manor, who frequently made examples of the depredators.*

Can the American mind picture a race of white men reduced to this condition? White men! Yes, of the highest and purest blood and breed of men. The very region I have described was once—before British civilization overtook us

---

* I have defended poor devils on charges of trespass by gathering sea-weed below high-water mark, and remember one case in which a number of farmers near the sea were indicted *for robbery*, on the charge of taking limestone from a rock uncovered at low-water only—to burn it, for spreading on their fields.

—the abode of the strongest and richest clans in Ireland; the Scotic MacCauras; the French Clan-Gerralt, (or Geraldin, or Fitzgerald)—the Norman MacWilliams (or De Burgo, or Burke)—the princely and munificent O'Briens and O'Donnells, founders of many monasteries, chiefs of glittering hosts, generous patrons of Ollamh, Bard, and Brehon; sea-roving Macnamaras and O'Malleys, whose ships brought from Spain wine and horses,—from England fair-haired, white-armed Saxon slaves, "tall, handsome women," as the chroniclers call them, fit to weave wool or embroider mantles in the house of a king.* After a struggle of six or seven centuries, after many bloody wars and sweeping confiscations, English "civilization" prevailed,—and had brought the clans to the condition I have related. The ultimate idea of English civilization being that "the sole *nexus* between man and man is cash payment,"—and the "Union" having finally determined the course and current of that payment, out of Ireland into England,—it had come to pass that the chiefs were exchanged for landlords, and the clansmen had sunk into able-bodied paupers.

The details of this frightful famine, as it ravaged those Western districts, I need not narrate;—they are sufficiently known. It is enough to say that in this year, 1846, not less than 300,000 perished, either of mere hunger, or of typhus-fever caused by hunger. But as it has ever since been a main object of the British Government to conceal the amount of the carnage (which, indeed, they ought to do if they can,) I find that the Census Commissioners, in their Report for 1851, admit only 2,041 "registered" deaths by famine alone, in 1846.

A Whig Ministry, however, was now in power; and the people were led to expect great efforts on the part of government to stay the progress of ruin. And I am bound to say that O'Connell used all his power to make the people depend upon that expectation. In August it became manifest that the potato-crop of '46 was also a total failure; but the products otherwise were most abundant,—much more than sufficient to feed all the people. Again, therefore, it became

---

* The monasteries still stand; the golden collars of chiefs are still turned up by the plough; the records may still be read,—the most authentic historic monuments in Western Europe. Yet it is customary with the English to deny, or laugh at the ancient civilization of Ireland! They are bound in policy, perhaps, to do so; but any literary man on the Continent of Europe would be ashamed to call it in question.

the urgent business of British policy to promise large "Relief," so as to ensure that the splendid harvest should be allowed peacefully to be shipped to England as before; and the first important measure of the Whigs was to propose a renewal of the *Disarming Act*, and a further increase in the Police-force. Apparently the outcry raised against this had the effect of shaming Ministers, for they suddenly dropped the Bill for this time. But the Famine could not be correctly administered without a Coercion Bill of some sort; so the next year they devised a machinery of this kind, the most stringent and destructive that had yet been prescribed for Ireland. In the meantime, for "Relief" of the Famine, —they brought forward their famous *Labor Rate Act*.

This was, in few words, an additional poor rate, payable by the same persons liable to the other poor rates; the proceeds to be applied to the execution of such public works as *the government* might choose; the control and superintendence to be entrusted to *government officers*. Money was to be in the meantime advanced from the Treasury, in order to set the people immediately to work; and that advance was to be repaid in ten years by means of the increased rate. There was to be an *appearance* of local control, inasmuch as barony sessions of landlords and justices were to have power to meet, (under the Lord Lieutenant's order,) and suggest any works they might think needful, provided they were strictly unproductive works; but the control of all was to be in the government alone.

Now, the class which suffered most from the potato-blight consisted of those small farmers who were barely able, in ordinary years, to keep themselves above starvation after paying their rents. These people, by the Labor-rate Act, had an additional tax laid on them; and not being able to pay it, could but quit their holdings, sink to the class of able-bodied paupers, and enrol themselves in a gang of government *navvys*,—thus throwing themselves for support upon those who still strove to maintain themselves by their own labor on their own land.

In addition to the proceeds of the new Poor Rate, Parliament appropriated a further sum of £50,000 to be applied in giving work in some absolutely pauper districts, where there was no hope of ever raising rates to repay it. £50,000 was just the sum which was that same year voted out of the

English and Irish revenue, to improve the buildings of the British Museum.

So there was to be *more* Poor Law, more Commissioners, (this time under the title of Additional Public Works Commissioners); innumerable officials in the Public Works, Commissariat and Constabulary departments; and no end of stationery and red tape;—*all* to be paid out of the rates. On the whole, it was hoped that provision was made for stopping the "Irish howl" this one season.

You have already been told that Irishmen of all classes had almost universally condemned the Poor Law at first; so, as they did not like Poor Law, they were to have *more* Poor Law. Society in Ireland was to be reconstructed on the basis of Poor Rates, and a broad foundation of able-bodied pauperism. It did not occur to the English—and it never will occur to them—that the way to stop Irish destitution is to Repeal the Union, so that Irishmen might make their own laws, use their own resources, regulate their own industry. It was in vain, however, that anybody in Ireland remonstrated. In vain that such journals as were of the popular party condemned the whole scheme. The *Nation* of that date treats it thus:—

"Unproductive work to be executed with borrowed money—a ten years' mortgage of a new tax, to pay for cutting down hills and filling them up again—a direct impost upon land proprietors in the most offensive form, to feed all the rest of the population, impoverishing the rich without benefiting the poor—not creating, not developing, but merely transferring, and in the transfer wasting the means of all;—perhaps human ingenuity, sharpened by intensest malignity, could contrive no more deadly and unerring method of arraying class against class in diabolical hatred, making them look on one another with wolfish eyes as if to prepare the way for '*aristocrates à la lanterne ;*'—killing individual enterprise,—discouraging private improvement,—dragging down employers and employed, proprietors, farmers, mechanics, and cottiers, to one common and irretrievable ruin."

Whether this view was justified by the result, will be seen hereafter

It may seem astonishing that the gentry of Ireland did not rouse themselves at this frightful prospect, and universally demand the Repeal of the Union. They were the same class, sons of the same men, who had, in 1782, wrested the independence of Ireland from an English Government, and enjoyed the fruits of that independence in honor, wealth, and prosperity, for eighteen years. Why not now? It is because, in 1782, the Catholics of Ireland counted as nothing: now they are numerous, enfranchised, exasperated; and the Irish landlords dare not trust themselves in Ireland without British support. They looked on tamely, therefore, and saw this deliberate scheme for the pauperization of a nation. They knew it would injure themselves; but they took the injury, took insult along with it, and submitted to be reproached for begging *alms*, when they demanded restitution of a part of their own means.

Over the whole island, for the next few months, was a scene of confused and wasteful attempts at relief: bewildered barony sessions striving to understand the voluminous directions, schedules, and specifications under which alone they could vote their own money to relieve the poor at their own doors; but generally making mistakes,—for the unassisted human faculties never could comprehend those ten thousand books and fourteen tons of paper; insolent Commissioners and Inspectors, and clerks snubbing them at every turn, and ordering them to study the documents: efforts on the part of the proprietors to expend some of the rates at least on useful works, reclaiming land or the like; which efforts were always met with flat refusal and a lecture on political economy; (for political economy, it seems, declared that the works must be strictly useless,—as cutting down a road where there was no hill, or building a bridge where there was no water,—until many good roads became impassable on account of pits and trenches):—plenty of jobbing and peculation all this while; and the laborers, having the example of a great public fraud before their eyes, themselves defrauding their fraudulent employers,—quitting agricultural pursuits and crowding to the public works, where they pretended to be cutting down hills and filling up hollows, and with tongue in cheek received half wages for doing nothing. So the labor was wasted; the laborers were demoralized; and the *next* year's famine was ensured.

Now began to be a rage for extermination beyond any former time; and many thousands of the peasants, who could still scrape up the means, fled to the sea, as if pursued by wild beasts, and betook themselves to America. The British army also received numberless recruits this year (for it is sound English policy to keep our people so low that a shilling a day would tempt them to fight for the devil, not to say the Queen): and insane mothers began to eat their young children, who died of famine before them. And still fleets of ships were sailing with every tide, carrying Irish cattle and corn to England. There was also a large importation of grain from England into Ireland, and the speculators and ship-owners had a good time. Much of the grain thus brought to Ireland had been previously exported *from* Ireland, and came back—laden with merchants' profits and double freights and insurance—to the helpless people who had sowed and reaped it. This is what Commerce and Free Trade did for Ireland in those days.

Two facts, however, are essential to be borne in mind —*first*, that the net result of all this importation, exportation, and re-importation, (though many a ship-load was carried four times across the Irish Sea, as prices "invited" it,) was, that England finally received our harvests to the same amount as before: and, *second*, that she gave Ireland—under free-trade in corn—less for it than ever. In other words, it took more of the Irish produce to buy a piece of cloth from a Leeds manufacturer, or to buy a rent-receipt from an absentee proprietor. They could do without much of the cloth; but, as for the rent-receipts, these they must absolutely buy; for the bailiff, with his police, was usually at the door, even before the fields were reaped; and he, and the Poor-rate Collector, and the Additional Poor-rate Collector, and the County-cess Collector, and the Process-server, with Decrees, were all to be paid out of the first proceeds. If it took the farmer's whole crop to pay them, which it usually did, he had, at least, a pocketful of receipts, and might see lying in the next harbor the very ship that was to carry his entire harvest and his last cow to England.

What wonder that so many farmers gave up the effort in despair, and sunk to paupers? Many Celts were cleared off this year, and the campaign was, so far, successful.

CHAPTER XIV.

LABOR-RATE ACT—DIGGING HOLES—ENGLAND BEGS FOR US—OUT-DOOR RELIEF—"FAST AND HUMILIATION"—QUARTER-ACRE CLAUSE—THE CALCULATIONS OF "POLITICAL CIRCLES"—TWO MILLIONS OF CELTIC CORPSES—AMERICA BAFFLED—PARISH COFFINS—REPUDIATION OF ALMS BY THE "NATION."

The Winter of 1846-7, and succeeding Spring, were employed in a series of utterly unavailing attempts to use the "Labor-rate Act," so as to afford some sensible relief to the famishing people. Sessions were held, as provided by the Act, and the landed proprietors liberally imposed rates to repay such government advances as they thought needful: but the unintelligible directions constantly interrupted them, and, in the meantime, the peasantry, in the wild, blind hope of public relief, were abandoning their farms and letting the land lie idle. For this I shall give a few authorities out of the mouth of the Conservative or British party. From Limerick we learn, through the Dublin *Evening Mail*:—

"There is not a laborer employed in the county, except on public works; and there is every prospect of the lands remaining untilled and unsown for the next year."

In Cork, writes the *Cork Constitution*:—

"The good intentions of the government are frustrated by the worst regulations—regulations which, diverting labor from its legitimate channels, left the fields without hands to prepare them for the harvest."

At a Presentment Session in Shanagolden, after a hopeless discussion as to what possible meaning could be latent in the Castle "instructions," and "supplemental instructions," the Knight of Glin, a landlord of those parts, said that, "While on the subject of mistakes," he might as well mention—

"On the Glin road some people are filling up the original cutting of a hill with the stuff they had taken out of it. That's another slice out of our £450."

Which he, poor knight, and the other proprietors of that barony had *to pay*. For you must bear in mind that all the advances under this act were to be strictly *loans*, repayable by the rates, secured by the whole value of the land—and at higher interest than the government borrowed the money so advanced.

The innocent Knight of Glin ascribed the perversions of labor to "mistake." But there was no mistake at all! Digging holes and filling them up again was precisely the kind of work prescribed in such case by the principles of political economy; and then there were innumerable regulations to be attended to before even this kind of work could be given. The Board of Works would have the roads torn up with such tools as they approved of, and none other—that is, with picks and short shovels: and picks and short shovels were manufactured in England, and sent over by ship loads for that purpose, to the great profit of the hardware merchants in Birmingham. Often there was no adequate supply of these on the spot: then the work was to be *task-work* ; and the poor people, delving macadamized roads with spades and turf-cutters, could not earn as much as would keep them alive, though, luckily, they were thereby disabled from destroying so much good road.

That all interests in the country were swiftly rushing to ruin was apparent to all. A committee of lords and gentlemen was formed, called a "Reproductive Committee," to urge upon the government, that, if the country was to tax itself to supply public work, the labor ought, in some cases, at least, to be employed upon tasks that might be of use. This movement was so far successful that it elicited a Letter from the Castle, authorizing such application, but with supplemental instructions so intricate and occult that this also was fruitless.

And the people perished more rapidly than ever. The famine of '47 was far more terrible and universal than that of the previous year. The Whig Government, bound by political economy, absolutely refused to interfere with market-prices, and the merchants and speculators were never so busy on both sides of the Channel. In this year it was that the Irish Famine began to be a world's wonder; and men's hearts were moved in the uttermost ends of the earth by the recital of its horrors. The London *Illustrated News* began to be adorned with engravings of tottering, windowless hovels, in Skibbereen and elsewhere, with naked wretches dying on a truss of wet straw; and the constant language of English Ministers and Members in Parliament created the impression abroad that Ireland was in need of *alms*, and nothing but alms: whereas Irishmen themselves uniformly protested that what they required was Repeal of the Union, so that the English might cease to devour their substance.

It may be interesting to you to know how the English people were faring all this while; and whether "that portion of the United Kingdom," as it is called, suffered much by the famine in Ireland and in Europe. Authentic *data* upon this point are to be found in the financial statement of Sir Charles Wood, Chancellor of the Exchequer, in February, 1847. In that statement he declares—and he tells it, he says, with great satisfaction—that "the English people and working classes" are steadily growing more comfortable, nay, more luxurious in their style of living. He goes into particulars even to show how rapidly a taste for good things spreads amongst English laborers, and bids his hearers "recollect that consumption could not be accounted for by attributing it to the higher and wealthier classes, but must have arisen from the consumption of the large body of the people and the working classes."

And what do you think constituted the regimen of the "body of the people and working classes" in that part of the world? And in what proportion had its consumption increased? Why, in the matter of *coffee*, they had used nearly seven million pounds of it more than they did in 1843; of *butter* and *cheese* they devoured double as much within the year as they had done three years before within the same period. "I will next," says the Chancellor of the Exchequer, "take *currants*," (for currants are one of the necessaries of life to an English laborer, who must have his pudding on Sunday at least;) and we find that the quantity of currants used by the "body of the people and working classes" had increased in three years from 254,000 cwt. to 359,000 cwt., by the year. Omitting other things, we come to the Chancellor's statement, that since 1843 the consumption of *tea* had increased by 5,400,000 lbs. It is unnecessary to say they had as much beef and bacon as they could eat, and bread *à discretion;*—and as for beer!—

So they live in merry England.

This statement was read by Sir Charles Wood at the end of a long speech, in which he announced the necessity of raising an additional loan to keep life in some of the surviving Irish; and he read it expressly in order " to dispel some portion of the gloom which had been cast over the minds of members," by being told that a portion of the surplus revenue must go to pay interest on a slight addition to the national debt. And the gloom *was* dispelled; and honorable members comforted themselves with the reflection that, whatever be the nominal debt of the country, after all, a man of the working classes can ask no more than a good dinner every day, and a pudding on Sundays.

One would not grudge the English laborer his dinner, nor his tea; and I refer to his excellent table only to remark that during those same three years, exactly as fast as the English people and working classes advanced to luxury, the Irish people and working classes sank to starvation: and further, that the Irish people were still sowing and reaping what they of the sister island so contentedly devoured, to the value of at least £17,000,000 sterling.

As an English farmer, artizan, or laborer began to insist on tea in the morning as well as in the evening, an Irish farmer, artizan or laborer, found it necessary to live on one meal a day. For every Englishman who added to his domestic expenditure by a pudding thrice a week, an Irishman had to retrench *his* to cabbage-leaves and turnip-tops. As dyspepsia creeps into England, dysentery ravages Ireland; " and the exact correlative of a Sunday dinner in England is a coroner's inquest in Ireland."

Ireland, however, was to have " alms." The English would not see their useful drudges perish at their very door for want of a trifle of alms. So the Ministry announced, in this month of February, a new loan of ten millions, to be used from time to time for relief of Irish Famine—the half of the advances to be repaid by rates—the other half to be a grant from the Treasury to feed able-bodied paupers for doing useless work or no work at all. As to this latter half of the ten millions, English newspapers and members of Parliament said that it was so much English money granted to Ireland. This, of course, was a falsehood. It

222   THE LAST CONQUEST

was a loan raised by the Imperial Treasury, on a mortgage of the taxation of the three kingdoms: the principal of it, like the rest of the "National debt;" was not intended to be ever repaid, and never can be; and as for the interest, Ireland would have to pay her proportion of it, as a matter of course.

This last Act was the *third* of the "Relief measures" contrived by the British Parliament, and the most destructive of all. It was to be put in operation as a system of out-door relief; and the various local boards of Poor Law Guardians, if they could only understand the documents, were to have some apparent part in its administration; but all, as usual, under the absolute control of the Poor Law Commissioners, and of a new Board, namely: Sir John Burgoyne, an Engineer; Sir Randolph Routh, Commissary-General; Mr. Twisleton, a Poor Law Commissioner; two Colonels, called Jones and M'Gregor, Police-Inspectors; and Mr. Redington, Under-Secretary.

In the administration of this system there were to be many thousands of officials, great and small. The largest salaries were for Englishmen; but the smaller were held up as an object of ambition to Irishmen; and it is very humiliating to remember what eager and greedy multitudes were always canvassing and petitioning for these.

In March, Lord John Russell announced in Parliament that, in view of the judgments afflicting her dominions, "Her Majesty had been graciously pleased to appoint a day of national fast and humiliation!" It needed no appointment of a day to make the Irish fast; and as for the English, the reader may wonder what *they* should fast for. But all this was to make an impression abroad.

In the new Act for the Out-door Relief, there was one significant clause. It was that if any farmer who held land should be forced to apply for aid under this Act, for himself and his family, he should not have it until he had first given up all his land to the landlord—except one quarter of an acre. It was called the Quarter-acre Clause, and was found the most efficient and the cheapest of all the Ejectment Acts. Farms were thereafter daily given up without the formality of a notice to quit, or summons before Quarter Sessions.

On the 6th of March, there were 730,000 *heads* of families on the public works. Provision was made by the last-recited

Act for dismissing these in batches. On the 10th of April, the number was reduced to 500,723. Afterwards batches of a hundred thousand or so were in like manner dismissed. Most of these had now neither house nor home; and their only resource was in the Out-door Relief. For this they were ineligible if they held but one rood of land. Under the new law it was able-bodied idlers only who were to be fed: to attempt to till even a rood of ground was death.

Steadily, but surely, the "Government" people were working out their calculation; and the product anticipated by "political circles" was likely to come out about September, in round numbers—*two millions of Irish corpses.*

That "Government" had at length got into its own hands all the means and materials for working this problem, is now plain. There was no longer any danger of the elements of the account being disturbed by external interference of any kind. At one time, indeed, there were odds against the Government sum coming out right; for charitable people in England and in America, indignant at the thought of a nation perishing of political economy, did contribute generously, and did full surely believe, good, easy men, that every pound they subscribed would give Irish famine twenty shillings worth of bread: they thought so, and poured in their contributions, and their prayers and blessings with them. In vain! "Government" and political economy got hold of the contributions (of prayers and blessings neither Government nor political economy takes any account), and disposed of them in such fashion as to prevent their deranging the calculations of political circles. For example: the vast supplies of food purchased by the "British Relief Association," with the money of charitable Christians in England, were everywhere locked up in Government stores. Government, it seems, contrived to influence or control the managers of that fund; and thus, there were thousands of tons of food rotting within the stores of Haulbowline, at Cork Harbor; and tens of thousands rotting without. For the market must be followed, not led (to the prejudice of our Liverpool merchants)!—private speculation must not be disappointed, nor the calculations of political circles falsified!

All the nations of the earth might be defied to feed or relieve Ireland, beset by such a Government as this. Suppose America tries another plan;—the ship "Jamestown" sails into Cork harbor, and discharges a large cargo, which actually begins to come into consumption; when, lo! Free Trade—another familiar demon of Government—Free Trade, that carried off our own golden harvests of the year before—comes in, freights another ship, and carries off from Cork to Liverpool a cargo *against* the American cargo. For the private speculators must be compensated; the markets must not be *led;* if these Americans will not give England their corn to lock up, why, she defeats them by "the natural laws of trade!" So many Briarean hands has Government;—so surely do official persons, understanding book-keeping by double entry, work their account.

Private charity, one might think, in a country like Ireland, would put out the calculating Government sadly; but that, too, was brought in great measure under control. The "Temporary Relief Act," *talking* of eight millions of money (*to be used if needed*),—distributing, like Cumæan Sybil, its mystic leaves by the myriad and the million,—setting charitable people everywhere to con its pamphlets, and compare clause with clause,—putting everybody in terror of its rates, and in horror of its inspectors,—was likely to pass the Summer bravely. It would begin to be partly understood about August; would expire in September:—and in September the "persons connected with Government" expected their round two millions of carcasses.

A further piece of the machinery, all working to the same great end, was the "Vagrancy Act," for the punishment of vagrants,—that is, of about four millions of the inhabitants,—by hard labor, "for any time not exceeding one month."

Many poor people were escaping to England, as deck-passengers on board the numerous steamers, hoping to earn their living by labor there; but "Government" took alarm about typhus fever—a disease not intended for England. Orders in Council were suddenly issued, subjecting all vessels having *deck-passengers* to troublesome examination and quarantine, thereby quite stopping up that way of escape;—and six days afterwards four steamship companies between England and Ireland, on request of the Government, raised the rate of passage for deck passengers. Cabin passengers were not interfered with in any way; for in fact it is the cabin passengers who spend in England five millions sterling *per annum*.

Whither now were the people to fly? Where to hide themselves? They had no money to emigrate; no food, no land, no roof over them; no hope before them. They began to envy the lot of those who had died in the first year's famine. The poorhouses were all full and much more than full. Each of them was an hospital for typhus fever; and it was very common for three fever patients to be in one bed, some dead and others not yet dead. Parishes all over the country being exhausted by rates, refused to provide coffins for the dead paupers, and they were thrown coffinless into holes; but in some parishes (in order to have, at least, the look of decent interment) a coffin was made, with its bottom hinged at one side, and closed at the other by a latch—the uses of which are obvious.

It would be easy to horrify the reader with details of this misery; but let it be enough to give the results in round numbers. Imagination must fill up the appalling picture. Great efforts were this year made to give relief by private charity; and the sums contributed in that way by Irishmen themselves far exceeded all that was sent from all other parts of the world beside. As for the ship-loads of corn generously sent over by Americans, I have already shown how the benevolent object was defeated. The moment it appeared in any port, prices became a shade lower; and so much the more grain was carried off from Ireland by "free trade." It was not foreign corn that Ireland wanted —it was the use of her own: that is to say, it was Repeal of the Union.

The arrangements and operation of the Union had been such that Ireland was bleeding at every vein; her life was rushing out at every pore; so that the money sent to her for charity was only so much added to landlords' rents and Englishmen's profits. American corn was only so much given as a handsome present to the merchants and speculators. That is, the English got it.

But, as I have said before, no Irishman begged the world for alms. The benevolence of Americans, and Australians, and Turks, and Negro slaves, was excited by the appeals of the English press and English members of Parliament; and in Ireland many a cheek burned with shame and indignation at our country being thus held up to the world, by the people who were feeding on our vitals, as abject

10*

beggars of broken victuals. The Repeal Association, low as it had fallen, never sanctioned this mendicancy. The true nationalists of Ireland, who had been forced to leave that Association, and had formed another society, the "Irish Confederation," never ceased to expose the true nature of these British dealings—never ceased to repudiate and spit upon the British beggarly appeals; although they took care to express warm gratitude for the well-meant charity of foreign nations; and never ceased to proclaim that the sole and all-sufficient " relief measure " for the country would be, that the English should let us alone.

On the 16th of March, for example, a meeting of the citizens of Dublin, assembled by public requisition at the Music Hall, presided over by the Lord Mayor, expressly to consider the peril of the country, and petition Parliament for proper remedies. It was known that the conveners of the meeting contemplated nothing more than suggestions as to importing grain in ships of war, stopping distillation from grain, and other trifles. Richard O'Gorman was then a prominent member of the Irish Confederation; and being a citizen of Dublin he resolved to attend this meeting, and if nobody else should say the right word, say it himself. After some helpless talk about the "mistakes" and "infatuation" of Parliament, and suggestions for change in various details, O'Gorman rose, and in a powerful and indignant speech, moved this resolution:—

"That for purposes of temporary relief, as well as permanent improvement, the one great want and demand of Ireland is, that foreign legislators and foreign Ministers shall no longer interfere in the management of her affairs."

In his speech he charged the Government with being the "murderers of the people," and said:—

"Mr. Fitzgibbon has suggested that the measures of government may have been adopted under an infatuation. I believe there is no infatuation. I hold a very different opinion on the subject. I think the British Government are doing *what they intend to do*."

The present writer, as another citizen of Dublin, seconded Mr. O'Gorman's resolution, and the report of my observations has these sentences:—

"I have listened with pain and disappointment to the proceedings of a meeting purporting to be a meeting of the citizens of Dublin, called at such a crisis, and to deliberate upon so grave a subject, yet at which the resolutions and speakers, as with one consent, have carefully avoided speaking out what nine-tenths of us feel to be the plain truth in this matter. But the truth, my lord, must be told—and the truth is, that Ireland starves and perishes simply because the English have eaten us out of house and home. Moreover, that all the legislation of their Parliament is, and will be, directed to this one end—to enable them hereafter to eat us out of house and home as heretofore. It is for that sole end they have laid their grasp upon Ireland, and it is for that, and that alone, they will try to keep her."

Greatly to the consternation of the quiet and submissive gentlemen who had convened the meeting, O'Gorman's resolution was adopted by overwhelming acclamation.

Take another illustration of the spirit in which British charity was received by the Irish people. The harvest of Ireland was abundant and superabundant in 1847, as it had been the year before. The problem was, as before, to get it quietly and peacefully over to England. Therefore the Archbishop of Canterbury issued a form of thanksgiving for an "abundant harvest," to be read in all churches on Sunday, the 17th of October. One Trevelyan, a Treasury Clerk, had been sent over to Ireland on some pretence of business; and the first thing he did when he landed was to transmit to England an humble entreaty that the Queen would deign to issue a royal "Letter," asking alms in all those churches on the day of thanksgiving. The petition was complied with; the *Times* grumbled against these eternal Irish beggars; and the affair was thus treated in the *Nation*, which certainly spoke *for the people* more authentically than any other journal:—

"Cordially, eagerly, thankfully we agree with the English *Times* in this one respect:—*there ought to be no alms for Ireland.*

"It is an impudent proposal, and ought to be rejected with scorn and contumely. We are sick of this eternal begging. If but one voice in Ireland should be raised against it, that voice shall be ours. To-morrow, to-morrow, over broad England, Scotland, and Wales, the people who devour our substance from year to year, are to offer up their canting thanksgivings for our 'abundant harvest,' and to fling us certain crumbs and crusts of it for charity. Now, if any church-going Englishman will hearken to us; if we may be supposed in any degree to speak for our countrymen, we put up our petition *thus:* Keep your alms, ye canting robbers;—button your pockets upon the Irish plunder that is in them;—and let the begging-box pass on. Neither as *loans* nor as *alms* will we take that which is our own. We spit upon the benevolence that robs us of a *pound*, and flings back a *penny* in *charity*. Contribute, now, if you will—these will be your thanks!

"But who has craved this charity? Why, the Queen of England, and her Privy Council, and two officers of her government, named Trevelyan and Burgoyne! No Irishman that we know of has begged alms from England.

"But the English insist on our remaining beggars. Charitable souls that they are, they like better to give us charity than to let us earn our bread! And consider the time when this talk of almsgiving begins:—our 'abundant harvest,' for which they are to thank God to-morrow, is still here; and there has been talk of keeping it here. So they say to one another—'Go to; let us promise them charity and church-subscriptions: they are a nation of beggars; they would rather have alms than honest earnings: let us talk of *alms*, and they will send us the bread from their tables, the cattle from their pastures, the coats from their backs!

"We charge the 'Government,' we charge the Cabinet Council at Osborne House, with this base plot. We tell our countrymen that a man named Trevelyan, a Treasury Clerk—the man who advised and administered the Labor-Rate Act—that this Trevelyan has been sent to Ireland, that he, an Englishman, may send over, from this side the Channel, a petition to the charitable in England. We are to be made to beg, whether we will or no. The Queen begs for us; the Archbishop of Canterbury begs for us; and they actually send a man to Ireland that a veritable *Irish* begging-petition may not be a-wanting.

"From Salt-hill Hotel, at Kingstown, this piteous cry goes forth to England. 'In justice,' Trevelyan says, 'to those who have appointed a general collection in the churches on the 17th, and still more in pity to the unhappy people in the western districts of Ireland,' he implores his countrymen to have mercy; and gets his letter published in the London papers (along with another from Sir John Burgoyne,) to stimulate the charity of those good and well-fed Christians who will enjoy the luxury of benevolence to-morrow.

"Once more, then, we scorn, we repulse, we curse, all English alms: and only wish these sentiments of ours could reach before noon to-morrow every sanctimonious thanksgiver in England, Scotland, Wales, and Berwick-upon-Tweed."

In the same number, the *Nation* took the pains to collect and present statistics by which it appeared that *every day*, one day with another, twenty large steamships, not counting sailing vessels, left Ireland for England, all laden with that "abundant harvest"—for which the English, indeed, might well give thanks in their churches.

Another example will finish the subject of alms. At a meeting of the Irish Confederation, it was determined to pass a resolution of thanks to those foreign nations, especially the Americans, who would have fed our people if they could only have reached them through the English Government. As many English people had also contributed largely, it was thought right to pass a vote of thanks even to them also; and to me was assigned by the Committee the duty of moving this latter resolution ; a delicate task, which was discharged in these words, as they appear in the newspaper report :—

"I have to move, sir, another vote of thanks for alms. We have thanked the kind citizens of that friendly country beyond the Atlantic ; we have now to thank, heartily and unfeignedly to thank, those benevolent individuals who have sent us relief from the hostile country of Great Britain. There is many a generous heart and many an open hand in England ; and if you look into the lists of contributors to our relief funds you will find large remittances, both from individuals and from congregations of every sect in England, which may put to shame the exertions of Irishmen themselves. There are amongst these, you may be sure, innumerable kind-hearted people, charitable women, and hard-working tradesmen, who have contributed according to their means, and without a thought of self-interest, to feed the hungry and reprieve the dying. Shall these people not be thanked ? Shall we not discriminate between the rulers who have conspired to keep from us the use of our own resources, and these good people who have ministered to us out of theirs ? In an assembly of Irishmen such questions need not be asked. Cordially, heartily, and unreservedly, we thank them. Now, sir, I wish I could stop here—I wish our thanks could be disencumbered of all ungracious restrictions, as in the case of America ; but here is a very obvious distinction to be taken ; and it is necessary there should be no mistake. Americans give us the produce of their own industry and energy. We have no claim upon them ;— America never wronged us, never robbed us ;—no American ever sought, save by fair competition, to ruin our trade that his might flourish ;—America has not the spending of our rents and revenues ; —Americans do not thrive by virtue of our beggary, and live by our death ;—Americans do not impose upon us laws that breed famine and pestilence, nor locust swarms of officials that exasperate famine and pestilence. In your thanks to the Americans let your whole hearts go with them. Let your acknowledgments be as ample and unconditional as their generosity (hear, and loud cheers). They have laid us under an obligation ; and if Heaven be good to us it shall be discharged (loud cheers). But Englishmen, sir, can well afford to give Ireland alms out of the spoils of Ireland. They are rich and may well be generous, because we have been such fools as to let them have our bread to eat and our money to spend for generations ;—because we have consented to use everything they can make, and to make little or nothing for ourselves ;—because we have sacrificed our tradesmen's wages, and our peasant's lives to the insatiable spirit of English—*commerce*, let me call it ; beggars must keep a civil tongue in their heads. Let me not be told that it is ungracious upon such an occasion to speak of the wrongs that England has done us. Sir, it is just upon such an occasion that it is needed most. Irishmen have been taught to look so long to England as the ruler and disposer and owner of all things Irish, that we absolutely scarce know our own plunder when the plunderers send a small pittance of it back to us in the form of alms. And let us be just; if we, in the depth of our distress, in the warmth of our gratitude, are almost forced to forget out of what funds these English alms are drawn, can we wonder if Englishmen forget it too, or even if they never knew it?—simple, exemplary country clergymen, benevolent women, ever prompt to do good, honest industrious tradesmen, who have learned their own handicraft, and little else,—can we believe that these people so much as know how their Government cared for them in times long past, at our expense; how provision was made to bring them over the rental of Ireland, to flow through the channels of English trade, enriching everybody as it passed ; how Irish manufacturers were broken down by systematic laws, in order that Englishmen might weave our wool into cloth, might clothe us from head to foot, yes, to the very buttons, in fabrics of their making, and keep us raising food wherewithal to pay them? Do you imagine our kind benefactors knew, or thought of all this? No : let it not be supposed that I mean to derogate from their merits, or to limit our thanks, when I tell them that, whether they know it or not, they are living upon Irish plunder, that, although the loss of one crop be a visitation from Heaven, Irish famine is a visitation from England—that the reason why we want relief, and they can give it, is just that our substance has been carried away, and that they have it. For every well-paid tradesman of Birmingham and Leeds there is a broken tradesman pining in the garrets of Dublin, or begging his bread in the streets of Cork. The well-fed laborer who sits down to his dinner in England never thinks that he is devouring whole families in Ireland. Aye, the very charitable spinster, annuitant or fundholder, who hastens to send her mite to Ireland, little dreams as she draws her quarter's dividend, that she is drawing the marrow from the bones of starving wretches in Kerry or Donegal. Hereafter, if Englishmen desire to benefit Ireland, let them know that the greatest charity they can do us, is to make their Government take its hand out of our pockets—its harpy claws off our tables. Let them compel it to draw off its commissioners, and its tens of thousands of gentlemanly officials, who swarm over the land, and eat up every green thing. Finally, let them make it restore that protecting legislature out of which it foully and fraudulently swindled us for their advantage. Let them do that, and we shall not need their alms for the future. But, my friends, you cannot expect that Englishmen will do all that for us. We must ourselves rescue our industry and redeem our lives from foreign oppression; we must banish the officials—we, *we* must Repeal the Union. We must repay their charity by raising ourselves above their charity—repay their charity by refusing them our food, and refusing them our custom—repay their charity by burning everything that comes from England, except coals—repay their charity by enabling ourselves to give them charity when they come to need it (loud cheers)."

I will only add that, during this year, coroners' juries in several counties repeatedly, on inquests over famine-slain corpses, found upon their oath verdicts of "Wilful Murder against John Russell, commonly called Lord John Russell."

Let no American ever believe, therefore, for the future, (what the English Press has diligently inculcated,) that our people, when smitten by famine, fell a-begging from England, or from America either; or wonder when he meets with Irishmen ungrateful for the "relief measures;"—and above all, if Ireland should again starve, (as she is most likely to do,) and should still be under British dominion—let America never, never send her a bushel of corn or a dollar of money. Neither bushel nor dollar will ever reach her.

futility of international aid

CHAPTER XV.

DEATH OF O'CONNELL—HIS CHARACTER—ARRANGEMENTS FOR THE NEXT YEAR'S FAMINE—EMIGRATION—REPORT OF A "SELECT COMMITTEE"—A NEW COERCION ACT—THE CRISIS APPROACHES.

In February, 1847, and amidst the deepest gloom and horror of the Famine, O'Connell, old, sick, and heavy-laden, left Ireland, and left it forever. Physicians in London recommended a journey to the South of Europe; and O'Connell himself desired to see the Pope before he died, and to breathe out his soul at Rome in the choicest odor of sanctity. By slow and painful stages he proceeded only as far as Genoa, and there died on the 15th of May.

For those who were not close witnesses of Irish politics in that day—who did not see how vast this giant figure loomed in Ireland and in England for a generation and a half—it is not easy to understand the strong emotion caused by his death, both in friends and enemies. Yet, for a whole year before, he had sunk low, indeed. His power had departed from him; and in presence of the terrible apparition of his perishing country, he had seemed to shrink and wither. Nothing can be conceived more helpless than his speeches in Conciliation Hall, and his appeals to the British Parliament during that time: yet, as I said before, he never begged *alms* for Ireland: he never fell so low as that; and I find that the last sentences of the very last letter he ever penned to the Association still proclaim the true doctrine:—

"It will not be until after the deaths of hundreds of thousands, that the regret will arise that more was not done to save a sinking nation.

"How different would the scene be if we had our own Parliament—taking care of our own people—of our own resources. But, alas! alas! it is scarcely permitted to think of these, the only sure preventatives of misery, and the only sure instruments of Irish prosperity."

Let me do O'Connell justice; bitter and virulent as may have been the hatred he bore to me in his last days of public life. To no Irishman can that wonderful life fail to be impressive,—from the day when, a fiery and thoughtful boy, he sought the cloisters of St. Omers for the education which penal laws denied him in his own land, on through the manifold struggles and victories of his earlier career, as he broke and flung off, with a kind of haughty impatience, link after link of the social and political chain that six hundred years of steady British policy had woven around every limb and muscle of his country,—down to that supreme moment of the blackness of darkness for himself and for Ireland, when he laid down his burden and closed his eyes among the palaces of the superb city, throned on her blue bay. Beyond a doubt, his death was hastened by the misery of seeing his proud hopes dashed to the earth, and his well-beloved people perishing; for there dwelt in that brawny frame tenderness and pity soft as woman's. To the last he labored on the "Relief Committees" of Dublin, and thought every hour lost unless employed in rescuing some of the doomed. The last time I saw him, he was in the Relief Committee Rooms, in Dame Street, sitting, closely muffled, in a chair, as I entered and found myself opposite to him and close by. Many months had gone by since we had spoken; and he had never mentioned me or any of my friends in that time without bitter reproaches. To my lowly inclination, I received in reply a chilling, stately bow, but no word.

Readers already know my estimate of his public character and labors. He had used all his art and eloquence to emasculate a bold and chivalrous nation; and the very gratitude, love, and admiration which his early services had won, enabled him so to pervert the ideas of right and wrong in Ireland, that they believed him when he told them that Constitutional "Agitation" was Moral Force—that bloodshed was immoral—that to set at naught and defy the London "laws," was a crime—that, to cheer and parade, and pay Repeal subscriptions, is to do one's *duty*—and that a people patient and quiet under wrong and insult is a virtuous and noble people, and the finest peasantry in the universe. He had helped the disarming policy of the English by his continual denunciations of arms, and had thereby degraded the manhood of his nation to such a point that to rouse them to resistance in their own cause was impossible, although still eager to fight for a shilling a day. To him and to his teachings, then, without scruple, I ascribe our utter failure to make, I do not say a revolution, but so much as an insurrection, two years after, when all the nations were in revolt, from Sicily to Prussia, and when a successful uprising in Ireland would have certainly destroyed the British Empire, and every monarchy in Europe along with it. O'Connell was, therefore, next to the British Government, the worst enemy that Ireland ever had,—or rather the most fatal friend. For the rest, no character of which I have heard or read was ever of so wide a compass; so capable at once of the highest virtues and the lowest vices—of the deepest pathos and the broadest humor—of the noblest generosity and most spiteful malignity. Like Virgil's oak-tree, his roots stretched down towards Tartarus, as far as his head soared towards the heavens; and I warn the reader, that whoso adventures to measure O'Connell must use a long rule, must apply a mighty standard, and raise himself up, by a ladder or otherwise, much above his own natural stature.

The clan O'Connell was an ancient sept in Kerry:

"O'Connell of the battalions of Munster,
Mighty are his mustering forces;
A Fenian armed warrior, frequent in the fight,
Commands the hosts of Hy Cuilein."

So the O'Connells of the twelfth century are described in the ancient topographical poem of O'Heerin. They did not keep a " Head Pacificator," nor would they have understood the modern O'Connell's method of using his mustering forces, in carrying out the "ethical experiment" of moral force. So much the better for them; the experiment proved a failure.

In the very same glens of Kerry, the clan O'Connell have dwelt for a thousand years; and a fragment of the ancient domain, which somehow escaped confiscation, remains in the family till this day. Many of the O'Connells had left Ireland in the time of the penal laws, and had taken service in Austria and in France. Count Daniel O'Connell was a General in the French service at the period of the great Revolution; wherein, like most of the Irish officers, he proved himself a staunch royalist. His cousin Daniel, of Irish fame, was always a monarchist also; and I have heard him say that he never could forget the shudder of horror that came upon him, when a student of St. Omers, because a young Irishman of the Mountain party displayed with triumph a handkerchief, which he had dipped in the blood of Louis, as it flowed fresh in the Place de la Concorde. In the Irish Rebellion of 1798, also, he had enrolled himself, not in the insurgent force, but in the lawyer's corps, to put the insurgents down; and never spoke of the gallant rebels of that era without execration.

O'Connell's body rests in Ireland; but without his heart. He gave orders that the heart should be removed from his body and sent to Rome. The funeral was a great and mournful procession through the streets of Dublin; and it will show how wide was the alienation which divided him from his former confederates, that when O'Brien signified a wish to attend the obsequies, a public letter from John O'Connell sullenly forbade him.

So long as John O'Connell continued to administer the dilapidated "agitation," his mode of persuading his followers to support him in any given measure, was, to threaten that he would raise his father's bones, and carry them away to the land where his heart is treasured.

In the year 1847, great and successful exertions were used to make sure that the next year should be a year of famine too. This was effected mainly by holding out the prospect of "out-door relief"—to obtain which tenants must abandon their lands and leave them untilled. A paragraph from a letter of Rev. Mr. Fitzpatrick, Parish Priest of Skibbereen, contains within it an epitome of the history of that year. It was published in the *Freeman*, March 12:—

"The ground continues unsown and uncultivated. There is a mutual distrust between the landlord and the tenant. The landlord would wish, if possible, to *get up his land;* and the unfortunate tenant is anxious to stick to it as long as he can. A good many, however, are giving it up, and preparing for America; and these are the substantial farmers who have still a little means left."

A gentleman travelling from Borris-in-Ossory to Kilkenny, one bright Spring morning, counts at both sides of the road, in a distance of twenty-four miles, "nine men and four ploughs" occupied in the fields; but sees multitudes of wan laborers, "beyond the power of computation by a mail-car passenger," laboring to destroy the road he was travelling upon. It was a "public work."—(Dublin *Evening Mail*.)

In the same month of March—"The land," says the Mayo *Constitution*, "is one vast waste: a soul is not to be seen working on the holdings of the poor farmers throughout the country; and those who have had the prudence to plough or dig the ground are *in fear* of throwing in the seed."

When the new "Out-door Relief" Act began to be applied, with its memorable Quarter-acre Clause, all this process went on with wonderful velocity, and millions of people were soon left landless and homeless. That they should be left landless and homeless was strictly in accordance with British policy; but then there was danger of the millions of outcasts becoming robbers and murderers. Accordingly, the next point was to clear the country of them, and diminish the poor-rates, by *emigration*. This is a matter somewhat interesting to Americans, so that I must give a clear account of it. If one should narrate how the cause of his country was stricken down in open battle, and blasted to pieces with shot and shell, there might be a certain mournful pride in dwelling upon the gallant resistance, as in the case of our Irish wars against Cromwell, against King William the Third, and against the power of Britain in '98;—but to describe how the spirit of a country has been broken and subdued by beggarly famine;—how her national aspirations have been, not choked in her own blood, nobly shed on the field, but strangled by red tape;—how her life and soul have been ameliorated and civilized out of her;—how she died of political economy, and was buried under tons of official stationery;—this is a dreary task, which I wish some one else had undertaken.

As it has been commenced, however, let the world hear the end. There began to be an eager desire in England to get rid of the Celts by *emigration;* for though they were perishing fast of hunger and typhus, they were not perishing fast enough. It was inculcated by the English Press that the temperament and disposition of the Irish people fitted them peculiarly for some remote country in the East, or in the West,—in fact, for any country but their own;—that Providence had committed some mistake in causing them to be born in Ireland. As usual, the *Times* was foremost in finding out this singular freak of nature! Says the *Times* (Feb. 22d, 1847):—

"Remove Irishmen to the banks of the Ganges, or the Indus—to Delhi, Benares, or Trincomalee,—and they would be far more in their element there than *in the country to which an inexorable fate has confined them.*"

Again, a Mr. Murray, a Scotch banker, writes a pamphlet upon the proper measures for Ireland. "The surplus population of Ireland," says Mr. Murray, "have been trained *precisely* for those pursuits which the unoccupied regions of North America require." Which might appear strange to anybody but a respectable banker;—a population expressly trained, and that *precisely*, to suit any country except their own!

But these are comparatively private and individual suggestions. In April of this year, however, six Peers and twelve Commoners, who called themselves Irish, but who included amongst them such "Irishmen" as Dr. Whateley and Mr. Godley, laid a scheme before Lord John Russell for the transportation of one million and a half of Irishmen to Canada, at a cost of nine millions sterling, to be charged on "Irish property," and to be paid by an income-tax.

Again, within the same year, a few months later, a "Select Committee," (and a very select one,) of the House of Lords brings up a Report "On Colonization from Ireland." Their lordships report that all former committees on the state of Ireland (with one exception) had agreed at least on this point,—that it was necessary to remove the "excess of labor." They say:—

"They have taken evidence respecting the state of Ireland, of the British North American colonies (including Canada, New Brunswick, Nova Scotia, Newfoundland), the West Indian islands, New South Wales, Port Philip, South Australia, Van Diemen's Land, and New Zealand. On some of these points it will be found that their inquiries have little more than commenced; on others, that those inquiries have been carried somewhat nearer to completion; but in no case can it be considered that the subject is as yet exhausted."

Far from it, indeed! In a later passage of the Report they say:—

"The committee are fully aware that they have as yet examined into many points but superficially, and that some, as, for example, the state of the British possessions in *Southern Africa* and in the *territory of Natal*, have not yet been considered at all. Neither have they obtained adequate information respecting what we sincerely hope may hereafter be considered as the prospering settlement of *New Zealand*. The important discoveries of Sir T. Mitchell in Australia have also been but slightly noticed."

Observe that any inquiry into the state of Ireland naturally called their Lordships to a consideration of very distant latitudes and longitudes. They could not conceive how Ireland was to be effectually ameliorated, without a full investigation of Nova Zembla, Terra del Fuego, and the Terra Australis Incognita.

Their Lordships further declare that the emigration which they recommend must be " voluntary," and also that " there was a deep and pervading anxiety for emigration exhibited by the people themselves."

A deep and pervading anxiety to fly, to escape any whither! From whom? Men pursued by wild beasts will show a pervading anxiety to go *anywhere* out of reach. If a country be made too hot to hold its inhabitants, they will be willing even to throw themselves into the sea. If men clear estates, and chase the human surplus from pillar to post, in such sort that out-door relief becomes the national way of living, you may be sure there will be a deep and pervading anxiety to get away: and then the exterminators may form themselves into a " committee " (select), and say to the public, " help us, you, to indulge the wish of our poor brethren: you perceive they *want* to be off. God forbid *we* should ship them away, save with their cordial concurrence!"

Remember all this while that there are from four to five millions of acres of improvable waste lands in Ireland; and that, even from the land in cultivation, Ireland was exporting food enough, every year, to sustain eight millions of people in England.

Their Lordships speak of *one* exception to the uniform testimony of Parliamentary Committees. I have already mentioned that Report of a Committee of the Commons, brought up in 1836, wherein their select Lordships say they find with surprise the following sentiments:

"It may be doubted *whether the country does contain a sufficient quantity of labor to develope its resources; and while the empire is loaded with taxation to defray the charges of its wars, it appears most politic to use its internal resources for improving the condition of its population*, by which the revenue of the exchequer must be increased, rather than encourage emigration, by which the revenue would suffer diminution, or than leave the laboring classes in their present state, by which poverty, crime, and the charges of government must be inevitably extended."

The same anomalous Report had expressed the strongest

opinion against Poor Laws, especially in the form of "outdoor relief,"—had reported, in short, directly against the whole system of British policy in Ireland. You may have a curiosity to know who were the members of so perverse a committee. They were twenty-four Irishmen to nine Englishmen; so no wonder they fell into so cursed a mistake. Among the Irish names, I find men of all parties; —Col. Conolly and Mr. O'Connell, Mr. Lefroy and Mr. Smith O'Brien, Lord Castlereagh and Feargus O'Connor: even Whigs,—Mr. Wyse, Mr. Shiel, and The O'Conor Don. This explains the Report, and explains further why the Imperial Parliament took care, afterwards, in all inquiries into Irish affairs, to employ Englishmen, on whom they could depend.

None of these vast public schemes of emigration were adopted by Parliament in their full extent, though aid was from time to time given to minor projects for that end: and landlords continued very busy all this year and the next, shipping off their "surplus tenantry," by their own private resources, thinking it cheaper than to maintain them by rates. The Irish Press, and especially the *Nation*, took up each of the schemes as it was propounded, and vehemently denounced it as part of the plan to clear our island of its own people, and confirm England in the peaceable possession of her farm.

There has been now, I think, laid before the reader a complete sketch, at least in outline, of the British Famine policy:—expectation of Government spoon-feeding at the point of police bayonets; shaking the farmers loose from their lands; employing them for a time on strictly useless public works; then disgorging them, in crowds of one hundred thousand at a time, to beg, or rob, or perish; then "out-door relief," administered in quantities altogether infinitesimal in proportion to the need; then that universal ejectment, the quarter-acre law; then the corruption of the middle class, by holding out the prize of ten thousand new government situations; then the vagrancy act, to make criminals of all houseless wanderers; then the " voluntary " emigration schemes; then the omnipresent police, hanging like a cloud over the houses of all "suspected persons," that is, all persons who still kept a house over their heads; then the quarantine regulations and increased fare for *deck* passengers to England, thus debarring the doomed race from all escape at that side, and leaving them the sole alternative, America or the grave;—this, I believe, gives something like a map or plan of the field, as laid out and surveyed for the Last Conquest.

What had become of the Repeal and our Parliament in College Green? Alas! Alas! the proud national aspirations that had stirred our people three years before had sunk into a dismal and despairing cry for food, or an impotent litany of execration upon our enemies. Yet the Repeal of the Union,—a Parliament in College Green,—this was still as ever the sole and single remedy for all our evils; and so it was still proclaimed by the Irish Confederation and by Smith O'Brien to the very last. For this the Repeal Members were taunted viciously, in Parliament, with complaining of everything, but having nothing to propose:— "nothing but what they knew the House would not adopt," said Mr. Roebuck. Indeed, they had nothing to propose but Repeal.

This same Roebuck, making a speech in Parliament during this year, in presence of Mr. O'Brien, reproached the Irish Members (falsely) with only asking *alms*, but suggesting no practical measures of manful self-help. "I pledge my faith," said the orator, "for the people of England, that they will give their immediate assent to any proposition which has a fair and honorable regard to the real interests of Ireland." There was one loud cry of "*hear!*" "Ah!" continued the speaker, "the honorable member opposite, the honorable member for Limerick, says *hear;*—and I know exactly what he means: he is going to propose Repeal: *I see it in his eye.*" Whereupon there was "laughter" and "renewed laughter."*

The Irish landlords were in dire perplexity. Many of them were good and just men; but the vast majority were fully identified in interest with the British government, and desired nothing so much as to destroy the population. They would not consent to Tenant-Right; they dared not trust themselves in Ireland without a British army. They may have felt, indeed, that they were themselves both injured and insulted by the whole system of English legislation; but they would submit to anything rather than fraternize with

* Debate of March 8th.

the injured Catholic Celts. A few landlords and other gentlemen met and formed an "Irish Council;" but these were soon frightened into private life again by certain revolutionary proposals of some members, and especially by the very name of Tenant-Right. At last, about the end of this year, seeing that *another* season's famine was approaching, and knowing that violent counsels began to prevail amongst the extreme section of the national party, the landlords, in guilty and cowardly rage and fear, called on Parliament for a new *Coercion Act.*

From this moment, all hope that the landed gentry would stand on the side of Ireland against England, utterly vanished.

In my next chapter, I shall have to tell how this deadly alliance between the landlords and the Government brought Irish affairs to a crisis,—how it broke up the "Confederation"—led to an attempt at insurrection—and a series of State trials—and the end of the hopeless struggle against British civilization for that time.

Before going further, however, I shall mention:—*First,* that by a careful census of the agricultural produce of Ireland for this year, 1847, made by Captain Larcom, as a Government Commissioner, the total value of that produce was £44,958,120 sterling; which would have amply sustained *double* the entire people of the island.* This return is given in detail, and agrees generally with another estimate of the same, prepared by John Martin, of Loughorn, in the County Down,—a gentleman whose name will be mentioned again in this narrative. *Second:* that at least 500,000 human beings perished this year of famine, and of famine-typhus †: and 200,000 more fled beyond the sea to escape famine and fever. *Third:* that the loans for relief given to the Public Works and Public Commissariat departments, to be laid out as they should think proper, and to be repaid by rates on Irish property, went in the first place to maintain ten thousand greedy officials; and that the greater part of these funds never reached the people at

---

* I do not possess this Return, as ordered by Parliament to be printed, but take an abstract of it given at the time in the London *Standard.* In Thom's Official Almanac and Directory, Government has taken care to suppress the statement of the gross amount.

† The deaths by famine of the year before I set down at 300,000. There is no possibility of ascertaining the numbers; and when the Government Commissioners pretend to do so, they intend deception.

all, or reached them in such a way as to ruin and exterminate them.

A kind of sacred wrath took possession of a few Irishmen at this period. They could endure the horrible scene no longer, and resolved to cross the path of the British car of conquest, though it should crush them to atoms.

CHAPTER XVI.

LORD CLARENDON, VICEROY—SUBTERRANEAN AGENCIES OF GOVERNMENT—MONAHAN, ATTORNEY-GENERAL—GALWAY ELECTION.

In the summer of this year, 1847, Lord Clarendon was sent over, as Lord Lieutenant, to finish the Conquest of Ireland,—just as Lord Mountjoy had been sent to bring to an end the wars of Queen Elizabeth's reign; and by the same means substantially,—that is, by corruption of the rich and starvation of the poor. The form of procedure, indeed, was somewhat different; for English statesmen of the sixteenth century had not learned to use the weapons of "amelioration" and "political economy;" neither had they then established the policy of keeping Ireland as a store-farm to raise wealth for England. Lord Mountjoy's system, then, had somewhat of a rude character; and he could think of nothing better than sending large bodies of troops to cut down the green corn and burn the houses. In one expedition into Leinster, his biographer, Moryson, estimates that he destroyed "ten thousand pounds' worth of corn," that is, wheat; an amount which might now be stated at £200,000 worth. In O'Cahan's country, in Ulster, as the same Moryson tells us, after a *razzia* of Mountjoy,—"We have none left to give us opposition, nor of late have seen any but dead carcases, merely starved for want of meat." So that Mountjoy could boast he had given Ireland to Elizabeth, "nothing but carcases and ashes."

Lord Clarendon's method was more in the spirit of the Nineteenth Century, though his slaughters were more terrible in the end than Mountjoy's. Again there was growing upon Irish soil a noble harvest; but it had been found more economical to carry it over to England by help of Free Trade, than to burn it on the ground. The problem then was, as it had been the last year and the year before, how to ensure its speedy and peaceful transmission. Accordingly, Lord Clarendon came over with conciliatory speeches, and large professions of the desire of "government," now at last to stay the famine. Sullen murmurs had been heard, and even open threats and urgent recommendations, that the Irish harvest must not be suffered to go another year: and there were rumors of risings to break up the roads, to pull down the bridges, in every way to stop the tracks of this fatal "commerce;" rumors, in short, of an insurrection. Some new method, then, had to be adopted to turn the thoughts and hopes of that too-credulous people once more towards the "Government." Lord Clarendon recommended a tour of agricultural "lecturers," the expense to be provided for by the Royal Agricultural Society, aided by public money. The lecturers were to go upon every estate, call the people together, talk to them of the benevolent intentions of his Excellency, and give them good advice. Their report was published in the following April: and irksome as are these details of one uniform and chronic misery, the due understanding of Lord Clarendon's policy will require some attention to this Report.

One lecturer, one Thomas Martin, travelled in Western Mayo. He writes:—" It was almost impossible to produce any impression in this wasted and neglected district." For why? The lecturer tells us—" For, from Bangor to Crossmolina, all was desolate and waste." Driving along " with the Rev. Mr. Stock, in his gig, he pointed out to me," says Martin, " a number of farm-houses in the Mullet, *all deserted*, and the land, too: nothing possibly could be done there, for the tenants *were gone*."

The grand object of all the lecturers was to get the people, those of them who remained, to till the land, instead of leaving it waste, to run to public works and out-door relief; for in truth it began to be feared in England, that the process was going too far, and that the sister country might even be defrauded of her usual tribute, if the Irish people *all* became able-bodied paupers. But, when Mr. Fitzgerald, another of those lecturers, urged this upon a meeting of tenants in Connemara, he tells us—" They all agreed that what I said was just; but they always had some excuse, [the good-for-nothing Celts!] : that they could not get seed, or had nothing to live on in the meantime."

These extracts are only samples of what the lecturers did, heard, and said, in all their districts. " I saw," says Mr.

Fitzgerald, "whole villages of roofless houses, and all I met told me they intended to give up their land, for they had neither food nor strength to till it." A certain Mr. Goode, lecturing in Connaught, informs us that:—

"The poor people here appeared to be in a most desponding state: *they always met me with the argument that there was no use in their working there, for they were going to be turned out in Spring, and would have their houses pulled down over them.* I used to tell them that I had *nothing to do with that;* that I was sent among them by some kind, intelligent gentlemen, barely to tell them *what course to pursue.*"

That was all. Lord Clarendon had not sent Mr. Goode down to lecture on Tenant-Right;—what business had they to obtrude their Jacobin principles on a Government lecturer? What had he to do with all that? They might as well have prated to him about the Repeal of the Union!

Another measure of my Lord Clarendon was to buy support at the Press with secret-service money. To the honor of the Dublin Press, this was a somewhat difficult matter. The government had at that time only one leading journal in the metropolis on which it could surely rely,—the *Evening Post.* Lord Clarendon wanted another organ, and of a lower species; for he had work to do which the comparatively respectable *Post* might shrink from. He sought out a creature named Birch, editor of the *World,* a paper which was never named nor alluded to by any reputable journal in the city. This Birch lived by *hush-money,* or black-mail of the most infamous kind;—that is, extorting money from private persons, men and women, by threats of inventing and publishing scandalous stories of their domestic circles. He had been tried more than once and convicted of this species of swindling. "I then offered him £100, if I remember rightly," says my Lord Clarendon,* "for it did not make any great impression on me at the time. He said that would not be sufficient for his purpose, and I think it was then extended to about £350." On further examination, his Lordship confessed that he had paid Birch "further sums" —in short, kept him regularly in pay; and finally, on Birch bringing suit against him for the balance due for "work and labor," had paid him in one sum £2,000, at the same time taking up all the papers and letters, (as he thought,) which

* See evidence on the trial of Birch against Sir T. Redington.

might bring the transaction to light. One can guess the nature of Birch's work and labor, and *quantum meruit*. His duty was to make weekly attacks, of a private and revolting nature, upon Smith O'Brien, upon Mr. Meagher, upon myself, and every one else who was prominent in resisting and exposing the Government measures. Further, the public money was employed in the gratuitous distribution of the *World*, for otherwise decent persons would never have seen it.. At the time, I was myself unaware of the man's attacks upon me, and did not even know him at all. It was during my exile in Van Diemen's Land that I learned, through the newspapers, how all this subterranean agency had come to light on the trial of one of the suits which Birch was forced to institute for recovery of his wages.

Concerning this Birch, I will only add, that he was subsequently employed and paid by Lord Palmerston also, for the same sort of services.

A third measure of the Viceroy was,—extreme liberality towards Catholic lawyers and gentlemen in the distribution of patronage; that so they might be the more effectually bought off from all common interest and sympathy with the "lower orders," and might stand patiently by and see their countrymen slain or banished. Amongst others, Mr. Monahan, an industrious and successful Catholic barrister, was made Attorney-General for Ireland,—from which the next step was to the Bench. Mr. Monahan became a grateful and useful servant.

Next came the Galway Election. It was essential that Mr. Monahan, being Attorney-General, should be also a Member of Parliament; and there was a vacancy in Galway city. The Repealers resolved to contest it; and Mr. Anthony O'Flaherty, a gentleman of Galway county, addressed the electors. It was resolved not only to contest this election with the Whig Attorney-General, but to fight it with the utmost vehemence and bitterness, in order to show the world how the "amelioration" Whig Government was appreciated in Ireland. But though nine-tenths of the people of Galway were Repealers, we knew that the enemy had great advantages in the struggle: because, in the first place, any amount of money would be at their command for bribery; and next, the *landlords* of the city and of the rural districts around were principally of the sort called "Catholic gentry,"—the very worst class, perhaps, of the Irish aristocracy.

The "Irish Confederation" sent down a number of its members to give gratuitous aid to Mr. O'Flaherty's law-agents and Committee. These were Dillon, Meagher, O'Gorman, Doheny, Barry, O'Donoghue, Martin O'Flaherty, and John Mitchel. In the depth of winter we travelled to Galway, through the very centre of that fertile island, and saw sights that will never wholly leave the eyes that beheld them:—cowering wretches, almost naked in the savage weather, prowling in turnip-fields, and endeavoring to grub up roots which had been left, but running to hide as the mail-coach rolled by: very large fields, where small farms had been "consolidated," showing dark bars of fresh mould running through them, where the ditches had been levelled:—groups and families, sitting or wandering on the high-road, with failing steps and dim, patient eyes, gazing hopelessly into infinite darkness; before them, around them, above them, nothing but darkness and despair: parties of tall, brawny men, once the flower of Meath and Galway, stalking by with a fierce but vacant scowl; as if they knew that all this ought not to be, but knew not whom to blame, saw none whom they could rend in their wrath; for Lord John Russell sat safe in Chesham Place; and Trevelyan, the grand commissioner and *factotum* of the pauper-system, wove his webs of red tape around them from afar. So cunningly does civilization work! Around those farm-houses which were still inhabited were to be seen hardly any stacks of grain; it was all gone; the poor-rate collector, the rent agent, the county-cess collector, had carried it off: and sometimes, I could see, in front of the cottages, little children leaning against a fence when the sun shone out,—for they could not stand,—their limbs fleshless, their bodies half-naked, their faces bloated yet wrinkled, and of a pale greenish hue,—children who would never, it was too plain, grow up to be men and women. I saw Trevelyan's claw in the vitals of those children: his red tape would draw them to death: in his Government laboratory he had prepared for them the typhus poison.

Galway is a very ancient but decayed city, with many houses yet standing, built in the old Spanish style, with high walls of solid stone, and an interior courtyard, entered by a low-browed arch. Foaming and whirling down from Lough Corrib, a noble river flows through many bridges into the broad bay; and the streets are winding and narrow, like the streets of Havana. When we arrived, the city, besides its usual garrison, was occupied by parties of cavalry and all the rural police from the country around;—they were to suppress rioters of O'Flaherty's party, and help those of Monahan's, cover their retreat, or follow up their charge. The landlords and gentry, Catholic and Protestant, were almost unanimous for Monahan, and highly indignant at strangers coming from Dublin to interfere with the election. Accordingly, in the Court-house, on the day of nomination, a young gentleman of spirit insulted O'Gorman, who forthwith went out and sent him a challenge. This was beginning a Galway election in regular form. The meeting, however, was prevented by some relative of the aggressor, who discovered the challenge; and they were both arrested. There was no further disposition to insult any of us. The tenantry of the rural district of the borough (which happened to be unusually large), were well watched by the agents and bailiffs; who, in fact, had possession of all their certificates of registry; and when the poor creatures came up to give their reluctant vote for the Famine candidate, it was in gangs guarded by bailiffs. A bailiff produced the certificates of the gangs which were under his care, in a sheaf, and stood ready to put forward each in his turn. If the voter dared to say, *O'Flaherty*, the agent scowled on him, and in that scowl he read his fate;—but he was sure to be greeted with a roaring cheer that shook the Court-house, and was repeated by the multitudes outside. Magistrates and Police-inspectors, pale with ferocious excitement, stood ready, eagerly watching for some excuse to precipitate the troops upon the people; and when the multitudes swayed and surged, as they bore upon their shoulders some poor farmer who had given the right vote, the ranks of infantry clashed the butts of their muskets on the pavement with a menacing clang, and the dragoons gathered up their bridles, and made hoofs clatter, and spurs and scabbards jingle, as if preparing for a charge.

I took charge of one of the polling-booths as O'Flaherty's agent. A gang of peasants came up, led or driven by the bailiffs. One man, when the oath was administered to him, that he had not been bribed, showed pitiable agitation. He spoke only Gaelic, and the oath was repeated, sentence by sentence, by an interpreter. He affected to be deaf, to be stupid, and made continual mistakes. Ten times at least the interpreter began the oath, and as often failed to have it correctly repeated after him. The unfortunate creature looked round wildly as if he meditated breaking away; but the thought, perhaps, of famishing little ones at home still restrained him. Large drops broke out on his forehead; and it was not stupidity that was in his eye, but mortal horror. Mr. Monahan himself happened to be in that booth at the time, and he stood close by his solicitor, still urging him to attempt once more to get the oath out of the voter. Murmurs began to arise, and at last I said to Mr. Monahan: "You cannot, and you dare not, take that man's vote. You know, or your solicitor knows, that the man was bribed. I warn you to give up this vote and turn the man out." In reply, he shrugged his shoulders, and went out himself. The vote was rejected; and, with a savage whisper, the bailiff who had marshalled him to the poll turned the poor fellow away. I have no doubt that man is long since dead, he and all his children.

The election lasted four or five days, and was a very close contest. The decent burghers of the town stood by us, and our friends were enabled to rescue some bands of voters out of the custody of the agents and bailiffs, whose practice it was to collect those of the several estates in large houses, set a guard over them, and help them to stifle thought and conscience with drink. Monahan had a mob hired,—the Claddagh fishermen,—so that we were obliged to organize a mob to counteract it. Of course there was much skirmishing in the streets. Monahan was run very close, and in the last two days his party spent much money in bribery; a kind of contest into which Mr. O'Flaherty did not enter with him. The Attorney-General won his election by four votes, out of a very large constituency; but his escape was narrow. If he had lost, he would have been thrown aside like any broken tool; but, as it chanced, he is now Chief Justice of the Common Pleas. More than this; he had the satisfaction, not many months after, of hunting into exile, or prosecuting (with packed juries) to conviction, every Irish Confederate who went down to hold out Galway against him—with a single exception. Ministers gave him *carte blanche* in the matter of those prosecutions, and he used it with much energy and legal learning.

The summer of '47 wore through wearily and hopelessly. All endeavors to rouse the landlord class to exertion entirely failed, through their coward fear of an outraged and plundered people: and, at last, when, out of the vast multitudes of men thrown from public works, houseless and famishing, a few committed murders and robberies, or shot a bailiff or an incoming tenant, the landlords in several counties besought for a new Coercion and Arms Act; so as to make that code more stringent and inevitable. Lord John Russell was but too happy to comply with the demand; but the landlords were to give something in exchange for this security. Addresses of confidence were voted by grand juries and county meetings of landlords. The Irish gentry almost unanimously volunteered addresses denouncing Repeal and Repealers, and pledged themselves to maintain the Union. At the same time ejectment was more active than ever; and it is not to be denied that, amongst the myriads of desperate men who then wandered houseless, there were some who would not die tamely. Before taking their last look at the sun, they could at least lie in wait for the agent who had pulled down their houses and turned their weeping children adrift: him, at least, they could send to perdition before them.

The crisis was come. The people no longer trusted the ameliorative professions of their enemies; and there were some, who zealously strove to rouse them now at last, to stand up for their own lives; to keep the harvest of '47 within the four seas of Ireland; and by this one blow to prostrate Irish landlordism and the British empire along with it.

How we felt ourselves justified in urging so desperate a measure, and how practically we meant to carry it out, must be explained in another chapter.

CHAPTER XVII.

DUBLIN DURING THE FAMINE—"YOUNG IRELAND"—ALARM OF THE MONEYED CLASSES—"S. G. O."—SUDDEN MEETING OF PARLIAMENT—NEW COERCION ACT—DIFFERENCES IN THE IRISH CONFEDERATION—BREAK-UP IN THE "NATION" OFFICE—O'BRIEN—THE "UNITED IRISHMAN."

After two years' frightful famine,—and when it was already apparent that the next famine, of 1847-48, would be even more desolating,—it may be imagined that Dublin city would show some effects or symptoms of such a national calamity. Singular to relate, that city had never before been so gay and luxurious; splendid equipages had never before so crowded the streets; and the theatres and concert-rooms had never been filled with such brilliant throngs. In truth, the rural gentry resorted in greater numbers to the metropolis at this time; some to avoid the sight and sound of the misery that surrounded their country-seats, and which British laws almost expressly enacted they should not relieve;—some to get out of reach of an exasperated and houseless peasantry. Any stranger, arriving in those days, guided by judicious friends only through fashionable streets and squares, introduced only to proper circles, would have said that Dublin must be the prosperous capital of some wealthy and happy country.

The band of friends, known to the outside world as "Young Ireland," now all scattered, exiled, or dead, at that time, over and above all the ordinary appliances of pleasure offered by a great city, met weekly at the house of one or the other; and there were nights and suppers of the gods, when the reckless gayety of Irish temperament bore fullest sway. Like the Florentines in plague-time, they would at least live while it was yet day; and that fiery life, if it must soon burn out, should burn brightly to the last. And here, I desire to say, once for all, that I have never heard or read of, neither do I expect to hear or to read of, any political party so thoroughly pure and disinterested, with aspirations so lofty, and effort and endeavor so single-hearted, as this same "Young Ireland." Those nights, winged with genial wit and cordial friendship, fade now, purple-hued, in the distance, and a veil of blackness is drawn over them ; but I avow myself much more proud of my association with that genial and generous brotherhood, than if I were a member even of the Atlantic Telegraph Company!

The new Poor Law was now on all hands admitted to be a failure;—that is, a failure as to its ostensible purpose. For its real purpose,—reducing the body of the people to "able-bodied pauperism,"—it had been no failure at all, but a complete success. Nearly ten millions sterling had now been expended under the several relief acts;—expended, mostly, in salaries to officials; the rest laid out in useless work, or in providing rations for a short time, to induce small farmers to give up their land ; which was the condition of such relief. Instead of ten millions in three years, if twenty millions had been advanced in the first year, and expended on useful labor (that being the sum which had been devoted promptly to turning wild the West India negroes,) the whole famine-slaughter might have been averted, and the whole advance would have been easily repaid to the Treasury. *

Long before the Government commissioners had proclaimed their law a failure, the writers in the *Nation* had been endeavoring to turn the minds of the people towards the only real remedy for all their evils,—that is, a combined movement to prevent the export of provisions, and to resist process of ejectment. This involved a denial of rent and refusal of rates ; involved, in other words, a root and branch revolution, socially and politically.

Such revolutionary ideas could only be justified by a desperate necessity, and by the unnatural and fatal sort of connection between Irish landlords and Irish tenants. The peasantry of England, of Scotland, and of Ireland, stand in three several relations towards the lords of their soil. In England they are simply the emancipated serfs and *villeins* of the feudal system : never knew any other form of social polity, nor any other lords of the soil, since the Norman conquest. As England, however, prosecuted her conquests

---

* Of these ten millions, about three have been repaid. In the case of the twenty millions for turning negroes wild, there was no expectation of repayment at all.

by degrees in the other two kingdoms, she found the free Celtic system of clanship; and, as rebellion after rebellion was crushed, her statesmen insisted upon regarding the chiefs of clans as feudal lords, and their clansmen as their vassals or tenants. In Scotland, the chiefs gladly assented to this view of the case; and the Mac Callum More became, nothing loath, Duke of Argyle, and owner of the territory which had been the tribe-lands of his clan. Owing mainly to the fact that estates in Scotland were not so tempting a prey as the rich tracts of Ireland,—and partly owing also to the Scottish people having generally become Protestants on the change of religion,—there was but little change in the ruling families; and the Scottish clansmen, now become "tenantry," paid their duties to the heads of their own kindred as before. So it has happened that, to this day, there is no alienation of feeling, or distinction of race, to exasperate the lot of the poor cultivators of the soil.

In Ireland, wherever the chiefs turned Protestant, and chose to accept "grants" of their tribe-lands at the hands of British kings (as the De Burghs and O'Briens), much the same state of things took place for a while. But Ireland never submitted to English dominion as Scotland has done; and there were continual "rebellions," (so the English termed our national resistance,) followed by extensive confiscations. Many hundreds of great estates in Ireland have thus been confiscated twice and three times; and the new proprietors were Englishmen, and, in a portion of Ulster, Scotchmen. These, of course, had no common interest or sympathy with the people, whom they considered, and called, "the Irish Enemy." Still, while Ireland had her own Parliament, and the landlords resided at home, the state of affairs was tolerable; but when the Act of "Union," in 1800, concentrated the pride and splendor of the empire at London, and made England the great field of ambition and distinction, most of our grandees resided out of Ireland, kept agents and bailiffs there, wrung the utmost farthing out of the defenceless people, and spent it elsewhere.

Now, it never would have entered the mind of any rational or just man, at this late date, to call in question the title to long ago confiscated estates; nor, supposing those titles proved bad, would it have been possible to find the right owners. But when the system was found to work so fatally,

—when hundreds of thousands of people were lying down and perishing in the midst of abundance and superabundance which their own hands had created,—I maintain that Society itself stood dissolved. That form of Society was not only a failure, but an intolerable oppression; and cried aloud to be cut up by the roots and swept away.

Those who thought thus, had reconciled their minds to the needful means,—that is, a revolution as fundamental as the French Revolution, and to the wars and horrors incident to that. The horrors of war, they knew, were by no means so terrible as the horrors of peace which their own eyes had seen; they were ashamed to see their kinsmen patiently submitting to be starved to death, and longed to see blood flow, if it were only to show that blood still flowed in Irish veins.

The enemy began to take genuine alarm at these violent doctrines,—especially as they found that the people were taking them to heart; and already, in Clare County, mobs were stopping the transport of grain towards the seaports. If rents should cease to be levied, it was clear that not only would England lose her five millions sterling *per annum* of absentee rents, but mortgagees, fundholders, insurance companies, and the like, would lose dividends, interest, bonus, and profits.

There was then in England a gentleman who was in the habit of writing able but sanguinary exhortations to Ministers, with the signature " S. G. O." His addresses appeared in the *Times*, and were believed to influence considerably the counsels of Government. In November, '47, this " S. G. O." raised the alarm, and called for prompt *coercion* in Ireland. Here is one sentence from a letter of his reverence —for S. G. O. was a clergyman:—

"Lord John may safely believe me; when I say that the prosperity, nay, almost the very existence, of many insurance societies, the positive salvation from utter ruin of many, very many *mortgagees*, depends on some instant steps to make life ordinarily secure in Ireland; of course, I only mean life in that class of it in which individuals effect insurances and give mortgages."

In short his reverence meant high-life. Lord Clarendon,— as Parliament was not then sitting,—issued an Admonitory Address, wherein he announced that:—

"The constabulary will be increased in all disturbed districts (whereby an additional burden will be thrown upon the rates), military detachments will be stationed wherever necessary, and efficient patrols maintained; liberal rewards will be given for information," etc.

In the meantime, large forces were concentrated at points where the spirit of resistance showed itself; for a sample of which I take a paragraph from a Tipperary paper:—

"A large military force, under the civil authority, has seized upon the produce of such farms in Boytonrath, as owed rent and arrears to the late landlord, Mr. Roe, and the same will be removed to Dublin, and sold there, if not redeemed within fourteen days. There are two hundred soldiers and their officers garrisoned in the mansion-house at Rockwell."—*Tipperary Free Press.*

Whereupon, in the *Nation*, I urged the people to begin calculating whether ten times the whole British army would be enough to act as bailiffs and drivers, everywhere at once; or whether, if they did, the proceeds of the distress might answer expectation. In fact, it was obvious that if the enemy should be forced to employ their forces in this way all over the island,—to lift and carry the whole harvest of Ireland, and that over roads broken up, and bridges broken down to obstruct them, and with the daily risk of meeting bands of able-bodied paupers to dispute their passage,—the service would soon have been wholly demoralized, and after three months of such employment, the remnant of the army might have been destroyed.

Parliament was called hastily together. Her Majesty told the Houses, "that there were atrocious crimes in Ireland,—a spirit of insubordination, an organized resistance to legal rights;" and of course, that she required "additional powers" for the protection of life,—that is, high-life.

The meaning of this was a new Coercion Bill. It was carried without delay, and with unusual unanimity; and it is instructive here to note the difference between a Whig in power and a Whig out. When Sir Robert Peel had pro-proposed his Coercion Bill, *the year before*, it had been vehemently opposed by Lord John Russell and Lord Grey. It was time to have done with coercion, they had said; Ireland had been "misgoverned;" there had been too many Arms Acts and Curfew Acts; it was "justice" that was wanted now, and they, the Whigs, were the men to dispense it. Earl Grey, speaking of the *last* Coercion Bill (it was brought in by the other party), said emphatically (*see debate in the*

Lords, March 23d, 1846), "that measures of severity had been tried long enough;" and repeated, with abhorence, the list of coercive measures passed since 1800, all without effect; how, in 1800, the Habeas Corpus Act was suspended, the Act for the Suppression of the Rebellion being still in force; how they were continued in 1801; continued again in 1804; how the Insurrection Act was passed in 1807, which gave the Lord Lieutenant full and legal power to place any district under Martial Law, to suspend trial by jury, and make it a transportable offence to be out of doors from sunset to sunrise;—how this act remained in force till 1810;—how it was renewed in 1814—continued in '15, '16, '17—revived in '22, and continued through '23, '24, and '25;—how another Insurrection Act was needed in 1833, was renewed in '34, and expired but five years ago. "And again," continued this Whig, "again in 1846, we are called on to renew it!" Horrible!—revolting to a Liberal out of place! "We must look farther," continued Earl Grey—vociferating from the Opposition bench—"we must look to the root of the evil; the state of the law and the habits of the people, *in respect to the occupation of land*, are almost at the roots of the disorder;—it was undeniable that the *clearance system* prevailed to a great extent in Ireland; and that such things could take place, he cared not how large a population might be suffered to grow up in a particular district, was *a disgrace to a civilized country.*"

And Lord John Russell, in the Commons, said: "if they were to deal with the question of the crimes, they were bound to consider also whether there were not measures that might be introduced which would reach *the causes of those crimes:*"—and he horrified the House by an account he gave them of "a whole village, containing 270 persons, razed to the ground, and the entire of that large number of individuals sent adrift on the high-road, to sleep under the hedges, without even being permitted the privilege of boiling their potatoes: or obtaining shelter among the walls of the houses." Disgusting!—to a Whig statesman in Opposition!

Now these very same men had had the entire control and government of Ireland for a year and a half. Not a single measure had been proposed by them in that time to reach " the causes of those crimes;" not a single security had been given "in respect of the occupation of land;" not one check to that terrible "clearance system," which was "a disgrace to a civilized country." On the contrary, every measure was carefully calculated to accelerate the clearance system; and the government had helped that system ruthlessly by the employment of their troops and police. They had literally swept the people off the land by myriads upon myriads; and now, when their relief acts were admittedly a *failure*, and when multitudes of homeless peasants, transformed into paupers, were at length making the landed men and mortgagees, and Jews, and insurance officers tremble for their gains,—the Liberal Whig Ministry had nothing to propose but more jails, more handcuffs, more transportation.

The new Coercion Bill was in every respect like the rest of the series; in Ireland, these Bills are all as much like one another as one policeman's carbine is like another. Disturbed districts were to be proclaimed by the Lord Lieutenant. He might proclaim a whole county, or the whole thirty-two counties. Once proclaimed, everybody in that district was to be within doors, (whether he had a house or not,) from dark till morning. Any one found not at home, to be arrested or transported. If arms were found about any man's premises, and he could not *prove* that they were put there without his knowledge,—arrest, imprisonment, transportation. All the arms in the district to be brought in, on proclamation to that effect, and piled in the police-offices. The Lord Lieutenant to quarter on the district as many additional police, inspectors, detectives, and sub-inspectors, as he might think fit;—offer such rewards to informers as he might think fit;—and charge all the expense upon the tenantry, to be levied by rates,—*no part* of these rates to be charged to the landlords;—Constabulary to collect them at the point of the bayonet;—and these rates to be in addition to poor-rates, cess, tithes, rent, and imperial taxes.

The story is now brought down to the point at which the "Irish Confederation,"—the only body in Ireland which gave the enemy the slightest apprehension,—became divided. And here it is needful that I speak somewhat more particularly of myself. I had been one of the founders of that Confederation, and had for two years written nearly all the political articles in the *Nation*. I had watched the progress of the Famine-policy of the Government, and could see nothing in it but a machinery, deliberately devised and skilfully worked, for the entire subjugation of the island,—the slaughter of a portion of its people, and the pauperization of the rest. Therefore, I had come to the conclusion that the whole system ought to be met with resistance at every point; and the means for this would be extremely simple; namely, a combination amongst the people to obstruct and render impossible the transport and shipment of Irish provisions; to refuse all aid in its removal; to destroy the highways; to prevent every one, by intimidation, from daring to bid for grain or cattle if brought to auction under "distress" (a method of obstruction which had put an end to church tithes before);—in short, to offer a passive resistance universally; but occasionally, when opportunity served, to try the steel. To recommend such a course would be extremely hazardous, and was besides in advance of the revolutionary progress made up to that time by Mr. Duffy, proprietor of the *Nation*. Therefore, in the beginning of December, I announced that I would write in the *Nation* no more. My friend, Devin Reilly, abandoned it also on the same day.

We still remained connected with the Confederation; and in the Clubs and Committee made no scruple to promulgate our views, and to recommend that the people should be advised not to give up their arms, but on the contrary provide more, especially *pikes*, for any contingency; seeing they might well be assured the Government sought to disarm them for the same reason that a highway robber disarms his victim.

Mr. Smith O'Brien earnestly remonstrated against this course. It would amount almost to a declaration of war; and he urged that the country was not "prepared" for war. Moreover, he honestly believed that the rents were justly due; and that the poor-rates, though a grievous blunder, were really a machinery for relief, not for slaughter. He came hastily up to Dublin, and introduced resolutions into the Confederation, disavowing certain letters written by Reilly and by myself, condemning our sentiments, and protesting against the club organization being made the medium of promulgating them.

I maintained that no law of the Confederation was violated by what we had done;—that there was no use in an Irish Confederation at all, unless it was prepared in so deadly an emergency to advise the general arming of the people, and to make them look for redress of their wrongs to this one agency,—the edge of the sword;—that if they were not prepared to fight pitched battles with the Queen's troops, they were as well prepared as they ever would be;—that if they were mowed down by shot and sabre, they would die a better death than was usual at that period;—for no carnage could be so hideous as the British Famine.

There was a two days' debate on O'Brien's Resolutions, John Martin occupying the chair. It was conducted with perfect courtesy and mutual respect, and it ended in the adoption of the resolutions, by no very great majority. The weight and authority which O'Brien's character deservedly gave him, influenced many: others were moved by the same considerations which acted upon him; and if I had not felt myself to be most exclusively and extremely right, I might have well doubted my position when Dillon, Meagher, and O'Gorman successively rose up and spoke, and voted for the Resolutions. The other side was maintained by Eugene O'Reilly, who has since been Colonel of a Turkish cavalry regiment in the Russian war, and by Devin Reilly, now in his grave at Washington.

We, therefore, and some two hundred other Confederates who voted with us, retired from the meetings of the Confederation; and I resigned my place on the Committee, and my office of Inspector of Clubs for the province of Ulster. Revolution, then, was ruled out; and I was cut off from the Confederation, as I had been from the Repeal Association before, and on the same question—physical force. This division took place on the 5th of February, 1848.— Three weeks after, Louis Philippe fled from before the face of an outraged people; and the tocsin was sounded for a Revolution all over Europe.

On the 12th of February appeared the first number of the *United Irishman*, a weekly paper established and owned by me. For contributors, I had not only Reilly, but Father Kenyon,—a good Tipperary priest, and one of the most accomplished scholars in Ireland;—John Martin, and James Clarence Mangan;—Catholics, Protestants, and Pagans, but all resolute Revolutionists.

The British Government had watched all these proceedings in the Confederation with some interest. They feared nothing in the world but pikes and rifles, and knew that so long as the Confederates confined themselves to "constitutional" operations, British dominion was safe. The first number of the *United Irishman* startled them a little; especially when they learned that the press, working night and day, could not keep pace with the demand; and that single copies were freely purchased at five times their cost. Lord Stanley [Earl Derby] brought up the first number into the House of Lords; and I may be pardoned for extracting a passage from his lordship's speech. After reading large extracts, he continues:—

"This paper was published at 5d, but, as I am informed, when the first number appeared, so much was it sought after, that, on its first appearance, it was eagerly bought in the streets of Dublin at 1s 6d and 2s a number. With the people of Ireland, my lords, this language will tell—(hear)—and I say it is not safe for you to disregard it. These men are honest; they are not the kind of men who make their patriotism the means of barter for place or pension. They are not to be bought off by the government of the day for a colonial place, or by a snug situation in the customs or excise. (Hear, hear.) No; they honestly repudiate this course; they are rebels at heart; and they are rebels avowed, who are in earnest in what they say and propose to do. My lords, this is not a fit subject, at all events, for contempt. My belief is, that these men are dangerous; —my belief is, that they are traitors in intent already, and if occasion offers, that they will be traitors in fact."

In calling us "rebels," his lordship was right;—but traitors we were not.

CHAPTER XVIII.

THE "UNITED IRISHMAN" NEWSPAPER—NATURE OF THE ENTERPRISE—EFFECT OF THE FRENCH REVOLUTION OF 1848—SITUATION OF THE GOVERNMENT—EXAMPLES.

THE enterprise to which the conductors of the *United Irishman* had committed themselves and their fortunes, may well be deemed hazardous and even desperate. No one could more fully appreciate its perils than they who undertook it. To rouse to armed resistance a poor and carefully disarmed people, whose country was occupied at every point by a numerous army, and whose " upper classes " were generally altogether devoted to British rule,—not for love of British rule, indeed, but for fear of their own countrymen, —and to attempt this in open day, and in defiance of the well-understood principle and practice of Irish law-courts, all in the full power and possession of the enemy,—was an undertaking which perhaps could end only in one way. But what then? Ireland was our country. The Irish race was our flesh and blood. The alternative was, either to see a foreign enemy scourge our people from the face of their own land, by famine and pestilence, "law," political economy, and red tape, or to set our backs to the wall and fight to the death.

As to our slender chances of success, they consisted mainly in this: The leading members of the Whig Administration, then in power, had uniformly, and with apparent sincerity, protested against the practice of *packing juries* in Ireland: and we were well aware that it would be with extreme reluctance they would prosecute the *United Irishman*, seeing they could hope for nothing but defeat if they gave a fair trial. Then if, through irresolution, or regard for " consistency,"—it would be too strong to say *conscience*,—they should forbear to prosecute for even a few months, until another harvest should be ripe and gathered, we made no doubt that we could in that time have the people as ripe as the harvest.

We know, indeed, that they were Whigs, "Liberals," and therefore treacherous as the wind, and false as the Father of Lies; but counted somewhat on their cowardice. We had yet to learn that every Englishman, even a Whig, could be brave in such a cause.

Here, I am not solicitous to avoid the appearance of egotism; and seeing the ignominious defeat of all our efforts, it is no great boast, Heaven knows, to have had "the carriage of the cause" in those days. But the mere fact is, that the English Government was fully conscious that the enemy they had now to deal with was the *United Irishman*, and the spirit and purpose which it excited and represented. This became more manifest when news burst in upon us of the February revolution in Paris, and the flight of King Louis Philippe; for between the French people and the Irish there has always been an electric telegraph, whose signals never fail; and British Statesmen had not forgotten that it was the first great French Revolution which cost them the Irish war of '98. The February revolution, also, at once obliterated the feuds of the Irish Confederation. Nobody would now be listened to there, who proposed any other mode of redress for Irish grievances than the sword. Reilly and myself, without ceremony, walked back into its meetings; and a resolution was passed with enthusiastic acclamation, that the Confederate clubs should become armed and officered, so that each man should know his right-hand and his left-hand comrade, and the man whose word he should obey. All the second-rate cities, as well as Dublin, and all the country towns, were now full of clubs, which assumed military and revolutionary names,—the "Sarsfield Club," the "Emmet Club," and so forth; and the business of arming proceeded with commendable activity. Such young men as could afford it, provided themselves with rifles and bayonets; those who had not the means for this got pike-heads made; and there was much request for ash poles. What was still more alarming to the enemy, the soldiers in several garrisons were giving unmistakable symptoms of sharing in the general excitement; not Irish soldiers alone, but English and Scottish, who had Chartist ideas. A large part of the circulation of the *United Irishman*, in spite of all the exertions of the officers, was in military barracks.

What was the "Government" to do? It was very plain

that the island would not long hold both the "Government" and me. Which, then, was to go? It is easy now to say *that* could hardly be doubted; but it was not easy then. New regiments were poured into Ireland, of course; and Dublin held an army of 10,000 men—infantry, cavalry, artillery, and engineers. The barrack accommodations being insufficient, many large buildings were taken as temporary barracks; the deserted palaces of the Irish aristocracy,—as Aldborough House, on the north-east; the deserted halls of manufactures and trade, in "The Liberty;" and the Linen Hall, were occupied by detachments. The Bank of Ireland, —our old Parliament House,—had cannon mounted over the entablatures of its stately Ionic colonnades; and the vast and splendid Custom House, not being now needed for trade (our imports being all from the "sister country," and our exports all to the same), was quite commodious as a barrack and arsenal. The quiet quadrangles of Trinity College were the scene of daily parades; and the loyal board of that institution gave up the wing which commands Westmoreland-street, College-street, and Dame-street, to be occupied by troops. Superb squadrons of hussars, of lancers, and of dragoons rode continually through and around the city; infantry practised platoon firing in the squares; heavy guns, strongly guarded, were for ever rolling along the pavements; and parties of horse artillery showed all mankind how quickly and dexterously they could wheel and aim, and load and fire at the crossings of the streets. These military demonstrations, and the courts of "Law," constituted the open and avowed powers and agencies of the enemy.

But there was a secret and subterranean machinery. The editor of the *World* was now on full pay, and on terms of close intimacy at the Castle and Viceregal Lodge—that is, private and back-door intimacy; for such a creature could by no means be admitted to decent society. His paper was gratuitously furnished to all hotels and public-houses by means of secret-service money. Dublin swarmed with detectives; they went at night to get their instructions at the Castle, from Colonel Brown, head of the police department; and it was one of their regular duties to gain admittance to the Clubs of the Confederation, where it afterwards appeared that they had been the most daring counsellors of treason and riot.

A man named Kirwan went to a blacksmith in the city, and gave him an order for some pikes, intimating mysteriously that they were wanted for the "revolution." The smith made the pikes, and Kirwan immediately brought them to the Castle. He was a paid detective and informer; but on this occasion, the detective was detected, through the vigilance of Mr. Arkins, who had him up before a bench of magistrates. A note-book was found in his possession full of memoranda connected with his pursuit, amongst which I saw several jottings concerning myself. In fact, for several months, I found myself haunted by detectives in various disguises, and never went into my own house, or out of it, without being watched. We have all heard much of the espionage of France or Austria. Neither of them is furnished with a police so omnipresent, so inevitable,—above all so treacherous,—as Ireland.

CHAPTER XIX.

MARCH, 1848—THE FRENCH REVOLUTION—WATERFORD ELECTION—AGGREGATE MEETING IN DUBLIN—PROSECUTION OF O'BRIEN, MEAGHER, AND MITCHEL—O'BRIEN IN THE ENGLISH PARLIAMENT—THE " TREASON-FELONY " ACT—TRIAL OF O'BRIEN AND MEAGHER FOR " SEDITION "—THE " UNITED IRISHMAN "—TRIALS FOR ILLEGAL DRILLING—PROSECUTION FOR " SEDITION " ABANDONED—ARREST OF MITCHEL FOR " TREASON-FELONY."

MARCH, '48, was a season of nervous tremor to the British Empire. The exciting news that came in every week from France, Germany, and Italy, intoxicated our people like wine; and the enemy knew that men's minds were entirely turned away from what used to be called "moral" agitation,—which had, indeed, been discovered to be extremely immoral. The structure of the British Parliament, and the delusive semblance of representation which Ireland possessed there, had been carefully calculated for the purposes of our enemy. That was a field expressly laid out and surveyed to ensure our eternal defeat. At the very moment that Europe shook with the crashing downfall of the Orleans throne, the Irish Confederation was using all its efforts, in prosecution of the policy deliberately adopted, to procure the return of Thomas Francis Meagher as representative of his native city, Waterford. He was opposed by *a Repealer* of the O'Connellite school.

You may ask what was the difference between the constitutionally agitating Repeal Association, and the constitutionally agitating Confederation? Why should they oppose one another in Waterford? Understand this distinction: the policy of the Repeal Association was to put men into Parliament who would crave office for themselves and their constituents at the hands of the enemy's government, professing all the while to be seeking for the Repeal. The Confederation was for returning men who would stand on terms of utter defiance towards the "Government," and use their position only to expose and frustrate, as far as possible, all British legislation for Ireland. With reluctance I opposed in the *United Irishman* the return of my friend, Mr. Meagher. To explain both his position and mine, I shall extract from the article in the *United Irishman*:—

"If Ireland had one single *chance* in contending with her ancient enemy upon his own chosen ground,—if Ireland had any *right* to send representatives to a British Parliament,—if Irishmen, there were indeed members of an Imperial senate, and not captives dragged at the chariot wheels of an Imperial ovation in the enemy's capital city,—if that Parliament were not a Lie, an imposture, an outrage, a game in which our part and lot must be disgrace and defeat forever, a shield and strong tower for its masters, but against us a two-edged sword,—if it were *anything* to Ireland besides a conduit of corruption, a workshop of coercion, a storehouse of starvation, a machinery of cheating, and a perpetual memento of slavery,—then we should congratulate the 'electors' of Waterford on this opportunity of doing honor to themselves, and conferring a trust on their most distinguished citizen.

"Mr. Thomas F. Meagher has offered himself as their representative. We give an extract from his address:

"'The grounds upon which I seek your trust are these: I shall not meddle with English affairs. I shall take no part in the strife of parties: all factions are alike to me. I shall go to the English House of Commons to insist upon the right of this country to be held, governed, and defended by its own citizens, and by them alone. Whilst I live, I shall never rest satisfied until the kingdom of Ireland has won a parliament, an army, and a navy of her own.

"'Of other things I shall not speak:—petty ameliorations—instalments of justice—scraps of government patronage;—if these things mingle in the burning hopes of the nation, the day for Ireland has not yet arrived, and I shall wait for other men and other times.

"'But if your thirst be, what I hope it is, for the pure and living waters,—and if you think that my youth and strength, my glory here and hope hereafter, would inspire my efforts to realize your wishes,—every personal objection to me will disappear. You will pledge your trust to my truth, and that obligation will, by its own holiness, compel me to fulfil it.'

"They are noble sentiments; and if there be faith in man, here is a man who will redeem his pledges. What glorious genius, indomitable courage, and passionate devotion to a sacred cause *can do*, we might expect to see done by Mr. Meagher.

"Yet we pray for his defeat. If Mr. Meagher were in Parliament, men's eyes would be attracted thither once more; some hope of 'justice' might again revive in this too easily deluded people. The nobler his genius, the more earnest his zeal, the more conspicuous his patriotism, just the more mischief would he do in propping up, through another session, perhaps through another famine, the miserable delusion of a 'parliamentary party.'"

Mr. Meagher's opponents were, first, one Pat. Costello, a placeman already, and one who desired to be a higher placeman, and to make as many as possible of his constituents placemen too—that is, hired servants of the enemy: second, Sir Henry Winston Barron, a Whig. A number of our principal Confederates went down to Waterford to conduct Meagher's election, as they had gone to Galway before, to oppose Monahan's. And again they were defeated more signally than in Galway. In vain the candidate, in vehement and impassioned language, appealed to the national spirit and patriotism of *the people*. The people ardently responded to his appeal. They would have given their blood for him; but they had *no votes*. The electoral body of Waterford was very limited, was in fact small enough to be reached and penetrated by the touch and the savor of official gold; and Barron was returned by a large majority.

Frankly, and at once, the Confederation accepted the only policy thereafter possible, and acknowledged the meaning of the European Revolutions. On the 15th of March, O'Brien moved an Address of Congratulation to the victorious French people; and ended his speech with these words:—

"It would be recollected that a short time ago he thought it his duty to deprecate all attempts to turn the attention of the people to military affairs, because it seemed to him that, in the then condition of the country, the only effect of leading the people's mind to what was called 'a guerilla warfare' would be to encourage some of the misguided peasantry to the commission of murder (hear, hear). Therefore it was that he declared he should not be a party to giving such a recommendation; but the state of affairs was totally different now, and he had no hesitation in declaring that he thought the minds of intelligent young men should be turned to the consideration of such questions as: how strong places can be captured, and weak ones defended;—how supplies of food and ammunition can be cut off from an enemy;—and how they can be secured to a friendly force (loud cries of hear). The time has also come when every lover of his country should come forward openly, and proclaim his willingness to be enrolled as a member of a national guard (hear and loud cheers). No man, however, should tender his name as a member of that national guard unless he was prepared to do two things—one, to preserve the state from anarchy; the other, to be ready to die for the defence of his country."

Two days after this meeting was St. Patrick's Day. A meeting of the citizens of Dublin was announced for that anniversary, to adopt a similar address, from Dublin to Paris, but was adjourned for two or three days to allow time for negotiations to unite all Repealers of the two parties in the demonstration. Lord Clarendon, doubtless under the advice of his privy-councillor of the *World*, thought it would be a good opportunity to strike terror by a military display. He pretended to apprehend that St. Patrick's Day would be selected for the first day of Dublin barricades; and the troops were kept under arms—the cavalry with horses ready saddled in all the barracks, waiting for the moment to crush the first movement in the blood of our citizens.

The meeting, as I said, was adjourned; but there was no intention of abandoning it; O'Brien had offered, even in case of a *Proclamation* forbidding it, to attend and take the chair; and what he promised the enemy well knew he would perform. In a letter to Lord Clarendon, I felt myself warranted in apprising him that the meeting would assuredly take place on the following Monday, whatever he might do or say to the contrary. It was held, in a vacant space near the river, below the Custom House, and was multitudinous and enthusiastic. No parade of troops was attempted; but we knew that the public buildings, and some private houses, were filled with detachments under arms. These addresses, both from the Confederation and from the city, were to be presented in Paris to the President of the Provisional government, M. de Lamartine; and O'Brien, Meagher, and an intelligent tradesman of high character and independence of mind, named Hollywood, were appointed a deputation to Paris.

All this, it was evident, could not go on long. The Clubs were, in the meantime, rapidly arming themselves with rifles; and blacksmiths' forges were prolific of pikeheads. We hoped, and the Government feared, that no armed collision would be made necessary until September, when the harvest would be all cut, and when the commissariat of the people's war, the cause of the war, and the prize of the war, would be all bound up in a sheaf together. But the foe we had to deal with was no weak fool. The Government understood our views thoroughly, and resolved to precipitate the issue somehow or other. On the morning after that meeting of Dublin citizens, three of us, Smith O'Brien, Mr. Meagher, and myself, were politely waited on by a police magistrate, and requested to give bail that we would stand our trial on a charge of sedition. The ground of prosecution in the two former cases was the language held at the meeting of the Irish Confederation (quoted above in part);—in my case, there were two distinct indictments, for two articles in the *United Irishman*. I was to have two trials, so that if one should fail another might happily succeed. Trials for sedition we regarded as child's play, and showed that we so regarded them. O'Brien and Meagher proceeded to France and presented their address. *

On their return, O'Brien walked into the British Parliament, and found that august body engaged in discussing a new Bill "for the further security of her Majesty's crown." Ministers, in fact, had determined to meet the difficulty by a new "law," the Treason-felony law, by which the writing and printing, or open and advised speaking, of incitements to insurrection in Ireland should be deemed "felony," punishable by transportation. The Bill was introduced by the Whigs, and was warmly supported by the Tories; Sir Robert Peel declaring that, what Ireland needed, was to make her national aspirations not only a crime, but an ignominious crime ; so as to put this species of offence on a footing with arson, or forgery, or waylaying with intent to murder. O'Brien rose to address the House, and never, since first Parliament met in Westminster, was heard such a chorus of frantic and obscene outcries. Honorable members crowed like cocks, lowed like cows, and brayed like jackasses, according to the custom of the Honorable House; but O'Brien, quite unmoved, persisted until he obtained a hearing; and I wish that my limits permitted me to present the whole of that manly and noble speech, in which he took care to reiterate all his "treasons" and "seditions." Take two or three extracts, with the interruptions, as recorded in the London papers of the time:—

* These were mere addresses of congratulation and of sympathy. De Lamartine made a highly poetic but rather unmeaning reply to them. He afterwards, in his History, violently misrepresented them ; being in fact a mere Anglo-Frenchman. Mr. O'Brien convicted him of these misrepresentations. I content myself here with pronouncing the two following sentences, poetic fictions: "Les Irlandais, unix anx Chartistes Anglais, se précipitaient sur le continent et cherchaient des complicités insurrectionnelles en France, à la fois parmi les demagogues au nom de la liberté, et parmi les chefs du parti Catholique au nom du Catholicisme." And again, "L'Angleterre n'attendait pas avec moins de solicitude la reception que ferait Lamartine aux insurgés Irlandais, partis de Dublin pour venir demander *des encouragements et des armes* à la République Française." If the poor feeble Lamartine had confined himself all his life to poetry,—I mean that species of composition in metre which holds itself out for poetry, and is intended to be called poetry,—himself and his France might have been spared the absurdities of that Provisional Government. Let no nation make a confirmed and inveterate poet its chief magistrate.

"Charges have been brought against me as an individual, and against the party with whom I act ('oh!' and ironical cheers). I am here to answer those charges, both for myself and for the party with which I act; and I will say this with regard to my companions in the noble struggle in which we are engaged,—(loud laughter)—that, though I have had an opportunity of seeing the most distinguished men of all parties in this House, I never met a number of men, acting for a great political object, who appeared to me, at least, to be animated by such pure and disinterested motives—(loud laughter)—as those with whom it is my pride to act. Now, sir, with regard to myself. I have been called a traitor—(a tremendous burst of cheers followed this sentence, twice renewed before silence was restored). I do not profess disloyalty to the Queen of England—(ironical applause). But if it be treason to profess disloyalty to this House, and to the government of Ireland by the Parliament of Great Britain—if that be treason, I avow the treason—('oh!' and great excitement). Nay, more, I say it shall be the study of my life to overthrow the dominion of this Parliament over Ireland—(hear, hear, and cries of 'oh!') . . . . . It has been stated I went to France for the purpose of enlisting French aid —(hear, hear)—that is to say, armed aid and succor for my countrymen in the struggle in which they are engaged. This is a misapprehension—(oh! oh! oh!). If I had gone to France asking for aid of an armed kind, believe me I should have come back accompanied by a tolerably large legion of troops—(some laughter, and 'oh! oh!'). You may believe what I say. I only wish you had been in France—(a laugh). The language I have held in Ireland and in France to my countrymen has been this—that Irish freedom must be won by Irish courage and Irish firmness. I had no desire to impose upon my country one description of servitude in the place of another—(hear, hear)—for I believe that the liberty of Ireland, and its redemption from its present position, were they won by foreign bayonets, could only be retained by foreign bayonets; and it is not my desire or intention to place my country under foreign dominion. . . . . . I trust that the Repealers of Ireland will accept that aid which the Chartists are universally prepared to give them. Now, I avow the fact,—I know not whether it be illegal or not,—that I have been instrumental in asking my countrymen to arm (marks of surprise and sensation). I conceive that under the present circumstances of all nations, it is the duty of every man to obtain the possession and learn the use of arms. There is not a nation, I believe, in Europe which does not make it part of its duty to instruct its citizens in the use of arms; and I conceive that it is the peculiar duty of the Irish people to obtain the possession of arms at a time when you tell them you are prepared to crush their expression of opinion, not by argument, but by brute force (loud cries of 'oh! oh!' and expressions of disapprobation)."

The bill was passed into "Law," of course, by immense majorities; and thereafter an Irish Repealer of the Union was to be a "felon." O'Brien returned to Dublin. The deputies were received by a multitudinous and enthusiastic meeting in the Dublin Music Hall; and Meagher presented to the citizens of Dublin, with glowing words, a magnificent flag, the Irish Tri-color, of Green, White, and Orange, surmounted by a pikehead. Of all the Confederates, Meagher was the sole orator, in the highest sense of that term; and those who have only heard him, in America, where his addresses were but rhetorical exercitations, and where the central fire of a great passion was wanting to lift him into a sublime self-abandonment, can ill conceive the effect of his speeches there, poured forth, bright and burning, upon ten thousand hearts whose fuel was so prompt to kindle.

Events hurried on; every day bringing in more and more deplorable accounts of wide-spread starvation and extermination of tenantry; and Dublin, as well as all the other seaports, saw pale and haggard crowds of emigrants trooping to the quays, to take shipping for America. Be generous to these ill-fated refugees! Oh, ye happy Americans, despise them not! Driven, like noxious vermin, from their hearths and the graves of their forefathers, let the great heart of your country open to embrace them,—to warm them to vitality, and illumine their darkened souls with hope.

Our trials approached. They were to be before special juries, struck by the process I have before described. O'Brien and Meagher were first tried; and, as their "sedition" had been so open and avowed,—and as the Whig government was extremely reluctant to pack juries *if they could help it*, —the Crown officers left on each of the two juries *one* Repealer. It was enough. A true Repealer knew that no Irishman *could* commit any offence against a foreign Queen; and in each case the one Repealer stood out, refused to convict, though he should be starved to death; and the traversers, amidst cheering multitudes, were escorted triumphantly from the Four Courts to the Confederate Committee Rooms, where they addressed the people, and promised to repeat and improve upon all their seditions. The excitement of the country was intense. The defeat of the "Government" was celebrated all over the country by bonfires and illuminations, and the clubs became more diligent in arming themselves; but Mr. Monahan, the Attorney-General, foamed and raged. Not only the British empire and the cause of general civilization, but (what was more important) the great cause of Monahan against the world was in danger.

My two trials were still to take place. It was plain to the enemy that there must be no failure here. The *United Irishman* was, by this time, by far the most widely circulated paper in Ireland. It was read in all military and police barracks,—was clubbed for in all parishes,—and duly read on Sundays to eager crowds in all chapel yards. It was in vain our enemy attempted to frighten the agents who sold it. One of them, in Enniskillen, had written that the police of that town had come into his shop and threatened him. I had published his letter, and taunted the "Government" with trying to intimidate mere tradesmen, while they suffered the principal offender to go unpunished. They caused clubmen to be arrested and marched through the streets to gaol, on charges of practising with rifles, or giving or receiving military instruction;—and I demanded to know why those humble men had been treated as common felons, while O'Brien, Meagher, and myself had been politely visited by a magistrate, and blandly requested to come and give bail. The policy of the "Government" at this time, I would characterize,—if I had not set out with the determination of narrating facts only, and using no abusive epithets,—as mean beyond all description. Police magistrates were ordered to arrest parties of young men practising at targets in the neighborhood of country towns, and march them in custody through the streets. Men in Dublin were seized upon and dragged to gaol on the charge of saying "halt" to the clubmen marching to a public meeting;—it was "training in military evolutions" under the Act;—and one young man was actually brought to trial and transported for seven years, on an indictment charging him, for that he had, in a private room in Dublin (not having the fear of God before his eyes, but being moved by the instigation of the devil), said to thirteen other young men, then and there ranged in line, these fatal words, "Right shoulders forward,"—contrary to the peace of our lady the Queen; and so forth.

On the 4th of May, at Thurles Quarter Sessions, in Tipperary, one Michael Gilfoyle was tried before the county judge (appointed by the Crown, of course), for having a *pike* in his possession, contrary to an act just passed prohibiting such articles. The "pike" was produced: it was a hay-fork with two prongs, such as is generally used in Ireland, but rather longer, stronger, and sharper in the prongs, than the police thought it prudent to let men turn hay withal. In fact, it was made upon a plan recommended by the *United Irishman*, as an improved kind of fork for *saving* the crop,— inasmuch as it would turn over, not only a truss of hay, but a policeman, bailiff, or dragoon. Mr. Howley, the county judge, in passing sentence of one year's imprisonment for this offence, took occasion to remark that the instrument was manifestly not intended for agricultural operations, but for civil war, and " was originated by the wicked advices of the *United Irishman*." He further expressed a hope that, when the finding of his Thurles jury, (that a fork is a pike,) should come to the ears of the writers in that incendiary publication, "perhaps it would have the effect of checking their insane career." In short, it was absolutely necessary to crush the incendiary publication, and that without delay.

The day arrived for striking the special juries for my two trials, on the charge of sedition; and I attended in the Crown office with my counsel. The Sheriff's clerk brought in the box purporting to contain cards having the names of all the special jurors of the city of Dublin; from which forty-eight names were to be drawn. The Crown officer blandly asked us whether we were satisfied that the box contained all the names,—a question which had never been answered in that office otherwise than in the affirmative. The Crown lawyers, therefore, and officials were surprised when I answered "No: I am not satisfied: I admit nothing: juries are packed here: I must see all the cards." The Queen's lawyers strongly objected to this course, and urged the officer to proceed to draw the names. After some time, he announced to me that such a question had never been raised before,—that he could not go out of the usual course,—that he would proceed with the business. Then I put on my hat, and said to Sir Colman O'Loghlen and Mr. O'Hagan, my counsel, " Come, then; —we cannot, even by our presence, countenance such a transaction as this: let us go; and they may make much of their jury." We went away. The matter was immediately reported to the Judges, then sitting in the Queen's Bench; and Judge Perrin (the same who had been so scandalized at the packing of juries before,) instantly ordered the officer to send for me, and count and compare the cards before me, though it should occupy all night. This was accordingly done. If there had been any villainy practised in the Sheriff's office, it had been rectified in the meantime. The two juries were struck; and it was instantly evident that on each of them would be men who would never convict me of any offence whatever against a foreign sovereign. The juries, in fact, were more favorable than those which had failed to do the Queen's business in the cases of O'Brien and Meagher; inasmuch as it was sure there would be two or three on each who desired the independence of their country. The enemy dared not go to trial with me before these juries. But what to do? Every week was heightening the spirit of the people, and increasing the number of pikes and rifles in the hands of the peasantry. The *United Irishman* had also forced the *Nation* to adopt the insurrectionary policy, and to publish plain instructions on pike-exercise, and the like,—or else go unread. Lord Clarendon was impatient; Birch, doubtless, was alarmed for "Law and Order;" and Monahan trembled for his due promotion. So they cut the matter short.

The scene at the Crown Office was on the 12th of May. The next day the "Government" abandoned the two prosecutions for sedition; and, about 5 o'clock in the evening, certain members of the detective police beset my house; one of them entered and arrested me on a charge of *Felony* under the new Act. There was no difficulty in finding overt acts; for every week's *United Irishman* contained as much of that saving doctrine which they called treason, as its sixteen pages would hold.

The arrest did not surprise me. It would have been easy for me to keep out of the way, or fly the country; but I was resolved to try conclusions with the "Whig" government in the matter of juries; knowing that they must either pack their jury so stringently as never was jury in this world, or I would obtain such a victory as would soon make the island untenable to them. Do not forget the speeches of Lord John Russell and Mr. Macaulay, denouncing all jury-packing, which I quoted before. Both these men were now Ministers of the Queen.

For the next two weeks, awaiting the result of this trial, all things stood still in Ireland, except the Famine, and the "Addresses of Confidence" from landlords, and the typhus-fever, and the clearing of estates, and the wail of the Banshee.

CHAPTER XX.

RAGE OF THE BRITISH PRESS—PROTESTANT REPEAL ASSOCIATIONS—LORD CLARENDON'S MANŒUVRES AMONG THE ORANGEMEN—PROCLAMATIONS AGAINST "COMMUNISTS"—THE CHARTISTS AND IRISH IN ENGLAND—LETTER TO THE PROTESTANTS OF THE NORTH—PROSECUTION.

It was May, '48: and in the opinion of our London enemies, the time had come to put an end to treason and sedition in Ireland by all or any means. They knew we would not commence an actual insurrection, until November; and they feared that by that time Ireland might be too strong for them. They betrayed their apprehensions in various ways. The *Morning Chronicle*, then a ministerial organ, to rouse the fear and rage of ignorant English readers, discoursed in this manner:—

"Let us suppose an Irish Republic established on the most democratic basis, and a government formed of the present heads of the Repeal party, Messrs. O'Brien, Meagher, and Mitchel, with, perhaps, an infusion of O'Connells and MacHales. Their avowed 'mission' is to break up the 'old British empire;' their appetites would have been *whetted by Saxon blood*, and their ambition flushed by success over Englishmen. An unemployed and desperate population would be on their hands;. and their only chance of existence would consist in expending its energies on foreign war. Let us proceed to reflect that they would then, as now, possess in every town of Great Britain an Irish garrison, and that then, as now, they would command the sympathies and assistance of all the disaffected part of our working population. . . . .

"Let any sensible man calmly ask himself what possible chances all these contingencies combined would leave for preserving peace. Well, then, say our opponents, let war come; we will reconquer Ireland. If you do, you will be exactly where you are now; but will you be able to conquer her? Recollect that if England would be the 'natural enemy' of an Irish Republic, France and America would be her 'natural allies.'

" . . . . We have great faith in the star of England, but—under these circumstances—we fear we should have to confess that Mr. Mitchel's sinister prophecies were on the point of accomplishment, and that the last hour of the 'old British empire' had struck. That would, indeed, be a glorious day for Ireland! The tables would be turned with a vengeance, when an Irish army of occupation should give the law in the British metropolis."

The whole British Press ran wild with furious imprecations against these Irish "traitors" and "rebels." The *Morning Post* suggested that :—

"A bill might be passed, enabling two or more magistrates, upon satisfactory proof of treasonable language having been spoken or written by any person, to commit that person forthwith to prison and hard labor for three months. Or a summary power *to flog* the persons guilty of the infamy of exciting the people to attack the government."

The British people were thoroughly aroused to their danger. Their organ, *Punch*, duly represented, for them, the Irish cut-throats, with every infamy of outrage that wood-engraving and types could express; and even the grave *Spectator* offered some *receipts* for settling matters with us; of which I shall give one as a sample :—

"HOW TO ROAST AN IRISH PATRIOT.

"Pick out a young one; speakers or editors are very good. Tie the arms behind the back, or close to the sides; but not too tight, or the patriot will be prevented from moving, and the ribs will not be done. Skewer down to the pile. You will want a strong, steady fire. Dry pine makes a very good blaze. When the fire gets low, throw in a little oil or fat. When nearly done, a little gunpowder thrown in will make the patriot skip: some cooks consider this important."

This is evidently a joke, and intended to be amusing: but such things show what was the temper of the British people. They had learned, as they believed, the real character of Irish agitators, through the articles which Lord Clarendon hired Birch to write about us; and were impatient to destroy such a gang. The Treason Felony Act had been supported eagerly in Parliament by both parties; it instantly passed through the House of Peers; and the *Illustrated News* had a large engraving, representing the queen signing her name to it with an air of vixenish spite, stamping her foot as she did it.

In Ireland, Lord Clarendon was getting up, through the Grand Masters of the Orangemen, loyal Addresses, and declarations against "rebels" and "traitors." In fact, the Orange farmers and burghers of the North were fast becoming diligent students of the *United Irishman ;* and although they and their Order had been treated with some neglect of late, both by England and by the Irish Aristocracy, they were now taken into high favor; and arms were secretly issued to some of their lodges, from Dublin Castle. *

But this needed prudence; for Protestant Repeal Associations had been formed in Dublin, in Drogheda, and even in Lurgan, a great centre of Orangeism. To counteract the progress we had made in this direction, the aristocracy and the clergy were incessant in their efforts, and the Protestants were assured that if Ireland should throw off the dominion of Queen Victoria, we would all instantly become vassals to the Woman who sitteth upon Seven Hills.

The Viceroy, at the same time, took care to frighten the moneyed citizens of Dublin and other towns by placards warning them against the atrocious designs of "Communists" and "Jacobins," whose only object, his lordship intimated, was plunder. † Lord Clarendon seemed to deliberate for some days whether he would *proclaim* and disarm Dublin, under the late Arms Act; or whether he would make one last desperate plunge into the "Law." The first course would have drenched the city in blood. Our Clubmen had not gone to so much trouble and expense in supplying themselves with arms, only to give them up to the enemy. The Chartists and Irish in England, too, were in dangerous humor; and if troops had once been let loose on the people in Ireland, many a city and factory would blaze high in England. On the whole, he resolved to begin with me. If I were once removed, he thought the difficulty would be more manageable.

A speech, a letter, a short article, all published in the *United Irishman*, formed the *corpus delicti* of the crime which the enemy undertook to prosecute. Of these it is enough to present the letter; a letter which any candid reader will admit to have been at least provoking, if not illegal. It was addressed to the Protestants of the North :—

---

* This was quite unknown to the Public at the time : one case of it only (so far as I know) ever came to light. It was a shipment of 500 stand of arms to the Belfast Orangemen.

† I attribute these placards to Lord Clarendon without scruple. They were printed by the Government printer, and paid for out of our taxes. But it is quite possible that the Viceroy, if charged with these things, would deny them, because they were done through a third party—perhaps Birch. In like manner he denied all knowledge of the shipment of muskets to the Belfast Orangemen: they were sent, however, from his Castle, and through a subordinate official of his household.

"My Friends,—Since I wrote my first letter to you, many kind and flattering addresses have been made to you by exceedingly genteel and very rich noblemen and gentlemen. Those of you, especially, who are Orangemen, seem to have somehow got into high favor with this genteel class, which must make you feel rather strange, I think;—you have not been used to much recognition and encouragement, of late years, from British Viceroys, or the noble and right worshipful Grand Masters. They rather avoided you; seemed, indeed, as many thought, somewhat ashamed of you and your old anniversaries. Once upon a time, no Irish nobleman or British Minister dared make light of the colors of Aughrim and the Boyne. But can you divine any cause for the sudden change of late? Do you understand why the Whig Lord Clarendon calls you so many names of endearment, and the Earl of Enniskillen tenderly entreats you as a father his only child? Can these men *want anything* from you?

"Let us see what the drift of their addresses generally is. Lord Clarendon, the English governor, congratulates you on your 'loyalty,' and your 'attachment to the Constitution,' and seems to calculate, though I know not why, upon a continuance of those exalted sentiments in the North. Lord Enniskillen, the Irish nobleman, for his part, cautions you earnestly against Popery and Papists, and points out how completely you would be overborne and swamped by Catholic majorities in all public affairs.

"My Lord Enniskillen does not say a word to you about what is, after all, the main concern, the *tenure of your farms;* not one word. It is about your Protestant interest he is uneasy. He is apprehensive, not lest you should be evicted by landlords, and sent to the poorhouse, but lest Purgatory and Seven Sacraments should be thrust down your throats. This is simply a Protestant pious fraud of his lordship's; merely a right worshipful humbug. Lord Enniskillen, and every other commonly informed man, knows that there is now no Protestant interest at all; that there is absolutely nothing left for Protestant and Catholic to quarrel for; even the Church Establishment is not a Catholic and Protestant question, inasmuch as all Dissenters, *and all plebeian churchmen*, are as much concerned to put an end to that nuisance as Catholics are. Lord Enniskillen knows, too, (or if he do not, he is the very stupidest Grand Master in Ulster,) that an ascendancy of one sect over another is from henceforth *impossible:* the fierce religious zeal that animated our fathers on both sides is utterly dead and gone. I do not know whether this is for our advantage or not: but, at any rate, it is gone; nobody in all Europe would now so much as understand it; and if any man talks to you now of religious sects, when the matter in hand relates to civil and political rights, to administration of government, or distribution of property,—depend on it, though he wear a coronet on his head, he means to cheat you.

"In fact, religious hatred has been kept alive in Ireland longer than anywhere else in Christendom, just for the simple reason that Irish landlords and British statesmen found their own account in it; and so soon as Irish landlordism and British dominion are finally rooted out of the country, it will be heard of no longer in Ireland, any more than it is in France or Belgium now.

"If you have any doubt whether Lord Enniskillen means to cheat you, I only ask you to remember: *first*, that he has written you a long and parental letter, upon the state of the country, and has not once alluded to your Tenant-right; and, *second*, that he belongs to that class of persons from whom *alone* can come any danger to your Tenant-right,—which is your life and property.

"As for Lord Clarendon and his friendly addresses, exhorting to 'loyalty' and attachment to the institutions of the country, I need hardly tell you that *he* is a cheat. What institutions of the country are there to be attached to? That all who pay taxes should have a voice in the outlay of those taxes, is not one of our institutions;—that those who create the whole wealth of the State by their labor, should get leave to live, like Christians, on the fruits of that labor, *this* is not amongst the institutions of the country. *Tenant-right* is not an institution of the country. No; out-door relief is our main institution at present—our *Magna Charta*—our Bill of Rights. A high-paid church and a low-fed people are institutions; stipendiary clergymen, packed juries, a monstrous army and navy, which we pay, not to defend, but to coerce us;—these are institutions of the country. Indian meal, too, strange to say, though it grows four thousand miles off, has come to be an institution of this country. Are these the 'venerable institutions' you are expected to shoulder your muskets to defend?

"But, then, 'Protestants have always been *loyal* men.' Have they? And what do they mean by 'loyalty'? I have never found that, in the north of Ireland, this word had any meaning at all, except that we, Protestants, hated the Papists, and despised the French. This, I think, if you will examine it, is the true theory of 'loyalty' in Ulster. I can hardly fancy any of my countrymen so totally stupid as to really prefer high taxes to low taxes,—to be really proud of the honor of supporting 'the Prince Albert' and his Lady, and their children, and all the endless list of cousins and uncles that they have, in magnificent idleness, at the sole expense of half-starved laboring people. I should like to meet the northern farmer, or laboring man, who would tell me, in so many words, that he prefers dear government to cheap government; that he likes the House of Brunswick better than his own house; that he would rather have the affairs of the country managed by foreign noblemen and gentlemen than by himself and his neighbors; that he is content to pay, equip, and arm an enormous army, and give the command of it to those foreign noblemen, and to be disarmed himself, or *liable* to be disarmed, as *you* are, my friends, at any moment. I should like to see the face of the Ulsterman who would say plainly that he deems himself unfit to have a voice in the management of his own affairs, the outlay of his own taxes, or the government of his own country. If any of you will admit this, I own he is a 'loyal' man, and 'attached to our venerable institutions;' and I wish him joy of his loyalty, and a good appetite for his yellow meal.

"Now, Lord Clarendon and Lord Enniskillen want you to say all this. The Irish noble and the British Statesman want the very same thing; they are both in a tale. The Grand Master knows that if you stick by your loyalty, and uphold British connection, you secure to him his coronet, his influence, and his rental—discharged of Tenant-right, and all plebeian claims. And Lord Clarendon knows, on his side, that if you uphold landlordism, and abandon Tenant-right, and bend all your energies to resisting the 'encroachments of Popery,' you thereby perpetuate British dominion in Ireland, and keep the 'Empire' going, yet a little while. Irish landlordism has made a covenant with British government, in these terms;—'Keep down for me my tenantry, my peasantry, my *masses*, in due submission, with your troops and laws;—and I will garrison the island for you, and hold it, as your liegeman and vassal forever.'

"Do you not know in your very hearts, that this is true? and still you are 'loyal' and attached to the institutions of the country!

"I tell you, frankly, that I, for one, am not 'loyal.' I am not wedded to the Queen of England, nor unalterably attached to the House of Brunswick. In fact, I love my own barn better than I love that House. The time is long past when Jehovah *anointed* Kings. The thing has long since grown a monstrous imposture, and has been already, in some civilized countries, detected as such, and drummed out accordingly. A modern King, my friends, is no more like an ancient anointed Shepherd of the People than an Archbishop's apron is like the *Urim* and *Thummim*. There is no divine right now but in the Sovereign People.

"And, for the 'institutions of the country,' I loathe and despise them; we are sickening and dying of these institutions, fast; they are consuming us like a plague, degrading us to paupers in mind, body, and estate,—yes, making our very souls beggarly and cowardly. They are a failure and a fraud, these institutions;—from the topmost crown-jewel to the meanest detective's note-book, there is no soundness in them. God and man are weary of them. Their last hour is at hand; and I thank God that I live in the days when I shall witness the utter downfall, and trample upon the grave, of the most portentous, the grandest, meanest, falsest, and cruellest tyranny that ever deformed this world.

"These, you think, are strong words: but they are not one whit stronger than the feeling that prompts them—that glows this moment deep in the souls of moving and awakening millions of our fellow-countrymen of Ireland; aye, and in *your* souls, too, Protestants of Ulster, if you would acknowledge it to yourselves. I smile at the formal resolution about 'loyalty to Queen Victoria,' so eagerly passed and hurried over as a dubious kind of form at Tenant-right meetings and 'Protestant Repeal' meetings. I laughed outright, here, on Tuesday night last, at the suspicious warmth with which Dublin merchants, as if half-afraid of themselves, protested so anxiously that they would yield in *loyalty* to none. They, democrats by nature and position, meeting there, without a nobleman to countenance them,—with the Queen's representative scowling black upon them from his castle,—are, they declare it with most nervous solemnity, *loyal* men. Indeed, it was easy to see that a vague feeling was upon them of the real meaning and tendency of all these meetings,—of what all this must end in, and to what haven they, and you, and we, are all, in a happy hour, inevitably drifting together.

"My friends, the People's Sovereignty, the land and sea and air of Ireland for the People of Ireland : this is the gospel that the heavens and the earth are preaching, and that all hearts are secretly burning to embrace. Give up forever that old interpretation you put upon the word 'Repeal.' Repeal is no priest-movement ; it is no sectarian movement ; it is no money swindle, nor 'Eighty-two' delusion, nor puffery, nor O'Connellism, nor Mullaghmast 'greencap' stage-play, nor loud-sounding inanity of any sort, got up for any man's profit or praise. It is the mighty, passionate struggle of a nation hastening to be born into new national life ; in which unspeakable throes all the parts, and powers, and elements of our Irish existence,—our Confederations, our Protestant Repeal Associations, our Tenant-right Societies, our Clubs, Cliques, and Committees,—amidst confusions enough and the saddest jostling and jumbling,—are all inevitably tending to one and the same illustrious goal, —*not* a local legislature—*not* a return to ' our ancient Constitution,' not a golden link or a patchwork Parliament, or a College Green chapel-of-ease to Saint Stephen's—but an Irish Republic, one and indivisible.

"And how are we to meet that day ? *In arms*, my countrymen, in arms. Thus, and not otherwise, have ever nations of men sprung to liberty and power. But why do I reason thus with you, —with you, the Irish of Ulster, who never have denied the noble creed and sacraments of manhood ? *You* have not been schooled for forty years in the fatal cant of moral force ; you have not been utterly debauched and emasculated by the clap-trap platitudes of public meetings, and the empty glare of ' imposing demonstrations.' You have not yet learned the litany of slaves, and the whine of beaten hounds, and the way to die a coward's death. No ; let once the great idea of our country's destiny seize on *you*, my kinsmen, and the way will be plain before you as a pike-staff twelve feet long.

"Yet there is one lesson you must learn :—fraternal respect for your countrymen of the South, and that sympathy with them, and faith in them, without which there can be no vital nationality in Ireland. You little know the history and sore trials and humiliations of this ancient Irish race ; ground and trampled first for long ages in the very earth, and then taught—expressly *taught*—in solemn harangues, and even in sermons, that it was their duty to die, and see their children die before their faces, rather than resist their tyrants as men ought. *You* can hardly believe that creatures with the gait and aspect of men could have been brought to this. And you cannot wonder that they should have been slow, slow, in struggling upward out of such darkness and desolation. But I tell you, the light has at length come to them : the flowery Spring of this year is the dawning of their day ; and before the cornfields of Ireland are white for the reaper, our eyes shall see the sun flashing gloriously, if the Heavens be kind to us, on a hundred thousand pikes.

"I will speak plainly. There are now growing on the soil of Ireland a wealth of grain, and roots, and cattle, far more than enough to sustain in life and in comfort all the inhabitants of the island. *That wealth must not leave us another year*,—not until every grain of it is fought for in every stage, from the binding of the sheaf to the loading of the ship. And the effort necessary to that simple act of self-preservation will at one and the same blow prostrate British dominion and landlordism together. 'Tis but the one act of volition;—if we resolve but *to live*, we make our country a free and Sovereign State.

"Will *you* not gird up your loins for this great national struggle, and stand with your countrymen for Life and Land? Will *you*, the sons of a warlike race, the inheritors of conquering memories, with the arms of freemen in all your homes, and relics of the gallant Republicans of 'Ninety-eight forever before your eyes,—will *you* stand folding your hands in helpless 'loyalty,' and while every nation in Christendom is seizing on its birthright with armed hand, will you take patiently your rations of yellow meal, and your inevitable portion of eternal contempt?

"If this be your determination, Protestants of Ulster, then make haste, sign addresses of loyalty and confidence in Lord Clarendon, and protest with that other Lord your unalterable attachment to 'our venerable institutions.'

"JOHN MITCHEL."

All this was open and outrageous "treason," of course; admitting that Queen Victoria was then the Queen of Ireland, and not a foreign tyrant. Yet, nine-tenths of the citizens of Dublin would have, on their oath, found the writer not guilty; and the liberal Whig Government were bound, by all their professions, *not* to pack juries. But they were still more strongly bound to crush the Press, and break the types, and fetter the hand which sent forth weekly addresses of this sort, to be read and laid to heart by at least a hundred thousand men.

How they solved this difficulty is to be told.

CHAPTER XXI.

JURIES IN IRELAND—WHIG PROFESSIONS OF IMPARTIALITY—IN THE DOCK—HOLMES CHALLENGING THE ARRAY—CLOSING SCENE—THE CLUBS RESTRAINED—MY LAST WEEK IN IRELAND.

IN this chapter I shall gladly take leave of myself; for the moment has arrived when I drop out of the history of Ireland, and disappear.

In provoking this legal contest with the enemy, my calculation was that I should obtain over them an easy, signal, and most perilous victory—provided they did not pack the jury. But, if they should pack the jury, and snatch what they call a conviction by the usual methods of British Government in Ireland, then I hoped the people were now too thoroughly roused to submit peaceably to such an outrage.

The matter of *juries* had always been a knotty one in Ireland, since the days of Edmund Spenser. The poet of the "Faëry Queene," being himself an English "undertaker," and the grantee of forfeited estates, and being, therefore, the natural enemy of all Irishmen, in his famous "View of the State of Ireland," observes, through the mouth of *Irenæus:—*

"Yet is the law of itself goode; and the first institution thereof being given to *all Englishmen* very rightfully; but now that the Irish have stepped into the very roomes of our English, wee are now to become heedful and provident in *iuryes.*" *

In fact, the difficulty was, that with Irishmen on juries, the English Sovereign never could obtain a verdict, either on inquisition into forfeited estates, or on criminal trials. Spenser, of course, attributes this to a natural turn for perjury among the Irish:—" they make no conscience to perjure themselves in their verdicts, and damne their soules." Yet Sir John Davies, Attorney-General of King James the First, in Ireland, another very hostile authority, bears testimony to the loyalty and love of law and justice which pre-

* Spenser's View, p. 34.

vailed in that island: "there being no nation under the sun that did love equal and indifferent justice better than the Irish, or that would rest better satisfied with the execution thereof, although it were against themselves, so as they might have the protection and benefit of the law, when upon a just cause they did desire it." *

These discrepancies are only to be explained by recollecting that the Irish never believed English "law" to be justice; but invariably found that "law" was at one side and justice at the other; which indeed they experience until this day. For some generations after Spenser's time, and during the whole period of the penal-laws, the British Government solved the difficulty by simply excluding Irish Catholics from juries. But Catholic Emancipation came; and liberal professions (especially from the Whigs) of a desire to administer law impartially. You have already had occasion to see how these professions were carried out on the trial of O'Connell. In the cases of O'Brien and Meagher, the Crown officers had admitted *one* Irish Repealer on each jury, and failed.

It was manifest that the Whig theory would not work; and in my case it was resolved that there must be no risk even of possible failure. Yet the Whig Ministers were extremely reluctant to part with their reputation for impartiality (which reputation, however, was false); and, accordingly, only two days before my "pretended trial," Lord John Russell, in answer to questions in the House of Commons, declared that he had written to "his noble friend" (Lord Clarendon) that "he trusted there would not arise any charge of any kind of unfairness, as to the composition of the juries; as, for his own part, he would rather see those parties acquitted, than that there should be any such unfairness."

Lord Clarendon, however, informed him that, for this once, he could not afford to adhere to the Whig maxims,—that a conviction must be had, *per fas aut nefas*. Not that the liberal and conciliatory Whigs would openly renounce their honest policy; on the contrary, they would pursue it more steadfastly than ever; but I must be out of the way first. His lordship counselled his colleagues, in this matter, as

---

* Sir John Davies His. Rel.

Ulysses counselled Neoptolemus, when the business was to procure the arms from Philoctetes under false pretences:—

> 'I know, indeed, that it is not your natural disposition
> To speak falsely, or to contrive injustice;
> But—it is sweet to be the winner;—
> Do it this once: and *afterwards* we will be honest."

During the two weeks that I awaited my trial, it became well known that the "Government" would pack my jury most carefully; and our Dublin Confederate Clubs were becoming violently excited. The boldest of them were for making an attack on Newgate prison; letting the struggle commence there and then; cutting the gas-pipes on some dark night; precipitating the clubs on Castle, barracks, and prisons; and either clearing out our metropolis of the English enemy, or perishing amidst its ruins and cinders. This was the right counsel. I thought so then; and, after many years, I deliberately think so still. The English Government had procured an "Act of Parliament" avowedly to make it felony to *say* what nine-tenths of our people thought and felt; and was now about to shut out those nine-tenths of our people from the exercise of the common civic office of Jurors, to crush one man (no matter what man) under a notoriously false pretence. When I say false pretence, it is not that I deny the matter charged to me, but that I deny having ever been tried at all. The false pretence was the "trial."

The Attorney-General resolved that the trial should take place at the regular Commission Court, or City Assizes; and that the jury should not be a special, but a common one. On the striking of special juries, he had discovered that I was fully able to expose, at least, if not defeat, the secret machinations of the Crown Officer; so I was to be arraigned before a common jury of Dublin citizens, selected by the Sheriff to serve on the pending Commission.

The Juror's Book, containing a list of all the qualified householders of Dublin, whose property entitled them to serve as jurors, had 4,570 names, of whom 3,000 were Catholics. Before my arrest, the Sheriff had designated one hundred and fifty of these jurors, and summoned them to attend on the Commission: but *after* my arrest, the Sheriff, knowing that important business was to be done—and being, as I have before explained, a creature of the

Crown,—altered that panel of one hundred and fifty names, removed from it most of the Catholic names, and filled their places not only with Protestants, (that would not suffice,) but with Orangemen, Englishmen, tradesmen to the Lord Lieutenant, in short, with people who were well known to be ready "to do the Queen's business," as that sort of transaction is called in Ireland. But it was not enough to pack the panel,—the jury was next to be carefully packed out of that panel; a thing which was easy enough; because the "Crown" in Ireland exercises the power of *unlimited challenge*, in making up common juries.

Matters being thus prepared, on the 25th of May, I was brought up from Newgate prison, by an underground passage, into the Court House, on Green Street. Outside, the streets were occupied by troops; and but few of my friends could gain admittance as spectators.

The imagination of every reader must help me out here. Let any high-spirited Irishman try to conceive himself in my place on that day: confronting that coarse mimicry of Law and Justice; on the brink of a fate worse than a thousand deaths; stationed in a dock between two thieves, for having dared to aspire to the privilege of freedom and manhood for myself and for my children; with all the horrible sufferings and high aspirations of my country crowding on memory and imagination, and the moan of our perishing nation seeming to penetrate even there, and to load the air I breathed; beholding the cause of our ancient nationhood brought to be decided, not, as I had hoped, by the proud array of our people in the field, but by the ignominious parchments of a dastard lawyer and the packed jury of a perjured Sheriff. Scorn almost overcame indignation, as I saw the exquisitely elaborated preparations of the enemy: and I felt that I would respect Lord Clarendon far more if he had hired one of his detectives to stab me in the dark. That would have been a crime; but surely not so vile and hideous a crime as this prostitution of the Courts and the name and forms of Justice.

The trial proceeded. The leading counsel for the defence was old Robert Holmes,—the brother-in-law of Robert Emmet,—the most eminent barrister in Ireland;—who had always refused the honor of a silk gown, and all other honors and promotions, at the hands of a government which he believed to be the mortal enemy of his country. Of course, he challenged the array of jurors on the ground of fraud; but the Attorney-general's brother, Stephen Monahan, clerk in the Attorney-General's office, and also one Wheeler, clerk in the Sheriff's office, had been carefully sent out of the city to a distant part of Ireland; and Baron Lefroy was most happy to avail himself of the defect of evidence to give his opinion that the panel was a good and honest panel. The Crown used its privilege of peremptory challenge to the very uttermost; *every* Catholic, and *most* Protestants, who answered to their names, were ordered to "stand by." There were thirty-nine challenges: nineteen Catholics,—*all* the Catholics who answered to their names, were peremptorily set aside, and twenty other gentlemen, who, though Protestants, were suspected of some national feeling, were also set aside:—that is to say, the Crown dared not go to trial with me before the People, Catholic or Protestant. The twelve men finally obtained by the sifting process had amongst them two or three Englishmen; the rest were faithful slaves of the Castle; and all Protestants of the most Orange dye.

Of course there was a "verdict" of Guilty; and a sentence of fourteen years' transportation. The facts charged were easily proved; they were patent, notorious, often repeated, and ostentatiously deliberate; insomuch that jurymen who felt themselves to be subjects of the Queen of England could not do otherwise than convict. On the other hand, any Irish Nationalist must acquit. Never before had the government of the foreign enemy and the Irish people met on so plain an issue. Never before was it made so manifest that the enemy's government maintains its supremacy over Ireland by systematically breaking the "law,"—even its own law; by turning its judicial trials into solemn farces, its ermined judges into bad actors, and its fountain of Justice into an obscene "mother of dead dogs."

Of course, both Mr. Holmes, and the prisoner on trial, took good care to manifest their sense of all this. Holmes informed the jury that they knew themselves to be well and truly packed; and when I was asked if I had anything to say why sentence should not be passed upon me, I remarked that I had not been *tried*. Baron Lefroy chose to interpret this as an impeachment of the jury for perjury: but I took care to contradict the judge. I could not, in that last moment of my life, afford to suffer any misrepresentation of the true issue: so I interrupted him to declare that I did not charge the jurors with perjury; but charged the sheriff (that is, another name for the Queen,) with empanelling only those who were well known to be my mortal enemies. When the sentence was passed, and every human being in court, friends and enemies, stood aghast at its murderous severity, I addressed the judges in a few sentences, wherein I concentrated all the disdain and defiance that had been gathering in my heart for two days:—

"'The law has now done its part, and the Queen of England, her crown and government in Ireland, are now secure, pursuant to act of parliament. I have done my part also. Three months ago I promised Lord Clarendon and his government, who hold this country for the English, that I would provoke him into his courts of justice, as places of this kind are called, and that I would force him, publicly and notoriously, to pack a jury against me to convict me, or else that I would walk a free man out of this court, and provoke him to a contest in another field. My lords, I knew I was setting my life on that cast; but I knew that, in either event, victory should be with me;—and it is with me. Neither the jury, nor the judges, nor any other man in this court presumes to imagine that it is a criminal who stands in this dock (murmurs of applause, which the police endeavored to repress). I have shown what the law is made of in Ireland. I have shown that her Majesty's government sustains itself in Ireland by packed juries—by partizan judges—by perjured sheriffs—'

"After an interruption from Baron Lefroy—who 'could not sit there,' to suffer the prisoner at that bar to utter very nearly a repetition of the offence for which he had been sentenced—Mitchel proceeded:

"'What I have now to add is simply this—I have acted all through this business, from the first, under a strong sense of duty. I do not repent anything I have done; and I believe that the course which I have opened is only commenced. The Roman who saw his hand burning to ashes before the tyrant, promised that three hundred should follow out his enterprise. Can I not promise for one, for two, for three?—'

"Indicating, as he spoke, Reilly, Martin, and Meagher. 'Promise for me'—'and me'—'and me, Mitchel,' rose around him in commingled tones of earnest solemnity, passionate defiance, and fearless devotion, from his friends and followers; and, embracing the exciting scene in a glance, he cried with proud eagerness:—

"'For one, for two, for three? Aye, for hundreds!'

"A scene of immense excitement followed, in the midst of

which the judges fled from the bench, the prisoner was huddled off, waving his hand to his friends; two of whom, Meagher and Doheney, were arrested for giving vent to the feeling impossible to suppress at such a moment.

"After they had been discharged, and when order was restored, Holmes rose to add his defiance to that of the prisoner. He said:—

"'My lords:—I think I had a perfect right to use the language I did yesterday. I wish now to state that what I said yesterday, as an advocate, I adopt to-day as my own opinion. I here avow all I have said; and, perhaps, under the late Act of Parliament, her Majesty's Attorney-General, if I have violated the law, may think it his duty to proceed against me in that way. I now say, with deliberation, that the sentiments I expressed with regard to England, and her treatment of this country, are my sentiments; and I here avow them openly. The Attorney-General is present—I retract nothing. These are my well-judged sentiments—these are my opinions as to the relative position of England and Ireland, and I have, as you seem to insinuate, violated the law by stating these opinions. I now deliberately do so again. Let her Majesty's Attorney-General do his duty to his government: I have done *mine* to my country.'"

Before dismissing *myself* from the scene forever, I will add that if anything had been wanted to justify me, in my own eyes, for all that I had done and meditated, the earnest and impassioned advocacy of the brave old Republican of '98 would have contented me well. It caused me to feel that my defeated life was at least one link in the unbroken chain of testimony borne by my country against foreign dominion; and with this consciousness I knew that my chains would weigh light. "In this island," exclaimed Meagher, "the English never, never shall have rest. The work begun by the Norman never shall be completed."

An armed steamer waited in the river on the day of my sentence; the whole garrison of Dublin was under arms, on pretence of a review in the Park; a place was secretly designated for my embarkation, below the city, where bridges over a canal, and over the entrance to the Custom House docks could be raised, to prevent any concourse of the people in that direction; and, two or three hours after the sentence, I was hurried off in a close omnibus filled with police, and carried by a circuitous route to the river, escorted by a force of cavalry and mounted police.

For two days before, the leaders of the Confederation had been earnestly engaged in restraining the natural impulse of our Clubs to attempt a rescue. Meagher and Reilly had been at first eager for this desperate enterprise. "I have but one life to give," exclaimed Reilly to his Club, "and I give it: let others swear the same." Meagher had declared that before the enemy should embark me in a convict-ship, Kingstown harbor would be one pool of blood. But O'Brien was absent from Dublin: some others of our Confederates sincerely believed it would be criminal to expose the citizens, not half-armed and not disciplined at all, to the hazard of so horrible a carnage: others still have been charged with opposing all movement out of personal hostility to me, or out of mere cowardice. I have no care to scrutinize motives: and it is enough to know that the most trusted men in the Confederation finally determined to restrain the Clubs, and suffer the last act of this elaborate national insult and outrage to be transacted in quiet. They came to me, the day before the trial, in my prison, entreating me to issue an Address to the Clubs under my own hand, that they should suffer me to be carried away peacefully: I refused utterly; and perhaps too bitterly.

Reilly fumed in silent rage. Meagher, being reluctantly coerced by the majority of his comrades to check the fierce impulse of his passion, labored like the rest, to calm the indignation of the Clubs: and it is just to give his own account of his own conduct. In a speech to the Confederation, a few days after my removal, he said:—

"In those feelings of depression and shame I deeply share; and from the mistrust with which some of you, at least, may regard the members of the late Council, I shall not hold myself exempt. If they are to blame, so am I. Between the hearts of the people and the bayonets of the government, I took my stand, with the members of the Council, and warned back the precipitate devotion which scoffed at prudence as a crime. I am here to answer for that act. If you believe it to have been the act of a dastard, treat me with no delicacy,—treat me with no respect. Vindicate your courage in the impeachment of the coward. The necessities and perils of the cause forbid the interchange of courtesies. Civilities are out of place in the whirl and tumult of the tempest.

"The address of the Council to the people of Ireland—the address signed by William Smith O'Brien—bears witness to your determination. It states that thousands of Confederates had pledged themselves that John Mitchel should not leave these shores but through their blood. We were bound to make this statement—bound in justice to you—bound in honor to the country. Whatever odium may flow from that scene of victorious defiance, in which the government played its part without a stammer or a check, none falls on you.

You would have fought, had we not seized your hands, and bound them.

"Let no foul tongue, then, spit its sarcasm upon the people. They were ready for the sacrifice; and had the word been given, the stars would burn this night above a thousand crimsoned graves. The guilt is ours;—let the sarcasms fall upon our heads.

"We told you in the Clubs, four days previous to the trial, the reasons that compelled us to oppose the project of a rescue. The concentration of 10,000 troops upon the city—the incomplete organization of the people—the insufficiency of food, in case of a sustained resistance—the uncertainty as to how far the country districts were prepared to support us—these were the chief reasons that forced us into an antagonism with your generosity, your devotion, your intrepidity. Night after night we visited the Clubs, to know your sentiments, your determination;—and to the course we instructed you to adopt, you gave, at length, a reluctant sanction.

"Now, I do not think it would be candid in me to conceal the fact, that the day subsequent to the arrest of John Mitchel, I gave expression to sentiments having a tendency quite opposite to the advice I have mentioned. At a meeting of the 'Grattan Club,' I said that the Confederation ought to come to the resolution to resist by force the transportation of John Mitchel; and if the worst befel us, the ship that carried him away should sail upon a sea of blood. I said this, and I shall not now conceal it. I said this, and I shall not shrink from the reproach of having acted otherwise. Upon consideration, I became convinced they were sentiments which, if acted upon, would associate my name with the ruin of the cause. I felt it my duty, therefore to retract them;—not to disown, but to condemn them;—not to shrink from the responsibility which the avowal of them might entail, but to avert the disaster which the enforcement of them would ensure.

"You have now heard all I have to say on that point; and with a conscience happy in the thought that it has concealed nothing, I shall exultingly look forward to an event—the shadow of which already encompasses us—for the vindication of my conduct, and the attestation of my truth. Call me coward,—call me renegade. I will accept these titles as the penalties which a fidelity to my convictions has imposed. It will be so for a short time only. To the end I see the path I have been ordained to walk: and upon the grave which closes in that path, I can read no coward's epitaph."

The enemy were themselves somewhat surprised at the ease with which they had borne me out of the heart of Dublin, at noonday, in chains; and evidently thought they would have but small trouble in crushing any attempts at insurrection afterwards. The Confederates waited until "the time" should come; and some of them, indeed, were fully resolved to make an insurrection in the harvest: yet, as might have been expected, "the time" never came. The individual desperation of Dillon, Meagher, O'Gorman,

Leyne, Reilly, could achieve nothing while the people were dispirited both by famine and by long submission to insolent oppression. "When will *the time* come?" exclaimed Martin, "the time about which your orators so boldly vaunt, amid the fierce shouts of your applause? If it come not when one of you, selected by your enemies as your champion, is sent to perish among thieves and murderers, for the crime of loving and defending his native land,—then it will never come—*never*."

Two or three other incidents of my last week on Irish ground will help to fill up the picture of the time. Reilly was arrested on the charge of saying to the members of his Club, when turning into their place of meeting—"Left wheel." It was a term of military drilling, though the Clubmen were without weapons. He was kept in a station-house all night; and bail was refused in the morning. In the course of the day he was fully committed for trial, and bail was taken. During the whole week, the large force of the city police had orders to stop all processions, to arrest citizens, on any or on no charges; and generally to "strike terror." In the meantime, every day was bringing in more terrible news of the devastation of the Famine, and evictions of the tenantry. "On Friday," says the *Tipperary Vindicator*, "the landlord appeared upon the ground, attended by the sheriff and a body of policemen, and commenced the process of ejectment," etc. On that morning, and at that spot, thirty persons were dragged out of their houses, and the houses pulled down. One of the evicted tenants was a widow— "a solvent tenant comes and offers to pay the arrears due by the widow; but a desire on Mr. Scully's part to *consolidate* prevented the arrangement."

The same week a writer in the *Cork Examiner*, writing from Skibbereen, says:—

"Our town presents nothing but a moving mass of military and police, conveying to and from the court-house crowds of famine culprits. I attended the court for a few hours this day. The dock was crowded with the prisoners, not one of whom, when called up for trial, was able to support himself in front of the dock. The sentence of the court was received by each prisoner with apparent satisfaction. Even transportation appeared to many to be a relaxation from their sufferings."

"One of the jurors," it is added, "proposed a resolution that the *government* were the authors of the misery, and hoped his brother jurors would mark their disapprobation of such a government." But his brother jurors would do nothing of the kind: too many of his brother jurors, no doubt, expected some small place about the great government "relief-works:" they could not afford to "mark their disapprobation."

On Tuesday, of the same week,—it being then well known that the Crown would pack their jury,—a meeting of the citizens of Dublin was held at the Royal Exchange to protest; and Mr. John O'Connell went so far as to move this Resolution:—

"*Resolved*, That we consider the right of trial by a jury as a most sacred inheritance; in the security of person, property, and character."

The meeting then proceeded to protest against "the practice of arranging juries to obtain convictions." During the same week the poorhouses, hospitals, gaols, and many buildings taken temporarily for the purpose, were overflowing with starving wretches; and fevered patients were occupying the same bed with famished corpses: but on every day of the same week large cargoes of grain and cattle were leaving every port for England. The Orangemen of the North were holding meetings to avow hostility to Repealers and to "Jezebel," and eagerly crying "To Hell with the Pope!" Thus British policy was in full and successful operation at every point, on the day when I left my country in the fetters of the enemy.

Henceforth, I know nothing of Irish affairs from personal observation; and must content myself with epitomizing the rest of the dreary story from other authorities.

CHAPTER XXII.

TRIUMPH OF THE ENEMY—THE "IRISH TRIBUNE"—THE EDITORS—HABEAS CORPUS SUSPENDED—NUMEROUS ARRESTS—O'BRIEN TAKES TO THE COUNTRY—CARRICK—KILLENAULE—BALLINGARRY—DISPERSION OF THE PEOPLE—NO INSURRECTION.

The whole British Press, which never strikes so viciously at an enemy as when he is down and in chains, sent after me on my dark voyage one continuous shriek of execration and triumph that came to my ear even in my Bermuda prison. The "government" was to have no trouble, as they fondly flattered themselves, thenceforth. Ireland, once cleared of *me*, was to be manageable. There was to be no more jury-packing *if possible*, and conciliatory government was to commence with Habeas Corpus, Trial by Jury, and other *Palladia* of the British Constitution.

But the enemy was somewhat too sanguine. The profound passion of wrath and shame, kindled throughout Ireland by the incidents of my pretended trial, could not sink down and allay itself so speedily as the ameliorative enemy hoped. At the next meeting of the Confederation, Meagher, in a most noble and intensely passionate speech which I have already cited, said:—

"We are no longer masters of our lives. They belong to our country,—to liberty,—to vengeance. Upon the walls of Newgate a fettered hand has inscribed this destiny. We shall be the martyrs or the rulers of a revolution. . . Once again they shall have to pack their jury-box; once again exhibit to the world the frauds and mockeries, the tricks and perjuries, upon which their power is based."

Once again! Yes, indeed, and more than once, they were to pack their jury. True, they felt reluctant to do it; but the alternative was,—to pack juries, or give up Ireland. This, indeed, had become too apparent. The open and audacious proceedings which had taken place on my trial made it clear that the enemy would, without scruple, "exhibit to the world frauds and mockeries, tricks and perjuries"—but that they could not bear to think of exhibiting to the world the spectacle of Ireland wrested out of the clutches of England.

The fierce enthusiasm of our Confederates was redoubled after my removal. They hoped, at least, that if they were restrained from action *then*, it was to some good end, with some sure and well-defined purpose; and, there were many thousands of men then in Ireland, who longed and burned, for that end and that purpose, to earn an honorable death. How the British system disappointed them even of an honorable death, remains still to be told. A man can die in Ireland of hunger, or of famine-typhus, or of a broken heart, or of *delirium tremens;* but to die for your country,—the death *dulce et decorum*,—to die on a fair field, fighting for freedom and honor,—to die the death even of a defeated soldier, as Hofer died; or so much as to mount the gallows like Robert Emmet, to pay the penalty of a glorious " treason,"—even this was an *euthanasia* which British policy could no longer afford to an Irish Nationalist.

Yet with all odds against them,—with the Irish gentry thoroughly corrupted or frightened out of their senses, and with the "government" enemy obviously bent on treating our national aspiration as an ignominious crime, worthy to be ranked only with the offences of burglars or pickpockets,—still there were men resolved to dare the worst and uttermost for but one chance of rousing that down-trodden people to one manful effort of resistance against so base and cruel a tyranny. The Irish Confederation re-constituted its Council, and set itself more diligently than ever to the task of inducing the people to procure arms, with a view to a final struggle in the harvest. And as it was clear that there was nothing the enemy dreaded so much as a bold and honest newspaper which would expose their plots of slaughter and turn their liberal professions inside out, it was before all things necessary to establish a newspaper to take the place of the *United Irishman.*

It was a breach as deadly and imminent as ever yawned in a beleaguered wall; but men were found prompt to stand in it. Within two weeks after my trial, the *Irish Tribune* was issued, edited by O'Doherty, Williams, and Antisell. In two weeks more, on the 24th of June, came forth another and perhaps the ablest of our revolutionary organs,—the *Irish Felon.* Its editor and proprietor was John Martin; a quiet country gentleman of the county Down, who had been for years connected with all national movements in Ireland, —the Repeal Association, the Irish Confederation,—but who had never been roused to the pitch of desperate resistance till he saw the bold and dashing atrocity of the enemy on the occasion of my pretended "trial." He came calmly to the conviction that the nation must now at last set its back to the wall; and that if no other would lead in this, *he* would. From the opening article, signed with Martin's name, I extract a paragraph or two, as sufficient indication of his position and purpose:—

"At the time when John Mitchel lay in Newgate prison, expecting what fate Lord Clarendon's 'loaded dice' might bring, I stated it as my opinion that if the Irish people permitted the English Ministry to consummate his legal murder, the national cause would be ruined for this generation. The transportation of a man as a felon, for uttering sentiments held and professed by at least five-sixths of his countrymen, seemed to me so violent and so insulting a national wrong, that submission to it must be taken to signify incurable slavishness. The English Government, the proclaimed enemy of our nationality, had deliberately selected John Mitchel to wreak their vengeance upon him as representative of the Irish nation. By indicting him for 'felony' they virtually indicted five-sixths of the Irish people for 'felony.' By sentencing him to fourteen years' transportation to a penal settlement, they pronounced five-sixths of the Irish people guilty of a crime worthy of such punishment; and they declare that every individual of the six millions of Irish Repealers who escapes a similar doom, escapes it not through right and law, but through the mercy or at the discretion of the English Minister. The audacity of our tyrants must be acknowledged. They occupy our country with military force, in our despite, making barracks of our very marts and colleges, as if to defy and to challenge any manly pride that might linger among our youth. They pervert our police force into an organization of street bullies, as if to drive all peace-loving, industrious citizens into the ranks of disaffection. They insult the poor dupes of 'legal and constitutional' agitation, and rudely open their eyes to the real nature of foreign rule, by such an outrage on public decency and justice as this 'trial,' aggravated as it must be by the official meanness, brutality, hypocrisy, and perjury, requisite for effecting their object. They took measures to provoke the active hostility of all Irishmen who loved justice, or respected religion. They defied and challenged all parties of the Irish people; and I did think that such a challenge could not honorably or prudently be refused, and that the abject submission of the Irish people in that matter might destroy the national cause for this generation.

"I must frankly say that I still disapprove of the policy pursued by the Repeal leaders on that occasion. But I believe that their motives, whether mistaken or not, were honorable; and I am satisfied that there is a strong and growing spirit of resistance among Repealers of all parties, as well as a spreading disaffection to the foreign tyranny among those Irishmen who have not yet pronounced for Ireland. And, on the whole, I perceive sufficient reasons for expecting the success of the national cause.

" That I do not now exile myself, is a proof that I hope to witness the overthrow, and assist in the overthrow, of that most abominable tyranny the world now groans under,—the British imperial system.

" To gain permission for the Irish people to care for their own lives, their own happiness and dignity,—to abolish the political conditions which compel the classes of our people to hate and to murder each other, and which compel the Irish people to hate the very name of the English,—to end the reign of fraud, perjury, corruption, and 'government' butchery,—and to make *law, order*, and *peace* possible in Ireland,—*The Irish Felon* takes its place among the combatants in the holy war now waging in this island against foreign tyranny. In conducting it, my weapons shall be—*the truth, the whole truth, and nothing but the truth, so help me God!*

"JOHN MARTIN."

Reilly was an ardent fellow-laborer with Martin; and James Finton Lalor, of Kildare county, came up to Dublin and threw himself into the work. Lalor was the most powerful political writer that our cause had yet called forth, if I except Davis only. These two journals established themselves in Trinity Street; one in my office, and the other next door to it: so that instead of one regular avowed organ of insurrection, the enemy had to deal with two. Mr. Duffy, also, in the *Nation*, became now as urgent and vehement in exciting the people to resistance as I had been, or as the *Tribune* or *Felon* themselves. For five weeks thereafter truth and manhood, that is, "treason-felony," were openly taught and enforced; but *six* weeks would have been too much. The police were ordered to forcibly stop the sale of papers by vendors in the streets; and warrants were issued for the arrest of all the Editors,—Martin, Duffy, O'Doherty, and Williams. The country was beginning to bristle with pikes; men were praying for the whitening of the harvest; and it was plain that, before the reign of "Law and Order" should begin, other terrible examples must be made; other juries must be packed; then, after *that*, a Whig "government" would surely begin to deal with Ireland in a conciliatory spirit!

Throughout all these scenes, the horrible famine was raging as it had never raged before;—and the police and military, both in towns and in the country, were busily employed in the service of ejecting tenants,—pulling down their houses,—searching out and seizing hidden weapons,—and escorting convoys of grain and provisions to the seaside, as through an enemy's country. Yet rumors began to grow and spread (much exaggerated rumors, as I fear,) of a very general arming amongst the peasantry and the Clubmen of the towns; and the police had but small success in their searches for arms; for in fact these were carefully built into stone walls, or carried to the graveyards, with a mourning funeral escort, and buried in coffins, shrouded in well-oiled flannel, "in hope of a happy resurrection."

The enemy thought it wisest not to wait for the harvest; and resolved to bring matters to a head at once. Accordingly, they asked Parliament to suspend the *Habeas Corpus* Act in Ireland, so as to enable them to seize upon any person or number of persons whom they might think dangerous, and throw them into prison without any charge against them. Parliament passed the Bill at once; and in truth it is an ordinary procedure for Ireland. It may occur as a curious reflection, that, whereas the British Constitution, that wonder and envy of surrounding nations, is said to hold out as its bulwark and palladium, those two immortal rights of Britons,—Trial by Jury, and the Habeas Corpus Act,—the same Constitution has never been able to maintain itself in Ireland, save by subverting Trial by Jury, and suspending the Habeas Corpus Act.

Instantly numerous warrants were placed in the hands of the omnipresent police; and in every town and village in Ireland sudden arrests were made. The enemy had taken care to inform themselves who were the leading and active Confederates all over the island,—the Presidents and Secretaries of Clubs, and zealous organizers of drilling and pike-exercise. These were seized from day to day, sometimes with circumstances of brutality, (which was useful to the enemy in "striking terror,") and thrust into dungeons, or paraded before their fellow-citizens in chains. Martin and the other editors were in Newgate prison, awaiting transportation as felons. Warrants were out against O'Brien and Meagher.

Well, *the time* had come at last. If Ireland had one blow to strike, now was her day. Queen Victoria would not wait till the Autumn should place in the people's hands the ample commissariat of their war; and decreed that if they *would* fight, they should, at least, fight fasting. O'Brien was at the house of a friend in Wexford county, when he heard of the suspension of the Habeas Corpus, and that a warrant had issued for his own arrest. He was quickly joined by Dillon and Meagher. Doheny and MacManus, with some others, betook themselves to the Tipperary hills, and "put themselves upon the country." O'Gorman hurried to Limerick and Clare, to see what preparation existed there for the struggle, and to give it a direction. Reilly and Smith ranged over Kilkenny and Tipperary, eagerly seeking for insurrectionary fuel ready to be kindled; sometimes in communication with O'Brien and his party, at other times alone. To O'Brien, on account of his character, his services, and his value to the cause, the leadership seemed to be assigned by common consent.

It comes very easy to men who sat at home in those days, and did and attempted to do nothing, to criticize the proceedings of O'Brien and those brave men who sought in his company for an honorable chance of throwing their lives away. But it must be obvious, from the narrative of the three years' previous famine, what a hopeless sort of material for spirited national resistance was then to be found in the rural districts of Ireland. Bands of exterminated peasants, trooping to the already too full poorhouses; straggling columns of hunted wretches, with their old people, wives, and little ones, wending their way to Cork or Waterford, to take shipping for America; the people not yet ejected, frightened and desponding; with no interest in the lands they tilled, no property in the house above their heads, no food, no arms, with the slavish habits bred by long ages of oppression ground into their souls, and that momentary proud flush of passionate hope kindled by O'Connell's agitation, long since dimmed and darkened by bitter hunger and hardship,—Ah! how could the storm-voice of Demosthenes, and the burning song of Tyrtæus rouse such a people as this! A whole Pentecost of fiery tongues, if they descended upon such a dull material, would fall extinguished in smoke and stench like a lamp blown out.

So one might well anticipate: and so it would assuredly be amongst any other peasantry on earth, who had been so long subjected to similar treatment. But there is in the Irish nature a wonderful spring and an intense vitality: insomuch that I believe, even now, the chances of a successful insurrection in '48 to have been by no means desperate. At any rate, O'Brien and his comrades were resolute to give the people a chance; knowing full well that though they should be mown down in myriads by shot and steel, it would be a better lot than poorhouses and famine-graves.

It is needful, here, to speak of the Irish priesthood and the part which they took in that last agony of our country. Hitherto I have not had occasion to say much of the Catholic Church, though it makes so potent an element in Irish life, for the reason that in all vehement popular movements it always follows the people, and never leads: unless the movement be strong and sweeping enough to command and coerce the clergy, the clergy keep aloof from it altogether. Instinctively, the Church adheres to what is established, opposes violent action, sympathizes only with success. Thus, in O'Connell's Repeal Agitation, several bishops held themselves neutral; and hundreds of priests, as was well known, were zealous Repealers against their will; only because the popular passion was too strong for them to resist. About the time of my imprisonment, and before the "government" had shown themselves thoroughly resolved to put forth all their resources both of force and fraud to crush us, many of the Catholic clergy had come over to the "Young Ireland" party, which then promised to be strong enough to command the services of the Church. Some of them, I am happy to acknowledge, being more Irishmen than Romans, did from the first fully sympathize with the national aspirations of their island,—did profoundly feel her wrongs, and burn to redress or avenge them. When the final scene opened, however, and the whole might of the empire was gathering itself to crush us, the clergy, as a body, were found on the side of the enemy. They hoped more *for their Church* in a union with monarchical and aristocratic England than in an Ireland revolutionized and republican; and having taken their part, they certainly did the enemy's business well.

It is plain, then, against what desperate odds O'Brien and his friends took the field. The utter failure to make, I do not say a revolution, but even insurrection, cannot be understood without explaining all these elements of the problem which had arisen to be solved.

On the 24th of July, O'Brien and Meagher came to the small town of Callan; marched to the Market-house; found it occupied by a party of the 8th Hussars.

"At the moment we entered, they were busy cleaning their bridles, saddles, carbines, sword-belts, and other accoutrements. Seeing the crowd approach the Market-house, some of them were for starting off, at first, and leaving the position in the hands of the 'enemy.'

"I told them there was no necessity for their leaving the building; that no advantage would be taken of them; that their arms were just as safe there as they would be in Dublin Castle; perhaps more so.

"'We know that, sir,' replied the young corporal, 'we know well you wouldn't take an unfair advantage of the poor soldiers; at any rate you wouldn't do it to the Irish-Hussars.'

"'Three cheers,' I cried out, going to the door, and calling upon the people, 'three cheers, boys, for the 8th Royal Irish Hussars!'"

The Hussars would probably have loved them much better if they had at once taken the arms and horses of the first troops they encountered, and proceeded to the next town.

A day or two afterwards, at Carrick-on-Suir:—

"A torrent of human beings, rushing through lanes and narrow streets; surging and boiling against the white basements that hemmed it in; whirling in dizzy circles, and tossing up its dark waves, with sounds of wrath, vengeance, and defiance; clenched hands, darting high above the black and broken surface, and waving to and fro, with the wildest confusion, in the air; eyes, red with rage and desperation, starting and flashing upwards through the billows of the flood; long tresses of hair—disordered, drenched, and tangled—streaming in the roaring wind of voices, and, as in a shipwreck, rising and falling with the foam; wild, half-stifled, passionate, frantic prayers of hope; invocations, in sobs, and thrilling wailings, and piercing cries, to the God of heaven, His Saints, and the Virgin Mary; challenges to the foe; curses on the Red Flag; scornful, exulting, delirious defiance of Death; all wild as the Winter gusts at sea, yet as black and fearful too; this is what I then beheld—these the sounds I heard—such the dream which passed before me!

"It was the REVOLUTION, if we had accepted it.

"Why it was not accepted, I fear, I cannot with sufficient accuracy explain."

The explanation is various. With what passionate enthusiasm soever this devoted band was at first welcomed, whether in city or country, the Catholic clergy (for which may God forgive them!) if they had recommended but a few hours before any decisive action, took care to cool it off, and succeeded in frightening the simple people. Then the people themselves were unprovided generally with arms and food; there was neither chest nor commissariat. Then, O'Brien resolutely refused to supply this want by the only resource in his power; refused to commence a struggle which he felt to be for man's dearest rights by attacking and plundering the estates and mansions of the gentry,—who, however, were then generally fortified and barricaded in their own houses, to hold the country for the enemy.

For several days he went from place to place, attended by his friends, followed sometimes by two or three hundred people, half-armed, always expecting to meet a party with a warrant for his arrest, in which case it would be *war*, both defensive and offensive, to the last extremity. All around him were country mansions of nobles and gentlemen who had openly avowed themselves (in their " Addresses of Confidence ") for the English, and against their own people, and who had publicly branded *him* as a rebel, and offered their lives and fortunes for the work of crushing him: and he, an outlaw, with arms in his hands, and a force gathering around him burning to begin the work—would not molest a single enemy, nor even exact contributions from them to feed his followers and hold them together. All this was resolved and done from the purest and most conscientious motives, undoubtedly; but it would have been much purer and *more* conscientious to make the people dip their hands deep at once in British blood, and beckon the nation to arms by the light of the blazing castles of Tipperary's exterminating landlords.

Another day we find them at the village of Killenaule. O'Brien and his few followers being then quartered in the place, news was brought that a party of dragoons was approaching. A primitive barricade was hastily thrown up across the village street, made of carts and rubbish: and Dillon commanded at the barricade. Mr. O'Brien's order was absolute—to let the dragoons pass on unless they carried a warrant to arrest some of the party. The officer rode up, and demanded passage. Dillon replied that he commanded there for O'Brien; and, if the officer would give his word of honor that he had no warrants for arrest, he might pass. As the officer imperiously demanded passage, Stephens suddenly raised his rifle and covered him: his finger was on the trigger: one moment, and Ireland was in insurrection. But Dillon sternly ordered him to lower his rifle, and, having removed some carts, he himself led the officer's horse through the barricade, as a sign to the people that the soldiers were not to be molested. The dragoons went on their way. O'Brien was not yet at war; and the villagers of Killenaule wondered what it meant.

All this while, from day to day, crowds of stout men, many of them armed, flocked to O'Brien's company; but they uniformly melted off, as usual, partly compelled by want of provisions, partly under the influence of the clergy. The last time he had any considerable party together was at Ballingarry, where forty-five armed police had barricaded themselves in a strong stone house, under the command of a certain Captain Trant, who certainly had the long-expected warrant to arrest O'Brien, but who was afraid to execute it until after the arrival of some further reinforcements. O'Brien went to one of the front windows and called on Captain Trant to surrender. Trant demanded half an hour to consider, *and got it.* During this half hour, some of the crowd had thrown a few stones through the windows; and Captain Trant, seeing that the people could not be controlled much longer by O'Brien, gave orders to fire. O'Brien rushed between the people and the window, climbed upon the window, and once more called on the police to surrender. At the first volley from the house two men fell dead, and others were wounded; and the crowd on that side fell back, leaving O'Brien almost alone in the garden before the house. [For a garden there certainly was; though whether the celebrated "cabbage" grew there, I shall not certainly avouch.] At the other side, Stephens and MacManus had been collecting some straw and piling it against the door, with the intention of burning the place and forcing the police out. But when O'Brien learned what they were about, he peremptorily forbade them to set fire to it. *Why,* I have never learned; but MacManus has since assured me that he almost kneeled to O'Brien for permission to go and fire his pistol into that straw; in vain. In the meantime, some priests made their appearance, and exhorted the people to go home and leave O'Brien to his fate: then, shortly after, sixty additional police marched up and relieved Captain Trant. "His friends, then," says Mr. Doheny, "pressed Mr. O'Brien to retreat, which he refused. By long and passionate entreaty, they induced him to mount the police officer's horse and retire."

Through all these scenes, O'Brien preserved the same calm and impassive demeanor, exposing himself ever foremost where there was danger, as he was always wont to do: but mere bravery is only one, and a quite minor one, of the qualities which fit a man to kindle an insurrection under such discouraging circumstances. Nor is it very clear that a Garibaldi could have gained victory, though he might have made, at least, a fight. Of course, the British were in high delight; and their Press, with its usual delicate irony, named O'Brien the "hero of the cabbage garden."

In fact, there was no insurrection. The people in those two or three counties did not believe that O'Brien meant to fight; and nothing would now persuade them of that but some desperate enterprise. Yet they were all ready and willing; and, indeed, are at all times ready and willing to fight against English dominion. The English ought to be grateful to O'Brien, that his extreme punctilio about not striking the first blow, and his tender regard for human life, suffered the passion of the people to cool, and enabled the enemy to draw their toils around him. If he had at once raised the green banner, with the *Lamh Laidhir* * on its folds, proclaimed Tenant-right, disarmed all the neighboring police-stations, and precipitated himself upon some garrison town, all Munster, Leinster, Connaught, and the half of Ulster, would have been in resistless insurrection within one week. The enemy might have overpowered a population, unarmed and half-starved, like ours; but at least the Last Conquest (Perhaps) would not have been consummated without one stalwart blow.

* The strong hand; the cognizance of the O'Briens.

CHAPTER XXIII.

ARREST OF O'BRIEN; OF MEAGHER; OF MACMANUS, ETC.—EXCUSE FOR MORE JURY-PACKING—EXCITEMENT IN ENGLAND—TRIAL OF CHARTISTS—SPECIAL COMMISSION IN CLONMEL—TRIAL OF O'BRIEN FOR HIGH TREASON—SENTENCE OF DEATH—TRIALS OF MACMANUS, O'DONOGHUE, AND MEAGHER—COMMUTATION OF THE SENTENCES OF DEATH—PLAN FOR A NEW "PLANTATION OF IRELAND"—SYSTEMATIC VILIFICATION OF THE CELTIC IRISH BY ENGLISH WRITERS.

From the first moment that the Repeal of the Habeas Corpus Act placed the liberties of all Irishmen at the disposal of Lord Clarendon, the police received secret orders to arrest all leading Confederates, both in town and country. A return was, in the beginning of the next year, 1849, made to Parliament of the number of persons, and their names, who were imprisoned under that law. There were 118 of them; including most of the very men on whom O'Brien might reasonably have relied to sustain his movement. They were all imprisoned in various gaols, without any charge, or one word of explanation; removed in batches from one prison to some other in a distant part of the island, with no other object, apparently, but to exhibit them in chains and strike a wholesome terror into all spectators.

After O'Brien's party had dispersed at Ballingarry, he seemed no longer to value his life, and used no means to escape or conceal himself. He went openly to the railroad station in Thurles, where he was immediately pointed out to the police—pointed out, as he himself believes, by a member of the Committee of the Confederation, a creature who appears to have some time before sold himself to the enemy.* Meagher, Leyne and O'Donoghue were soon captured also; MacManus, after having almost escaped in an

---

* His name is John Donnellan Balfe. His reward was a colonial appointment under the government, in the very distant colony of Van Diemen's Land, where the evil odor of his crime could not annoy the more reputable servants of the government by too close association.

American ship, was at length taken. Dillon, O'Gorman, Reilly and Doheny, all escaped out of the island, though long and closely pursued. I was, for months before, safe in my cell at Bermuda; Martin, Duffy, Williams, and O'Doherty, were all in their Newgate dungeon awaiting trial. Nobody was left at large over all the island, capable of initiating a bold movement; and indeed the peasantry were by this time so dispirited, so feeble, and so poor, that no such movement could have been attempted through their means. The priests were signalizing their royalty by calming down all indignant feeling, and heartily abusing the defeated rebels: the middle classes were frightened and corrupted;—and the Conquest was consummated.

There remained for the enemy now only to confirm that conquest, and then to make a profitable use of it for England. First, the Editors must be brought to trial under the new "Treason-Felony" Act; and O'Brien and his immediate comrades, under the Common Law, for the crime of "High Treason," having appeared in arms against the "government." Our enemies would gladly have dispensed with these trials, and removed their captives out of the way by a more summary process. But they were not to forget that they were a "liberal" government, and had a reputation to support before the world. Ireland was not Naples, (would to God she had been!) and political offenders could by no means be suffered to perish by long confinement, in subterranean dungeons, without trial. But, then, arose the question of juries; and the "government" knew full well that no jury in Ireland impartially empanelled according to law, and really representing the nation, would convict one of those men for any offence whatever against a foreign government.

They could not refuse a trial; but one thing they could do, which the King of Naples had never learned,—they could pack the juries. No doubt, it was painful to have to pack juries *again:* how could Whig reputation endure it? But they hoped this would be the last time. They knew that in the eyes of Englishmen, the extreme urgency of the occasion would justify this one last tremendous fraud; and, like Ulysses, they could be honest afterwards. When I say "in the eyes of Englishmen," I mean the ruling classes of Englishmen, namely, the landed interests and the monied and mercantile interests;—I mean, in short, those Englishmen whose opinions and interests are alone consulted in the government of that country. To *them* it was an absolute necessity of their existence that Irish national movements should be crushed down by any means and all means— but it would be unjust to charge the mass of Englishmen with approving of the system of British Government in Ireland. Most of them know nothing about it. Those people of the industrious classes, who do interest themselves somewhat in public affairs—that is, the Chartists— were utterly powerless, and were held in the profoundest contempt by those who own them, and own their industry and their lives. In truth, of the three Peoples whom our enemies pretend to govern, they fear none but the Irish. The government, accordingly, gave the Chartists a significant hint, immediately after my "trial," that they were to mind their own business, and leave the settlement of Irish affairs to their betters. A large Chartist meeting was held in London, and indignant speeches were made, protesting against the packing of the "jury." Amongst others, Mr. Ernest Jones had said, (and the detective police had taken down his words) that the People would triumph yet,—that a day would come when John Mitchel would return in triumph to his country, and Lord John Russell and Lord Clarendon would be transported in his place! He was immediately brought to trial, convicted for sedition, and expiated his rash words by two years in a dungeon.

The Whig Government, in short, felt that if they satisfied the men of rank and money in England, they did the whole duty of Whigs: and the men of rank and money were eagerly crying out to have the last embers of that long national struggle stamped out.

O'Brien, Meagher, MacManus, and O'Donohoe were to have their trial before a special commission in Clonmel, the capital of Tipperary. On the details of these trials I need not dwell; because they were on the same pattern with other scenes of this same kind which I have narrated. The officials of the Crown showed a stern, dogged determination to disregard every remonstrance, to refuse every application, and to do the work intrusted to them in the most coarse, insolent, and thoroughgoing style. For example, Mr. Whiteside, O'Brien's counsel, reminded the court " that, *in England* persons charged with high treason are allowed a copy of the Jurors' panel, and a list of the witnesses to be examined on the part of the Crown." Take one extract from the report of the "trial":—

"The learned counsel put it to the Court whether Mr. O'Brien, under trial in a country said to be under the same government and laws as England, should not have the same privilege which he would enjoy as a matter of right, if he happened to be tried on the other side of the Channel.

"The Court decided *that the prisoner was not entitled to the privilege.*"

When the clerk read the names of the jury-panel, Mr. O'Brien of course challenged the array, on the ground of fraud; and, of course, the Court ruled against him.

"Mr. Whiteside stated that it made little difference whether his client would be tried by a jury selected from a panel thus constituted, or taken and shot through the head on the high-road. No less than one hundred Catholics had been struck off the panel, and so few left on, that Mr. O'Brien's right to challenge was now little better than a farce. This objection was also overruled; Chief Justice Blackburne having decided that the panel was properly made out."

O'Brien, whose mind was made up to meet any fate, stood in the dock during this nine days' trial, with a haughty calmness. What thoughts passed through that proud heart, as the odious game proceeded, no human eye will ever read: but of one thing I am sure,—his grief, shame, and indignation were not for himself, but for the down-trodden country, where such a scene could be enacted in the open day and against the will of nine-tenths of its inhabitants.

There was a verdict of guilty: and O'Brien slightly bowed to the Jury. He was re-conducted to his prison, where he met Meagher, who eagerly sought to read the result in his face. But nothing is to be read there: it wears the same steady, cheerful smile as ever,—so cheerful that Meagher hopes for a moment that he brings good news. O'Brien presses his hand, merely saying, "*Guilty*, Meagher—guilty! as we all are, of not having sold our country." The next morning he stands before the Judge; is asked if he has anything to say why sentence should not pass; replies that he has nothing to say, save that his conscience is clear; that he has done only what was the duty of every Irishman; "and now," he adds, "proceed with your sentence."

Chief Justice Blackburne puts on his black cap, which becomes him well. I give the precise words of the sentence:—

"That sentence is, that you, William Smith O'Brien, be taken from hence to the place from whence you came, and be thence drawn on a hurdle to the place of execution, and be there hanged by the neck until you are dead; and that afterwards your head shall be severed from your body, and your body divided into four quarters, to be disposed of as her Majesty shall think fit. And may the Lord have mercy on your soul."

O'Brien hears it unmoved as a statue: again inclines his head in a stately bow; politely takes leave of his counsel and returns to his prison.

Again, and again, and again, the same process was performed in all its parts. MacManus was next tried, then O'Donohoe, then Meagher: their juries were all carefully packed; they were all sentenced to be hanged; and they all met the announcement of their fate as men ought. For more than a month these trials went on, from day to day; and it was the 23d of October when the last sentence was pronounced. A strong garrison of cavalry, infantry, and artillery occupied the town, and enclosed the scene with a hedge of steel. Outside, the people muttered deep curses, and chafed with impotent rage. A few daring spirits, headed by O'Mahony, once contemplated an attack and rescue; but the people had been too grievously frightened by the priests (on account of their miserable pauper souls), and too effectually starved by the government, to be equal to so dashing an exploit: and so that solemn and elaborate insult was once more put upon our name and nation; and the four men who had sought to save their people from so abject a condition lay undisturbed in Clonmel gaol, sentenced to death. Considering which humiliating picture, one might be tempted to repeat the bitter words of Don Juan D'Aguila—"Surely Christ never died for *this* people!" Yet whosoever has studied even the imperfect sketch which I have given of the potent and minutely elaborated system of oppression that pressed upon that nation at every point, and tied down every limb, watching over every man, woman, and child, at their uprising and downlying, so as to be enabled to foresee and to baffle even the slightest approach to combination for a national purpose*—will assuredly forbear to taunt us, and will bless

---

* So far back as 1602, Attorney-General Davies thus described that espionage, which is one principal arm of British power—"Notice is taken of every person that is able to do either good or hurt. It is known not only how they live and what they do, but it is foreseen what they purpose or intend to do."

God that he was born in a land where men are free to will and to act.

The newspaper Editors were still to be "tried,"—that is, to be transported. In the months of October and November, 1848, Duffy, of the *Nation,* Williams and O'Doherty, of the *Tribune,* and Martin, of the *Felon,* were successively brought up for trial in the City Court-house, of Green-street. Their newspapers had been suppressed weeks before, their offices broken into, their types and presses and books seized.

O'Doherty and Martin were "convicted" by well-packed juries, containing not a single Catholic. In the cases of Duffy and Williams, the enemy ventured to leave one or two Catholics on the juries. Williams was acquitted: Duffy's jury disagreed, and he was retained in prison till a more tractable jury could be manufactured. Again he was brought to trial, and again the jury disagreed. Still he was kept in custody, though his health was rapidly failing; and, at last, when all apprehension of trouble seemed to be over, and the more dangerous conspirators were disposed of, the "government" yielded to a memorial on his behalf, and abandoned the prosecution.

In the matter of those who were sentenced to death, the enemy after much deliberation decided on sparing their lives and commuting their punishment to transportation for life. This, I believe, was done under the false pretence of clemency; but it was in truth the most refined cruelty; it was, moreover, illegal,—there being no law to authorize such a commutation. The prisoners, therefore, objected through their counsel: they had no use for life under such circumstances; and demanded to have the extreme benefit of the law. Ministers, however, were resolved to be merciful,—introduced an Act into Parliament, empowering the Queen to transport them,—had it passed at once,—and immediately shipped them off to herd with felons in the penal colony of Van Diemen's Land. O'Doherty and Martin, having been originally sentenced to ten years' transportation, were sent away at the same time, but in another ship; and for more than five years, in the most degrading bondage, they expiated the crime of "not having sold their country." If they had prudently sold that commodity, there were no Irishmen in our day who could have made so profitable a bargain.

What to do now with this Ireland, thus fallen under the

full and peaceful possession of her "sister island," was the subject of serious thought in England. The famine was still slaying its tens of thousands; and the government emigration scheme was drawing away many thousands more, and shooting them out naked and destitute on the shores of the St. Lawrence: so that it was hoped the "Celts" would soon be thinned out to the proper point. The very danger so lately escaped, however, brought home to the British Government, and to the Irish landlords, the stern necessity of continued extermination. It was better, they felt, to have too few hands to till the ground, than too many for the security of law and order.

A plan was promulgated by Sir Robert Peel for a new "Plantation of Ireland"—that is for replacing the Irish with good Anglo-Saxons; and this idea was warmly advocated by no less a person than Thomas Carlyle. *Væ Victis!* was the word. "Ireland," said Carlyle, "is a starved rat that crosses the path of an elephant: what is the elephant to do? squelch it, by Heaven! squelch it!" From this time commenced that most virulent vilification of the Celtic Irish, in all the journals, books, and periodicals of the "sister island," which has been so faithfully reproduced (like all other British cant) in America, and which gave such venom to the Know-Nothing agitation. Then, more than ever, English writers were diligent in pointing out and illustrating the difference of "race" between Celt and Saxon; which proved to their own satisfaction that the former were born to be ruled by the latter. A peculiar feature in this species of literature, is, that the most zealous apostles and preachers of it have been themselves Celts of the Celts: Carlyle himself, for example, a Scotchman of Dumfries-shire, and with a name that convicts him of kindred with the Celtic people of Cumbria; and still more manifestly Macaulay, who was, by the father's side, at least, of the MacAmhlaidhs of the Highlands; but who wrote of the whole Celtic family—pandering to the ignorant pride of the English—with a real venom and affected contempt, which one might explain upon the theory that early in his life some Celt had crossed him in love, or pulled his nose, or done both the one and the other,—but which I am inclined to account for on a more commercial principle: he wrote his books *for* Anglo-Saxons and for those who ignorantly believe they are Anglo-Saxons.

The bitterness and spite exhibited against the Irish Celt in all British literature, especially since '48, has, however, a parallel. It is precisely the same kind of animosity, and founded on the same reasons, as that which appears against the Scottish nation in all English books of the last century—that is, while Scotland remained disaffected against English rule, and discontented with the Scottish Union. Nothing so much pleased the magnanimous British at that time, as ridicule and denunciation of the Scotch. The Lord Macaulay himself informs us that " when the English condescended to think of him (the Highlander) at all—and it was seldom that they did so, they considered him as a filthy, abject savage, a slave, a Papist, a cut-throat, and a thief." And further, he says:—

"This contemptuous loathing lasted till the year 1745 (that is, until the last outrising of the Highlanders against the English) and was then for a moment succeeded by intense fear and rage. England, thoroughly alarmed, put forth her whole strength. The Highlanders were subjugated rapidly, completely, and forever. During a short time, the English nation, still heated by the recent conflict, breathed nothing but vengeance. The slaughter on the field of battle, and on the scaffold, was not sufficient to slake the public thirst for blood. The sight of the tartan inflamed the populace of London with hatred, which showed itself by unmanly outrages to defenceless captives."

This writer, however, takes care to justify, and so far as in him lies, to perpetuate, this horror and hatred of the Celt. He enlarges upon the filth of the dwellings and the persons of the Gael, in a manner which would have delighted Doctor Johnson himself; and, with a singular sort of filial piety, likens his own fathers to the Esquimaux and the Samoyedes.

Now, those volumes of Macaulay were written since '48. They are in all their matter and scope, not a history, but a political pamphlet; and the zealous and diligent depreciation of Celts, both in his accounts of Scottish and Irish transactions, has a manifest bearing upon our Last Conquest. It is intended not only to soothe and flatter the English with the belief that they are the " superior race," but also to turn aside and make ridiculous the sympathy of all civilized mankind, if peradventure mankind should be so misguided as to throw away its sympathies upon so abject a race as these starved-out Celts. But, in truth, the calculated care and diligence of the British literary class in defaming all Celts, has had of late years a far more urgent motive than it ever had in the case of the Scottish people, for they are painfully aware that myriads upon myriads of the exterminated Irish, having found refuge here in America, have filled this continent with cursing and bitterness against the English name; and a strong political necessity is upon them to make Americans hate us, and, if possible, despise us, as heartily as they do themselves. As for us, expatriated and exterminated Irish, we have every day occasion to feel that our enemy pursues us into all lands with unrelenting vengeance; and, though we take the wings of the morning, we can nver escape it—never until Ireland shall become, as Scotland is, a contented province of the British Empire, thoroughly subdued, civilized, emasculated, and "ameliorated" to the very heart's core.

To return from this slight digression, the plan of Sir Robert Peel for a new "Plantation" in Ireland was anxiously revolved in the councils of our enemy. It began to be believed that the peasant class being now almost sufficiently thinned out—and the claim of tenants to some sort of right or title to the land they tilled, having been successfully resisted and defeated;—that the structure of society in Ireland having been well and firmly planted upon a basis of able-bodied pauperism (which the English, however, called "independent labor"), the time was come to effect a transfer of the real estate of the island from Irish to English hands. This grand idea afterwards elaborated itself into the famous "Incumbered Estates Act."

14

CHAPTER XXIV.

CONSUMMATION OF THE "CONQUEST"—THE QUEEN'S SPEECH IN 1849—MORE COERCION—MORE POOR-LAW—DEPOPULATION—CONDITION OF THE PEOPLE, AS DESCRIBED BY MR. DUFFY IN 1849—LORD JOHN RUSSELL'S "RATE-IN-AID"—THE "INCUMBERED ESTATES ACT"—RESULT TO IRELAND OF INCUMBERED ESTATES COURT—QUEEN'S VISIT TO IRELAND IN 1849—POPULAR FEELING IN DUBLIN SUPPRESSED BY THE POLICE—IRELAND "TRANQUIL," "IMPROVING," AND "PROSPEROUS"—STATISTICS, RECAPITULATION, CONCLUSION.

The Conquest was now consummated—England, great, populous, and wealthy, with all the resources and vast patronage of an existing government in her hands—with a magnificent army and navy—with the established course and current of commerce steadily flowing in the precise direction that suited her interests—with a powerful party on her side in Ireland itself, bound to her by lineage and by interest—and, above all, with her vast brute mass lying between us and the rest of Europe, enabling her to intercept the natural sympathies of other struggling nations, to interpret between us and the rest of mankind, and represent the troublesome sister island, exactly in the light that she wished us to be regarded—England prosperous, potent, and at peace with all the earth besides—had succeeded (to her immortal honor and glory) in anticipating and crushing out of sight the last agonies of resistance in a small, poor, and divided island, which she had herself made poor and divided, carefully disarmed, almost totally disfranchised, and totally deprived of the benefits of that very British "law" against which we revolted with such loathing and horror. England had done this; and whatsoever credit and prestige, whatsoever profit and power could be gained by such a feat, she has them all. "Now, for the first time these six hundred years," said the London *Times*, "England has Ireland at her mercy, and can deal with her as she pleases."

It was an opportunity not to be lost, for the interests of British civilization. Parliament met late in January, 1849.

The Queen, in her "speech," lamented that "*another* failure of the potato crop had caused severe distress in Ireland: and thereupon asked Parliament to continue, "for a limited period," the extraordinary power; that is, the power of proclaiming any district under martial law, and of throwing suspected persons into prison, without any charge against them. The Act was passed, of course.

Then, as the famine of 1848 was fully as grievous and destructive as any of the previous famines;—as the rate-payers were impoverished, and in most of the "unions" could not pay the rates already due—and were thus rapidly sinking into the condition of paupers; giving up the hopeless effort to maintain themselves by honest industry, and throwing themselves on the earnings of others; as the poorhouses were all filled to overflowing, and the exterminated people were either lying down to die or crowding into the emigrant-ships;—as, in short, the Poor Law, and the New Poor Law, and the Improved Poor Law, and the Supplementary Poor Law, had all manifestly proved a "failure," Lord John Russell's next step was to give Ireland *more* Poor Law.

When I say that the whole code of poor laws was a *failure*, I must qualify that expression, as before.—They were a failure for their professed purpose—that of relieving the famine; but were a complete success for their real purpose—that of uprooting the people from the land, and casting them forth to perish. I have not much faith in the "government" statistics of that country, but as some may wish to see how much our enemies were willing to admit, I shall give some details from a report furnished in '48 by Captain Larcom, under the orders of the government, and founded on local reports of police inspectors. I find the main facts epitomized thus, for one year:—

"In the number of farms, of from *one* to *five* acres, the decrease has been 24,147; from *five* to *fifteen* acres, 27,379; from *fifteen* to *thirty* acres, 4,274; whilst of farms *above* thirty acres the *increase* has been 3,670. Seventy thousand occupiers, with their families, numbering about three hundred thousand, were rooted out of the land.

"In Leinster, the decrease in the number of holdings not exceeding one acre, as compared with the decrease of '47, was 3,749; above one, and not exceeding five, was 4,026; of five, and not exceeding fifteen, was 2,546; of fifteen to thirty, 391: making a total of 10,617.

"In Munster, the decrease in the holdings, under thirty acres, is stated at 18,814; the increase over thirty acres, 1,399.

"In Ulster, the decrease was 1,502; the increase, 1,134.

"In Connaught, where the labor of extermination was least, the clearance has been most extensive. There, in particular, the roots of holders of the soil were never planted deep beneath the surface, and consequently were exposed to every exterminator's hand. There were in 1847, 35,634 holders of from one to five acres. . In the following year there were less by 9,703; there were 76,707 holders of from five to fifteen acres, less in one year by 12,891; those of from fifteen to thirty acres were reduced by 2,121 ; a total depopulation of 26,499 holders of land, exclusive of their families, was effected in Connaught in one year."

On this report it may be remarked that it was a list of killed and wounded in one year of carnage only—and of one class of people only. It takes no account of the dead in that multitudinous class thinned the most by famine, who had no land at all, but lived by the labor of their hands, and who were exposed before the others, as having nothing but life to lose. As for the landlords, already encumbered by debt, the pressure of the poor-rates was fast breaking them down. In most cases, they were not so much as the receivers of their own rents, and had no more control over the bailiffs, sheriffs, and police, who plundered and chased away the people, than one of the pillars of their own grand entrance gates.

Take one paragraph now from amongst the commercial reports of the Irish papers; which will suggest more than any labored narrative could inculcate:—

"Upwards of one hundred and fifty ass hides have been delivered in Dublin from the county Mayo, for exportation to Liverpool. *The carcasses, owing to the scarcity of provisions, had been used as food!*"

But those who could afford to dine upon famished jackasses were few, indeed. During this Winter of '48–9, hundreds of thousands perished of hunger. During this same Winter the herds and harvests raised on Irish ground were floating off to England on every tide : and, during this same Winter, almost every steamship *from* England daily carried Irish paupers, men, women, and children, away from Liverpool and Bristol, to share the good cheer of their kinsmen at home.

It was in this state of things that Lord John Russell, having first secured a continued suspension of the Habeas

Corpus Act, proposed an additional and novel sort of poor-rate for Ireland. It was called the "Rate-in-aid." That is to say, poor-law unions, which were still solvent, and could still in some measure maintain their own local poor, were to be rated for relief of such unions as had sunk under the pressure. Assuming that Ireland and England are two integral parts of an "United Kingdom," (as we are assured they are,) it seems hard to understand why a district in Leinster should be rated to relieve a pauper territory in Mayo—and a district in Yorkshire not. Or to comprehend why old and spent Irish laborers, who had given the best of their health and strength to the service of England, should be shipped off to Ireland to increase and intensify the pauperism and despair. But so it was: the maxim was that "the property of Ireland must support the poverty of Ireland;" without consideration of the fact that the property of Ireland was all this time supporting the luxury of England.

The next measure passed in the same session of Parliament was the "Incumbered Estates Act:" the Act of 12th and 13th Victoria, c. 77. Under this, a royal commission was issued, constituting a new court "for the sale of Incumbered Estates;" and the scope and intent of it were to give a short and summary method of bringing such estates to sale, on petition either of creditors or of owners. Before that time the only mode of doing this was through the slow and expensive proceedings of the Court of Chancery; and the number of incumbered landlords had grown so very large since the famine began, their debts so overwhelming, and their rental so curtailed, that the London Jews, money-brokers, and insurance offices, required a speedier and cheaper method of bringing their property to the hammer. What I wish to be fully understood is, that this Act was not intended to relieve, and did not relieve, anybody in Ireland; but that, under pretence of facilitating legal proceedings, it contemplated a sweeping confiscation and new "Plantation" of the Island. The English press was already complacently anticipating a peaceable transfer of Irish land to English and Scotch capitalists; and took pains to encourage them to invest their money under the new Act. Ireland, it was now declared, had become tranquil: "the Celts were gone:" and if any trouble should arise, there was the Habeas Corpus Suspension Act; and the horse, foot, and artillery, and the juries. Singular to relate, however, the new Act did not operate satisfactorily in that direction. English capitalists had a wholesome terror of Tipperary, and of the precarious tenure by which an Irish landlord holds his life; insomuch that the great bulk of the sales made by the Commissioners were made to Irishmen:—and in the official return of the operations of the court, up to Oct., 1851, I find that while the gross amount produced by the sales had been more than three and a half millions sterling, there had been only fifty-two English and Scottish purchasers, to the amount of £319,486.

Down to the 25th May, 1857, there had been given orders for sale to the number of 3,197: the property had been sold to 7,216 purchasers, of whom 6,902 were Irish—the rest English, Scotch, or other foreigners. The estates already sold had brought upwards of twenty millions sterling, which was almost all distributed to creditors and other parties interested. The result to Ireland is simply this—about one-fifteenth part of the island has changed hands; has gone from one landlord and come to another landlord: the result to the great tenant class is simply *nil*. The new landlord comes over them armed with the power of life and death, like his predecessor: but he has no local or personal attachment which in some cases used to mitigate the severity of landlord rule;—and he is bound to make interest on his investment. The estates have been broken up, on an average, into one-half their former size: and this has been much dwelt upon as an "amelioration:" but I have yet to learn that small landlords are more mild and merciful than great ones. On the whole, I maintain that the "Incumbered Estates Act" has benefited only the money-lenders of England.

As to "Tenant-right," the salutary custom which I explained before, and which did once practically secure to the tenantry in some portions of Ulster a permanency of tenure on payment of their rent, our Parliamentary patriots have been agitating for it, begging for it, conferring with Ministers about it, eating public dinners, making speeches and soliciting votes on account of it; but they have never made, and never will make, an approach by one hair's-breadth to its attainment.* It is absolutely essential to the existence

---

* Mr. Gladstone's Law, pretending to secure something like a Tenant-right, is, in fact, only an example and a confirmation of the judgment given in the text.

of the British Empire, that the Irish peasant class be kept in a condition which will make them entirely manageable—easy to be thinned out when they grow too numerous, and an available *matériel* for armies. This, I say, is necessary to the British commercial and social governmental system—but I do not say it by way of complaint. Those who are of opinion that British civilization is a blessing and a light to lighten the world, will easily reconcile themselves to the needful condition. Those who deem it the most base and horrible tyranny that has ever scandalized the earth, will probably wish that its indispensable prop—Ireland—were knocked from under it.

In the meantime, neither the Incumbered Estates Act, nor any other act, made or to be made by an English Parliament, has done or aimed to do anything towards giving the Irish tenant-at-will the smallest interest in the land he tills; but, on the contrary, the whole course of the famine legislation was directed to the one end of shaking small leaseholders loose from the soil, and converting them into tenants-at-will, or into "independent laborers," or able-bodied paupers, or lean corpses. Let it be understood further, that the condition of an Irish "Tenant-at-Will" is unique on the face of the globe,* is utterly unintelligible to most civilized Europeans, and is only to be found within the sway of that Constitution which is the envy of surrounding nations. The German, Von Raumer, making a tour in Ireland, thus tries to explain the thing:—

"How shall I translate *tenants-at-will? Wegjagbare?* Expellable? Serfs? But in the ancient days of vassalage, it consisted rather in keeping the vassals attached to the soil, and by no means in driving them away. An ancient vassal is a lord compared with the present tenant-at-will, to whom the law affords no defence. Why not call them *Jagdbare* (*chaseable*)? But this difference lessens the analogy—that for hares, stags, and deer there is a season during which no one is allowed to hunt them;—whereas tenants-at-will are hunted all the year round. And if any one would defend his farm, (as badgers and foxes are allowed to do,) it is here denominated *rebellion*."

In 1849, it was still believed that the depopulation had not proceeded far enough; and the English Government was fully determined, having so gracious an opportunity, to make

---

* Paralleled in some sort only by the *ryots* of India—another people privileged to enjoy the blessings of British rule.

a clean sweep. One of the provisions of Lord John Russell's *Rate-in-Aid* Bill was for imposing an additional rate of two shillings and sixpence in the pound, to promote *emigration*. During the two years, 1848-9, the Government Census Commissioners admit 9,395 deaths by famine alone; a number which would be about true if multiplied by twenty-five. In 1850 there were nearly 7,000, as admitted by the same authorities; and in the first quarter of 1851, 652 deaths by hunger, they say, " are recorded."

In the very midst of all this havoc, in August, 1849, her Majesty's Ministers thought the coast was clear for a Royal Visit. The Queen had long wished, it was said, to visit her people of Ireland; and the great army of persons, who, in Ireland, are paid to be loyal, were expected to get up the appearance of rejoicing. Of course there were crowds in the streets; and the natural courtesy of the people prevented almost everything which could grate upon the lady's ear or offend her eye. One Mr. O'Reilly, indeed, of South Great George's-street, hoisted on the top of his house a large *black* banner, displaying the crownless Harp; and draped his windows with black curtains, showing the words *Famine* and *Pestilence:* but the police burst into his house, tore down the flag and the curtains, and thrust the proprietor into gaol. One other incident of the royal visit will be enough:—

"The *Freeman* says, that, on passing through Parkgate-street, Mr. James Nugent, one of the Guardians of the North Union, approached the Royal carriage (which was moving rather slowly), and, addressing the Queen, said—'Mighty Monarch, pardon Smith O'Brien.' Before, however, he had time to get an answer, or even to see how her Majesty received the application, Lord Clarendon rode up and put him aside; and the *cortège* again set out at a dashing pace, which it maintained until it drew up opposite the Vice-regal Lodge in the Park."

On the whole, however, the Viceroy's precautions against any show of disaffection, were, I take shame to say it, complete and successful. Nine out of ten citizens of Dublin eagerly hoped that her Majesty would make this visit the occasion of a " pardon " to O'Brien and his comrades. Lord Clarendon's organs, therefore, and his thousand placemen and agents of every grade, diligently whispered into the public ear, that the Queen would certainly pardon the State prisoners if she were not insulted by Repeal demonstrations —in short, if there was not one word said about those prisoners. The consequence was that no whisper was heard about Repeal, nor about the State prisoners—except only the exclamation of silly Mr. Nugent to his "Mighty Monarch."

Although there was no chance of Tenant-Right, no chance of Ireland being allowed to manage her own affairs—yet towards Catholics of the educated classes there was much liberality. Mr. Wyse was sent ambassador to Greece: Mr. More O'Ferrall was made Governor of Malta: many barristers, once loud in their patriotic devotion at Conciliation Hall, were appointed to Commissionerships and other minor offices; and Ireland became "tranquil" enough. For result of the whole long struggle, England was left, for a time, more securely in possession than ever, of the property, lives, and industry of the Irish nation. She had not parted with a single atom of her plunder, nor in the slightest degree weakened any of her garrisons, either military, civil, or ecclesiastical. Her "Established Church" remained in full force—the wealthiest church in the world, quartered upon the poorest people, who abhor its doctrine, and regard its pastors as ravening wolves. It had, indeed, often been denounced in the London Parliament, by Whigs out of place: Mr. Roebuck had called it "the greatest ecclesiastical enormity in Europe;" Mr. Macaulay had termed it "the most utterly absurd and indefensible of all the institutions now existing in the civilized world." But every one knows what value there is in the liberal declarations of Whigs out of place. Once in place and power, they felt that the "enormity" of the Established Church, absurd and indefensible as it was, constituted one of their greatest and surest holds upon the Irish aristocracy, to whose younger sons and dependants it afforded a handsome and not too laborious livelihood. The Archbishop of Armagh alone continued yearly to receive his £14,664—almost thrice the salary of the President of the United States; and the Bishop of Derry nearly double as much as the President—and ten other Bishops, emoluments varying from £7,600 down to the lowest, £2,310. Then every parish must have its "rector," though in a great many parishes there are no congregations; and the poor Catholic people, over and above rents, rates, and taxes, must pay these sinecure pastors out of their poor stackyards—the remedy for non-payment being distress by the landlord.* The Orangemen, also, have been maintained in full force. They are all armed: for no Bench of Magistrates will refuse a good Protestant the liberty of keeping a gun; and lest they might not have enough, the government sometimes supplies arms for distribution among the lodges. The police and detective system is more highly organized than ever; and the Government Board of "National" Education, more diligently than ever inculcates the folly and vice of national aspirations.

Yet Ireland, we are told, is "improving" and "prosperous." Yes; it cannot be denied that three millions of the people having been slain or driven to seek safety by flight, the survivors begin to live better for the present. There is a smaller supply of labor, with the same demand for it— therefore wages are higher. There is more cattle and grain for export to England, because there are fewer mouths to be fed; and England (in whose hands are the issues of life and death for Ireland) can afford to let *so many* live. Upper classes, and lower classes, merchants, lawyers, state-officials, civil and military, are indebted for all that they have, for all that they are, or hope for, to the sufferance and forbearance of a foreign and hostile nation. This being the case, every one must see that the prosperity of Ireland, even such ignominious prosperity as it is, has no guarantee or security. Whenever Irishmen grow numerous again (as they surely will), and whenever "that ancient swelling and desire of liberty," as Lord Mountjoy expressed it, shall once more stir their souls (as once more it certainly will), why, the British Government can crush them again, with greater ease than ever; for the small farmers are destroyed; the middle classes are extensively corrupted; and neither stipendiary officials nor able-bodied paupers ever make revolutions.

This very dismal and humiliating narrative draws to a close. It is the story of an ancient Nation stricken down by a war more ruthless and sanguinary than any seven years' war, or thirty years' war, that Europe ever saw. No sack of Magdeburg, or ravage of the Palatinate, ever approached in horror and desolation to the slaughters done in

---

* In the matter of the Established Church, also, the late Gladstone law ("Disestablishment and Disendowment") is a mere subterfuge and imposture. It has diminished the emoluments of some of the bishops, but has not relieved the people of any part of this burden on account of that church; no, not to the amount of a single farthing.

Ireland by mere official red tape and stationery, and the principles of Political Economy. A few statistics may fitly conclude this dreary subject.

The Census of Ireland, in 1841, gave a population of 8,175,125. At the usual rate of increase, there must have been, in 1846, when the Famine commenced, at least eight and a half millions; at the same rate of increase, there ought to have been, in 1851 (according to the estimate of the Census Commissioners), 9,018,799. But in that year, after five seasons of artificial famine, there were found alive only 6,552,385—a deficit of about two millions and a half. Now, what became of those two millions and a half?

The "government" Census Commissioners, and compilers of returns of all sorts, whose principal duty it has been, since that fatal time, to conceal the amount of the havoc, attempt to account for nearly the whole deficiency by emigration. In Thom's Official Almanac, I find set down on one side, the actual decrease from 1841 to 1851 (that is, without taking into account the increase by births in that period), 1,623,154. Against this, they place their own estimate of the emigration during those same ten years, which they put down at 1,589,133. But, in the first place, the decrease did not *begin* till 1846—there had been till then a rapid increase in the population: the government returns, then, not only ignore the increase, but set the emigration of *ten* years against the depopulation of *five*. This will not do: we must reduce their emigrants by one-half, say to six hundred thousand—and add to the depopulation the estimated increase *up* to 1846, say half a million. This will give upwards of two millions whose disappearance is to be accounted for—and six hundred thousand emigrants in the other column. Balance unaccounted for, *a million and a half*.

This is without computing those who were born in the five famine years, whom we may leave to be balanced by the deaths from *natural* causes in the same period.

Now, that million and a half of men, women, and children, were carefully, prudently, and peacefully *slain* by the English Government. They died of hunger in the midst of abundance, which their own hands created; and it is quite immaterial to distinguish those who perished in the agonies of famine itself from those who died of typhus fever, which in Ireland is always caused by famine.

Further, I have called it an artificial famine: that is to say, it was a famine which desolated a rich and fertile island, that produced every year abundance and superabundance to sustain all her people and many more. The English, indeed, call that famine a "dispensation of Providence;" and ascribe it entirely to the blight of the potatoes. But potatoes failed in like manner all over Europe; yet there was no famine save in Ireland. The British account of the matter, then, is first, a fraud—second, a blasphemy. The Almighty, indeed, sent the potato blight, but the English created the famine.

And lastly, I have shown, in the course of this narrative, that the depopulation of the country was not only encouraged by artificial means, namely, the Out-door Relief Act, the Labor-rate Act, and the emigration schemes, but that extreme care and diligence were used to prevent relief coming to the doomed Island from abroad; and that the benevolent contributions of Americans and other foreigners were turned aside from their destined objects—not, let us say, in order that none should be saved alive, but that no interference should be made with the principles of political economy.

The Census Commissioners close their last Report with these words:—

"In conclusion, we feel it will be gratifying to your Excellency, to find, that, although the population has been diminished in so remarkable a manner, by famine, disease, and emigration, and has been since decreasing, the results of the Irish census are, *on the whole, satisfactory*."

The Commissioners mean that the Census exhibits an increase in sheep and cattle for the English market—and that while men are lean, hogs are fat. "The good of this," said Dean Swift—more than a century ago—"the good of this is, that the more sheep we have, the fewer human creatures are left to wear the wool or eat the flesh. Ajax was mad when he mistook a flock of sheep for his enemies; but we shall never be sober until we have the same way of thinking."

The subjection of Ireland is now probably assured until some external shock shall break up that monstrous commercial firm, the British Empire; which, indeed, is a bankrupt firm, and trading on false credit, and embezzling the goods of others, or robbing on the highway, from Pole to Pole;

but its doors are not yet shut; its cup of abomination is not yet running over. If any American has read this narrative, however, he will never wonder hereafter when he hears an Irishman in America fervently curse the British Empire. So long as this hatred and horror shall last—so long as our island refuses to become, like Scotland, a contented province of her enemy, Ireland is not finally subdued. The passionate aspiration for Irish nationhood will outlive the British Empire.

THE END.

INDEX TO

CRUSADE OF THE PERIOD.

PAGE

CHAPTER I. Froude *versus* Ireland—The Mock Trial—Plan of the "Crusade"—Meaning of the "Crusade"—The "Crusader" Himself—"Taking Charge of the Irish"—The "Inverted Commas".. 7

CHAPTER II. Conspiracy against the "First Historian"—John P. Prendergast—Colonel Meline—Attitude of the "Historian"—He Marches off—His Book—The "Normans"—The "Massacre" of 1641—"Protestants," Good and Bad.. 20

CHAPTER III. Making the Issue—The Pretended Massacre—Froude's "Chamber of Horrors"................................ 31

CHAPTER IV. The Swearers—The "Ghosts of the Bann"—Dean Maxwell—More "Murders by Papists"—Froude's Treatment of the Evidence.. 38

CHAPTER V. Too much Froude—The "Cloud of Witnesses"—Sir John Temple—Doctor Petty—Who "Pared the Forests"... 50

CHAPTER VI. The Pretended and the Real Massacre—Island-Magee—Owen Roe O'Neill—The Battle of Benburb...... 61

PAGE

CHAPTER VII. "Clan Oliver"—Froude's "Were Wolves"—
The Irish Transported to Barbadoes—Perils of the Irish
Episcopate—Secret of English Toleration—Froude's Fears
for the Future.................................... 71

CHAPTER VIII. Religious Liberty in Ireland—King James's
Parliament—The King's "Artful Language"—The Irish
Governor of New York—Religious Liberty in America—
Farewell to Froude................................. 81

INDEX TO

LAST CONQUEST OF IRELAND, (PERHAPS.)

                                                          PAGE

CHAPTER I. Introduction—Address of the American Congress "To the People of Ireland," in 1775—Statistics and Condition of Ireland—Ireland in 1843—O'Connell—The Repeal Debate in the Corporation of Dublin—The "Monster Meetings" in 1843—Opinion in the English Parliament—Sir Robert Peel's Declaration in Answer to Mr. Bernal [Osborne].. 93

CHAPTER II. "Repeal Year" (1843)—Resources of O'Connell—Clare Election, and Catholic Emancipation—Shiel—"Young Ireland"—Davis, Dillon, Duffy—The "Nation"—Resources of the English—Disarming Laws............ 101

CHAPTER III. "The Repeal Year," still—O'Brien's Motion—Arms Bill—Sir Edward Sugden—Dismissed Magistrates—Arbitrators—More Monster Meetings.................... 110

CHAPTER IV. O'Connell's Oratory—Its Themes—The Whigs—Davis and the "Nation"—The Young Agitators—Tara Meeting—Council of Three Hundred—The Queen's Speech against Repeal—Great Meeting at Mullaghmast—Meeting at Clontarf forbidden............................. 119

CHAPTER V. Determination of the Enemy—Clontarf—The "Projected Massacre"—Arrest of O'Connell and the "Conspirators"—Opening of "Conciliation Hall"—O'Brien joins the Repealers—Preparation for the Trials.......... 128

PAGE

CHAPTER VI. The Trial—System of "Selecting" a Jury in Ireland—Verdict against O'Connell—Debate in Parliament on the State of Ireland—Operation of the Arms Act—Sentence and Imprisonment of O'Connell........................ 137

CHAPTER VII. O'Connell in Prison—Davis; his Misgivings—Reversal of the Judgment—Whig Law Lords—Rejoicings in Dublin—The People disappointed—Federalism—O'Brien... 146

CHAPTER VIII. Approach of the Famine, in 1845—Repeal prospects after the liberation of O'Connell—Irish Produce exported to England in 1844—Arms and Detectives in return for it—"Landlord and Tenant" Commission—Ejectment Legislation—Condition of Ireland in 1845—The Devon Commission—The Tenant-Right of Ulster—Conspiracy of Landlords and Legislators—Sir Robert Peel..... 155

CHAPTER IX. Land-Tenure Report—O'Brien—Eighty-two Club—Grey Porter—A National Militia—President Polk and Oregon Territory—Robert Tyler—Colleges Bill—MacNevin—James Haughton—John O'Connell and General Jackson—Lord Stanley's Bill—"Surplus Population"—Death of Davis—Famine........................... 166

CHAPTER X. Davis; his influence, aims, and labors—His opinion of "Imposing Demonstrations"—His Letters—His Death—Fate of MacNevin.......................... 176

CHAPTER XI. Duties of Government—Alms—Playfair and Lindley—Memorial of the Corporation and Citizens of Dublin—Lord Heytesbury—O'Connell's proposals—O'Brien's—Meeting of Parliament—Coercion Bill—Repeal of the Corn Laws—Relief............................ 186

CHAPTER XII. Loss of the Irish crops—Accounts between England and Ireland—Rapid export of Irish harvest and cattle—Sir Robert Peel's "Remedial Measures"—O'Brien in Parliament—English Press on "Alms"—Sir Robert Peel's two weapons—Repeal Association—Resistance to the Coercion Bill—Extermination in Connaught—The "Nation," and Young Ireland—Another State Prosecution—Change of Ministry............................ 197

CHAPTER XIII. "Relief of Famine"—Importations of grain—Imprisonment of O'Brien—Destruction of the Repeal Association—The Labor-rate Act—More Poor-Law Extermination—Recruiting....................................... 207

CHAPTER XIV. Labor-rate Act—Digging holes—England begs for us—Out-door relief—"Fast and humiliation"—Quarter-acre clause—The Calculations of "Political Circles"—Two millions of Celtic corpses—America baffled—Parish coffins—Repudiation of alms by the "Nation"............ 218

CHAPTER XV. Death of O'Connell—His character—Arrangements for the next year's famine—Emigration—Report of a "Select Committee"—A New Coercion Act—The Crisis approaches.. 232

CHAPTER XVI. Lord Clarendon, Viceroy—Subterranean agencies of Government—Monahan, Attorney-General—Galway election... 243

CHAPTER XVII. Dublin during the Famine—"Young Ireland"—Alarm of the Moneyed Classes—"S. G. O."—Sudden meeting of Parliament—New Coercion Act—Differences in the Irish Confederation—Break up in the "Nation Office"—O'Brien—The "United Irishman"............. 251

CHAPTER XVIII. The "United Irishman" Newspaper—Nature of the enterprise—Effect of the French Revolution of February, 1848—Situation of the Government—Examples. 261

CHAPTER XIX. March, 1848—The French Revolution—Waterford election—Aggregate Meeting in Dublin—Prosecution of O'Brien, Meagher, and Mitchel—O'Brien in the English Parliament—The "Treason-Felony" Act—Trial of O'Brien and Meagher for "Sedition"—The "United Irishman"—Trials for illegal drilling—Prosecution for "Sedition" abandoned—Arrest of Mitchel for "Treason-Felony"..... 265

CHAPTER XX. Rage of the British Press—Protestant Repeal Associations—Lord Clarendon's Manœuvres among the Orangemen—Proclamations against "Communists"—The Chartists and Irish in England—Letter to the Protestants of the North—Prosecution...................... 275

CHAPTER XXI. Juries in Ireland—Whig professions of impartiality—In the Dock—Holmes—Challenging the array—Closing Scene—The Clubs restrained—Meagher's Account—My last week in Ireland........................ 283

CHAPTER XXII. Triumph of the Enemy—The "Irish Tribune"—The Editors—Habeas Corpus suspended—Numerous Arrests—O'Brien takes to the Country—Carrick—Killenaule—Ballingarry—Dispersion of the people—No Insurrection. 294

CHAPTER XXIII. Arrest of O'Brien; of Meagher; of MacManus, etc.—Trials—Excuse for more Jury-packing—Excitement in England—Trial of Chartists—Special Commission in Clonmel—Trial of O'Brien for High Treason—Sentence of Death—Trials of MacManus, O'Donohoe, and Meagher—Commutation of the Sentences of Death—Plan for a New "Plantation of Ireland"—Systematic vilification of the Celtic Irish by English writers.................... 305

CHAPTER XXIV. Consummation of the "Conquest"—The Queen's Speech in 1849—More coercion—More Poor-law—Depopulation: condition of the people, as described by Mr. Duffy, in 1849—Lord John Russell's "Rate-in-aid"—The "Incumbered Estates Act"—Result to Ireland of Incumbered Estates Court—Queen's visit to Ireland in 1849: Popular feeling in Dublin suppressed by the Police—Ireland "tranquil," "improving," and "prosperous"—Statistics—Recapitulation—Conclusion...................... 314

www.ingramcontent.com/pod-product-compliance
Lightning Source LLC
Chambersburg PA
CBHW021208230426
43667CB00006B/617